Balancing Competing Human Rights Claims in a Diverse Society

Balancing Competing Human Rights Claims in a Diverse Society

Institutions, Policy, Principles

edited by
Shaheen Azmi, Lorne Foster, & Lesley Jacobs

IRWIN LAW

Ontario
Human Rights Commission
Commission ontarienne des droits de la personne

Balancing Competing Human Rights Claims In A Diverse Society:
Institutions, Policy, Principles

Published in 2012 by

Irwin Law Inc.
14 Duncan Street
Suite 206
Toronto, ON
M5H 3G8

www.irwinlaw.com

ISBN: 978-1-55221-311-7

Library and Archives Canada Cataloguing in Publication

Balancing competing human rights claims in a diverse society : institutions, policy, principles / edited by Shaheen Azmi, Lorne Foster, & Lesley Jacobs.

Includes bibliographical references and index.

ISBN 978-1-55221-311-7

1. Human rights—Canada. 2. Human rights—Ontario.

I. Azmi, Shaheen, 1961– II. Foster, Lorne III. Jacobs, Lesley A

JC599.C3B34 2012 323.0971 C2012-906506-4

The publisher acknowledges the financial support of the Government of Canada through the Canada Book Fund for its publishing activities.

We acknowledge the assistance of the OMDC Book Fund, an initiative of Ontario Media Development Corporation.

Printed and bound by CPI Group (UK) Ltd, Croydon, CR0 4YY

1 2 3 4 5 16 15 14 13 12

Table of Contents

Editors' Introduction

Shaheen Azmi, Lorne Foster, Lesley Jacobs

In the context of globalization, diversity has become an increasingly valued characteristic of contemporary societies. Diverse societies are viewed as remarkable for their variety in terms of religious practices, spoken languages, ethnicities, sexualities, and expressions of multiculturalisms. Such societies are said to allow for a measure of openness and adaptability that enable them to meet efficiently and effectively the ever changing needs and demands of a global economy.

Yet, as societies have embraced and indeed aspire towards diversity, certain challenges and tensions have become visible that were not fully anticipated. This book focuses on one of those challenges, the challenge of balancing competing human rights claims. The practice of human rights has taken on increasing complexity in Canada and other diverse societies because more and more often around the world the claim to a right of one individual or group directly affects the claim to the human rights of another group. Such competing human rights claims can be played out in many places, from the classroom to workplaces, from the public square to the international stage, wherever individuals or groups actively claim the recognition of rights that may interfere with the access to rights of others.

Examples of these sorts of competing human rights should be familiar to all of us. Think about religious individuals or organizations that object on the grounds of the right to religious beliefs and practice, to prohibitions of discrimination against gays and lesbians, or measures aimed at promoting the inclusion of women. The rights of parents to excuse their children from exposure to topics like world religions or evolutionary biology in schools provide other examples. Imagine likewise a situation where an individual with a Seeing Eye dog seeks to enter the taxi of a driver who is allergic to dog hair. The rights of one person with a disability are here in competition with the rights of someone else with a different sort of disability. The rights of individuals to wear certain types of religious dress or carry symbolic weapons in public places such as schools or courts may compete with the rights of others to security or a fair trial. Claims from immigrant groups to be protected from expressions of racism or hate can compete with the rights of journalists or academics to express critical or controversial views about immigration policy or practices.

Recognition that human rights claims can come into conflict or be in competition with each other is not new. Among rights theorists, the potential for conflict between rights claims has been an important theme in philosophical debates throughout the twentieth century. But the conflict was conceived of in a particular way, that is to say, between the right to liberty and the right to equality, or the right to private property and the right to equality. These debates yielded innovative approaches to thinking about these conflicts. Some philosophers such as John Rawls argued that in the case of conflicts, some rights to basic liberties should have lexical priority over others.[1] Others argued that these conflicts should be resolved in favour of a calculation about what rights serves the greatest overall good for society.[2] Others still such as Isaiah Berlin believed that there is no single principle for resolving conflicting rights claims and that we should draw on our

---

1 John Rawls, *A Theory of Justice* (Cambridge, MA: Harvard University Press, 1971).

2 LW Sumner, *The Moral Foundation of Rights* (Oxford, UK: Oxford University Press, 1988).

intuitions in particular instances to decide what to do.[3]

Competing human rights claims in diverse societies are, in our view, not best thought of abstractly in terms of a conflict between the demands of equality and/or liberty but rather as arising from different beliefs about how people should best lead their lives and what sorts of accommodations should be made for persons with different beliefs out of respect for human dignity and mutual recognition. These sorts of differences are not new but in diverse societies people with these differences live together in close proximity, which brings the possibilities for conflicts and competing human rights claims to the forefront.

Unlike the conflict between equality and liberty, balancing or reconciling competing human rights claims in diverse societies has received scant systematic academic attention nor has it been the site for significant policy development and innovation. Instead, until recently, the popular media and the courts have been the major forums for discussing how to balance competing human rights claims in diverse societies. Those discussions have rarely been careful or probed deeply into what it means for human rights claims to be in competition or how best to balance them in a diverse society. This book is designed to help remedy these shortcomings in two ways. First, it presents a concrete example of a new innovative policy for balancing competing human rights claims developed by a major human rights institution, the Ontario Human Rights Commission. Second, it offers theoretically oriented insights by academics, lawyers, and policy makers, organized thematically, to further our understanding of why competing human rights claims are so pressing in diverse societies and how they might be best addressed.

---

3 Isaiah Berlin, *Concepts and Categories* (Oxford, UK: Oxford University Press, 1979).

Institutions and Policy

Issues of competing human rights claims have become important and pressing in Canada. Different provinces have responded in different ways. In Quebec, for example, the provincial government mandated in 2007 the Bouchard-Taylor Consultation Commission on Accommodation Practices Related to Cultural Differences to hear from the public on "reasonable accommodations" of religious and ethnic minorities and to issue a report of their findings and recommendations. The Commission reported back to the Quebec Government in 2008 but few of its recommendations have been followed.[4] In Ontario, in contrast, the Ontario Human Rights Commission (OHRC) took the lead to develop the first policy in Canada to address competing human rights claims, beginning in 2005. This policy development included extensive consultation with the public, academics, human rights commissions elsewhere in the country, and stakeholders in the human rights community in Ontario. These efforts by the OHRC resulted in a policy for Ontario, released in April 2012.

Part One of this book presents this policy[5] and a series of chapters that provide instructive background for the development of the policy. Shaheen Azmi, director of Policy, Education, Monitoring, and Outreach at the OHRC, explains in Chapter 2 the approach to balancing competing human rights that the OHRC took in its development of the policy. Janet Epp Buckingham, a professor at Trinity Western University, explores the similarities

---

4 For the abridged Final Report of the Bouchard-Taylor Commission, see Québec, Commission de Consultation sur les Pratiques d'Accommodement Reliées aux Différences Culturelles, *Building the Future: A Time for Reconciliation*, Gérard Bouchard and Charles Taylor (Gouvernement du Québec, 2008) online: http://postmediaottawacitizen.files.wordpress.com/2011/03/rapport-final-abrege-en.pdf.

5 See Chapter 1.

between the *Ontario Human Rights Code*[6] and the *Canadian Charter of Rights and Freedoms*[7] on competing rights claims in Chapter 3. Richard Moon, a professor of law at the University of Windsor, describes the criticisms and attacks human rights commissions across Canada have been subject to in the course of addressing competing human rights claims in Chapter 4. In Chapter 5, Patricia Hughes, executive director of the Ontario Law Commission, describes how public consultation is a fundamental ingredient in policy development in Ontario. Gary Yee, chair of Ontario's Licence Appeal Tribunal, provides insight based on the institutional structure that underpins tribunals in Ontario to help situate the OHRC's policy development in Chapter 6.

Principles and Applications

Part Two broadens the scope of the discussion by exploring broad principles at stake when human rights compete in a diverse society, as well as some more fine-grained applications of those principles. Shauna Van Praagh, a professor of law at McGill University, explores how urban spatial metaphors capture the essence of the competition between human rights claims in a diverse society in Chapter 7. In Chapter 8, Lorne Foster, an associate professor of public policy and equity studies at York University, and Lesley Jacobs, a professor of law & society and political science at York University, argue that shared social citizenship is important to making sense of how to balance competing human rights. Errol Mendes, a professor of law at the University of Ottawa as well as a Commissioner for the Ontario Human Rights Commission, develops his idea that it is possible to strike a measure of equilibrium between rights claims in Canada in Chapter 9.

---

6 RSO 1990, c H.19.

7 *Canadian Charter of Rights and Freedoms*, Part I of the *Constitution Act, 1982*, being Schedule B to the Canada Act 1982 (UK) 1982, c 11 [*Charter*].

Patricia Hughes, executive director of the Law Commission of Ontario, provides a different framework for reconciling competing rights claims in Chapter 10. In Chapter 11, B.J. Wray, who now works for the Government of Canada's Department of Justice, provides one possible framework for addressing conflicting human rights in Ontario.

Fine-grained applications are developed by four other contributors. Miriam Smith, a professor of law & society at York University, closely examines the treatment of the competing human rights claims involving sexual orientation and religion in Chapter 12. In Chapter 13, Iain Benson, a senior legal counsel at Miller Thompson LLP, Canada, considers how religious viewpoints can be represented in the public sphere. In Chapter 14, Lauren Bates, a staff lawyer for the Law Commission of Ontario, examines how human rights claims compete in the context of disability. Finally, in Chapter 15, Richard Moon dicusses the balancing of human rights in the context of hate speech regulation in Canada.

Acknowledgements

This book grew out of the partnership between the Ontario Human Rights Commission and the York Centre for Public Policy and Law at York University in Toronto. We are grateful for the support of many people both at the OHRC and York University. Barbara Hall, Chief Commissioner of the OHRC, has provided unwavering support for this initiative. Our greatest debt is to Dora Nipp, a lawyer and Human Rights Education and Change Specialist at the OHRC, who pushed us to complete the volume so that it could be published by Irwin Law. At York, we are grateful to Noel Badiou and Selwyn McSween at the Centre for Human Rights and Robin Smith at the Centre for Public Policy and Law for their help on numerous dimensions of the project. Nicole Alywin and Aaron Jacobs did excellent copy editing work on the contributions by individual authors.

Part I

Institutions and Policy

Chapter 1
Policy on Competing Human Rights

Ontario Human Rights Commission

Summary

As people better understand their rights and wish to exercise them, some of those rights may come into conflict with the rights of others. This is especially true in Ontario's increasingly diverse and complex society. Conflicts can begin when an individual or group tries to enjoy or exercise a right, interest, or value in an organizational context (e.g. in schools, employment, housing). At times, these claims may be in conflict, or may appear to be in conflict with other claims. Depending on the circumstances, for example, the right to be free from discrimination based on creed or sexual orientation or gender may be at odds with each other or with other rights, laws, and practices. Can a religious employer require an employee to sign a "morality pledge" not to engage in certain sexual activity? Can an accuser testify wearing a *niqab* (a face veil worn by some for religious reasons) at the criminal trial of her accused? How do you resolve a situation where a professor's guide dog causes a severe allergic reaction in a student?

The Canadian *Charter of Rights and Freedoms*, provincial human rights legislation (including the Ontario *Human Rights Code*), and the courts recognize that no rights are absolute and no one right is more important than another right. Our laws guarantee rights such as freedom of expression as well as protection against discrimination and harassment based on gender, creed, sexual orientation and disability, among other grounds. They require we give all rights equal consideration. The law also recognizes that rights have limits in some situations where they substantially interfere with the rights of others.

The courts have said we must go through a process on a case-by-case basis to search for solutions to reconcile competing rights and accommodate individuals and groups, if possible. This search can be challenging, controversial, and sometimes dissatisfying to one side or the other. But it is a shared responsibility and made easier when we better understand the nature of one another's rights and obligations and demonstrate mutual respect for the dignity and worth of all involved. Finding the best solution for maximizing enjoyment of rights takes dialogue and even debate.

Ontario's *Human Rights Code* says the Ontario Human Rights Commission's mandate includes reducing tension and conflict in Ontario's communities and encouraging and co-ordinating plans, programs, and activities to do this. The OHRC has developed this *Policy on Competing Human Rights* to help organizations and individuals address difficult situations involving competing rights.

Goals of policy

The *Policy on Competing Human Rights* is intended to be a useful tool for individuals and organizations as they deal with different types of conflict. It sets out a process to analyze and reconcile competing rights that emphasizes specific objectives and considerations.

For example, everyone involved should:

- show dignity and respect for one another
- encourage mutual recognition of interests, rights, and obligations
- facilitate maximum recognition of rights, wherever possible
- help parties to understand the scope of their rights and obligations
- address stigma and power imbalances and help to give

marginalized individuals and groups a voice
- encourage cooperation and shared responsibility for finding agreeable solutions that maximize enjoyment of rights.

The approach in the policy can help organizations and decision-makers resolve and even avoid rights conflicts altogether. Where litigation cannot be avoided, the policy provides a framework that can be used by courts and tribunals as they deal with these types of conflicts.

Practical steps to reduce potential for conflict

Employers, housing providers, educators, and other responsible parties covered by the Ontario *Human Rights Code* have the ultimate responsibility for maintaining an inclusive environment that is free from discrimination and harassment, and where everyone's human rights are respected. As part of this, organizations and institutions operating in Ontario have a legal duty to take steps to prevent and respond to situations involving competing rights.

Organizations can reduce the potential for human rights conflict and competing rights situations by:

- being very familiar with the Ontario *Human Rights Code* and with their obligations under it
- taking steps to educate and train responsible individuals on competing rights situations and the OHRC's *Policy on Competing Human Rights*
- having in place a clear and comprehensive competing rights policy that:
  * sets out the process to be followed when a competing rights situation arises
  * alerts all parties to their rights, roles, and responsibilities
  * commits the organization to deal with competing rights matters promptly and efficiently.

Taking proactive and effective steps to address competing rights matters will help to protect organizations from liability if they are ever named as a respondent in a human rights claim involving competing rights.

What are competing rights?

In general, competing human rights involve situations where parties to a dispute claim that the enjoyment of an individual or group's human rights and freedoms, as protected by law, would interfere with another's rights and freedoms. This complicates the normal approach to resolving a human rights dispute where only one side claims a human rights violation. In some cases, only one party is making a human rights claim, but the claim conflicts with the legal entitlements of another party or parties.

While many situations may at first appear to involve competing rights, one must recognize that not all claims will be equal before the law: some claims have been afforded a higher legal status and greater protection than others. For example, international conventions, the Canadian *Charter of Rights and Freedoms*, provincial human rights legislation, and legal decisions all recognize the paramount importance and unique status of human rights.

Other non-human rights-related rights may also be protected in legislation, but may not have the same status that human rights do. Claims may also be based on interests or values held by individuals or groups.

While there are many situations in which rights, interests, and values may seem to conflict or compete, when evaluating situations of competing rights, human rights and other legally codified rights will usually hold a higher status than interests and values. The OHRC's *Policy on Competing Human Rights* is meant mainly to be a tool for resolving situations where there is a conflict of human rights and rights that are legally protected.

Examples of competing rights situations[1]

A competing human rights situation exists when legally protected rights are present in both claims, and at least one of the claims connects to human rights law. Based on this definition, allegations of competing human rights scenarios might include:

1. *Code* right v *Code* right
2. *Code* right v *Code* legal defence
3. *Code* right v other legislated right
4. *Code* right v *Charter* right
5. *Code* right v common law right
6. International treaty right v *Code/Charter* defence
7. *Charter* right v *Charter* right.

Key legal principles[2]

While the courts have not set a clear formula or analytical approach for dealing with competing rights, legal decisions have identified a number of fundamental principles that provide direction on how to deal with these types of scenarios, as well as what to avoid. The courts have recognized that the specific facts will often determine the outcome of the case and claims should be approached on a case-by-case basis. The main legal principles that organizations must consider when they deal with competing rights situations are:

1. No rights are absolute
2. There is no hierarchy of rights
3. Rights may not extend as far as claimed
4. The full context, facts, and constitutional values at stake

---

1 See section 4.2 of the *Policy on Competing Human Rights* for examples and discussion of each of these situations.

2 See section 5 of the *Policy on Competing Human Rights* for detailed discussion and examples of each of these principles.

must be considered
5. Must look at extent of interference (only *actual* burdens on rights trigger conflicts)
6. The core of a right is more protected than its periphery
7. Aim to respect the importance of both sets of rights
8. Statutory defences may restrict rights of one group and give rights to another.

Analysis for addressing competing human rights situations

The *Policy on Competing Human Rights* includes a framework for addressing competing rights that the OHRC developed based on international human rights principles, caselaw, social science research, and consultation with community partners and stakeholders.[3] The following table summarizes the framework's three-stage, five-step process for recognizing and reconciling competing human rights claims:

Process for addressing competing human rights situations
Stage One: Recognizing competing rights claims
Step 1: What are the claims about?
Step 2: Do claims connect to legitimate rights? (a) Do claims involve individuals or groups rather than operational interests? (b) Do claims connect to human rights, other legal entitlements, or *bona fide* reasonable interests? (c) Do claims fall within the scope of the right when defined in context?

3 The framework is set out in a summarized chart at Appendix C of the *Policy on Competing Human Rights*. See Section 6 of the *Policy* for a detailed discussion of the analysis that underlies the framework.

Step 3: Do claims amount to more than minimal interference with rights?

Stage Two: Reconciling competing rights claims

Step 4: Is there a solution that allows enjoyment of each right?

Step 5: If not, is there a "next best" solution?

Stage Three: Making decisions

- Decisions must be consistent with human rights and other laws, court decisions, human rights principles, and have regard for OHRC policy
- At least one claim must fall under the *Ontario Human Rights Code* to be actionable at the Human Rights Tribunal of Ontario

By implementing the OHRC's proposed approach, organizations can be confident that they have a conflict resolution process in place that is consistent with human rights principles.

Organizational process for addressing competing rights[4]

Many competing rights situations can be quickly resolved through an informal process that may involve no more than one or two meetings. At the outset, organizations should consider whether the situation is suited to an informal and expedited process. For example, the facts of the situation and the framing of each claim may be straightforward and not in dispute. The parties may already be well-informed about each other's claims, rights, and obligations. They may have shown respect for each other's interests and be willing to engage in discussions about solutions without delay.

A quick process will generally involve running through the analysis with both parties in a quick way. The focus here is less

---

4 The case examples included in Appendix D can help organizations as they work through this part of the process. The case examples are presented in an analysis template that can help organizations frame the issues and assess all relevant considerations.

on a precise analysis of the rights at play, and more on finding solutions that benefit all sides and respect human rights. If the informal, quick process does not resolve the issue, then the organization may decide to use a full and more formal process. However, it is important to consider a quick resolution process first because workable solutions can be found relatively quickly in most cases of competing rights claims.

In a full, more formal process, the framework is applied more rigorously at Stage One to find out if a genuine competing human rights situation exists. If, after going through Stage One, an organization concludes that a competing human rights situation does exist, Stage Two will help guide it through the reconciliation process. The *Policy on Competing Human Rights* proposes an alternative dispute resolution (ADR) model to guide organizations through the Three Stage Analysis.

Conclusion

Competing human rights situations will inevitably arise in many different contexts, including workplaces, housing, and schools. By following the approach outlined in the *Policy on Competing Human Rights*, organizations may be able to resolve tension and conflict between parties at an early stage. Resolving conflict early helps organizations to address matters before they fester and become entrenched. This in turn helps ensure the health and functioning of an organization, and can avoid costly and time-consuming litigation.

"All human beings are born free and equal in dignity and rights."[5]

1. Introduction

As they interact with each other, individuals and organizations will encounter situations of tension and conflict. This is especially true in Ontario's increasingly diverse and complex society. Conflicts can begin when an individual or group tries to enjoy or exercise a right, interest, or value in an organizational context (e.g. in schools, employment, housing). At times, these claims may be in conflict, or may appear to be in conflict with other claims. Depending on the circumstances, for example, the rights to be free from discrimination based on creed or sexual orientation or gender may be at odds with each other or with other rights, laws, and practices. How do you resolve a situation where a religious employer requires an employee to sign a "morality pledge" not to engage in certain sexual activity? Or, where a woman wants to testify wearing a *niqab* (a face veil worn by some for religious reasons) at the criminal trial of her accused? Or, where a professor's guide dog causes a student to have a severe allergic reaction?

The Canadian *Charter of Rights and Freedoms* (the *Charter*), provincial human rights legislation, and the courts recognize that no rights are absolute and no one right is more important than another right. Our laws guarantee rights such as freedom of expression and protection against discrimination and harassment based on gender, creed, sexual orientation, and disability, among other grounds. They require that all rights be given equal consideration. The law also recognizes that rights have limits in some situations, particularly where they substantially interfere with the

---

5 UN General Assembly, *Universal Declaration of Human Rights*, 10 December 1948, 217 A (III), Article 1; online: www.unhcr.org/refworld/docid/3ae6b3712c.html [accessed 17 January 2012].

rights of others.

In recent years, competing human rights claims have emerged as a challenging issue for human rights commissions across Canada. The Ontario Human Rights Commission (the OHRC) has found that human rights claims increasingly involve situations where it appears that multiple claims are at stake. For example, a claimant may say that their statutory human rights have been violated by a respondent who then, in turn, claims a defence that is also established by human rights legislation. The human rights grounds most often cited in competing human rights claims include gender, creed, sexual orientation, and disability, although other grounds and legal rights have also been invoked.

Ontario's *Human Rights Code* (the *Code*) says the OHRC's mandate includes reducing tension and conflict in Ontario's communities and encouraging and co-ordinating plans, programs, and activities to do this. The OHRC has developed this policy to help address difficult situations involving competing rights.

Caselaw dealing with competing human rights claims has been developing slowly in Canada. The courts have said we must go through a process on a case-by-case basis to search for solutions to reconcile competing rights and accommodate individuals and groups, to the greatest extent possible. This search can be challenging, controversial, and sometimes dissatisfying to one side or the other. But it is a shared responsibility and will be made easier when we better understand the nature of one another's rights and obligations and show mutual respect for the dignity and worth of everyone involved. Finding the best solution for maximizing enjoyment of rights takes dialogue and even debate. To this end, there is a clear need for human rights policy guidance to supplement legal interpretation.

The OHRC has found that public debates on competing rights often relate to the presence of minority communities and how far the dominant culture should accommodate the rights of these groups. For example, in the post 9/11 world, various cultural and religious practices of Muslims have been called "inappropriate" or "unacceptable" by elements of the majority culture. These scenarios have commonly been referred to as matters of "competing rights" in the media. Others have questioned the extent to which publicly-funded schools ought to incorporate recognition of and respect for sexual diversity, including diverse family forms such as same-sex families.

The Right Honourable Beverley McLachlin, the Chief Justice of the Supreme Court of Canada, has extensive experience in the areas of human and *Charter* rights. She has written:

> We need human rights. Whether we like it or not, religious, ethnic and cultural diversity is part of our modern world — and increasingly, part of our national and community reality. Human rights and the respect for every individual upon which they rest, offer the best hope for reconciling the conflicts this diversity is bound to generate. If we are to live together in peace and harmony — within our nations and as nations in the wider world — we must find ways to accommodate each other.[6]

The OHRC engaged in extensive background work to develop this policy. In addition to conducting legal and social science research, the OHRC developed a detailed caselaw review on competing rights.[7] The OHRC also met with a wide range of individuals and organizations that either deal directly with competing rights situations, or have significant expertise in the area. For more detail on the policy development process, see Appendix B.

---

6 The Right Honourable Beverley McLachlin, P.C., Chief Justice of Canada, "Human Rights Protection in Canada," (2009) *Osgoode Hall Review of Law and Policy* (Vol. 2, Issue 1) at 20.

7 See *The Shadow of the Law: Surveying the Case Law Dealing with Competing Rights Claims*. This publication is available online: www.ohrc.on.ca/en/issues/reconciling/shadow.

2. Practical steps to reduce potential for conflict

Employers, housing providers, educators, and other responsible parties covered by the *Code* have the ultimate responsibility for maintaining an inclusive environment that is free from discrimination and harassment, and where everyone's human rights are respected. Organizations and institutions operating in Ontario have a legal duty to take steps to prevent and respond to situations involving competing rights.

There are proactive and practical steps that organizations should take to help reduce the potential for human rights conflict and competing rights. Organizations should be very familiar with the *Code* and with their obligations under it. They should take steps to educate and train responsible individuals on competing rights situations and the OHRC's *Policy on Competing Human Rights.*

It may be helpful for organizations to think of their responsibility to deal with competing rights matters as parallel to their already existing responsibilities relating to the human rights accommodation process. Organizations might consider assigning the responsibility for handling competing rights situations to the same people that are already responsible for dealing with accommodation issues. It could be the job of these people to educate and train others (including new staff), to monitor their environments to detect trends relating to competing rights, etc.

Employers, housing providers, educators, and other responsible parties can help promote a healthy and inclusive environment for individuals protected by the *Code* by having a clear and comprehensive competing rights policy. The policy should include the process to be followed when a competing rights situation arises, alert all parties to their rights, roles and responsibilities, and commit the organization to deal with competing rights matters promptly and efficiently. An effective competing rights policy supports the equity and diversity goals of organizations and institutions and makes good business sense. For more detail on the suggested contents of an internal policy, see Appendix E of this policy.

Everyone in an organization should be aware of the policy and the steps for resolving complaints. This can be done by:

- giving policies to everyone as soon as they are introduced
- making all employees, tenants, students, etc. aware of them by including the policies in any orientation material
- training people, especially people in positions of responsibility, on the contents of the policies, and providing ongoing education on competing rights issues.

Tribunals and courts often find organizations liable, and assess damages, based on failure to respond appropriately to address discrimination and harassment. Some things to consider when deciding whether an organization has met its duty to respond to a human rights claim include:

- what procedures were in place to deal with discrimination and harassment
- how promptly the organization responded to the complaint
- how seriously the complaint was treated
- what resources were made available to deal with the complaint
- whether the organization provided a healthy environment for the person who complained
- how well the action taken was communicated to the person who complained.

Taking proactive and effective steps to address competing rights matters will help to protect an organization from liability if it is ever named as a respondent in a human rights claim involving competing rights.[8]

---

8 The OHRC's *Guidelines on Developing Human Rights Policies and Procedures* provides more information to help organizations meet their human rights obligations and take proactive steps to make sure

3. Goals of this policy

The main goal of this policy is to provide clear, user-friendly guidance to organizations, policy makers, litigants, adjudicators, and others on how to assess, handle, and resolve competing rights claims. The policy will help various sectors, organizations, and individuals deal with everyday situations of competing rights, and avoid the time and expense of bringing a legal challenge before a court or human rights decision maker.

It is in keeping with promoting social harmony to ensure that effective conflict resolution mechanisms are in place to address various types of conflict. This policy provides a framework for addressing competing rights situations that can be used as is, or adapted to meet the specific needs of individual organizations.

The courts have been clear that context is crucial in competing rights cases and each situation must be assessed on a case-by-case basis. This policy is intended to be a useful tool for individuals and organizations as they deal with different types of conflict.

It sets out a process, based in existing caselaw, to analyze and reconcile competing rights. This process is flexible and can apply to any competing rights claim under the Canadian *Charter of Rights and Freedoms*, provincial or federal human rights legislation or another legislative scheme.

The process builds in specific objectives and considerations for the organizations and individuals involved. They should:

- show dignity and respect for one another
- encourage mutual recognition of interests, rights, and obligations
- facilitate maximum recognition of rights, wherever possible
- help parties to understand the scope of their rights and obligations

---

their environments are free from discrimination and harassment. The guidelines are available online: www.ohrc.on.ca/en/resources/Policies/gdpp/view

- address stigma and power imbalances and help to give marginalized individuals and groups a voice
- encourage cooperation and shared responsibility for finding agreeable solutions that maximize enjoyment of rights.

The approach in this policy can help organizations and decision makers resolve and even avoid apparent rights conflicts altogether. But in some cases litigation may be unavoidable, particularly where matters prove to be too complex to resolve informally, where parties are not willing to take part in the reconciliation process, or where all concerned may want the guidance of a court or tribunal.

4. What are competing rights?

In general, competing human rights involve situations where parties to a dispute claim that the enjoyment of an individual or group's human rights and freedoms, as protected by law, would interfere with another's rights and freedoms. This complicates the normal approach to resolving a human rights dispute where only one side claims a human rights violation. In some cases, only one party is making a human rights claim, but the claim conflicts with the legal entitlements of another party or parties.

4.1 Defining terms

Although there may be a perception that a competing rights situation exists, one must recognize that not all claims will be equal before the law: some claims have been afforded a higher legal status and greater protection than others. For example, after World War II, the United Nations enshrined the paramount importance of human rights in the *Universal Declaration of Human Rights.* The *Declaration* opens:

> Whereas recognition of the inherent dignity and of the equal and inalienable rights of all members of the human family is

the foundation of freedom, justice and peace in the world . . .[9]

Legal systems around the world have responded to this universal commitment to world peace by granting special protection to human rights. Canada recognizes the unique status of human rights in its *Charter of Rights and Freedoms*, a comprehensive list of rights and fundamental freedoms entrenched in the Constitution of Canada that is intended to unify Canadians around a set of principles that embody those rights.

In Ontario, the provincial legislature included a primacy clause in the Ontario *Human Rights Code*, giving it the ability to trump other provincial legislation. Courts have also commented on the "quasi-constitutional" status of human rights legislation and stated the importance of interpreting the guaranteed rights in a broad and purposive manner that best ensures that society's anti-discrimination goals are reached.

The following frequently used terms are defined in an attempt to show how they are distinguishable from one another.

Human rights

Human rights are inalienable, indivisible, universal entitlements codified in international and domestic law. In Canada, they are protected and interpreted through:

- the Canadian *Charter of Rights and Freedoms*
- provincial-territorial human rights legislation
- decisions of tribunals and courts
- human rights commission policy statements, interventions, and other mandated functions
- international law/instruments (ratified treaties, treaty body comments/decisions, international, and other jurisdictional court decisions).

Statutory human rights are also accompanied by defences, as set out in human rights legislation, and sections of the

9 *Universal Declaration of Human Rights*, above note 5.

Charter. For example, the right to freedom of expression guaranteed by section 2(b) of the *Charter* may be circumscribed by reasonable limits as contemplated in section 1 of the *Charter.*[10] A person's right to freedom of expression may be limited, for example, where their views incite hatred toward an identifiable group.

Legal entitlements

For the purposes of this policy, legal entitlements are non-human rights-related rights that are also codified in legislation (e.g. the *Occupational Health and Safety Act* and the *Residential Tenancies Act*), and the common law (i.e. caselaw). They are rights that are legally actionable: for example, the violation of a person's right to "reasonable enjoyment" of their rental housing could be litigated in Ontario before the Landlord and Tenant Board, the adjudicative body that administers the *Residential Tenancies Act.*

Interests

An interest is a matter in which someone has a personal concern, share, portion, or stake. Interests may be societal and/or individual. Although interests are not legal rights, they are sometimes misunderstood and misclassified as such. In some cases, an interest could be elevated to the status of a right, if it is validated by a legal body. For example, a court or tribunal could find that an interest is *bona fide* (genuine) and reasonable in the circumstances: "the best interests of the child" have been given a high legal status and used by courts and tribunals to determine a wide range of issues involving children. Or, a court could find that an interest is of such magnitude that it constitutes a reasonable limit under section 1 of a *Charter* right. For example, the Supreme Court of Canada has held that a requirement that all licensed drivers be photographed,

10 Section 1 of the *Charter* states: "The *Canadian Charter of Rights and Freedoms* guarantees the rights and freedoms set out in it subject only to such reasonable limits prescribed by law as can be demonstrably justified in a free and democratic society": *The Constitution Act, 1982,* being Schedule B to the *Canada Act 1982* (UK), 1982, c 11.

even though it interfered with the right to freedom of religion of Hutterites, was justified under section 1 of the *Charter* due to the state's interest in preventing identity theft and fraud.[11]

Values

Values are moral principles, standards, and/or things that a person (or group) believes are vital for achieving "the good" or excellence in any sphere of life. Some values may be reflected in law. For example, the Preamble to the *Code* is informed by the principles of mutual respect and the recognition of the dignity and worth of every person. Generally, however, values are subjective and not legally actionable in and of themselves. Understanding the individual or social values that may underlie a human rights claim will help parties and may inform its ultimate disposition. For example, in *Ross v New Brunswick School District No. 15*, the Supreme Court of Canada gave special recognition to the importance of public education and the vulnerability of children when it unanimously upheld a human rights Board of Inquiry finding that a teacher's off-duty anti-Semitic comments undermined his ability to fulfill his functions as a teacher. The Court concluded that the Board of Inquiry was correct in concluding that his continued employment as a teacher constituted discrimination in public education.[12]

There are many situations in which rights, interests, and values seem to conflict or compete. When evaluating situations of competing rights, human rights and other legally codified rights will usually hold a higher status than interests and values. However, in some circumstances, interests and values may represent reasonable limits on rights and human rights, as envisioned by section 1 of the *Charter*. This policy is meant mainly to be a tool for resolving situations where there is a conflict of human rights and rights that are legally protected.

---

11 *Alberta* v *Hutterian Brethren of Wilson Colony*, 2009 SCC 37.

12 *Ross* v *New Brunswick School District No. 15*, [1996] 1 S.C.R. 825.

4.2 Examples of competing rights situations

A competing human rights situation exists when legally protected rights are present in both claims, and at least one of the claims connects to human rights law. Based on this definition, allegations of competing human rights scenarios might include the following:

4.2.1 *Code* right v *Code* right

The Ontario *Human Rights Code* prohibits discrimination based on fifteen grounds: race, ancestry, place of origin, colour, ethnic origin, citizenship, creed, sex, sexual orientation, age, marital status, family status, disability, receipt of public assistance (in housing only), and record of offences (in employment only). Competing rights claims may potentially arise relating to any *Code* ground. However, situations of conflict often involve creed, sex, gender identity, sexual orientation, marital status, or disability.

Example: A civil marriage commissioner objects to performing a marriage ceremony for a same-sex couple, claiming that it violates his religious beliefs. He claims that under the *Code*, he has the right to be free from discrimination based on religion in employment. The couple wishing to receive the service claims that their right under the *Code* to be free from discrimination because of sexual orientation in services is being breached.[13]

---

13 The Saskatchewan Court of Appeal recently considered whether civil marriage commissioners should have the right to refuse to perform same-sex marriage ceremonies based on their religious beliefs: *Marriage Commissioners Appointed Under the Marriage Act (Re)*, 2011, SKCA 3 (CanLII). In two separate decisions, all five judges of the court found that proposed amendments to Saskatchewan's *The Marriage Act, 1995*, which would have allowed individual marriage commissioners to refuse to conduct a marriage ceremony if doing so would be contrary to their religious beliefs, violated the equality rights provision (s. 15) of the

It is also possible for competing claims to involve the same ground.

Example: A college professor's guide dog is affecting one of her students who has a severe allergy to dogs. Both individuals might make *Code*-based human rights claims on the ground of disability.

4.2.2 *Code* right v *Code* legal defence

In addition to providing protection from discrimination based on specific enumerated grounds, the *Code* includes exemptions that may act as a defence to a claim of discrimination. In many cases, these exemptions are deliberate attempts by those who wrote the legislation to address and help resolve situations where rights might compete.[14]

Example: A religious organization, providing supportive group living to persons with disabilities of any denomination, requires staff to abide by a religious code of behaviour. The organization dismisses a support worker once it learns she is in a same-sex relationship. The dismissed worker might claim *Code*-based discrimination on the ground of sexual orientation while the religious organization might claim a *Code* defence under section 24(1)(a) that allows restrictions on terms of employment for religious and other types of organizations in certain circumstances.[15]

Charter. Consistent with the general approach to reconciling competing rights under the *Charter*, both decisions then balanced the right to be free from discrimination based on sexual orientation against the religious rights of the marriage commissioners under s. 1 of the *Charter* and concluded, for slightly different reasons, that the equality rights infringement could not be justified despite the goal of addressing the religious objections of the marriage commissioners. See also *Nichols v M.J.*, 2009 SKQB 299 (CanLII).

14 See section 5.8 of this policy entitled "Defences found in legislation may restrict rights," for more detailed information.

15 *Ontario Human Rights Commission v Christian Horizons*, 2010 ONSC

4.2.3 *Code* right v other legislated right

In some cases, competing rights claims may involve *Code* grounds and other legal entitlements.

Example: Some parents want the Ministry of Education to modify its sex education curriculum so it does not interfere with their beliefs: some for religious-based reasons, some for personal reasons. Other parents support the new curriculum changes: some based on the *Code* ground of family status and sexual orientation. Others want the new curriculum, based on the legislated right to public education. Parents opposed to certain types of sex education because of their beliefs might claim discrimination on

---

2105 (CanLII) dealt with the ability of a religious organization that operates residential homes and camps for persons with developmental disabilities to rely on the special employment defence in section 24(1)(a) of the *Code* in defence of a claim of discrimination because of sexual orientation. Connie Heintz, a support worker in a community living residence operated by Christian Horizons, had signed a Lifestyle and Morality Statement required by Christian Horizons. The statement identified, among other things, "homosexual relationships" as inappropriate behaviour rejected by Christian Horizons. Several years after beginning her employment, Ms. Heintz came to an understanding of her sexual orientation and entered into a same-sex relationship. When this became known to the employer, she was offered counselling to assist her to comply with the Lifestyle and Morality Statement prohibiting "homosexuality." Ms. Heintz alleged that after that, she was unfairly disciplined for her attitude and performance and exposed to a poisoned work environment. For Christian Horizons to rely on this defence it had to show: (1) that it is a "religious organization"; (2) it is "primarily engaged in serving the interests of persons identified by" their creed and employs only people who are similarly identified; and (3) religious adherence is a reasonable and *bona fide* qualification because of the nature of the employment. On appeal, the Divisional Court found that Christian Horizons failed to meet the third element of the s. 24(1)(a) defence and discrimination was found.

the *Code* ground of creed. Other parents might claim a *Code* right based on family status, sexual orientation, and a legislated right to a curriculum based on the broader purpose and requirements of the *Education Act*.

4.2.4 *Code* right v *Charter* right

There may be situations where rights that are protected under the *Code* may compete with rights guaranteed by the *Charter*.

Example: A man describing himself as a "born again" Christian often discusses his new religious enthusiasm with his employees. He has tried several times to encourage workers to come to his church meetings, and for Christmas gives each employee a Bible as a gift. Employees have made it clear that they do not welcome or appreciate his comments and conduct in their secular workplace.

The employees could argue that the *Code* right to be free from discrimination based on creed includes the right not to be subjected to proselytizing at work. The employer might argue that he is exercising his freedom of expression rights under the *Charter.*

4.2.5 *Code* right v common law right

In some cases, a right protected by the *Code* may bump up against a right established by common law.

Example: A Jewish family is asked to remove a temporary *sukkah* hut placed on their balcony for religious celebration because it does not comply with the condominium's bylaws and is said to be interfering with the neighbours' enjoyment of their balcony. The Jewish family claims discrimination on the ground of creed while the condominium co-owners might claim a right to peaceful enjoyment of property based on common law.[16]

---

16 *Syndicat Northcrest v Amselem*, 2004 SCC 47

4.2.6 International treaty right v *Code/Charter* defence

Canada has signed and ratified many different international human rights conventions, some of which include complaint mechanisms. There may be situations where rights set out in these treaties conflict with domestic rights and obligations.

Example: Non-Catholic religious school users claim a right to non-discriminatory religious school funding based on provisions of the United Nations' *International Covenant on Civil and Political Rights*.[17] The UN treaty body responsible for the Covenant found that Ontario's public funding of the Catholic school system to the exclusion of all other religions was discriminatory.[18] The Ontario government relied on provisions of the *Education Act*, an exemption in the *Human Rights Code*, the *Charter* and related caselaw in its defence.

---

17 UN General Assembly, *International Covenant on Civil and Political Rights*, 16 December 1966, United Nations, Treaty Series, vol. 999, p. 171, available online: www.unhcr.org/refworld/docid/3ae6b3aa0.html [accessed 17 January 2012].

18 Consideration of Reports Submitted by States Parties. Under Article 40 of the Covenant, *Concluding Observations of the Human Rights Committee*, Canada, CPR/C/CAN/CO/5, 20 April 2006, at para. 21: The Committee expressed concern about the State party's responses relating to the Committee's views in the case *Waldman v Canada* (Communication No. 694/1996, Views adopted on 3 November 1999), requesting that an effective remedy be granted to the author eliminating discrimination on the basis of religion in the distribution of subsidies to schools (arts. 2, 18, and 26). The State party should adopt steps in order to eliminate discrimination on the basis of religion in the funding of schools in Ontario. Note, however, that in *Adler v Ontario*, [1996] 3 S.C.R. 609, the Supreme Court of Canada considered the constitutional obligation to fund private denominational education and found that the *Ontario Schools Act* did not violate sections 2(a) or 15(1) of the *Canadian Charter of Rights and Freedoms*.

4.2.7 Charter right v *Charter* right

There may be situations where one person's rights under the *Charter* may compete with another person's *Charter* rights.

Example: A number of decisions dealing with the production of medical or other sensitive records in court or tribunal proceedings have considered the relationship between privacy and equality rights and the right to make full answer and defence, all rights protected by the *Charter*. In *R. v O'Connor*, a case in which the accused was charged with a number of sexual offences, the Supreme Court of Canada established a procedure for determining when a victim's medical and therapeutic records, in the possession of third parties such as physicians, must be released to the accused for meaningful full answer and defence.[19]

5. Key legal principles[20]

While the courts have not set a clear formula or analytical approach for dealing with competing rights, they have provided some guidance. Where rights appear to be in conflict, *Charter* principles require decision makers to try to "reconcile" both sets of rights. Although there are no "bright-line rules"[21] for dealing with competing rights claims, legal decisions have identified a number of fundamental principles that provide direction in how to deal with these types of scenarios, as well as what to avoid.[22] The courts

---

19 *R. v O'Connor*, [1995] 4 S.C.R. 411.

20 The information in this section has been adapted from the OHRC publication, *The Shadow of the Law: Surveying the Case Law Dealing with Competing Rights Claims, supra,* note 7, which provides a more detailed discussion of the case law dealing with competing rights.

21 *R. v N.S.*, 2010 ONCA 670 at para 97. Leave to appeal to the Supreme Court of Canada granted: 2011 Can LII 14361 (SCC). The appeal was heard by the Supreme Court on 8 December 2011.

22 Examples of "what not to do" in a competing rights scenario include:

have recognized that the specific facts will often determine the outcome of the case. Therefore many of the principles are abstract, and allow for some flexibility in approaching claims on a case-by-case basis. While many of these principles arose in the context of *Charter* litigation, they also provide guidance for other types of human rights conflicts:

1. No rights are absolute
2. There is no hierarchy of rights
3. Rights may not extend as far as claimed
4. The full context, facts, and constitutional values at stake must be considered
5. Must look at extent of interference (only *actual* burdens on rights trigger conflicts)
6. The core of a right is more protected than its periphery
7. Aim to respect the importance of both sets of rights
8. Statutory defences may restrict rights of one group and give rights to another

Organizations must consider these legal principles when they deal with competing rights situations.

5.1 No rights are absolute

A consistent principle in the caselaw is that no legal right is absolute, but is inherently limited by the rights and freedoms of others.[23] In *R. v Mills*, Supreme Court of Canada Justice McLachlin (as she then was) and Supreme Court of Canada Justice Iacobucci stated:

---

(1) treating any right as absolute; (2) regarding any rights as inherently superior to another; (3) accepting a hierarchy of rights; and (4) approaching rights in the abstract or in a factual vacuum.

23 *Trinity Western University v British Columbia College of Teachers*, [2001] 1 S.C.R. 772 at para. 29; *P. (D.) v S. (C.)*, [1993] 4 S.C.R. 141 at 182; *B. (R.) v Children's Aid Society of Metropolitan Toronto*, [1995] 1 S.C.R. 315 at para. 226.

> At play in this appeal are three principles, which find their support in provisions of the Charter. These are full answer and defence, privacy, and equality. No single principle is absolute and capable of trumping the others; all must be defined in light of competing claims. As Lamer C.J. stated in Dagenais "... When the protected rights of two individuals come into conflict .... Charter principles require a balance to be achieved that fully respects the importance of both sets of rights." This illustrates the importance of interpreting rights in a contextual manner — not because they are of intermittent importance but because they often inform, and are informed by, other similarly deserving rights or values at play in particular circumstances.[24]

Justice Iacobucci emphasizes this point in an article entitled "'Reconciling Rights': The Supreme Court of Canada's Approach to Competing *Charter* Rights," when he states: "A particular Charter right must be defined in relation to other rights and with a view to the underlying context in which the apparent conflict arises."[25]

Example: A person has a right to freedom of expression under the *Charter*, but they do not have a right to make child pornography.

In the context of freedom of belief or religion, the courts have found that the "freedom to hold beliefs is broader than the freedom to act upon them" where to do so would interfere with the rights of others.[26]

The Ontario *Human Rights Code* protects against discrimination on the basis of creed. But this protection does not extend to religious belief that incites hatred or violence against other indi-

---

24 *R. v Mills*, 1999 CanLII 637 (SCC) at para. 61.

25 The Honourable Justice Frank Iacobucci, "'Reconciling Rights' The Supreme Court of Canada's Approach to Competing Charter Rights," *Supreme Court Law Review* (2003), 20 S.C.L.R. (2d) 137 at 139.

26 *Trinity Western*, above note 23 at para. 29.

viduals or groups, or to practices or observances that are said to have a religious basis, but which contravene the *Criminal Code* or international human rights principles.

Other examples include limiting the right to freedom of expression guaranteed by section 2(b) of the *Charter* where the expression could compromise a fair trial guaranteed by section 11(d) and section 7 of the *Charter*,[27] incite hatred as defined in the *Criminal Code of Canada* and some human rights legislation,[28] or result in discrimination against a minority group in our society.[29]

5.2 No hierarchy of rights

The Supreme Court of Canada has also been clear that there is no hierarchy of rights[30] — all rights are equally deserving and an approach that would place some rights over others must be avoided.[31] No right is inherently superior to another right.[32]

Example: In *Dagenais v Canadian Broadcasting Corporation*, the Supreme Court of Canada was asked to order a publication ban. The ban would have prevented the CBC from airing a mini-series showing a fictional account of sexual and physical abuse at a Catholic boy's school in Newfoundland during the trial of

---

27 *Dagenais v Canadian Broadcasting Corp.*, [1994] 3 S.C.R. 835.

28 *Canada (Human Rights Commission) v Taylor*, [1990] 3 S.C.R. 892; *R. v Keegstra*, [1990] 3 S.C.R. 697.

29 *Ross*, above note 12.

30 Note that there may be a hierarchy of *Charter* vs. non-*Charter* rights and *Code* vs. non-*Code* rights. The *Charter* has primacy over all laws in Canada. As well, quasi-constitutional rights contained in human rights laws generally have primacy over non-constitutional legal rights (see for example s. 47(2) of the Ontario *Human Rights Code*, R.S.O. 1990, c H. 19).

31 *Dagenais,* above note 27; *Mills*, above note 24 at para. 61.

32 *R. v N.S.*, above note 21 para 48. See also *Mills*, *ibid.*; *Dagenais*, *ibid.* at 877; *R. v Crawford*, [1995] 1 S.C.R. 858 at para. 34.

several members of a Catholic religious order. They were charged with physical and sexual abuse of young boys at schools in Ontario. The request for the publication ban required the court to balance the key constitutional rights of free expression (s 2(b) of the *Charter*) and the right to a fair trial (s 11(d)). Chief Justice Lamer stated:

> A hierarchical approach to rights, which places some rights over others, must be avoided, both when interpreting the Charter and when developing the common law. When the protected rights of two individuals come into conflict . . . Charter principles require a balance to be achieved that fully respects the importance of both sets of rights.[33]

5.3 Rights may not extend as far as claimed

When faced with a competing right scenario, organizations must assess whether the rights extend as far as the parties claim. This validation process has two main components:

1. Does the claim engage a genuine legal right?
2. When the evidence is examined, can the individual with the claim bring himself or herself within the asserted right?[34]

---

33 *Dagenais, ibid.*

34 For example, a claim that there is an interference with freedom of religion may not be found to be legitimate if, on the facts of the case and in the relevant context, the asserted religious belief is not found to be sincerely held. In *Bothwell v Ontario (Minister of Transportation)*, 2005 CanLII 1066 (ON S.C.D.C.), the Court considered all the evidence relating to the claimant's objection to a digital driver's licence photograph for religious reasons and found that the claimant did not meet his burden of establishing a sincerely held religious belief as set out in the Supreme Court decision in *Amselem*, above note 16. The Court was influenced, in part, by the fact that the claimant had raised a number of privacy, rather than religious, concerns and that his actions were not consistent with his asserted religious beliefs. Another example

The courts have suggested that for a competing rights scenario to arise at all, a legal right must first be found to exist.[35] When the facts and law are set out clearly, in context, not every rights claim will be found to be legally valid.

Human rights tribunals have considered and rejected several justifications for discriminatory conduct which could appear to be competing rights. For example, decision makers have not accepted "customer preference" or "business or economic interests" as a valid competing right in cases involving discrimination contrary to human rights legislation.[36]

Example: Organizations and individuals objecting to breastfeeding in public have claimed a "right" to request that a woman cover herself, move to a private area, etc. This right has sometimes been articulated as a freedom of expression claim. At first glance, there appears to be a conflict between freedom of expression and freedom from discrimination based on sex. But a careful consideration tells a different story. Court and Tribunal decisions have clearly established a woman's right to breastfeed in public.[37] These decisions have concluded that actions which prevent a woman from breastfeeding in public are discriminatory. These precedents mean that in the absence of a compelling, equally valid right (or a *Code* defence such as health and safety),

---

of failing to bring oneself within the right would be if asserting the right to free expression concerning activity that (a) does not convey or attempt to convey a meaning, and thus has no expressive content, or (b) that conveys a meaning but through a violent form of expression; see *Irwin Toy Ltd. v Quebec (Attorney General)*, [1989] 1 S.C.R. 927.

35 *R. v N.S.*, above note 21 at paras. 49 and 65.

36 See for example: *Giguere v Popeye Restaurant*, 2008 HRTO 2 (CanLII) citing a number of other human rights decisions. In *Giguere*, the Tribunal stated at para. 77: "Economic interests and rights do not trump human rights, unless there is a specific exemption in the legislation."

37 See, for example, *Quebec et Giguere v Montreal (Ville)* (2003) 47 C.H.R.R. D/67.

a woman has an unqualified right to breastfeed in public. Freedom of expression is not a valid counter-claim because there is no established positive legal right to individual preference. In other words, you may have an opinion about a woman breastfeeding in public, but you cannot use your preference to stop an activity that is already recognized as an established equality right.

If the claim does engage a legal right, it is then necessary to consider whether on the facts of the case, the individual can bring him or herself within that right. Evidence may need to be called to prove that the claim falls within the parameters of the right unless the engagement of the right is clear from the circumstances.[38]

In the case of *Grant v Willcock*, a refusal to sell property to a racialized person did not fall under the right to liberty guaranteed by section 7 of the *Charter*. A human rights tribunal (formerly the "Board of Inquiry") found in the circumstances of the case that liberty rights did not extend to the liberty to discriminate based on a prohibited ground in the public sale of private property.[39]

---

38 In *R. v N.S.*, the court noted that unlike an accused person's right to make full answer and defence in a fair trial, a witness' right to freedom of religion is not inherently triggered by taking part in the criminal justice process. A witness who seeks to exercise a religious practice while testifying must establish that the practice falls within the scope of the right to freedom of religion. That inquiry must almost inevitably involve testimony from the witness explaining the connection between the practice and his or her religious beliefs, although in most cases the inquiry would be relatively straightforward; *R. v N.S.*, above note 21 at paras. 65-66. In a BC Human Rights Tribunal decision, the applicant was found not to have alleged facts "from which a nexus could be inferred" between the alleged adverse treatment she received and her religious beliefs. Therefore, there was insufficient evidence to establish that a religious right was engaged; *Chiang v Vancouver Board of Education*, 2009 B.C.H.R.T. 319 at para 115.

39 *Grant v Willcock* (1990), 13 C.H.R.R. D/22 (Ont. Bd.Inq.).

5.4 Consider full context, facts, and constitutional values

5.4.1 Context and facts

Once the competing issues are identified and described, the rights must be defined in relation to one another by looking at the context in which the apparent conflict arises.[40] This approach is critical — the courts have repeatedly held that *Charter* rights and human rights do not exist in a vacuum and must be examined in context to settle conflicts between them.

Example: The Ontario Court of Appeal stated clearly in *R. v N.S.*: "reconciling competing *Charter* values is necessarily fact-specific. Context is vital and context is variable."[41]

Supreme Court of Canada Justice Frank Iacobucci expressed a similar view:

> The key to rights reconciliation, in my view, lies in a fundamental appreciation for *context*. Charter rights are not defined in abstraction, but rather in the particular factual matrix in which they arise.[42]
>
> . . .
>
> Courts must be acutely sensitive to context, and approach the Charter analysis flexibly with a view to giving fullest possible expression to all the rights involved.[43]

Even slight variations in context may be critical in determining how to reconcile the rights. For example, in a situation that measures the right to freedom of expression against the impact of that expression on a vulnerable group, the precise tone, con-

---

40 *Mills*, above note 24; *Trinity Western*, above note 23.

41 *R. v N.S.*, above note 21 at para. 97.

42 Above note 25 at 141.

43 *Ibid* at 167.

tent and manner of delivery of the impugned message all have a significant impact on assessing its effect and the degree of constitutional protection it should be afforded. As noted by Justice Rosalie Abella in her dissenting judgment in *Bou Malhab v Diffusion Métromédia CMR Inc.*, "[T]here is a big difference between yelling 'fire' in a crowded theatre and yelling 'theatre' in a crowded fire station."[44]

5.4.2 Underlying constitutional and societal values

As part of understanding the context, the constitutional and societal values at stake must be appreciated and understood.[45] This "scoping of rights" allows some rights conflicts to be resolved.

Several considerations come into play in scoping the rights. A contextual analysis will often involve weighing the underlying values of Canadian society incorporated in various legal instruments and caselaw. For example, as the Supreme Court of Canada stated in *R. v Oakes*, a case that set out the test for determining whether an infringement of *Charter* rights can be justified in a free and democratic society:

> The Court must be guided by the values and principles essential to a free and democratic society which I believe embody, to name but a few, respect for the inherent dignity of the human person, commitment to social justice and equality, accommodation of a wide variety of beliefs, respect for cultural and group identity, and faith in social and political institutions which enhance the participation of individuals and groups in society.

---

44 *Bou Malhab v Diffusion Métromédia CMR Inc.*, [2011] 1 S.C.R. 214 at para. 96.

45 *Danson v Ontario (Attorney General)*, [1990] 2 S.C.R. 1086 at 1099–1101; *MacKay v Manitoba*, [1989] 2 S.C.R. 357 at 362–63, 366; *Canadian Council of Churches v Canada (Minister of Employment and Immigration)*, [1992] 1 S.C.R. 236 at 253–55.

> The underlying values and principles of a free and democratic society are the genesis of the rights and freedoms guaranteed by the Charter and the ultimate standard against which a limit on a right or freedom must be shown, despite its effect, to be reasonable and demonstrably justified.[46]

The Preamble to the Ontario *Human Rights Code*, adapted from the *Universal Declaration of Human Rights*, also reflects societal values with respect to human rights and equality. To this end, four key principles emerge from the Preamble:

1. recognizing the dignity and worth of every person
2. providing equal rights and opportunities without discrimination that is contrary to law
3. creating a climate of understanding and mutual respect, so that
4. each person feels a part of the community and able to contribute fully to the development and well-being of the community and the province.

Inherent in these values is a balancing[47] of individual and group rights. The Preamble describes relational rights where the equality of each individual exists alongside community development and well-being. These values are not seen as hierarchical; one establishes and gives meaning to the other. In other words, the equality of each individual is fostered by creating a climate of mutual respect. At the same time, the community is fostered through the recognition of the inherent dignity and worth of each

---

46 *R. v Oakes*, [1986] 1 S.C.R. 103. It is significant that these words very closely echo those that describe the values and principles underlying human rights as found in the preamble to the Ontario *Human Rights Code* and human rights statutes across the country.

47 The term "balancing" has been used in a number of legal decisions involving competing rights: see, for example, *Ross*, above note 12 at paras. 73 and 74.

individual. The Preamble makes clear that human rights legislation does not simply deal with violations of equality rights — it is also designed to foster an inclusive climate of mutual respect.[48]

International human rights law can also be an indicator of a society's underlying values. By endorsing an international convention, for example, Canada has publicly stated its commitment to uphold the values the convention contains.[49]

There have been cases where a person's objections to what they see as a violation of their rights have not been successful because their views are not consistent with society's underlying values on human rights and equality. Decision makers should apply a contextual analysis that considers constitutional values and societal interests including equality rights of women, negative stereotyping of minorities, access to justice, and public confidence in the justice system.[50]

Example: *Chamberlain v Surrey School District No. 36*[51] involved a challenge to a school board's decision not to approve three books showing same-sex parented families as supplementary resources for use in teaching the family life curriculum. The Supreme Court of Canada noted that, while religious concerns of some parents could be considered, they could not be used to deny equal recognition and respect to other members of the community. The majority decision recognized the right to *hold* religious views, including the view that the practices of others are undesirable. But it emphasized that if a school is to function in

---

48 For a more detailed discussion on this point, see Ontario Human Rights Commission, "Balancing Conflicting Rights: Towards an Analytical Framework," (2005) at 7; available online: www.ohrc.on.ca/en/resources/discussion_consultation/balancingrights/pdf

49 For a more detailed discussion, see Sebastian Poulter, "Ethnic Minority Customs, English Law and Human Rights," (1987) 36 *International and Comparative Law Quarterly*, 589 at 596.

50 See *R. v N.S.*, above note 21.

51 *Chamberlain v Surrey School District No. 36*, [2002] 4 S.C.R. 710.

an atmosphere of tolerance and respect, these views could not become the basis of school policy.

In *Bruker v Marcovitz*,[52] the Supreme Court of Canada dealt with the relationship between freedom of religion and gender equality rights. A domestic dispute arose out of a husband's refusal to give his wife a religious divorce. The couple had signed an agreement to resolve their matrimonial disputes. The agreement included a term that the husband would give his wife a *get*.[53] However, for more than fifteen years the husband refused to honour his commitment and argued that a civil court could not enforce the agreement he signed without violating his religious rights. The majority of the judges of the Supreme Court of Canada disagreed. They found that the contract was a valid and binding obligation and that the husband was not protected from liability for breaching the agreement based on freedom of religion. In doing so, they suggested that the wife's rights were a factor, and so too were fundamental values in Canadian society.[54] The judges noted that the husband had "little to put on the

52 *Bruker v Marcovitz*, [2007] 3 S.C.R. 607.

53 A *get* is a Jewish divorce that would release a wife from marriage and allow her to remarry within the faith. Only a husband can give a *get* and there is no other process within the Jewish faith for releasing a wife from the marriage.

54 The majority of the Court noted that while courts would be reluctant to interfere in "strictly spiritual or doctrinal" religious matters, they will intervene when property or civil rights are engaged. They went on to question the husband's religious rights claim, stating they were having "difficulty discerning" how requiring him to comply with his agreement to give a *get* could conflict with a sincerely held religious belief and have non-trivial consequences for him. However, even if he could establish this, his claim of a religious right had to be balanced against competing values or harm that would result. The OHRC's *Policy on Creed and the Accommodation of Religious Observances* also recognizes limits on religious freedom and states at page 5 that it "does not extend

scales" both because he had freely entered into an agreement which he later claimed violated his rights, and because to allow him to back out of it would offend public policy:

> The public interest in protecting equality rights, the dignity of Jewish women in their independent ability to divorce and remarry, as well as the public benefit in enforcing valid and binding contractual obligations, are among the interests and values that outweigh Mr. Marcovitz's claim that enforcing [the agreement] would interfere with his religious freedom.

Not all competing rights decisions deal with discrimination issues directly. But many of the values underlying human rights protections — respect for human dignity, commitment to social justice and equality, accommodating a wide variety of beliefs and circumstances, protecting vulnerable persons and minority groups — are important when deciding how to reconcile or appropriately limit rights.

5.5 Look at extent of interference

When rights appear to be in conflict, a key consideration is to determine if there is an actual intrusion of one right on the other, and the extent of the interference. If the interference is minor or trivial, the right is not likely to receive much, if any, protection.

Example: In *Syndicat Northcrest v Amselem*, a Jewish family was asked to remove a *sukkah* (a temporary hut placed on their

---

to religions that incite hatred or violence against other individuals or groups, or to practices or observances that purport to have a religious basis but which contravene international human rights standards or criminal law." The Policy refers to female genital mutilation as a violation of human rights that is not protected on the ground of creed. The OHRC's *Policy on Creed and the Accommodation of Religious Observances* is available online: www.ohrc.on.ca/en/resources/Policies/PolicyCreedAccomodEN/pdf.

balcony for religious celebration) because it did not comply with the condominium's bylaws and was interfering with the neighbours' enjoyment of their balcony. The Supreme Court refused to engage in a balancing process under section 1 of the *Charter* between freedom of religion as it affected the right to peaceful enjoyment and free disposition of property, since, in the Court's view, the effect on the Jewish family was substantial while the effect on the co-owners was "at best, minimal," and therefore limiting religious freedom could not be justified.[55]

Unless there is a substantial impact on other rights, there is no need to go further in the resolution process.

Example: Providing rainbow stickers (which show support for lesbian, gay, bisexual, transsexual, transgender, intersex, queer, questioning, two-spirited, and allied communities) to a teacher, who could choose to display the stickers or not, was found not to create any burden or disadvantage on religious rights.[56]

Recognizing the rights of one group (e.g. the legalization of same-sex marriage) cannot, in itself, violate the rights of another (e.g. religious groups that do not recognize the right of persons of the same sex to marry) unless there is an actual impact on the rights of another (e.g. religious officials being asked to perform same-sex marriages). In *Reference re Same-Sex Marriage*, the Supreme Court of Canada stated:

> [T]he mere recognition of the equality rights of one group cannot, in itself, constitute a violation of the rights of another. The promotion of *Charter* rights and values enriches our society as a whole and the furtherance of those rights cannot undermine the very principles the *Charter* was meant to foster.[57]

---

55 *Amselem*, above note 16 at paras. 57 and 60.

56 *Chiang*, above note 38 at para 36.

57 *Reference re Same-Sex Marriage*, 2004 SCC 79 at para. 46. In *S.L. v Commission scolaire des Chênes*, 2012 SCC 7, the Supreme Court of

Similarly, speculation that a rights violation *may* occur is not enough – there must be evidence, and not just an unsupported assumption, that the enjoyment of one right will have a harmful effect on another.

Example: Requiring teaching students in a religious teacher's college to follow certain "community standards" prohibiting "homosexual activity" does not mean that graduates of the teaching program will discriminate against or show intolerance towards their students based on sexual orientation.[58]

5.6 Core of right more protected than periphery

If there is a substantial interference with the rights in question, the rights must be weighed or balanced; one right will give way to the other or both rights will be compromised. It appears from the law that one set of rights is more likely to be restricted when an action would be contrary to the "core," or a fundamental aspect, of another individual's rights. For example, the courts have said that requiring religious officials to perform same-sex marriages contrary to their religious beliefs[59] is different than allowing a person operating a business to refuse to offer his

---

Canada dismissed a challenge under s 2(a) of the Canadian *Charter of Rights and Freedoms* by parents who argued that a mandatory course on ethics and religion would interfere with their ability to pass on their Catholic faith to their children. The Court found that a person must prove, through objective evidence, that there is an interference with a religious right. While the parents sincerely believed that they had an obligation to pass on the precepts of their religion to their children, they did not objectively demonstrate that their ability to do so had been interfered with. The Supreme Court also stated that children's exposure to views that are different than what they have been taught by their families does not in itself violate religious rights (at para. 40).

58 *Trinity Western,* above note 23.

59 *Reference re Same-Sex Marriage*, above note 57.

printing services to a same-sex organization on the basis that it violates his religious beliefs. In the latter case, the court noted that commercial enterprise is at the "periphery" of freedom of religion, and therefore, the religious rights had to give way to the right to be free from discrimination in services based on sexual orientation.[60]

The court stated:

> The further the activity is from the core elements of the freedom, the more likely the activity is to impact on others and the less deserving the activity is of protection. Service of the public in a commercial service must be considered at the periphery of activities protected by freedom of religion.[61]

The courts have consistently acknowledged that individuals are free to hold religious beliefs or express their opinions - but they have also made it clear that there are limits to how these beliefs and opinions may be acted upon where they may deny equal recognition and respect to other marginalized members of society. To this end, the private exercise of a right is generally given greater protection than the public exercise of a right.

Example: The rights to freedom of expression and religion have been limited where the inherent dignity and equality of individuals protected under human rights legislation is significantly

---

60 In *Brockie v Brillinger (No. 2)*, (2002), 43 C.H.R.R. D/90 (Ont. Sup. Ct.), the Divisional Court noted that Mr. Brockie's exercise of his right to freedom of religion in the commercial marketplace is, at best, at the fringes of the right. Therefore, limits on his right to freedom of religion were found to be justified where it would cause harm to others, namely by infringing their *Code* right to be free from discrimination based on sexual orientation. The court left open the possibility that a different conclusion could be reached if the material being printed contained material that "might reasonably be held to be in direct conflict with the core elements of Mr. Brockie's religious beliefs." (at para. 56)

61 *Brockie v Brillinger (No. 2), ibid.* at para. 51.

engaged, such as where the writings of a teacher were found to have poisoned the educational environment for his Jewish students.[62]

For one right to prevail over another, the impact on the core of the right must be shown to be real and significant in the circumstances. Yet, even where this is found to be the case, there is still a duty to accommodate the yielding right as much as possible.

5.7 Respect importance of both sets of rights

Where rights appear to be in conflict, *Charter* principles require an approach that respects the importance of both sets of rights, as much as possible.[63] As noted in Supreme Court of Canada Justice Frank Iacobucci's article, and as cited with approval by the Ontario Court of Appeal:[64]

> . . . it is proper for courts to give the fullest possible expression to all relevant *Charter* rights, having regard to the broader factual context and to the other constitutional values at stake. [65]

However, potential compromises to both sets of rights, recently described as "constructive compromises" by the Ontario Court of Appeal, are part of the reconciliation process. These compromises "may minimize apparent conflicts . . . and produce a process in which both values can be adequately protected and respected."[66] Searching for compromises involves exploring measures that may lessen any potential harm to each set of rights.

This process of looking for options to reconcile competing human rights resembles the analysis under section 1 of the *Char-*

62 *Ross*, above note 12.

63 *Trinity Western,* above note 23 at para. 31; *Dagenais,* above note 27 at p. 877.

64 *R. v N.S.*, above note 21 at para. 47.

65 Above note 25 at 140.

66 *R. v N.S.*, above note 21 at para. 84.

ter and the process that must be followed as part of the duty to accommodate under human rights law. Similarly, in cases such as *Dagenais v Canadian Broadcasting Corp.*,[67] the Supreme Court directed courts considering a request for a publication ban to search for a "reasonably available and effective alternative measure" which would achieve the important objectives at stake.

When rights are in true conflict, some balancing may be required. One right may give way to another, or constructive compromises to both sets of rights may be found. In *R. v O'Connor*,[68] a case involving a victim's right to privacy in medical records and an accused person's right to make full answer and defence, a balance was achieved by first providing the disputed records to the court to review.

There may be rare cases where reconciling the rights in question is not possible. For example, in *R. v N.S.*,[69] the Ontario Court of Appeal acknowledged that while all rights are to be treated as equal at the outset, if there is no way to reconcile them, one right may be forced to give way to another. For example, when a conflict arises that truly harms an accused person's *Charter* right to make full answer and defence, that right will prevail. The countervailing right will have to yield as our justice system has always held that the threat of convicting an innocent person strikes at the heart of the principles of fundamental justice.[70]

---

67 *Dagenais*, above note 27.

68 *O'Connor*, above note 19.

69 *R.* v. *N.S.*, above note 21. The Supreme Court of Canada has granted leave to appeal the decision of the Ontario Court of Appeal. It will, therefore, soon have the opportunity to comment on or revise the approach to the competing rights at issue.

70 *R.* v. *N.S.*, *ibid.* at paras. 88-89; *Mills*, above note 24 at para. 89.

5.8 Defences found in legislation may restrict rights

Human rights laws and the *Charter* contain exceptions that allow differential treatment in certain circumstances. In many cases, these defences were put into legislation to recognize competing rights and may reflect lawmakers' efforts to reconcile a conflict between different rights.[71]

Often, statutory defences have been created to protect collective rights.[72] They typically deal with matters such as religious education, the ability of certain types of organizations serving the interests of a particular group to restrict their membership to persons who belong to that group; the ability to restrict access to certain facilities and shared housing by sex; and the rights of religious officials to refuse to conduct marriage ceremonies contrary to their religious beliefs.

The Ontario *Human Rights Code* also includes provisions that appear to be attempts by the Legislature to reduce competing rights conflicts. The Preamble to the *Code* offers initial guidance for addressing conflicting rights by reflecting the values underlying the *Code* and human rights legislation in general. The *Code* also contains several exceptions that help to avoid situations

---

71 Legislators are often in a good position to address the potential for rights to compete. As opposed to decision-makers, legislators have the ability to proactively address conflicts before they occur by drafting legislative language that can prevent conflicts from occurring in the first place. However, as one author notes, "Opting for the legislature as a preferential forum for dealing with conflicts of human rights may restrict the scope of the problem for the courts, but will not exclude it. There will always be cases in which the legislator does not foresee the negative implications that a rule protecting one right may have on another right": see Eva Brems, "Conflicting Human Rights: An Exploration in the Context of the Right to a Fair Trial in the European Convention for the Protection of Human Rights and Fundamental Freedoms," *Human Rights Quarterly* 27 (2005) 294 at 305.

72 See *Caldwell v Stewart*, [1984] 2 S.C.R. 603.

where rights could potentially compete. The exceptions under the *Code* that most often emerge in competing rights cases are sections 13, 18, 18.1, 20(3), and 24. The eligibility criteria contained in each of these sections restricts to whom and in what circumstances these exceptions will apply.

For example, section 13 of the *Code* attempts to balance a prohibition on an announced intention to discriminate with the freedom of expression of opinion.

> 13. (1) A right under Part I is infringed by a person who publishes or displays before the public or causes the publication or display before the public of any notice, sign, symbol, emblem, or other similar representation that indicates the intention of the person to infringe a right under Part I or that is intended by the person to incite the infringement of a right under Part I.
>
> (2) Subsection (1) shall not interfere with freedom of expression of opinion.

In recognition of the importance of freedom of expression as set out in this section, the OHRC intervened at the Human Rights Tribunal of Ontario in *Whitely v Osprey Media Publishing Inc. and Sun Media Corporation*. The case involved an allegation that an editorial in *The County Weekly News* discriminated against people who have moved to Prince Edward County from elsewhere. The applicant alleged discrimination in services because of place of origin. The OHRC argued that section 13 of the *Code* does not restrict newspapers from printing opinions that some people may not like. In its decision, the Tribunal agreed, saying ". . . publication of opinion in the media is a matter at the core of freedom of expression and freedom of the press in a democratic society."[73]

In another example, section 18 of the *Code* addresses "special interest organizations":

73 *Whiteley v Osprey Media Publishing*, 2010 HRTO 2152 (CanLII).

> The rights under Part I to equal treatment with respect to services and facilities, with or without accommodation, are not infringed where membership or participation in a religious, philanthropic, educational, fraternal or social institution or organization that is primarily engaged in serving the interests of persons identified by a prohibited ground of discrimination is restricted to persons who are similarly identified.

This section applies only to services and facilities that are restricted based on membership or participation in an organization that primarily serves the interests of persons identified by a prohibited ground of discrimination (e.g. an Italian club for older persons). To qualify for an exception under this section, membership and participation must be restricted to persons who are similarly identified with the primary service interests of the organization. Therefore, this provision accommodates religious freedoms by allowing religious institutions to grant preferences in their admission policies or membership based on religion.[74] The interpretation of this section in the caselaw balances freedom of association with equality rights. Like each of the other exception sections, this section considers the relationship between the private and public spheres. The public's right to be treated without discrimination must be considered against a private organization's right to limit its membership to an identified group.[75]

Section 1 is the primary site of internal balancing in the *Charter*. This section, also known as the "reasonable limits clause," allows the government to limit an individual's *Charter* rights. When the government has limited an individual's right, it has an

---

74 For example, under section 18, a private Christian post-secondary school can restrict its admissions to students who agree that "homosexuality" is a sin and undertake to refrain from "homosexual" practices.

75 *Martinie v Italian Society of Port Arthur* (1995), 24 C.H.R.R. D/169 (Ont. Bd. Of Inquiry). Note, this section could also apply to other organizations; for example, women's groups, ethnic organizations, etc.

onus to show, on a balance of probabilities, that the limitation was prescribed by law and is a reasonable limit in a free and democratic society. This is done by applying the "*Oakes* test." Simply put, the *Oakes* test considers:

1. Whether there is a serious and important government objective
2. Whether the way the government is trying to reach that objective is proportional (i.e. reasonable and justified). This consideration determines whether:
   a. the government's measures are carefully designed to reach the objective
   b. the approach used impacts on the rights at issue as little as possible
   c. the benefits from the government's measures outweigh the seriousness of the impact on the rights.[76]

In a competing rights situation, the *Oakes* test should be applied flexibly to find a balance between the infringed right and the right the state seeks to foster to justify the infringement. Once again, this requires close attention to the full context in the particular circumstances of the case before the court.

Example: The majority of the Supreme Court in *B. (R.) v Children's Aid Society*[77] found that the parents' decision to refuse a potentially life-saving blood transfusion for their baby was protected by freedom of religion. Using a process under the *Child*

---

76 The exact language for the test as set out in *R.* v. *Oakes*, above note 46 at para. 70 is:

1. There must be a pressing and substantial objective
2. The means to achieve that objective must be proportional
   a. The means must be rationally connected to the objective
   b. There must be minimal impairment of rights
   c. There must be proportionality between the infringement and objective

77 *B. (R.)*, above note 23.

Welfare Act, the child had been made a temporary ward of the Children's Aid Society which had consented to the blood transfusion. However, despite the serious contravention of the parents' section 2(a) rights, the infringement was justified under section 1 of the *Charter*. The state interest in protecting children at risk was balanced against the parents' rights and found, in this case, to outweigh them.

Several things are clear when one reads the decisions that consider defences to discrimination in human rights statutes. First, unlike human rights defences that limit an individual's right based on other interests (such as financial undue hardship),[78] defences that also recognize and promote the competing rights of other groups in society must not be interpreted overly narrowly. Second, despite this approach to interpretation, the defence has to be found to actually apply in the case at issue. Finally, this last point requires a full consideration of context based on the evidence in the circumstances of the case. In particular, the organization seeking to rely on the defence must be able to show, through objective evidence, the link between the actions that have a discriminatory impact on others and its enjoyment of its group right.

6. Analysis for addressing competing human rights situations

This section is based on a framework for addressing competing rights that the OHRC developed based on international human rights principles, caselaw, social science research, and consulta-

78 Section 17(2) of the *Code* prescribes three considerations in assessing whether an accommodation would cause undue hardship. These are: cost; outside sources of funding, if any; and health and safety requirements, if any.

tion with community partners and stakeholders.[79] The framework is set out in a summarized chart form at Appendix C.

The framework was developed with organizational settings in mind. This is where most competing rights situations happen and where they are best resolved. Employers, service providers, housing providers, unions, and others have a legal obligation to address all human rights matters that may arise. This policy outlines a process to help organizations recognize and reconcile competing human rights claims. It is also an analysis tool that can be used by lawyers, mediators, and adjudicators.

It is critical that all parties involved have a chance to be heard and to hear the perspectives of opposing parties. As the Ontario Court of Appeal has noted:

> If a person has a full opportunity to present his or her position and is given a reasoned explanation for the ultimate course of conduct to be followed, the recognition afforded that person's rights by that process itself tends to validate that person's claim, even if the ultimate decision does not give that person everything he or she wanted.[80]

---

79 The OHRC has already taken steps to promote its framework in different legal proceedings involving competing rights. The OHRC intervened in the case of *R. v N.S.*, above note 21, involving a witness who wore a *niqab*. In its facta submitted to the Court of Appeal for Ontario and the Supreme Court of Canada, the OHRC advanced a legal approach to resolving competing human rights claims consistent with the framework. Relevant portions of the Court of Appeal factum are available on the OHRC's website and were reflected in the decision of the Court of Appeal. The OHRC also relied on the framework's reasoning and analysis in its intervener factum filed with the Supreme Court of Canada in *Saskatchewan Human Rights Commission v William Whatcott*, 2010 CanLII 62501 (SCC). The appeal was heard by the Supreme Court on 12 October 2011.

80 *R. v N.S.*, above note 21 at para. 83.

By implementing the OHRC's proposed approach, organizations can be confident that they have a conflict resolution process in place that is consistent with human rights principles. The framework helps organizations recognize and address any power imbalances that may exist and take steps to empower all parties involved. Also, having an objective process removes some of the elements of individual discretion on the part of each decision maker, and helps parties to feel they are being treated fairly and in accordance with standard procedures.

By following the approach outlined in the framework, organizations can take steps to resolve tension and conflict between parties at an early stage. Resolving conflicts early helps organizations to address matters before they fester and become entrenched. This in turn helps ensure the health and functioning of an organization, and can avoid costly and time-consuming litigation.

The following table summarizes the framework's three-stage, five-step process for recognizing and reconciling competing human rights claims:

Process for addressing competing human rights situations

Stage One: Recognizing competing rights claims

Step 1: What are the claims about?

Step 2: Do claims connect to legitimate rights?
- (a) Do claims involve individuals or groups rather than operational interests?
- (b) Do claims connect to human rights, other legal entitlements, or *bona fide* reasonable interests?
- (c) Do claims fall within the scope of the right when defined in context?

Step 3: Do claims amount to more than minimal interference with rights?

Stage Two: Reconciling competing rights claims

Step 4: Is there a solution that allows enjoyment of each right?

Step 5: If not, is there a "next best" solution?

Stage Three: Making decisions

- Decisions must be consistent with human rights and other laws, court decisions, human rights principles, and have regard for OHRC policy
- At least one claim must fall under the *Ontario Human Rights Code* to be actionable at the Human Rights Tribunal of Ontario

6.1 Stage One: Recognizing competing rights claims

At one point or another, most organizations will face situations where the values, interests, and rights of individuals come into conflict. Stage One guides organizations to three areas of inquiry to help determine whether claims amount to competing human rights.

Recognizing whether the claims involve legal "rights" is a preliminary consideration separate from reconciling claims. This is a crucial part of the analysis, even if the organization does not believe the situation involves competing rights. It helps educate parties about their human rights and responsibilities, an especially important goal given the general lack of public awareness and ambiguity around rights and related language. This in turn may help parties frame their claims properly.

At the outset, parties should try to be open and suspend judgment. Often there is a tendency for rivals to deny the legitimacy of each other's rights claims. Working through this stage in a respectful and earnest way gives people a voice, helps diminish power imbalances (especially for historically marginalized groups), shows genuine consideration of different positions, and promotes the dignity of all claimants. It also encourages a spirit of cooperation that is very important for the reconciliation stage.

6.1.1 Step 1: What are the claims about?

Step 1 of the framework helps organizations draw out a detailed picture of each claim and the underlying situation or context. Parties should include facts, their perceptions about what happened, and views about the potential rights, values, and/or interests that may underlie the situation. It is important for parties to take part fully in this step. As one author notes:

> Hearing directly from the people affected is crucial to developing effective and responsive ways to resolve tensions between or among rights claims. Those who experience a denial of their rights have a unique perspective on why that is the case and appropriate remedies.[81]

A broad, inclusive approach will help to give a full appreciation of the social and factual context in which the conflict arises. Such an approach also helps to avoid dismissing relevant factors prematurely, and helps to frame claims properly. Only then can it be determined if the situation is actually one of competing rights.

6.1.2 Step 2: Do claims connect to legitimate rights?

Once the claims and context become clear under Step 1, organizations move to Step 2 to consider three questions to determine whether the claims connect to actual rights:

a) Do claims involve individuals or groups rather than operational interests?
b) Does at least one claim fall under a human right?
c) Do claims fall within the scope of the right?

---

81 Patricia Hughes, "Competing Rights Policy: The Law Commission of Ontario Approach," *Canadian Diversity*, Volume 8:3, Summer 2010 at 54.

(a) Do claims involve individuals or groups rather than operational interests?

Under the *Code*, many organizations, including employers, service providers, housing providers, and unions have a duty to accommodate the *Code*-related needs of individuals. As part of determining what each claim is about, organizations must distinguish between claims that solely affect business operations from competing claims that affect the rights of other individuals and groups. Claims that affect business operations alone are properly considered within the scope of the duty to accommodate (i.e. whether an accommodation is appropriate or amounts to an undue hardship) and are not competing human rights claims.

Example: An employee claims discrimination when her employer denies her request for modified work hours to meet child care responsibilities. Her request does not appear to affect the legal rights of others. Therefore, this situation is not a "competing rights" claim, but rather is one involving a request for human rights accommodation. The employer might argue undue hardship based on financial impact for his business, which could limit his duty to accommodate.

A request for accommodation may turn out to be a competing rights situation if, while dealing with the accommodation request, it turns out that the rights of another person or group might also be affected.

(b) Does at least one claim fall under a human right?

As part of this step, organizations must identify whether their claims are legally recognized (in other words, whether they are protected by the law). Rights might be guaranteed by the Constitution (including the *Charter*), legislation, international treaties, or court decisions. It may help to ask: if the allegations were true, which rights would be violated? This may be straightforward in most cases. For example, one party might identify that they have a need that requires accommodation under the Ontario *Human Rights Code*. Another party might identify a *Charter* right, such as the right to make full answer and defence. Other claims may not fall under a legislated right, but could connect to situations already dealt with by a court, such as the right to peaceful enjoyment of public parks in the midst of a demonstration.

(c) Do claims fall within the scope of the right?

Organizations must determine whether each claim falls within the "scope" of the right. There may be a general right at play, but does it extend as far as the claim made in a particular situation? Are the rights claims characterized appropriately? Organizations should examine the claims in their context and compare the situation with any parameters already set by legislation or courts for similar situations. As mentioned earlier, sometimes legislation itself will put limits on rights it seeks to protect, or will provide defences to proactively address situations where rights may potentially compete.

Example: The scope of the right to non-discrimination in employment under the *Code* does not extend to personal care attendants hired directly by people in need. A person may hire someone of the same sex, for example, to provide their personal care.[82]

Other times, the setting or sector may affect the limits on the exercise of a right.

Example: A woman objected to an inscription on a monument donated by a Catholic men's organization that was located on property owned by the Catholic Church. She stated that the reference to life "from conception until natural death" is a statement against abortion, which is offensive and discriminatory because it denounces, victimizes, and excludes women. She also claimed that the inscription violated her right to be free from religious coercion, including religious messages. The inscription could not

---

82 Section 24(1)(c) of the Ontario *Human Rights Code*, above note 30.

be read from the public sidewalk and could only be read by a person on church property. In a summary hearing process, the Human Rights Tribunal of Ontario dismissed the claim saying it has no jurisdiction to examine the content of religious teaching and beliefs, particularly where these are conveyed on the premises of a religious organization.[83]

The breadth of the right to freedom of expression as it relates to communicating offensive language will also vary depending on the context. For example, in media commentary, the right might be interpreted very broadly, but in a school or workplace it may be interpreted more narrowly. The *Criminal Code* sets out limitations on expressions of hate in both contexts.

In accordance with accepted rules of statutory interpretation, when considering the scope of rights, organizations should interpret rights broadly and defences narrowly (except where defences also recognize and promote the competing rights of other groups in society). The answer might be in previous tribunal or court decisions, which have decided limits in similar circumstances.

Many apparent rights conflicts may be resolved by asking whether the claims actually fall within the scope of the right in the particular context. Properly delineating or making reasonable

---

83 The HRTO described both the positive component (the right to express and disseminate beliefs) and the negative dimension (the right to be free from coercion to accept or adopt any beliefs, practices, or forms of worship) of the competing rights at issue. In doing so, it noted that the applicant was asserting a *Code* right that engages issues that are at the core of others' *Charter* rights, namely the respondent's right to display a message consistent with its religious beliefs on the grounds of a religious institution. The HRTO stated that in interpreting the applicant's rights under the *Code*, it must be careful not to strip the respondent's positive religious rights of any meaning. The Tribunal concluded that it is not an appropriate use of human rights protections set out in the *Code* to challenge the Catholic Church's belief system and teachings: *Dallaire v Les Chevaliers de Colomb*, 2011 HRTO 639 (CanLII).

adjustments to the rights may make it possible to resolve any conflict between them. After properly scoping the boundaries of the rights, there might be no actual intrusion of one right onto the other. As Justice Iacobucci has noted:

> *B. (R.)* is a classic example of definitional reconciliation. Where a parent's right to religion is defined as not extending to the right to allow for religious medical choices which can harm a child, there really is no conflict between freedom of religion and life, liberty, and security of the person. This sentiment was echoed in *Trinity Western* where the Supreme Court noted that "this is a case where any potential conflict should be resolved through a proper delineation of the rights and values involved. In essence, *properly defining the scope of the rights avoids a conflict in this case* (emphasis in original)."[84]

Interpreting whether the scope of a right extends to claims made in a particular situation will often be open to debate. Again, the OHRC's framework encourages parties not to prematurely dispose of a claim unless there is a solid legal basis for doing so.[85]

6.1.3 Step 3: Do claims amount to more than minimal interference with rights?

Where the scoping exercise does not resolve the conflict, it is necessary to determine the extent of the interference with the rights in question. If interference with a right is minor or trivial, the right is not likely to receive protection. There is no conflict unless there is a sufficient interference with, burden or intrusion on a right. Where the impact on one right is minimal or insignificant,

84 Above note 25 at 163.

85 See the OHRC publication, *The Shadow of the Law: Surveying the Case Law Dealing with Competing Rights Claims*, above note 7, which provides a detailed discussion of the caselaw dealing with competing rights.

that right must give way to the other.[86] If enjoying one right does not result in a real burden or impact on the other, the rights are not actually in conflict and do not need to be reconciled.[87] It is instructive to ask whether the "core" or fundamental aspect of a right is engaged. Where the conduct is at the "periphery" of a right, it will more likely need to give way to a right whose core values are engaged.[88]

Organizations need to determine whether a situation amounts to more than minimal interference on a claimant's rights. For this interference to be found, a relevant rights-related distinction or factor must exist, flowing from either claim, that imposes burdens, obligations, or disadvantages not imposed upon others, or withholds or limits access to opportunities, benefits, and advantages available to others.[89] Sometimes parties perceive interference where none really exists.

Example: Courts have generally rejected arguments made against same-sex marriage legislation on the basis that it offends religious rights. The courts generally agree that permitting such marriages for others does not substantially interfere with the religious rights of people opposed to same-sex marriage, unless religious organizations must perform those marriages.

If there is substantial interference with the rights in question, then the decision maker must shift to a reconciliation exercise.

---

86 *Amselem*, above note 16 at para. 84; *Bruker*, above note 52.

87 This was the conclusion of the Supreme Court of Canada in *Reference re Same-Sex Marriage*, above note 57 and *Trinity Western*, above note 23.

88 *Brockie v Brillinger (No. 2)*, above note 60 at para. 51.

89 The OHRC's framework relies on the analysis in *R. v Kapp*, [2008] 2 S.C.R. 483 (S.C.C.)

6.2 Stage Two: Reconciling competing rights

If the inquiries in Stage One show that a competing human rights situation exists, then organizations should move to Stage Two to see if rights can be reconciled. Ideally, reconciliation would result in neither side having to give up anything substantial. As a next best solution, it might involve parties having to give up things that are perhaps negotiable or at the periphery of a right, this being determined by legal principles or jurisprudence. Step 4 sets out the considerations involved in finding an "ideal" reconciliation. Step 5 looks at finding a "next best" solution when an ideal resolution is not possible.

6.2.1 Step 4: Is there a solution that allows enjoyment of each right?

Reconciliation is a process for exploring options to reduce or eliminate interference and allow full or at least "substantial" exercise of the rights of all parties within the given context. Often, reconciliation will involve changing conditions or adjusting the way one or both parties enjoy their rights. This may look like a multi-party human rights accommodation process involving secondary changes such as altering schedules, working conditions, activity locations, and so on.

Example: A woman with a disability uses a service dog to perform her work duties as a teacher, but a student in the classroom has her disability (allergies) triggered by the presence of the service dog. The *Code* requires employers to accommodate the needs of employees with disabilities, and it would also require educational institutions to accommodate the needs of students with disabilities. The *Code* does not prioritize these needs or requirements — one is as important as the other. However, these competing rights claims might be resolved by assessing the needs of both parties.

The employer/service provider would first need to look at the accommodation needs of both the employee and the student in the context of the classroom to find out if the needs of the two parties are actually in conflict. In what ways is the service dog assisting the employee in the classroom? Are there other ways that support could be provided without the service dog?[90] Alternative options for meeting the student's needs should be similarly looked at. In this case, there may be other instructors the student can study with, or other sessions she could attend. The employer/service provider should then explore a combination of solutions for accommodating both, allowing each to enjoy their rights.

6.2.2 Step 5: If not, is there a next best solution?

If the reconciliation process does not lead to an ideal solution, there is still a duty to explore options that least impair or compromise a right. Even if one right prevails in the circumstances, there may still be a duty to accommodate the other claim to some degree.

Exploring ideal and next best solutions inevitably involves limiting or compromising rights. Organizations should apply established principles from human rights caselaw and OHRC policy. Undoubtedly, selecting, weighing, and applying principles can lead to differing results. One human rights principle alone may not provide an answer. Consider principles together with the full context in mind. The following principles, which are discussed in greater detail in the "Key legal principles" section of this policy,

---

90 Section 4.3 of the OHRC's *Policy and Guidelines on Disability and the Duty to Accommodate* notes that "if there is a choice between two accommodations which are equally responsive to the person's needs in a dignified manner, then those responsible are entitled to select the one that is less expensive or that is less disruptive to the organization." The Disability Policy is available online: www.ohrc.on.ca/en/resources/Policies/PolicyDisAccom2/pdf.

will assist organizations as they search for next best solutions:

1. No rights are absolute
2. There is no hierarchy of rights
3. Aim to respect the importance of both sets of rights
4. The full context, facts, and constitutional values at stake must be considered
5. Must look at extent of interference (only *actual* burdens on rights trigger conflicts)
6. The core of a right is more protected than its periphery
7. Statutory defences may restrict rights

The OHRC's framework offers a fluid approach to recognizing and reconciling competing rights. Organizations may need to go back to previous steps in the framework to test options for solutions; for example, whether a proposed option would now make the impact on rights insignificant.

Any limitation of a right should consider human rights values, including respect for human dignity, inclusion of all, community and social harmony, and the collective interests of minority or marginalized groups.

6.3 Stage Three: Making decisions

When it comes to addressing competing rights, organizations are not a neutral third party. They have a legal obligation to deal with competing human rights claims just like any other human rights matter that may arise in their environment. Ultimately, organizations will need to decide on and endorse an outcome. Along the way, they must remember their legal obligations and make sure parties understand the process. They must also make sure that any resolution reflects OHRC policy and is consistent with human rights and other law, court decisions, and human rights principles.

By acting in accordance with human rights principles, organizations are taking steps to protect themselves from liability if they are ever named as a party in a case before the Human Rights Tribunal of Ontario or a higher court.

Other parties – potential claimants, respondents and unions, where applicable – also have a shared responsibility to act in good faith, show dignity and respect for one another, and cooperate in a process to recognize rights and find solutions for everyone involved. In other words, you cannot expect respect for your rights without respecting the rights of others.

After working through Stage One, organizations may find that competing human rights are not ultimately involved. The organization should communicate this assessment to the parties, but should still consider addressing the matter. In fact, in many cases, the organization may have a legal obligation to do so. Even if a claim is not interfering with someone else's rights, the organization will still have a duty to maintain a non-discriminatory, harassment-free environment and to accommodate any *Code*-related needs a person may have.

In other cases, an organization may assess the situation and decide that engaging claimants in a process is not needed, not desirable, or impossible. For example, the organization may have already dealt with a similar situation before and now has a policy on how to deal with these matters going forward. Or, the organization may decide the situation is too contentious or complex to reconcile and it may wish to seek legal advice instead.

Some claimants may raise claims that the organization feels lack merit, they may be unwilling to take part in a reconciliation process, or parties might not be able to reach agreement. While the organization might take action unilaterally, it should consider the decision to do so carefully and communicate clear reasons to the parties involved. One or both parties may not be satisfied and they may ask the organization to reconsider the decision. Parties may also have the option of taking their case to the Human Rights Tribunal of Ontario or another legal decision maker.

For a party to bring their competing rights claim to a human rights tribunal, at least one of the claimed rights must fall under a human right established by law. For example, if one of the parties wishes to bring the matter to the Human Rights Tribunal of Ontario, then their claim must connect to the Ontario *Human Rights Code.*

In most cases, the organization will find it beneficial to engage in a process that tries to recognize and reconcile competing rights rather than make a unilateral decision.

7. Organizational process for addressing competing rights

7.1 Quick resolution

Many competing rights situations can be resolved quickly through an informal process that may involve no more than one or two meetings. At the outset, organizations should consider whether the situation is suited to an informal and expedited process. For example, the facts of the situation and the framing of each claim may be straightforward and not in dispute. The parties may already be well-informed about each other's claims, rights, and obligations. They may have shown respect for each other's interests and be willing to engage in discussions about solutions without delay. A quick process will generally involve running through the analysis with both parties in a quick way. The focus here is less on a precise analysis of the rights at play, and more on finding solutions that benefit all sides and respect human rights.

Example: A community centre plans to celebrate National Aboriginal Awareness Day on June 21. They partner with the local Aboriginal cultural centre for a full day of events about programs and services and the rich heritage of Aboriginal peoples. The day will open with a "smudging" ceremony. Notices go out encouraging staff and clients to take part. One staff worker raises concern about her asthma and the presence of smoke. Both sides recognize the legitimacy and importance of the other's interests. The worker wants the ceremony to proceed and the Aboriginal centre wants the worker to take part. They work together on a solution to move the opening ceremony outdoors and redirect smoke away from the audience and the worker.

If the informal, quick process does not resolve the issue, then the organization may decide to use a full and more formal process. However, it is important to consider a quick resolution process first because in the OHRC's experience, working through a full, formal process is usually not necessary. Workable solutions can be found relatively quickly in most cases of competing rights claims.

7.2 Full process

In a full, more formal process, the framework is applied more rigorously at Stage One to find out if a genuine competing human rights situation exists. The case studies included in Appendix D can help organizations as they work through this part of the process. The case studies are presented in an analysis template that can help organizations frame the issues and assess all relevant considerations. For detailed information on the legal disposition of different types of competing rights cases, see the OHRC's document, *The Shadow of the Law: Surveying the Case Law Dealing with Competing Rights Claims*.[91]

If, after going through Stage One, an organization concludes that a competing human rights situation does exist, Stage Two will help guide it through the reconciliation process. This policy proposes an alternative dispute resolution (ADR) model to guide organizations through the Three Stage Analysis.

---

91 Above note 7.

7.3 Alternative Dispute Resolution (ADR) models

ADR models for reconciling competing rights claims *		
Types	**When to use**	**Why to use**
(1) Negotiation A voluntary process of dispute resolution that does not involve a neutral party facilitator. **Core elements:** • Recognition by the parties that they both have rights and obligations • Power balancing self-restraint by party with greater power in situation (usually the organization) • Takes place in "the shadow of the law" • Aims at remediation and prevention	Two possible scenarios: • **Two parties** are involved (an organization and a claimant); **OR** • **Three parties (or more)** are involved (an organization and two or more claimants)	Parties cannot reconcile competing rights unilaterally Parties want to control the process of reconciling competing claims and also make their own decisions about how competing claims are reconciled rather than have a third party control the process and impose decisions on them Transaction costs (money, time, stress) of litigating before tribunals and courts are much higher Principled negotiation is a collaborative method of negotiation designed to preserve the core competing rights of both/all parties; if this is not possible, then aim is to ensure partial enjoyment of the competing rights of both/all parties The most durable settlements are the ones the negotiating parties make themselves

* The OHRC wishes to thank Desmond Ellis, Lesley Jacobs, Lorne Foster, and Robin Smith of The York Centre for Public Policy and Law for their insights and contributions to this section.

ADR models for reconciling competing rights claims *		
Types	**When to use**	**Why to use**
(2) Conciliation (also referred to as "mediation") An impartial third party facilitates constructive communication and problem-solving aimed at reconciling the claims of competing rights claimants **Core elements:** • Parties recognize that they both have rights and obligations • Parties are involved in crafting terms included in settlements of competing rights claims • An impartial third party (e.g. mediator, conciliator) facilitates principled negotiation • Impartial third party conducts power-balancing interventions • Settlements are legally enforced • Takes place in "the shadow of the law" • Aims at remediation and prevention	• When attempts at negotiation reach an impasse	Parties could not settle their competing rights claims themselves by taking part in principled negotiation; or, organization may not have capacity to negotiate, and/or situation is too complex to address without outside expertise The transaction costs (money, time, stress, relationship damage) associated with litigation are higher, sometimes much higher Self-determination, i.e. parties still make decisions about terms of settlement, as with principled negotiation, but a conciliator (with no authority to make decisions on terms of settlement) will help parties to overcome the barriers to settlement they experienced when taking part in principled negotiation Conciliation is designed to preserve the core competing rights of both/all parties; if this is not possible, then the aim is to ensure both/all parties partially enjoy the competing rights The most durable settlements are made by the negotiating parties themselves

This ADR approach follows the mixed interest- and rights-based mediation model that is often used to address human rights claims. Under this model, mediators help parties to first frame their positions and understand each other's rights before guiding them through a formal mediation process. The process involves searching for mutually agreed-upon solutions that factor relevant considerations into the context.

Mixed interest- and rights-based ADR is particularly well-suited to address competing human rights claims where no one claimant can assert that they are the only party affected. Rather, it requires creative and cooperative efforts to reach agreement on solutions. These efforts are more likely than litigation to uncover relatively harmonious and durable solutions. When parties work together to resolve a dispute, each side feels a sense of ownership of and commitment to the solution, and this fosters good will and mutual respect. Experts in the field of ADR have noted:

> Seeing different claimants as fellow citizens and viewing those citizens in a way that is empathetic holds much greater promise than an adversarial process where there are only winners and losers.[92]

Once an organization decides that an ADR process is appropriate, and claimants agree to take part, it will then need to select the type of ADR that best suits the nature of the dispute. Where two or more competing claimants come forward, a conciliation approach might be best. Conciliation is another term for mediation and is defined as a facilitated negotiation involving a neutral or impartial third party. The term conciliation is preferred in this context as it better relates to the idea of "reconciling" claims already recognized as competing human rights under Stage One.

---

92 Lorne Foster and Lesley Jacobs, "Shared Citizenship as the Context for Competing Human Rights Claims: Towards a Social Policy Framework," *Canadian Diversity*, Volume 8:3, Summer 2010 at 13.

Even if only one claimant has come forward with a human rights claim, the organization might recognize that the claim may affect the rights of others. In this case, the organization may need to "wear two hats" and represent the rights of other individuals or groups potentially affected while negotiating with the claimant. Alternatively, it may choose to involve the individuals or groups potentially affected in the process in some way.

In some situations, it may not be prudent for the organization to take on the role of mediator, particularly where one or more of the parties believe that the organization has played a role in creating or worsening the problem. In some cases, it may be more constructive and to the greater satisfaction of all parties to bring in an external conciliator. This may be the case, for example, where the organization has expressed a view or an interest that creates a perception of bias.

Despite the best efforts of organizations, there will be some cases where ADR methods fail to resolve competing rights claims. Parties may not be willing to make concessions to the other parties involved; they may not be willing to respect or recognize the dignity of the other party or parties. They may believe, rightly or wrongly, that they will "get a better deal" by going to a tribunal or a court. In some cases, litigation is unavoidable. Where competing rights situations do end up before a tribunal or a court, the OHRC's policy and approach can be a useful tool for decision makers as they try to resolve these matters in a formal legal setting.

Flow Chart for Competing Human Rights Conciliation

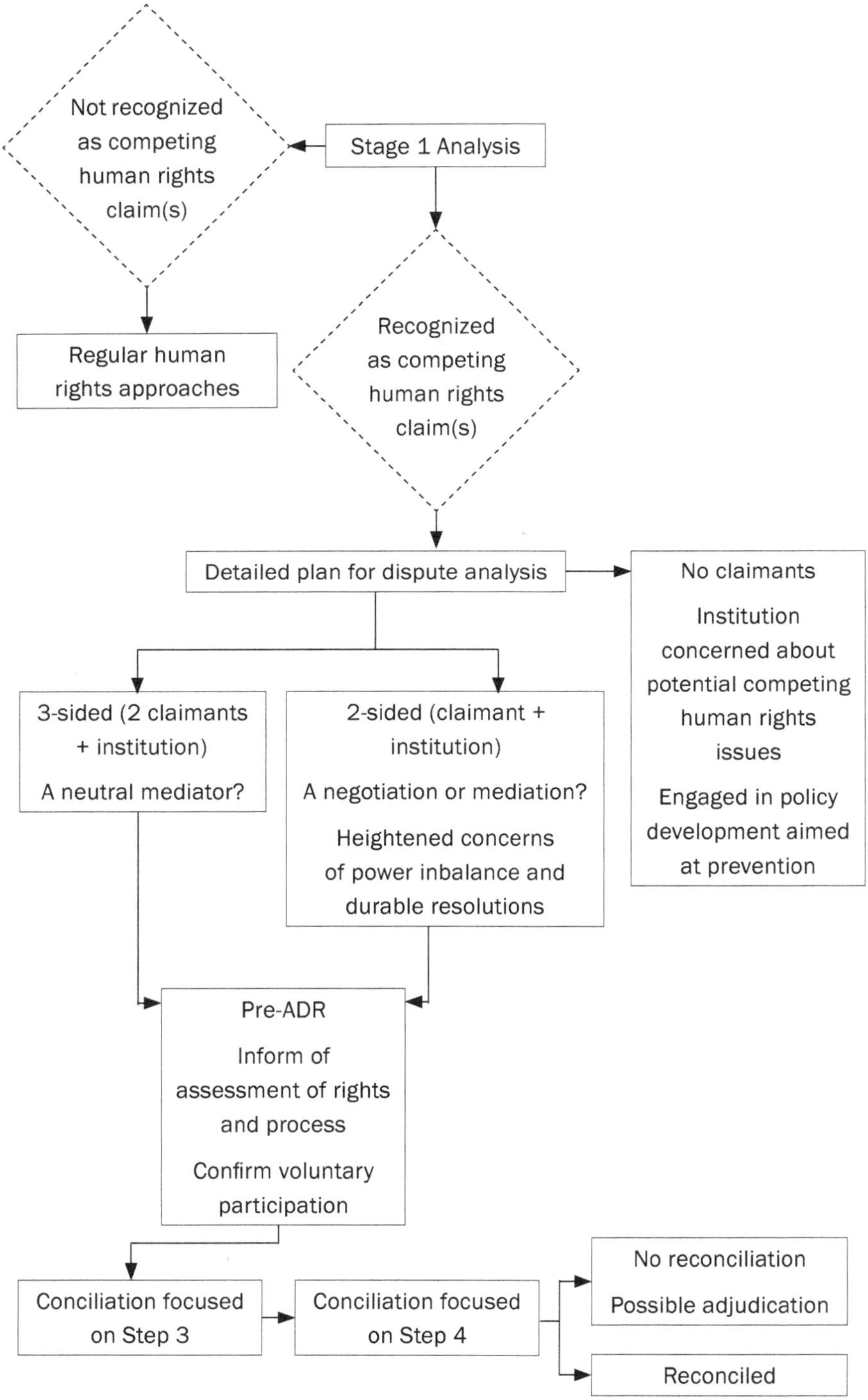

8. Conclusion

Competing human rights situations will inevitably arise in many different contexts, including workplaces, housing, and schools. Employers, housing providers, educators, and other responsible parties covered by the *Code* have the ultimate responsibility for maintaining an inclusive environment that is free from discrimination and harassment, and where everyone's human rights are respected. Organizations and institutions operating in Ontario have a legal duty to take steps to prevent and respond to situations involving competing rights.

This policy is intended to provide clear, user-friendly guidance to organizations, policy makers, litigants, adjudicators, and others on how to assess, handle, and resolve competing rights claims. It sets out a process for addressing competing rights situations, based in existing caselaw, that organizations can use as is or adapt to meet their own specific needs. Taking prompt, proactive, and effective steps to address competing rights matters will help organizations to resolve tension and conflict before it escalates, and can help to avoid costly and time-consuming litigation. Where litigation is unavoidable, taking these steps will help organizations to protect themselves from liability.

Appendix A: Purpose of OHRC's policies

Section 30 of the Ontario *Human Rights Code* authorizes the OHRC to prepare, approve, and publish human rights policies to provide guidance on interpreting provisions of the *Code*. The OHRC's policies and guidelines set standards for how individuals, employers, service providers, and policy makers should act to ensure compliance with the *Code*. They are important because they represent the OHRC's interpretation of the *Code* at the time of publication.[93] Also, they advance a progressive understanding of the rights set out in the *Code*.

Section 45.5 of the *Code* states that the HRTO may consider policies approved by the OHRC in a human rights proceeding before the HRTO. Where a party or an intervener in a proceeding requests it, the HRTO *shall* consider an OHRC policy. Where an OHRC policy is relevant to the subject matter of a human rights application, parties and interveners are encouraged to bring the policy to the HRTO's attention for consideration.

Section 45.6 of the *Code* states that if a final decision or order of the HRTO is not consistent with an OHRC policy, in a case where the OHRC was either a party or an intervener, the OHRC may apply to the HRTO to have the HRTO state a case to the Divisional Court to address this inconsistency.

OHRC policies are subject to decisions of the Superior Courts interpreting the *Code*. OHRC policies have been given great deference by the courts and the HRTO,[94] applied to the facts of the

---

93 Note that caselaw developments, legislative amendments, and/or changes in the OHRC's own policy positions that took place after a document's publication date will not be reflected in the hard copy of that document. The OHRC is moving toward having up-to-date electronic versions of its documents available on its website. For more information, please contact the Ontario Human Rights Commission.

94 In *Quesnel v London Educational Health Centre* (1995), 28 C.H.R.R. D/474 at para. 53 (Ont. Bd. Inq.), the tribunal applied the United States

case before the court or the HRTO, and quoted in the decisions of these bodies.[95]

Appendix B: Policy development process

Over the past several years, the OHRC has taken many steps to advance understanding of how best to address competing rights. In 2005, the OHRC began the dialogue by releasing a research paper entitled, *Balancing Conflicting Rights: Towards an Analytical Framework.*[96] The paper provided the public with preliminary information that would promote discussion and further research without taking any firm policy positions.

In 2007–08, the OHRC conducted a detailed literature review scanning relevant articles from the fields of law, philosophy,

---

Supreme Court's decision in *Griggs v Duke Power Co.*, 401 U.S. 424 (4th Cir. 1971) to conclude that OHRC policy statements should be given "great deference" if they are consistent with *Code* values and are formed in a way that is consistent with the legislative history of the *Code* itself. This latter requirement was interpreted to mean that they were formed through a process of public consultation.

95 The Ontario Superior Court of Justice has quoted at length excerpts from the OHRC's published policy work in the area of mandatory retirement and stated that the OHRC's efforts led to a "sea change" in the attitude to mandatory retirement in Ontario. The OHRC's policy work on mandatory retirement heightened public awareness of this issue and was at least partially responsible for the Ontario government's decision to pass legislation amending the *Code* to prohibit age discrimination in employment after age sixty-five, subject to limited exceptions. This amendment, which became effective December 2006, made mandatory retirement policies illegal for most employers in Ontario: *Assn. of Justices of the Peace of Ontario v Ontario (Attorney General)* (2008), 92 O.R. (3d) 16 at para. 45. See also *Eagleson Co-Operative Homes, Inc. v Théberge,* [2006] O.J. No. 4584 (Sup.Ct. (Div.Ct.)) in which the Court applied the OHRC's *Policy and Guidelines on Disability and the Duty to Accommodate*, above note 90.

96 Above note 48.

conflict resolution, and political science. This review revealed a wealth of information on how competing rights claims have been and might be looked at from a variety of perspectives. At the same time, caselaw in Canada and the United States has continued to develop and some preliminary analysis has been conducted. Very recently, the OHRC developed a competing rights caselaw review and made it available to the public.[97]

In many cases, the OHRC has also been actively involved in developing this caselaw. For example, the OHRC litigated *Ontario (Human Rights Commission) and Heintz v Christian Horizons*,[98] a case that dealt with religious rights of an organization and the rights of a lesbian employee. The OHRC has also intervened in relevant legal cases that examine competing rights questions. For example, the OHRC intervened before the Ontario Superior Court, the Ontario Court of Appeal, and the Supreme Court of Canada in *R. v N.S.*,[99] a case considering whether a woman wearing a *niqab* while testifying against the men alleged to have sexually assaulted her interferes with their right to make full answer and defence. The OHRC also intervened before the Supreme Court of Canada in *Saskatchewan Human Rights Commission v Whatcott*,[100] a case considering whether freedom of expression and religion include the right to distribute pamphlets alleged to contain hate speech targeting gays and lesbians.

The OHRC has also conducted one-on-one interviews with a number of individuals who were known to be very familiar with situations of competing rights claims from a variety of stakeholder, legal, and academic perspectives. These interviews represented initial efforts to identify issues and concerns emerging from the perspectives of groups associated with the *Code* grounds of gender, creed, sexual orientation, and disability, while

---

97 Above note 7.

98 *Christian Horizons*, above note 15.

99 Above note 21.

100 Above note 79.

also helping to identify individuals and groups who could take part in future public consultation activity to ensure a complete discussion.

In March 2010, the OHRC partnered with York University's Centre for Public Policy and the Law to hold a policy dialogue on competing human rights. Academics and researchers were recruited to develop articles within set parameters and to present these at the policy dialogue. These people represented different stakeholder groups and social and institutional perspectives. The Association of Canadian Studies and the University of British Columbia Press both published research papers from the policy dialogue.[101]

After this dialogue, OHRC staff developed a draft policy framework for reconciling competing human rights that aimed to address the issues raised by its preliminary consultation and research. In December 2010, the OHRC tested its draft framework at a two-day workshop with representatives from Ontario's education sector and others. Over the past year, the OHRC has continued its dialogue with various groups and received positive feedback and constructive comment on its framework proposal. The framework represents the OHRC's recommended approach to addressing competing rights situations and provides the foundation for this policy. The OHRC has also used this approach in its interventions before the courts in high-profile competing rights cases.[102]

---

101 The Association of Canadian Studies, *Canadian Diversity*, Vol. 8:3, Summer 2010. The UBC publication is forthcoming.

102 Above notes 21 and 79.

Appendix C: OHRC framework

<table>
<tr><th colspan="7">Framework for Addressing Competing Human Rights</th></tr>
<tr><th rowspan="2">Stage</th><th rowspan="2">Goals</th><th rowspan="2">Analysis</th><th colspan="2">Organizational Process</th><th rowspan="2">Legal Principles</th><th rowspan="2">Definitions</th></tr>
<tr><th>Informal</th><th>Formal</th></tr>
<tr><td rowspan="4">Recognizing rights</td><td rowspan="4">• Mutual recognition of interests & rights promotes mutual dignity & respect
• Helps frame rights
• Gives marginalized voice
• Diminishes power imbalances
• Reduces stigma
• Rights & obligations awareness</td><td>1. What are the claims about?</td><td colspan="2" rowspan="2">• Inquire into each claimant's story
• Values, beliefs, interests, feelings, context
• Determine whether informal or formal process appropriate</td><td rowspan="4">• No rights are absolute
• No hierarchy of rights
• Right may not extend as far as claim
• Must consider full context/facts & constitutional values at stake
• Rights defined in relation to one another & extent of interference
• Core more protected than periphery</td><td rowspan="4">Some claims may have higher legal status than others . . .
• Beliefs: opinions firmly held as truth; belief not legally actionable, right to hold it is
• Values: individual/social moral principles & standards; may reflect in/inform law or claim; not legally actionable</td></tr>
<tr><td>2. Do claims connect to legitimate rights & interests?</td></tr>
<tr><td>a. Individuals or groups rather than operational interests?</td><td rowspan="2">If claimants understand their rights, recognize each other's claims as legitimate, & demonstrate dignity & respect for each other, then...</td><td rowspan="2">Before dispute resolution
• Analyse situation:
• Could org. policy development help?
• Negotiation or conciliation?
• Internal or external conciliator?</td></tr>
<tr><td>b. Human rights, legal entitlements or bona fide reasonable interests?</td></tr>
</table>

Framework for Addressing Competing Human Rights

Stage	Goals	Analysis	Organizational Process		Legal Principles	Definitions
			Informal	Formal		
Recognizing rights (continued)	• Maximum recognition of rights • Encourages spirit of cooperation	c. Context of claim falls within scope of right or interest?	Frame issues together	Identify parties & inform them of situation, roles & responsibilities & consequences of not participating…	• Usually no ”bright lines” • Courts have drawn some for particular case types • Statutory defences may also restrict rights • Aim to respect importance of both sets of rights • Search for “constructive compromises” (procedural duty)	• Interests: individual/ social concerns or stakes; may elevate to legal entitlement if *bona fide* & reasonable in circumstances or satisfies legal limit or exemption • Legal entitlements: codified in law or interpreted through court tribunal decision
		3. Amounts to more than minimal interference with right?				

<table>
<tr><th colspan="7">Framework for Addressing Competing Human Rights</th></tr>
<tr><th rowspan="2">Stage</th><th rowspan="2">Goals</th><th rowspan="2">Analysis</th><th colspan="2">Organizational Process</th><th rowspan="2">Legal Principles</th><th rowspan="2">Definitions</th></tr>
<tr><th>Informal</th><th>Formal</th></tr>
<tr><td rowspan="2">Reconciling rights</td><td rowspan="2">• Claimants & organization engage in shared responsibility to find agreeable solutions</td><td>4. Is there a solution that allows enjoyment of each right?</td><td rowspan="2">Explore/discuss & attempt to reach mutually agreeable solutions that are ideal or next best</td><td rowspan="2">Conduct dispute resolution</td><td rowspan="5"></td><td rowspan="5">• Human rights: inalienable, indivisible, universal legal entitlements; include limits & exemptions; usually have higher status than other legal entitlements; both have higher legal status than interests, values, beliefs</td></tr>
<tr><td>5. If not, is there a next best solution for one or both rights?</td></tr>
<tr><td rowspan="3">Making decisions</td><td rowspan="3">• Organizations take responsibility for: corporate liability; substantive & procedural duties; policies; training
• Protection from litigation</td><td rowspan="3">• Must be consistent with human rights and other law, court decisions, human rights principles, and have regard for OHRC policy
• At least one claim must fall under Code to be actionable at Human Rights Tribunal</td><td colspan="2">Internal decision</td></tr>
<tr><td colspan="2">Internal appeal</td></tr>
<tr><td colspan="2">External appeal/complaint/decision at tribunal or higher court</td></tr>
</table>

Appendix D: Case examples for resolving competing rights

SCENARIO 1: The Prom	Matt's Claim	Catholic School Board Claim
Recognizing Rights		
1. What are the claims about?	Matt is a gay 17-year-old student attending a publicly funded Catholic high school. He wishes to go to the prom with a same-sex date. The prom is being held at a rental hall off school property. He is considering seeking a court injunction because the prom is only weeks away.	The school principal and the school board have said no on the grounds that this would be endorsing conduct contrary to the Catholic Church's teachings. Matt believes that this is a violation of his human rights.
2. Do claims connect to legitimate rights and interests?		
a. Does the situation involve individuals or groups rather than only operational interests?	• Matt and his boyfriend who attends another school • Matt's school friends and peers can bring their opposite sex dates • Other LGBTQ students who might have liked to bring dates • Matt's parents and parents of other LGBTQ students who are involved in school life and look forward to this "rite of passage" for their children • School staff who have worked hard with students and want to support their celebration • LGBTQ community members and advocates who could not bring same sex dates to their proms and continue to experience stigma and discrimination	• Catholic school principal who under-stands his job responsibilities to cover instilling a religious environment across extracurricular and social activities • Catholic school board members who understand their responsibilities to include upholding religious teachings through board policy and practice • Catholic Church which sees its role as the spiritual guide to school board policy and practice over religious matters • Other students, staff, and parents who are concerned about maintaining a Catholic environment and not promoting the "gay lifestyle" • Other schools in the board may have to address similar requests and are watching the outcome of this case

SCENARIO 1: The Prom	Matt's Claim	Catholic School Board Claim
b. What human rights, other legal entitlements or *bona fide* and reasonable interests might be invoked?	• Freedom from discrimination based on sexual orientation including poison-free environment under Ontario *Human Rights Code* s. 1 & *Charter* equality rights s. 15(1) • Freedom of expression, *Charter* s. 2(b) • Freedom of association, *Charter* s. 2(d) • Reasonable limits on rights, *Charter* s.1 • Right to and requirement for elementary and secondary school education from age 6 to 18 under Ontario *Education Act* • Right to education without discrimination under *UN Convention on Economic Social and Cultural Rights* articles 2 and 13.1 & 2 • Freedom of religion only limited by need to protect rights of others, *UN Convention on Civil and Political Rights* article 18.3 • School sanctioned extracurricular and social activities may be a *bona fide* reasonable benefit of school life	• Separate (Catholic) school rights preserved under Ontario *Human Rights Code* s. 19, *Charter* s. 29, 1867 Constitution Act s. 93 • *Education Act* provisions and regulations relating to Roman Catholic Boards • Freedom of conscience and religion under *Charter* s. 2(a), and under *UN Convention on Civil and Political Rights* article 18.1

SCENARIO 1: The Prom	Matt's Claim	Catholic School Board Claim
c. Does the claim fall within the scope of the right or other entitlement in this context?	• Extracurricular/social activities held off school premises not at the core of teaching • Prom is not a religious event, is not educational in nature, and is held off of school property • Diversity and inconsistency of Catholic opinion and practice: school accepts gay students but wishes to suppress all activity connected with their sexuality	• Catholic school rights include full board discretion over religious matters • All school sanctioned activities, on or off site, must promote and uphold religious teachings • School board practice has been consistent with policy, even if diversity of Catholic opinion exists
3. Amounts to more than minimal interference with a right?	• Unlike other students, he is not free to choose his date for school social functions, would have to go without his boyfriend • Prohibiting a same-sex date substantially interferes with the nature of a prom which typically involves bringing a date and or dancing with a partner of choice • Would miss out on this end of school/ graduation "rite of passage" • Differential treatment based on sexual orientation amounts to serious injury of dignity	• Allowing same-sex date at extracurricular/social activities would impede school's ability to promote religious school environment and teach religious curriculum consistent with tenets of the faith during core hours • Would have broad impact on other Catholic schools and Catholic Church

SCENARIO 1: The Prom	Matt's Claim	Catholic School Board Claim
Reconciling Rights		
4. Is there a solution that allows enjoyment of each right?	Option 1 • Prohibit non-LGBTQ students from bringing formal "dates" to the prom as well • Allow any student to bring a "guest" who is not a student of that school • Require all students to refrain from intimate behaviour • Such neutral terminology and inclusive policy approach could help avoid further stigmatizing individuals based on their sexual orientation • School would otherwise limit upholding formal Catholic board policy and Church position • on religious tenets to educational settings and core hours • Board could maintain position that a "don't ask don't tell" guest policy would not prejudice Catholic school rights Option 2 • Change school/board policy to no longer sanction/organize/fund proms as official school events; such events would be left entirely as a student-initiated responsibility held off-site without any formal connection to the Catholic school or board	
5. If not, is there a next best solution for one or both rights?	• Allow Matt to attend with a "guest" friend of his choice while allowing other students to attend with their formal opposite sex "date"	• Comply with any court injunction and allow Matt to attend the prom with his "boyfriend" in this case only • Take the position that such an injunction does not prejudice Catholic school rights • Examine Church doctrine more closely against school/board policy to deem whether proms are at the core or periphery of Catholic school rights

SCENARIO 1: The Prom	Matt's Claim	Catholic School Board Claim
Making Decisions		
• Must be consistent with human rights and other law, court decisions, legal principles and have regard for OHRC policies	• *Hall v Powers*, Ont. Superior Court 2002 (injunction order allowing Hall to attend prom with same-sex date) • *Smith v Knights of Columbus*, BCHRT 2005 (re: scope of organizational obligations on versus off premises)	• *Hall v Powers*, Ont. Superior Court 2002 (did not rule on Catholic school rights) • *Ross v New Brunswick School District* No. 15, SCC 1996 (re: poisoned environment)
• At least one claim must fall under the *Code* to be actionable at the Human Rights Tribunal	• Schools fall under *Code* s. 1 "service" • Matt's claim involves *Code* ground of sexual orientation	• Catholic board claim falls under *Code* s. 19 defence

SCENARIO 2: College Admission Standards	Christian Teachers' College Claim	Provincial Governing Body Claim
Recognizing Rights		
1. What are the claims about?	A private Christian teachers' college claims the provincial governing body is discriminating based on religion by refusing to certify the college's program because of the college's admissions policy prohibiting homosexual behaviour for its student teachers. This would discourage those wishing to pursue teacher training in a religious institution by denying them certification and the opportunity to work in the public school system.	The governing body claims the college's prohibition on homosexual behaviour is discriminatory based on sexual orientation. Approving their teaching program would be contrary to the public interest because these teacher graduates may exhibit bias, prejudice, and intolerance towards LGBTQ students or their LGBTQ parents and be seen to poison the learning environment in the public school system.
2. Do claims connect to legitimate rights and interests?		
a. Does the situation involve individuals or groups rather than only operational interests?	• The college's religious students, faculty, and administrative staff who wish to follow the tenets of the faith • Other public or private Canadian colleges and universities with traditional religious affiliations, Christian churches and religious organizations	• LGBTQ students (and their parents) and teachers in the public school system • Prospective LGBTQ or non-Christian students to the college • Teacher education governing bodies and other accreditation boards across Canada • Other self-governing professional bodies across Canada

SCENARIO 2: College Admission Standards	Christian Teachers' College Claim	Provincial Governing Body Claim
b. What human rights, other legal entitlements or *bona fide* and reasonable interests might be invoked?	• Freedom from discrimination in services and employment based on creed under Ontario *Human Rights Code* ss. 1, 5 and 9 • Defence for religious organizations under *Code* s. 18 • Freedom of conscience and religion under *Charter* s. 2(a) and under *UN Convention on Civil and Political Rights* article 18.1 • Equality rights under *Charter* s. 15 based on religion • Right to free expression under *Charter* 2.b • Liberty to choose religious education under *UN Convention on Economic, Social and Cultural Rights* article 13.3	• Freedom from discrimination in services based on sexual orientation including a poison-free classroom environment under Ontario *Human Rights Code* s. 1 • Equality rights under *Charter* s. 15 based on religion • Right to education directed to strengthen respect for human rights under *UN Convention on Economic, Social and Cultural Rights* article 13.1
c. Does the claim fall within the scope of the right or other entitlement in this context?	• Freedom to hold beliefs is broader than the freedom to act on them • The college's policy only prohibits homosexual activities of students while they attend the college • The college's policy says nothing about proselytizing against homosexual behaviour or otherwise singling out or treating LGBTQ students differently in the public school system • There is no evidence that other graduates have engaged in such behaviour	• Adhering to the college's policy prohibiting homosexual behaviour can lead to intolerant and discriminatory behaviour and even a poisoned environment in the public school environment • Governing body and schools/boards have legal obligations under the *Code* to ensure welcoming environments free from discrimination and harassment

SCENARIO 2: College Admission Standards	Christian Teachers' College Claim	Provincial Governing Body Claim
3. Amounts to more than minimal interference with a right?	• Denial of program certification for a religious teachers' college would bar graduates from pursuing employment and a career in teaching • They would have to be trained at a certified "secular" teachers' college instead, denying them the freedom of religion they could have otherwise enjoyed while attending a religious teachers' college	• Public school students who identify as LGBTQ are already extremely marginalized and face extensive harassment and discrimination. They also experience higher rates of mental illness and suicide. • Schools and governing bodies should not condone certification and employment of teachers who might not respect, protect, and promote equality and freedom from discrimination and harassment for LGBTQ students
Reconciling Rights		
4. Is there a solution that allows enjoyment of each right?	• Without limiting the religious college's policy against homosexual behaviour, certify the college's teaching program therefore allowing graduates to seek employment at public schools • Assume the college's graduates will not harass or discriminate or otherwise fail to respect, protect, and promote the human rights of LGBTQ students • If such behaviour does happen, address it quickly through normal complaint mechanisms and performance reviews including discipline up to and including dismissal • Educate all staff and students about their human rights obligations and ensure they promote equality, respect, and a welcoming environment for LGBTQ students	

SCENARIO 2: College Admission Standards	Christian Teachers' College Claim	Provincial Governing Body Claim
5. If not, is there a next best solution for one or both rights?	• Amend the college's policy to be silent on any prohibition against homosexual behaviour altogether • Add to the amended policy, or to the existing policy, a provision that student teachers have human rights obligations to respect, protect, and promote the *Code* rights of LGBTQ and other students	• Certify the religious college's teaching program regardless of the college's prohibitive policy • At the same time, require its graduates to complete additional requirements regarding their human rights obligations • Or, require all teacher training programs regardless of religious affiliation to include requirements on teachers' human rights obligations
Making Decisions		
• Must be consistent with human rights and other law, court decisions, and legal principles and have regard for OHRC policies	• *Trinity Western University v British Columbia College of Teachers*, SCC 2001	• *Chamberlain v Surrey School District No. 36*, SCC 2002 • *Ross v New Brunswick School District No. 15*, SCC 1996 • *R v Jones*, SCC 1986 (public interest in maintaining and improving supportive environments in the classroom)
• At least one claim must fall under the *Code* to be actionable at the Human Rights Tribunal	• College would need to argue that the governing body's certification power is a "service" within the meaning of the *Code* and make a claim based on creed accordingly	• LGBTQ students and/or their parents/guardians, or someone or some group on their behalf, would have to make out a claim against either the school/board and/or the governing body in "services" on the ground of sexual orientation and/or sex (gender identity)

SCENARIO 3: County Newspaper Editorial	Goods Importer's Claim	County Newspaper's Claim
Recognizing Rights		
1. What are the claims about?	A goods importer claims that his local county newspaper discriminated against him based on his place of origin when they published an editorial about the negative economic impact of goods and services imported into their community from the big city.	The newspaper says it has freedom of the press to write what it wants in its editorials based on the right to freedom of expression.
2. Do claims connect to legitimate rights and interests?		
a. Does the situation involve individuals or groups rather than only operational interests?	• The goods importer in this claim • Other goods importers living and/or doing business in the county • Immigrants or visitors to the county	• The county newspaper publisher, its editorial board, and staff • The county newspaper's corporate parent • Other media publishers and journalists
b. What human rights, other legal entitlements or *bona fide* and reasonable interests might be invoked?	• Right to equal treatment with respect to services, goods, and facilities without discrimination based on place of origin and possibly other related grounds under section 1 of the *Code* • *Code* s. 13(1) prohibits announced intention to discriminate by a person who publishes or displays before the public or causes the publication or display before the public of any notice, sign, symbol, emblem, or other similar representation that indicates the intention of the person to infringe a right under Part I	• Section 13 (2) of the *Code* protects opinion and says section 13 (1) shall not interfere with freedom of expression of opinion • Right to freedom of expression under section 2(b) of the *Charter*

SCENARIO 3: County Newspaper Editorial	Goods Importer's Claim	County Newspaper's Claim
c. Does the claim fall within the scope of the right or other entitlement in this context?	• The goods importer would have to show how the content of the editorial amounts to a notice, sign, symbol, emblem, or other similar representation that indicates the intention of a person to discriminate in employment, housing or services • Editorial based on a prohibited ground of discrimination such as place of origin • He might also have to show why the right to freedom of expression under section 2 (b) of the *Charter* should be limited under section 1 of the *Charter* in this circumstance	• Editorials are "opinion." They are not a "service" within the meaning of the *Code* • Even it were a service, the editorial cannot be considered a "similar representation" to a sign, notice or symbol under s. 13 (1) • Nor does the editorial declare an intent to discriminate in employment, housing, services, etc. • Nor does the editorial violate the hate provisions of the *Criminal Code*
3. Amounts to more than minimal interference with a right?	• The goods importer might argue, for example, how the editorial would result in the local community refusing to buy from those who import goods from outside the county putting them out of business without economic means to support themselves and their families. • He might also argue there is a negative impact on business people who are perceived to be "foreigners" because of race or related grounds	• Any limit on editorials, outside of *Criminal Code* provisions against hate, would put a chill on a newspaper's ability to operate freely and independently on the basis of free expression in a democratic society

SCENARIO 3: County Newspaper Editorial	Goods Importer's Claim	County Newspaper's Claim
Reconciling Rights		
4. Is there a solution that allows enjoyment of each right?	• The goods importer's claim does not appear to fall within the scope of the right to be free from announced intent to discriminate under the *Code* • The goods importer does not have a competing right that requires consideration for reconciliation • Publication of opinion in the media is a matter at the core of freedom of expression and freedom of the press in a democratic society. Any ambiguity should be resolved in favour of the exclusion of such matters from the *Code*	
5. If not, is there a next best solution for one or both rights?	• The newspaper in its discretion might consider printing letters to the editor written by non- country residents, giving opportunity for these individuals to oppose the editorial opinion	• Not required
Making Decisions		
• Must be consistent with human rights and other law, court decisions, legal principles and have regard for OHRC policies	• None applicable to the goods importer's claim	• *Whiteley v Osprey Media Publishing*, HRTO 2010 • In 2008, OHRC concluded it did not have jurisdiction under the *Code* to proceed with complaints about an article in *Maclean's* magazine
• At least one claim must fall under the *Code* to be actionable at the Human Rights Tribunal	• The goods importer's claim could not be made out under s. 13(1) of the *Code*	• Freedom of expression of opinion protected under s. 13(2) of the *Code*

Appendix E: Suggested contents of an internal policy

Under the Ontario *Human Rights Code*, education providers, employers, housing providers, and other responsible parties have the ultimate responsibility for maintaining an inclusive environment that is free from discrimination and harassment. As part of this, they have a legal duty to take steps to prevent and respond to situations involving competing rights. Having in place an effective "competing rights policy" is one concrete and practical way that organizations can fulfil their responsibilities under the *Code.* The OHRC's *Policy on Competing Human Rights* provides guidance to organizations when they are developing their own internal policies. While each organization should tailor its policy, taking into account such factors as its mandate, size, resources, and culture, the following are suggested basic features of an effective policy:

1) A vision statement setting out the organization's commitment to maintaining a fair and equitable environment where everyone's human rights are respected, and where discrimination, harassment, and competing rights situations are dealt with promptly and effectively.

Example: We recognize and value the diversity of Ontario and of our own [workplace, school, apartment building, etc.] We strive for equality in our [employment, education, housing, etc.] practices and delivery of services. We recognize that sometimes rights may come into conflict with one another. Therefore, we will equip management and all [employees, students, tenants, etc.] with knowledge and skills to recognize and address competing rights in our [workplace, school, apartment building, etc.] and service delivery.

We will foster respect on a daily basis amongst management and all [employees, students, tenants, etc.]. We will ensure that management staff understand their legal responsibilities to act immediately to deal with competing rights situations. We will continually monitor and assess progress in recognizing and addressing competing rights situations in our organization.

2) A clear statement of the goals of the policy, namely:

- show dignity and respect for one another;
- encourage mutual recognition of interests, rights and obligations;
- facilitate maximum recognition of rights, wherever possible;
- help parties to understand the scope of their rights and obligations;
- address stigma and power imbalances and help to give marginalized individuals and groups a voice;
- encourage cooperation and shared responsibility for finding agreeable solutions that maximize enjoyment of rights; and
- a commitment on the part of the organization to make sincere efforts to achieve these goals when addressing competing human rights scenarios.

3) A statement of rights and obligations under the Ontario *Human Rights Code*.

Example: We recognize that under the Ontario *Human Rights Code*, we have the ultimate responsibility for maintaining an inclusive environment that is free from discrimination and harassment, and where everyone's human rights are respected. As part of this, we have a legal duty to take steps to prevent and respond to situations involving competing rights.

Example: Under the *Code*, [employees, students, tenants, etc.] have the right to file a human rights claim with the Human Rights Tribunal of Ontario if they believe that they have experienced discrimination in [employment, housing, education, other services, etc.].

4) A list of the prohibited grounds of discrimination listed in the *Code*.

Example: The *Code* prohibits discrimination based on fifteen grounds: race, ancestry, place of origin, colour, ethnic origin, citizenship, creed, sex, sexual orientation, age, marital status, family status, disability, receipt of public assistance (in housing only), and record of offences (in employment only). Competing rights claims may potentially arise relating to any *Code* ground.

5) A definition of "competing human rights" (see section 4 of this *Policy*).

Example: In general, competing human rights involve situations where parties to a dispute claim that the enjoyment of an individual or group's human rights and freedoms, as protected by law, would interfere with another's rights and freedoms. This complicates the normal approach to resolving a human rights dispute where only one side claims a human rights violation. In some cases, only one party is making a human rights claim, but the claim conflicts with the legal entitlements of another party or parties.

6) Examples of competing rights scenarios that are meaningful and relevant in the organization's context.

7) A description of who the policy applies to (such as employers, employees, unions, etc.).

8) How internal complaints and competing rights situations will be handled with details on:

- who to complain to and/or raise competing right concerns with
- an assurance that the person handling complaints and/or competing rights concerns should be independent, expert, etc.
- confidentiality
- reassurance that the person(s) making a complaint and/or raising competing rights concerns will be protected from reprisal or threat of reprisal

- help that is available for parties
- the availability of alternative dispute resolution, such as mediation, to resolve a complaint and/or competing rights situation (see section 7.3 of this *Policy*)
- how the complaint and/or competing rights situation will be investigated
- how long the process will take
- a commitment that decisions made and/or actions taken by the organization will be communicated to the parties.

9) A commitment to act in accordance with the following key competing rights legal principles:

- No rights are absolute
- There is no hierarchy of rights
- Rights may not extend as far as claimed
- The full context, facts, and constitutional values at stake must be considered
- Must look at extent of interference (only *actual* burdens on rights trigger conflicts)
- The core of a right is more protected than its periphery
- Aim to respect the importance of both sets of rights
- Statutory defences may restrict rights of one group and give rights to another, and a recognition of the obligation to consider these legal principles when dealing with competing rights situations, and to stay apprised of caselaw developments (the OHRC will provide on-line legal updates to this *Policy* at www.ohrc.on.ca). (See section 5 of this *Policy* for more detail.)

10) A commitment to use the OHRC's analysis when addressing competing human rights situations (see section 6 of this *Policy*).

11) A statement reinforcing the right of individuals to file other types of complaints, such as:

- a human rights application with the Human Rights Tribunal of Ontario at any time during the internal process, as well as an explanation of the one-year time limit in the *Code*
- a complaint under the *Occupational Health and Safety Act*, if applicable
- a grievance under a collective agreement, if applicable
- criminal charges, if applicable.

Appendix F: Table of cases

Adler v Ontario, [1996] 3 S.C.R. 609

Alberta v Hutterian Brethren of Wilson Colony, 2009 SCC 37

Assn. of Justices of the Peace of Ontario v Ontario (Attorney General) (2008), 92 O.R. (3d) 16

B. (R.) v Children's Aid Society of Metropolitan Toronto, [1995] 1 S.C.R. 315

Bothwell v Ontario (Minister of Transportation), 2005 CanLII 1066 (ON S.C.D.C.)

Bou Malhab v Diffusion Métromédia CMR Inc., [2011] 1 S.C.R. 214

Brockie v Brillinger (No. 2), (2002), 43 C.H.R.R. D/90 (Ont. Sup. Ct.)

Bruker v Marcovitz, [2007] 3 S.C.R. 607

Caldwell v Stewart, [1984] 2 S.C.R. 603

Canada (Human Rights Commission) v Taylor, [1990] 3 S.C.R. 892

Canadian Council of Churches v Canada (Minister of Employment and Immigration), 1992 CanLII 116 (S.C.C.)

Chamberlain v Surrey School District No. 36, [2002] 4 S.C.R. 710

Chiang v Vancouver Board of Education, 2009 B.C.H.R.T. 319

Dagenais v Canadian Broadcasting Corp., [1994] 3 S.C.R. 835

Dallaire v Les Chevaliers de Colomb, 2011 HRTO 639 (CanLII)

Danson v Ontario (Attorney General), 1990 CanLII 93 (S.C.C.)

Eagleson Co-Operative Homes, Inc. v Théberge, [2006] O.J. No. 4584 (Sup.Ct. (Div.Ct.))

Giguere v Popeye Restaurant, 2008 HRTO 2 (CanLII)

Grant v Willcock (1990), 13 C.H.R.R. D/22 (Ont. Bd. Inq.)

Griggs v Duke Power Co., 401 U.S. 424 (4th Cir. 1971)

Hall v Durham Catholic District School Board, 2005 CanLII 23121 (ON SC)

Irwin Toy Ltd. v Quebec (Attorney General), [1989] 1 S.C.R. 927

MacKay v Manitoba, 1989 CanLII 26 (S.C.C.)

Marriage Commissioners Appointed Under the Marriage Act (Re), 2011, SKCA 3 (CanLII)

Martinie v Italian Society of Port Arthur (1995), 24 C.H.R.R. D/169 (Ont. Bd. Of Inquiry)

Nichols v M.J., 2009 SKQB 299 (CanLII).

Ontario Human Rights Commission v Christian Horizons, 2010 ONSC 2105 (CanLII)

P. (D.) v S. (C.), [1993] 4 S.C.R. 141

Quebec et Giguere v Montreal (Ville) (2003) 47 C.H.R.R. D/67

Quesnel v London Educational Health Centre (1995), 28 C.H.R.R. D/474

R. v Crawford, 1995 CanLII 138 (SCC)

R. v Kapp, [2008] 2 S.C.R. 483

R. v Keegstra, [1990] 3 S.C.R. 697

R. v Mills, 1999 CanLII 637 (SCC)

R. v N.S., 2010 ONCA 670

R. v O'Connor, [1995] 4 S.C.R. 411

R. v Oakes, [1986] 1 S.C.R. 103

Reference re Same-Sex Marriage, 2004 SCC 79

Ross v New Brunswick School District No. 15, [1996] 1 S.C.R. 825

Syndicat Northcrest v Amselem, 2004 SCC 47

Trinity Western University v British Columbia College of Teachers, [2001] 1 S.C.R. 772

Whiteley v Osprey Media Publishing, 2010 HRTO 2152 (CanLII)

Chapter 2

Addressing Competing Human Rights Claims: The Policy Approach of the Ontario Human Rights Commission

Shaheen Azmi

A. Introduction

The Ontario Human Rights Commission (OHRC) released its *Policy on Competing Human Rights* in April 2012,[1] culminating a six-year program of research and consultation focused on detailing effective ways to address competing human rights claims. In general, competing human rights claims are situations in which legally codified human rights are claimed by two or more parties to a dispute, thus complicating the normal approach to resolving a human rights dispute where only one side claims a human right in relation to an alleged violator of rights.

This chapter reviews the nature of human rights policy and its development by the OHRC, discusses the OHRC's rationale for becoming involved in this policy activity, and reviews the ongoing process employed to develop and promote this policy. The policy development process employed by the OHRC included a policy dialogue that was convened in March 2010, and for which most of the chapters in this publication were developed.

The OHRC is the statutory human rights commission established by the Ontario *Human Rights Code*.[2] When it enacted the

---

1 Ontario Human Rights Commission, *Policy on Competing Human Rights* (OHRC, 2012 online: OHRC www.ohrc.on.ca/en/policy-competing-human-rights.

2 RSO 1990, c H.19 [*Code*].

Code in 1962, Ontario was one of the earlier Canadian provinces to introduce human rights legislation. Currently, the federal government, as well as all provinces in Canada, save British Columbia, have passed human rights legislation that establishes a human rights commission. The OHRC's mandate is to promote and protect human rights through a variety of powers, which, until July 2008, included the responsibility to take and process human rights complaints. This included mediation, investigation, and referral of complaints to the Human Rights Tribunal of Ontario (HRTO) and litigation of complaints before the HRTO and the courts. Changes to the *Code* in 2008 resulted in the responsibility for processing complaints being passed to the HRTO, leaving the OHRC to focus on the promotion of human rights. Promotion methods include: establishing human rights policy, conducting research and inquiry, intervening in legal proceedings, and providing public education. The OHRC is the only human rights commission in Canada that no longer receives and processes human rights complaints.

B. What Is Human Rights Policy?

Human rights policies provide cutting-edge and innovative interpretations of human rights law. They open up possibilities for expanding the protections of the *Code*, address new and emerging human rights issues and trends, incorporate international perspectives on human rights, and provide a broad understanding of the social and economic aspects of human rights. Fundamentally, they aim to provide clear policy direction in new unexplored areas or in areas of ambiguity for a wide variety of audiences.

Section 30 of the *Code* authorizes the OHRC to prepare, approve, and publish human rights policies and to provide guidance on interpreting its provisions. The power to develop policies is part of the OHRC's broader responsibility under section 29 to promote, protect, and advance respect for human rights in Ontario, to protect the public interest, and to eliminate discriminatory practices. Section 45.5 of the *Code* states that the HRTO may consider policies approved by the OHRC in an HRTO proceeding. Where a party or an intervener in a proceeding requests it, the HRTO *shall* consider an OHRC policy. Where an OHRC policy is relevant to the subject matter of a human rights application, parties and interveners are encouraged to bring the policy to the HRTO's attention for consideration. Section 45.6 of the *Code* states that if a final decision or order of the HRTO is not consistent with an OHRC policy, in a case where the OHRC was either a party or an intervener, the OHRC may apply to have the HRTO state a case to the Divisional Court to address this inconsistency.

Although OHRC policies and guidelines are not binding on the HRTO or on courts, they are often given great deference and applied to the facts of human rights cases before courts or tribunals, and are quoted in the decisions of these bodies. In addition, the OHRC's policies contain practical guidance relevant to the everyday lives of Ontarians. They aim to influence social behaviour to prevent human rights violations before they occur and to promote social change. They set standards for how individuals, employers, housing providers, service providers, and policy makers should act to ensure compliance with the *Code*. OHRC policies are widely used as a source of guidance by those responsible for applying the *Code*, such as lawyers, unions, human resource managers, and others. They are perceived as useful and instructive because they respond to day-to-day human rights issues.

As the largest provincial human rights commission in Canada, the OHRC has become a leader in the development of human rights policy in the country. There are currently twenty-one Commission-approved policies that are accessible through the OHRC's website.[3] The first of these was the *Policy on Height*

3 Ontario Human Rights Commission, online: OHRC www.ohrc.on.ca.

and Weight Requirements, which was released in 1989,[4] and the most recent of these was the *Policy on Rental Housing and Human Rights* released in 2009.[5] These policies range in style from short, focused policy positions on issues such as drug and alcohol testing, to comprehensive and detailed policy documents addressing multiple issues and positions related to major *Code* grounds like "race" or "disability," or significant social areas such as "employment." These more substantive policies typically contain sections on historical, legal, and social context, linguistic and conceptual clarification, identification of specific types of discrimination, and detailing of best practices and approaches to addressing these types of discrimination. The most widely used OHRC policies such as the *Policy and Guidelines on Disability and the Duty to Accommodate*,[6] the *Policy and Guidelines on Racism and Racial Discrimination*,[7] and *Human Rights at Work*,[8] are more substantive in nature.

---

4 This policy was revised December 2009. See Ontario Human Rights Commission, *Policy on Height and Weight Requirements* (OHRC, 1996), online: OHRC www.ohrc.on.ca/en/policy-height-and-weight-requirements.

5 Ontario Human Rights Commission, *Policy on Rental Housing and Human Rights* (OHRC, 2009), online: OHRC www.ohrc.on.ca/en/policy-human-rights-and-rental-housing.

6 Ontario Human Rights Commission, *Policy and Guidelines on Disability and the Duty to Accommodate* (OHRC, 2000), online: OHRC www.ohrc.on.ca/en/policy-and-guidelines-disability-and-duty-accommodate.

7 Ontario Human Rights Commission, *Policy and Guidelines on Racism and Racial Discrimination* (OHRC, 2005), online: OHRC www.ohrc.on.ca/en/policy-and-guidelines-racism-and-racial-discrimination.

8 Ontario Human Rights Commission, *Human Rights at Work*, 3d ed (Toronto: Thomson/Carswell, 2008), online: OHRC www.ohrc.on.ca/en/human-rights-work-2008-third-edition.

C. How Are Human Rights Policies Developed?

Human rights policy development is triggered and informed by a broad range of factors including: inquiries and human rights claims received from the public; public education and outreach activities; academic and social science research; monitoring of social issues and trends; caselaw development; and, of course, the provisions of the *Code* and the *Canadian Charter of Rights and Freedoms*.[9]

Human rights policy development in a specific area of concern is often highly contextual. However, generally speaking, there are three key sources of guidance: legal review, academic and social science research, and public consultation.

The legal reference points for policy development include primarily the *Code* and the *Charter*, human rights caselaw, and international human rights instruments. Policy development usually begins with an effort to determine the current law on the matter. However, the law is not always clear. While the law often provides limits to policy development, gaps and inconsistencies in the law can be prime areas for policy development. For example, in the context of mandatory retirement, the OHRC's policy development led to legislative efforts to overturn the mandatory retirement age of sixty-five that was protected as a legitimate form of discrimination in the *Code* itself. In 2008, in *Assn of Justices of the Peace of Ontario v Ontario (Attorney General)*,[10] the Ontario Superior Court of Justice quoted from the OHRC's *Policy on Discrimination against Older People Because of Age*.[11] The

---

9 *Canadian Charter of Rights and Freedoms*, Part I of the *Constitution Act, 1982*, being Schedule B to the *Canada Act 1982* (UK) 1982, c 11 [*Charter*].

10 *Assn of Justices of the Peace of Ontario v Ontario (Attorney General)* (2008), 92 OR (3d) 16 (SCJ).

11 Ontario Human Rights Commission, *Policy on Discrimination against Older People Because of Age* (OHRC, 2002), online: OHRC www.ohrc.

court stated that the OHRC's efforts led to a "sea change" in the attitude to mandatory retirement in Ontario, which led to the Ontario government's decision to pass legislation amending the *Code* to prohibit age discrimination in employment after age sixty-five, subject to limited exceptions.

Academic and social science research provides another key reference point for policy development. Research of this type may identify historical factors, changing perceptions and understandings of terms and concepts, and alternative approaches to addressing and resolving concerns. For example, human rights policy positions that relate to medical conditions may vary considerably depending on the latest medical knowledge. Human rights policy positions regarding treatment of individuals with HIV/AIDS is a specific example of how policy positions evolved as medical understanding and treatment developed. In another context, growing social scientific understanding of the social construction of "race" and "disability" led to major changes in how discrimination relating to these two human rights grounds was understood and determined by tribunals and courts; OHRC policy demonstrates this shift in understanding and depicts these grounds as socially constructed, rather than biologically determined.

The last of the key reference points — public consultation — has been referred to by tribunals as the key element that obligates tribunals and courts to show deference to human rights policies. For example, in *Quesnel v London Education Health Centre*,[12] the Board of Inquiry, as the HRTO was then known, found that the OHRC's *Policy and Guidelines on Disability and the Duty to Accommodate*[13] were entitled to "great deference" by interpreters of the *Code* because they carry forward the meaning and intent of the *Code*, they were developed in a manner consistent with its

---

on.ca/en/policy-discrimination-against-older-people-because-age.

12 *Quesnel v London Education Health Centre* (1995), 28 CHRR D/474 (Ont Board of Inquiry).

13 See above note 6.

legislative history, and their development was informed by broad public consultation.

The OHRC regularly consults with a broad range of stakeholders, including employers and employer organizations, unions, public and private service providers, human resources professionals, community groups, advocacy organizations, lawyers, academics, provincial and municipal governments, housing providers, social service agencies, education service providers, consumer groups, and others. Public consultations identify key issues and concerns for the OHRC, as well as possible approaches and best practices.

Formal public consultation relating to policy development aims to gather information, test policy positions, and assess the value and usefulness of policy documents. Consultations may take a variety of forms including interviews, surveys, focus groups, town hall meetings, public presentations, distribution of discussion papers and consultation reports, written submissions, and policy dialogues. The development of discussion papers for public input and the subsequent publishing of a consultation report have been common tools employed by the OHRC when developing major policies that requiring significant input from the wider public. Social issues that have led the OHRC to employ these policy development techniques include: age-based discrimination, disability and education, rental housing, and human rights and public transit.

Policy dialogues are another of the favoured tools employed by the OHRC. This tool brings together individuals from key stakeholder groups including academics, government representatives, and human rights workers to focus on a defined policy area in a concentrated period of time, usually two or three days. Prepared presentations by experts or key informants are followed by policy-focused discussion led by the OHRC's policy analysts. This type of consultation is particularly useful when stakeholders are clearly identifiable and where complex notions requiring detailed explanation and testing are involved. For example, the OHRC's policy development in the area of the ground of "race" included a three-day policy dialogue to help meet its public consultation needs.

Although testing of human rights policy positions occurs informally throughout the development of a policy, in many cases, specific testing of key positions or documents is needed. Testing often takes the form of the consultation formats identified above that are specifically geared to testing. For example, the OHRC may release a draft policy document for public consultation prior to finalizing it. In some cases contentious or controversial ideas or approaches are tested through focus groups and interviews.

After a policy has been developed, reviewed, and approved by the commissioners for public release, the OHRC will launch a phase of promotion. Promotion is critical to raising public awareness and for ensuring that a policy is a vital force that influences society, tribunals, and courts. Typically, a major launch or series of launches are planned in partnership with key organizations and groups. Shorter plain language and user-friendly communication and media documents are also produced and distributed, and public education and training events are planned. The bulk of public education requests that the OHRC receives relate to training for community groups and organizations on the OHRC's policies. The inability of the OHRC to respond to all such requests has led to the recent development of e-learning as a new format to provide public education relating to human rights policy. All new policies of the OHRC will be accompanied by e-learning modules available through the OHRC's website.

Another way for the OHRC to promote its policies is through intervention in human rights cases before the HRTO and the courts. The OHRC actively monitors ongoing human rights cases, in part to identify which cases would facilitate the confirmation of key policy positions. For example, the OHRC intervened in the

Supreme Court of Canada case, *Syndicat Northcrest v Amselem*,[14] to promote its policy positions regarding accommodation of religious belief.

Given that social and legal developments occur often, human rights policy is subject to considerable change. The OHRC periodically updates its policies, usually in response to new caselaw or changes in legislation. However, it has had difficulty doing so in a timely fashion for all documents, particularly as most of these documents have been primarily conceived as hard texts. In response to this dilemma, the OHRC is exploring using its website to post official versions of its policy which can be updated much more quickly and frequently.

D. Why the Policy Focus on Competing Human Rights Claims?

The matter of competing human rights claims has emerged as a challenging issue for human rights commissions across Canada, primarily in the context of complaint handling and litigation. Like these other commissions, the OHRC has found that human rights complaints presented by the public sometimes involve scenarios in which complainants allege violations of their statutory human rights by respondents who would then claim defence on the basis of human rights grounds also established by human rights legislation. Such situations are of many types and configurations. The human rights grounds most often cited relating to competing human rights claims include the grounds of "creed," "sexual orientation," "disability," and "gender." Although other grounds and legal rights could also be invoked, competing human rights claims have been particularly challenging for human rights commissions to handle as normal approaches and processes are often unable to provide adequate guidance. Although caselaw on

14 *Syndicat Northcrest v Amselem*, [2004] 2 SCR 551, 2004 SCC 47.

the matter of competing human rights claims has slowly been developing in Canada, it is clear that there is a need for human rights policy guidance to supplement legal interpretation.

Another major factor that led the OHRC to address the issue of competing rights claims was the recognition of the need to update its widely used *Policy on Creed and the Accommodation of Religious Observances*.[15] This policy needs considerable updating to reflect changing caselaw and the emergence of new scenarios related to an increasingly diverse Canadian social context. The development of several highly charged controversial scenarios where creed human rights seemed to conflict with other human rights, particularly rights associated with sexual orientation and gender, was one of the major human rights concerns that drew attention to competing rights claims. The OHRC recognized that providing some guidance on such competing claims was one essential component to updating the OHRC's Creed Policy.

At the same time, the emergence of a variety of public debates relating to what have been termed "competing rights" led the OHRC to be further concerned with ways to address competing human rights claims. These debates often relate to the presence of minority communities and how far the rights of these groups should be accommodated by the majority culture. For example, in the post-9/11 world, various cultural and religious practices of Muslims have been questioned as inappropriate or unacceptable by elements of the majority culture; such scenarios have commonly been termed as scenarios of "competing rights" in the media. Although these public debates are broader in nature than the OHRC's focus, they indicate popular conceptions that must be factored in when developing effective human rights policy.

15 Ontario Human Rights Commission, *Policy on Creed and the Accommodation of Religious Observances* (OHRC, 1996), online: OHRC www.ohrc.on.ca/en/policy-creed-and-accommodation-religious-observances [Creed Policy].

E. What was the Policy Development Process for Addressing Competing Human Rights Claims?

Like many policy projects, the OHRC entered into a formal process of policy development, with respect to competing human rights claims, with a number of preliminary steps to help guide the way.

Because competing human rights scenarios often emerge in relation to the human rights grounds of sexual orientation and creed, the OHRC first addressed the matter of competing rights briefly in its *Policy on Discrimination and Harassment Because of Sexual Orientation*.[16] However, it is obvious that more substantial policy development in this area is required. To this end, the OHRC contracted with a law student to develop a policy paper on what was termed at the time "balancing rights." This led to a paper entitled, "Balancing Conflicting Rights: Towards an Analytical Framework" that was posted on the OHRC's website in August 2005.[17] It was intended to provide public information that would promote discussion and further research without elaborating any firm policy positions.

After some delay, due to the restructuring of the human rights system in Ontario, the OHRC continued its work in the area of competing rights more formally. In 2007, initial steps taken for the formal policy development process included a detailed literature review scanning relevant articles from the fields of law,

16 Ontario Human Rights Commission, *Policy on Discrimination and Harassment because of Sexual Orientation* (OHRC, 2000), online: OHRC www.ohrc.on.ca/en/policy-discrimination-and-harassment-because-sexual-orientation.

17 Ontario Human Rights Commission, "Balancing Conflicting Rights: Towards an Analytical Framework" (OHRC, 2005), online: OHRC www.ohrc.on.ca/en/balancing-conflicting-rights-towards-analytical-framework. A revised version of this paper by BJ Wray is contained in Chapter 11 of this book.

philosophy, conflict resolution, and political science. This review revealed a wealth of information relating to how competing rights claims have been conceived from a variety of perspectives, and how competing human rights claims might be conceived. At the same time, Canadian and US caselaw has continued to develop and some preliminary analysis has been conducted. In many cases, OHRC counsel have themselves been actively involved in the development of this caselaw: for example, the OHRC litigated *Ontario (Human Rights Commission) v Christian Horizons*.[18] In addition, detailed scoping interviews were conducted with ten key informants who were known to be familiar with situations of competing human rights claims from a variety of stakeholder, legal, and academic perspectives. These interviews represented initial efforts to identify issues and concerns emerging from the perspectives of groups associated with the *Code* grounds of creed, sexual orientation, gender, and disability, while also helping to identify individuals and groups who should participate in future public consultation activity.

The initial policy development activities led to the identification of the following goals for a policy framework:

1) Provide clear, user-friendly guidance to a broad spectrum of community and organizational needs on how to frame, handle, and potentially resolve competing human rights claims across multiple contexts.
2) Provide policy interpretation of the *Code* to policy makers, litigants, and adjudicators on how to frame, handle, and potentially resolve competing human rights claims.

Early in the planning it was recognized that the public consultation technique that best fit the need of development of such a policy framework was a policy dialogue process referred to earlier. Competing human rights claims present complex and some-

18 *Ontario (Human Rights Commission) and Heintz v Christian Horizons*, 2010 ONSC 2105.

what abstract scenarios involving multiple types of stakeholders who are often in situations of conflict. An effectively planned and convened policy dialogue process would allow for a concentrated process to detail the full range of the complexity involved and allow at the same time for direct stakeholder input on key policy issues.

A partnership was struck with the York Centre for Public Policy and Law to organize and convene a policy dialogue. Key areas for academic presentation were identified based on previous research and consultation, and policy-focused questions were identified to guide the discussion that would follow. Academics and researchers were recruited to develop articles within the parameters identified and to present these to the policy dialogue conference. Individuals recruited for the policy dialogue represented different stakeholder groups and relevant social and institutional perspectives. Senior policy and legal staff of the OHRC focused and guided discussion and recorded the proceedings.

The two-day policy dialogue was held at York University in Toronto in March 2010. The proceedings were attended by a total of sixty-eight invited participants. Members of the general population were invited to view the proceedings via a video feed into a nearby auditorium. The proceedings proved to be riveting and rich with material for the development of a policy framework. Comments from participants indicated that the event was an unusual opportunity for individuals, often on conflicting sides of disputes, to engage in constructive debate directly with each other and work towards a common purpose.

The framework was extensively tested in relation to real world circumstances. A two-day testing symposium of representatives from school boards and other stakeholder groups from across Ontario was convened at York University in December 2010. Attendees at this event were trained in the framework and were given opportunities to test out the framework in relation to competing human rights scenarios derived from practical scenarios drawn from educational settings. A refined framework was further tested in consultation sessions conducted with representatives of a wide variety of stakeholder groups in the summer of 2011. These summer consultation sessions led to the final version of the framework that was then elaborated upon to form the policy document released in April 2012.

F. What Are the Next Steps?

With the release of the policy the OHRC's focus will now shift to promotion of this policy. This type of policy, with its novel subject matter and inherent complexity, will require an extensive multi-year program of public education and training initiatives to ensure that the policy becomes a truly effective human rights instrument.

Promotion of the policy has already included the publication of shortened articles from the policy dialogue in a dedicated edition of the publication *Canadian Diversity/Diversité Canadienne*.[19] A number of post-policy release activities are being planned as of the writing of this chapter. E-learning training modules are being developed to supplement the policy that will be made available on the OHRC's website. A series of launch events are being organized across the province of Ontario. Partnerships with major organizations are being negotiated to help them implement policy guidance within their policy and organizational structures. Education and training activities are being organized for multiple locations and settings over the next few years.

In addition, efforts to promote the elements of the framework have already begun in legal proceedings. The OHRC intervened in the Ontario Court of Appeal niqab case of *R v NS*[20] and, in its factum submitted to the court, advanced a legal approach to competing human rights claims consistent with the draft frame-

19 See the Fall 2010 issue of the publication.

20 2010 ONCA 670.

work. Relevant portions of this factum are posted on the OHRC's website.[21] The OHRC will continue to look for further opportunities to advance its policy and framework in legal proceedings as they present themselves.

21 Above note 3.

Chapter 3

Oil and Vinegar: Resolving Conflicting Rights under the *Charter* and Ontario's *Human Rights Code*

Janet Epp Buckingham

A. Introduction

Religion has long been a "hot button issue" in Canadian society with issues of religious conflict garnering significant media attention and raising considerable controversy across the country. In the context of Canadian human rights law, religion enjoys strong protection but religious rights invariably compete for recognition alongside other rights protected under Canadian law. Religious rights and these other rights, of course, make up our tolerant, free, and just Canadian social fabric but a little like oil and vinegar; together they can make either a fine-flavoured vinaigrette or a powerfully unpleasant mixture with both the oil or the vinegar competing for dominance and drowning out the nuances of the salad beneath. When religious human rights go head-to-head with other human rights protected by Canadian law, as claimed under either the *Canadian Charter of Rights and Freedoms*[1] or provincial human rights codes or both, the results, like those of a salad dressing, can be either a harmonious blend pleasing to the palate or an unpleasant conflict leaving a bad taste in one's mouth. This paper unpacks the current state of the law in Canada with respect to the protection of religious rights when they come into conflict with other rights and suggests that if a sound,

---

1 *Canadian Charter of Rights and Freedoms*, Part I of the *Constitution Act, 1982*, being Schedule B to the *Canada Act 1982* (UK) 1982, c 11 [*Charter*].

logical, and transparent mechanism exists to resolve disputes or conflicts between religious rights and other rights, then conflicts are minimized, competing groups in society are not left marginalized, and one can enjoy "une bonne salade à la canadienne." Bon appétit.

Ontario's *Human Rights Code*[2] provides one mechanism for the peaceful resolution of such conflict. Under the *Code*, everyone in Ontario has the right to equal treatment in employment,[3] accommodation,[4] and services[5] without discrimination on the basis of, *inter alia*, creed. They also have the right to be free from harassment in relation to accommodation[6] and employment[7] on the basis of, *inter alia*, creed. Anyone who believes they have been discriminated against may file an application with the Human Rights Tribunal of Ontario (HRTO). The HRTO will first attempt to mediate the dispute, failing which a panel will be assigned to adjudicate the matter.

HRTO decisions must always recognize the broad protection for freedom of religion and freedom from discrimination on the basis of religion as set out in the *Charter*, which guarantees that governments will protect religious rights and freedoms. The interpretation of the enumerated ground "creed" under the *Code* is generally synonymous with the definition of "religion" found in the *Charter*. Until recently, it appeared that cases addressing accommodation of religion under the *Charter* were converging with cases under provincial human rights codes that dealt with accommodation of religion. However, a recent Supreme Court of Canada decision signals that these two streams of similar cases are diverging.

---

2 *Human Rights Code*, RSO 1990, c H.19 [*Code*].

3 *Ibid*, s 5(1).

4 *Ibid*, s 2(1).

5 *Ibid*, s 1.

6 *Ibid*, s 2(2).

7 *Ibid*, s 5(2).

Competing rights arise most frequently as conflicts between rights guaranteed by the *Charter* and rights protected by the *Code*. As many rights are protected under both, there is no single way that these cases arise. A complaint of discrimination on the basis of creed can be adjudicated under the *Code* and then be challenged on the basis that the decision violates a *Charter* right, religious or otherwise. Similarly, a tribunal decision finding discrimination on another enumerated basis can be challenged on the basis that it violates religious freedom. The Supreme Court of Canada has resorted to building a framework for resolving such conflicts under section 1 of the *Charter* but as the parameters of religious freedom are still being defined, it is in the formative stages.

Complaints of discrimination on the basis of creed have tended to fall into one of several categories: holy days, religious dress, and conscientious objection to certain types of work or activities. Previous board and tribunal decisions have set out some broad guidelines that provide a maximum scope for religious practices and observances while protecting the health and safety of others. This paper will address accommodation of religious practices under these categories and then examine the resolution of competing rights.

B. Definition of "Creed" under the *Code*

The term "creed" is used in the *Code* as the prohibited ground of discrimination relating to "religion." The *Code* was originally enacted in 1962, predating the *Charter* by two decades. This term generally refers to a system of beliefs, thereby avoiding the concept of a religion of one person. The Ontario Human Rights Commission's (OHRC) accepted definition for "creed" is:

> Creed is interpreted to mean "religious creed" or "religion." It is defined as a professed system and confession of faith, including both beliefs and observances or worship. A belief in a God

> or gods, or a single supreme being or deity is not a requisite.
>
> Religion is broadly accepted by the OHRC to include, for example, non-deistic bodies of faith, such as the spiritual faiths/practices of aboriginal cultures, as well as *bona fide* newer religions (addressed on a case-by-case basis).
>
> The existence of religious beliefs and practices are both necessary and sufficient to the meaning of creed, if the beliefs and practices are sincerely held and/or observed.[8]

The current OHRC *Policy on Creed and the Accommodation of Religious Observances* states, "'Creed' is defined subjectively." It goes on to indicate that religious practices are protected "even if they are not essential elements of the creed."[9]

While many complaints are on the basis of traditional religions, tribunals have addressed both new religions and the outer bounds of "creed." For example, Falun Gong has been found to be included in the meaning of "creed."[10] The tribunal in that case considered both objective evidence, that being an expert in new religions, and subjective evidence, that being the complainant who testified that Falun Gong was a deeply held belief with spiritual meaning.

An HRTO has also found that Rastafarianism falls within the meaning of "creed"[11] but the Tribunal provided little analysis. The Tribunal accepted that the complainant's beliefs were sincerely held. Another case raised the issue whether tarot card

---

8 Ontario Human Rights Commission, *Policy on Creed and the Accommodation of Religious Observances* (OHRC, 1996) at 4 (approved by the Commission 20 October 1996 with minor revisions in December 2009), online: www.ohrc.on.ca/en/resources/Policies/PolicyCreedAccomodEN/pdf.

9 *Ibid* at 5.

10 *Huang v 1233065 Ontario Inc (Ottawa Senior Chinese Cultural Association)* (2006), 55 CHRR D/216, 2006 HRTO 1.

11 *Henry v Kuntz*, [2004] OHRTD No 7, 2004 HRTO 7.

reading for third parties could be part of "creed"[12] but the case was decided on another issue. In *Jazairi v Ontario (Human Rights Commission)*,[13] the Ontario Court of Appeal put some outer limits on the meaning of "creed," determining that it does not include political opinions.

C. The Basis for Protecting Religious Rights under the *Charter*

The interpretation and application of the prohibition of discrimination on the basis of creed has been complicated by similar protection offered by the *Charter*. The *Charter* can apply directly as human rights commissions, boards of inquiry, and tribunals are government agents and thus are subject to the *Charter*. The application of the *Code* must be in accordance with the *Charter*.[14] In some instances, a complaint could have given rise to an action under the *Charter* or under the *Code*, where the allegation is against a school board, for example. The *Charter* can also come into play when the alleged discriminator claims a competing right guaranteed by the *Charter*.

Two sections of the *Charter* protect religious rights. The first is section 2(a), which guarantees "freedom of conscience and religion" as a fundamental freedom. Section 15 protects individuals from discrimination on the basis of religion. It guarantees that every individual is

> equal before and under the law and has the right to the equal protection and equal benefit of the law without discrimina-

---

12 *Sauve v Ontario (Training, Colleges and Universities)*, [2009] OHRTD No 1385, 2009 HRTO 1415.

13 (1999), 175 DLR (4th) 302 (Ont CA).

14 *Vriend v Alberta*, [1998] 1 SCR 493 stands for the proposition that provincial human rights codes will be interpreted in light of the human rights guarantees in the *Charter*.

> tion and, in particular, without discrimination based on race, national or ethnic origin, colour, *religion*, sex, age or mental or physical disability. [emphasis added]

The seminal case on the interpretation of section 2(a) is *Big M.*[15] Justice Dickson, writing for the majority, set out the two guiding principles for religious freedom: broad freedom and non-coercion.

> The essence of the concept of freedom of religion is the right to entertain such religious beliefs as a person chooses, the right to declare religious beliefs openly and without fear of hindrance or reprisal, and the right to manifest religious belief by worship and practice or by teaching and dissemination . . . . Freedom can primarily be characterized by the absence of coercion or constraint.[16]

The Supreme Court more fully defined "religion" and "freedom of religion" in *Syndicat Northcrest v Amselem*.[17] While the definition of "creed" need not match that of "religion," it seems likely that the courts would anticipate a definition at least as broad:

> Defined broadly, religion typically involves a particular and comprehensive system of faith and worship. Religion also tends to involve the belief in a divine, superhuman or controlling power. In essence, religion is about freely and deeply held personal convictions or beliefs connected to an individual's spiritual faith and integrally linked to one's self-definition and spiritual fulfilment, the practices of which allow individuals to foster a connection with the divine or with the subject or object of that spiritual faith.[18]

The current subjective interpretation of "creed" appears correct in light of Justice Iacobucci's statement on whether one must

15 *R v Big M Drug Mart*, [1985] 1 SCR 295 [*Big M*].

16 *Ibid* at paras 94–95.

17 *Syndicat Northcrest v Amselem*, [2004] 2 SCR 551 [*Amselem*].

18 *Ibid* at para 39.

prove that a certain religious practice is required by the religion:

> To summarize up to this point, our Court's past decisions and the basic principles underlying freedom of religion support the view that freedom of religion consists of the freedom to undertake practices and harbour beliefs, having a nexus with religion, in which an individual demonstrates he or she sincerely believes or is sincerely undertaking in order to connect with the divine or as a function of his or her spiritual faith, irrespective of whether a particular practice or belief is required by official religious dogma or is in conformity with the position of religious officials.[19]

And further:

> It is the religious or spiritual essence of an action, not any mandatory or perceived-as-mandatory nature of its observance, that attracts protection. An inquiry into the mandatory nature of an alleged religious practice is not only inappropriate, it is plagued with difficulties.[20]

The current OHRC policy on creed mirrors the definition of religious freedom under the *Charter*.

D. Accommodation of Religious Rights under the *Charter* and the *Code*

The Supreme Court of Canada appears to be wrestling with the relationship between the interpretation of section 2(a) when specifically applied to religious accommodation and the interpretation of accommodation of religion under human rights codes. There is a significant body of caselaw on the interpretation of these two sections, particularly as it applies to accommodating religious practices. While the relationship between the cases

---

19 *Ibid* at para 46.

20 *Ibid* at para 47.

under the *Charter* and those under human rights codes can be confusing, until the recent case, *Alberta v Wilson Colony of Hutterian Brethren*,[21] it appeared that there was convergence between the two. This case brings the convergence into doubt and introduces uncertainty and confusion into this area of law.

Numerous cases have been brought under the *Charter* that allege a violation of the *Charter* guarantee of religious freedom and request a remedy that effectively engages the court in determining how the individual can be accommodated. It is natural, then, that there be some correlation between how human rights codes determine accommodation and how it is determined under the *Charter*.

Two previous cases, *Eldridge v British Columbia*[22] under section 15(1) and *Multani v Commission scolaire Marguerite-Bourgeoys*[23] under section 2(a), used a deliberately convergent approach to human rights interpretation of reasonable accommodation. Justice Charron, writing for the majority in *Multani*, says:

> In *Eldridge*, at para. 79, this Court stated that, in cases concerning s. 15(1) of the *Canadian Charter*, "reasonable accommodation" was equivalent to the concept of "reasonable limits" provided for in s. 1 of the *Canadian Charter*.
>
> In my view, this correspondence between the legal principles is logical. In relation to discrimination, the courts have held that there is a duty to make reasonable accommodation for individuals who are adversely affected by a policy or rule that is neutral on its face, and that this duty extends only to the point at

21 *Alberta v Wilson Colony of Hutterian Brethren*, 2009 SCC 37 [*Wilson Colony*].

22 *Eldridge v British Columbia (Attorney General)*, [1997] 3 SCR 624 [*Eldridge*].

23 *Multani v Commission scolaire Marguerite-Bourgeoys*, [2006] 1 SCR 256 [*Multani*].

> which it causes undue hardship to the party who must perform it. Although it is not necessary to review all the cases on the subject, the analogy with the duty of reasonable accommodation seems to me to be helpful to explain the burden resulting from the minimal impairment test with respect to a particular individual, as in the case at bar.[24]

The most recent case from the Supreme Court of Canada concerning religious accommodation is *Wilson Colony*. Chief Justice McLachlin, writing for the majority in *Wilson Colony*, took the opportunity to explain "reasonable accommodation":

> Reasonable accommodation is a concept drawn from human rights statutes and jurisprudence. It envisions a dynamic process whereby the parties — most commonly an employer and employee — adjust the terms of their relationship in conformity with the requirements of human rights legislation, up to the point at which accommodation would mean undue hardship for the accommodating party.[25]

The majority is critical of the approach of the Alberta Court of Appeal, which applied a "reasonable accommodation" approach when considering the minimal impairment branch of the *Oakes* test. Rather, "reasonable accommodation" is only helpful to fashion an appropriate remedy under section 24(1) because under this section, the court is fashioning a remedy "*with respect to a particular individual*."[26] As this case was brought under section 52, where the validity of legislation or, in this case, regulations, was at issue, "reasonable accommodation" was not applicable. This either signals that "reasonable accommodation" under human rights codes will develop independently of similar

24 *Ibid* at paras 52–53.

25 *Wilson Colony*, above note 21 at para 68.

26 *Ibid* at para 67 [emphasis in the original].

complaints brought against governments under the *Charter*,[27] or it is specific to cases challenging constitutional validity that will be narrowly applied.

Despite the potential divergence between the application and interpretation of *Charter* rights vis-à-vis human rights code rights, the *Charter* sets a minimum standard for rights guarantees in Canada. The *Charter* applies to government action and human rights tribunals are part of government. Therefore, human rights tribunals must be aware of and apply these minimum standards.

E. Discrimination on the Basis of Creed under the *Code*

1) The General Rule on Accommodation

Infringements of the right to be free from discrimination on the basis of creed can be direct or adverse effect discrimination. An example of direct discrimination is a bus company that refuses all religious advertising because it is "too controversial." More common are general policies, such as dress requirements or holiday policies, which have an adverse effect on those with religious requirements.

The leading case on adverse effect discrimination is *Re Ontario Human Rights Commission and Simpsons-Sears (sub nom O'Malley v Simpsons-Sears)*.[28] Mrs. O'Malley had worked full time for a large retail outlet, which required her to work regular Friday evening and Saturday shifts. When she became a member of the Seventh-day Adventist Church, O'Malley informed her supervisor that her religion required that she observe a Sabbath from sundown on Friday through to sundown on Saturday. Her

---

27 See Janet Epp Buckingham, "Drivers Needed: Tough Choices from *Alberta v Wilson Colony of Hutterian Brethren*" (2010) 18 Const Forum Const 109.

28 *Re Ontario Human Rights Commission and Simpsons-Sears (sub nom O'Malley v Simpsons-Sears)*, [1985] 2 SCR 536 [*O'Malley*].

supervisor told her she would have to quit but subsequently offered her part-time employment with reduced salary and benefits. The Supreme Court of Canada found that this was discrimination on the basis of creed contrary to the *Code*.[29] While the employer had reasonable business reasons for requiring Friday evening and Saturday work, the effect on this employee was discriminatory. In contrast to direct discrimination, adverse effect discrimination does not require an intention to discriminate. The employee must communicate religious needs to the employer,[30] and then the employer is under a duty to accommodate the needs of the employee up to the point of undue hardship.[31]

The Supreme Court of Canada challenged the distinction between direct and adverse effect discrimination in the case known as *Meiorin*.[32] It ruled that the "accommodationist" approach left discriminatory "neutral rules" in place while singling out those on whom they had a discriminatory impact. Under the new standard, the neutral rules themselves will be under scrutiny and the employer will be required to show that it is not possible to have

---

29 *Code*, above note 2, s 4(1)(g).

30 *Strauss v Ontario (Liquor Licence Board)* (1994), 22 CHRR D/169 (Ont Board of Inquiry).

31 For an example where a board of inquiry found that there was undue hardship, see *MacEachern v St. Francis Xavier University* (1994), 24 CHRR D/226 (NS Board of Inquiry). For cases where the employer was found not to have accommodated the employee see *Gohm v Domtar Inc.* (1992), 39 CCEL 213, 89 DLR (4th) 305; *Shepherd v Pines Motel* (1993), 22 CHRR D/343 (Ont Board of Inquiry); *Smart v T. Eaton Ltée* (1993), 19 CHRR D/446 (TDPQ); *Drager v IAM, Automotive Lodge 1857* (1994), 20 CHRR D/119 (BC Human Rights Council); *Québec (Commission des droits de la personne) c. Autobus Legault Inc.* (1994), 25 CHRR D/337 (TDPQ).

32 *British Columbia (Public Service Employee Relations Commission) v BCGSEU*, [1999] 3 SCR 3 [*Meiorin*].

a less stringent rule that allows accommodation within the rule itself.[33]

a) Observance of Holy Days

It is now settled law that employers must accommodate their employees' holy days and days of observance (Sabbath). Following *O'Malley*, the Supreme Court of Canada extended the requirement to accommodate religious observances. In the 1992 case *Central Okanagan School District No 23 v Renaud*[34] the Court required both an employer and a union to accommodate Sabbath observance by a Seventh-day Adventist. The employer had been willing to create a unique shift for Mr. Renaud, a school custodian, but the union would not agree. The Court found not only that the union should have agreed to the accommodation but that the employer should have accommodated the employee even if it had to defend a union grievance to do so. In the 1994 case *Commission scolaire régionale de Chambly v Bergevin*[35] the Supreme Court of Canada held that a school calendar requiring Jewish teachers to work on Yom Kippur was discriminatory. While the school board was willing to grant the teachers the day off without pay, that was not sufficient. The collective agreement under which the teachers worked allowed the school board to grant days off work with pay if the employee had a "good or valid reason." The school board was ordered to grant the teachers a day off with pay so they could celebrate their holy day.

The challenge is that statutory holidays are based on the

---

33 See Alvin Esau, "'Islands of Exclusivity': Religious Organizations and Employment Discrimination" (2000) 33 UBC L Rev 719 at 785–94, for analysis and commentary on what changes this might make to the law of discrimination on the basis of religion.

34 *Central Okanagan School District No 23 v Renaud*, [1992] 2 SCR 970.

35 *Commission scolaire régionale de Chambly v Bergevin*, [1994] 2 SCR 525.

dominant Christian holy days: Good Friday and Christmas Day. Many workplaces offer Sunday, or weekends, as the common pause days. The OHRC argues, "A workplace schedule that is based on the majority faith, but then requires everyone else to negotiate their own accommodation, is not consistent with *Meiorin* principles."[36] The OHRC recommends that employers offer two days per year of paid leave available for religious holy days. However, all workplaces are not alike and there is no hard-and-fast rule that can be applied in all circumstances. In some workplaces, shifts can be changed to accommodate religious holy days. In other workplaces, personal days or special paid leaves of absence are available. Not only that but some religious adherents require more than two days per year for religious observances.

The Ontario Court of Appeal applied the *Meiorin* principles in *Ontario (Ministry of Community and Social Services) v O.P.S.E.U.*[37] Tratnyek observed eleven holy days over the calendar year but his employer provided two paid days for observances. The employer allowed him to make use of the compressed work week for the additional nine days and gave flexibility to its usual practice by allowing him to take the days off when he required them for religious observances. The court found that the scheduling policy had a discriminatory effect because it only allowed single days to be taken off at a time. But the employer accommodated Tratnyek by allowing him to take the days off when he required.

Ensuring that all employees have an equal right to observe the holy days of their religion is a shared responsibility of employers and employees. Employers are required to have policies that allow flexibility for employees, accommodating the "individual needs of members of minority religions . . . without having to lose wages or encroach on pre-existing earned entitlements such as vacation time."[38] Employees must make their requirements

36 *Markovic v Autocom Mfg*, 2008 HRTO 64 at para 14.

37 (2000), 50 OR (3d) 560 [*Tratnyek*].

38 *Ibid* at para 30.

known to the employer and must take advantage of the flexibility offered by their employer.

b) Dress Requirements

Some religions have specific dress requirements. Adverse effect discrimination has been found where employers have neutral dress requirements that conflict with religious dress requirements. Sikh men, for example, are required by their religion to wear turbans on their heads, not to cut their hair, and to carry a kirpan, a small ceremonial dagger. Muslims must dress "modestly," which is generally considered to include being covered to the ankles and wrists. Many Muslim women wear head coverings, the hijab, and some wear face coverings as well, the niqab.

The first challenge to a dress requirement was brought by KS Bhinder, [39] who challenged a safety helmet requirement as discriminatory on the basis of religion under the *Canadian Human Rights Act*.[40] The railway argued that the safety helmet requirement was a *bona fide* occupational requirement. To find that a certain requirement is a *bona fide* occupational requirement, the court applied a two-fold test:[41] a subjective test that the requirement was imposed honestly and in good faith, and an objective test that the requirement was related to the efficient and economical performance of the job. The majority decision of the Supreme Court of Canada had no difficulty finding that the subjective part of the test was met. The hard hat requirement was applied to everyone honestly and in good faith. The objective part of the test was also met. The requirement for employees to wear

39 *Re Bhinder and Canadian National Railway*, [1985] 2 SCR 561 [*Bhinder*].

40 RSC 1985, c H-6.

41 This test was originally enunciated in *Ontario Human Rights Comm'n v Borough of Etobicoke*, [1982] 1 SCR 202.

hard hats promoted safety.[42] The majority also said that there was no duty to accommodate the religious beliefs of Bhinder based on the particular wording of the *bona fide* occupational qualification section.

The Supreme Court of Canada reversed *Bhinder* in 1990. In *Central Alberta Dairy Pool v Alberta (Human Rights Commission)*,[43] the Supreme Court of Canada specifically held that *Bhinder* was erroneous and that there was a duty to accommodate religious practices under the wording of any human rights legislation.

Several years later, the federal government exempted Sikhs from having to wear the required "Mountie hat" [44] as part of the dress requirements to be an officer of the Royal Canadian Mounted Police (RCMP). Other RCMP officers challenged this exemption, arguing on the strength of the *Big M*[45] case that the regulation had a religious purpose and should be struck down.[46] The Federal Court of Appeal upheld the trial decision that the regulation gave a religious exemption. It did not force any religious action on any officer of the RCMP. Merely because a regulation had a religious purpose, it did not infringe religious freedom. In fact, the contrary argument could be made that the federal government was required to make this exemption under laws that prohibit discrimination.

---

42 See also *Toor v Finlay Forest Industries Ltd.* (1984), 6 CHRR D/2873 (BC Board of Inquiry).

43 [1990] 2 SCR 489. This case dealt with an employee who was required by his religion to take Easter Monday as a holy day. As this is not a statutory holiday in Canada, his employer required that he work that day or lose his job. The Supreme Court of Canada found that the employer should have accommodated the employee's religious beliefs.

44 Reg SOR/90-182 under the *Royal Canadian Mounted Police Act*, RSC 1985, c R-10.

45 *Big M*, above note 15.

46 *Grant v Canada (Attorney General)* (1995), 81 FTR 195, aff'd 125 DLR (4th) 556, 96 FTR 239 (FCA).

While a Sikh complainant was successful in British Columbia in challenging the mandatory motorcycle helmet law,[47] the Ontario equivalent survived a *Charter* challenge when a Sikh man faced a fine for not wearing a helmet.[48] Justice Blacklock found that the requirement to wear a motorcycle helmet infringed religious freedom for Sikhs but found that the provision was saved under section 1. Clearly, the provision exists to protect the safety of motorcycle riders. However, given that the *Code* does not have a limitation clause, the outcome might be different if the requirement came under the scrutiny of a human rights tribunal.

There have been several cases involving the discriminatory effect on Sikh men of a job requirement of clean-shaven faces. When the issue is purely aesthetic, a taxi company that does not hire men with beards or long hair for example, the company was required to consider the complainant's application for employment.[49] The issue is different when it involves health and safety, however. Where the job could necessitate wearing self-contained breathing apparatus in the event of a gas leak in a pulp mill[50] or to lead correctional facility inmates to safety[51] the requirement that employees be clean-shaven has been upheld because failure to do so endangers the lives of others.

The Sikh requirement to wear a ceremonial dagger, the kirpan, has been more problematic as it is a weapon. Kirpans are not permitted on Canadian airplane flights.[52] Judges can exclude

---

47 *Dhillon v B.C. (Min. of Transportation and Highways, Motor Vehicle Branch)* (1999), 35 CHRR D/293 (BCHRT).

48 *R. v Badesha* (2008), 168 CRR (2d) 164 (Ont Ct J), aff'd 2011 ONCJ 284.

49 *Khalsa v Co-op Cabs* (1980), 1 CHRR D/167 (Ont Board of Inquiry); *Pannu v Prestige Cab Ltd.* (1986), 8 CHRR D/3709 (Alta Board of Inquiry).

50 *Pannu v Skeena Cellulose Inc.*, [2000] BCHRTD No 56.

51 *Re Singh and the Crown in Right of Ontario (Ministry of Correctional Services)* (1980), 27 LAC (2d) 295 (Ontario Crown Employees Grievance Board).

52 *Nijjar v Canada 3000 Airlines Ltd.*, [1999] CHRD No 3 (CHRT).

kirpans from the courtroom.[53] Calgary's Telus Centre cancelled a concert featuring Gurdas Maan, a Punjabi star, when kirpan-carrying Sikhs were turned away at the gate.[54] The City of Calgary is reviewing its kirpan policy.

In 2006, the Supreme Court of Canada upheld the right of a Sikh boy to wear the kirpan at school, requiring an exemption from a "no weapons" policy.[55] This case was decided under the *Charter* but Quebec's *Charter of Human Rights and Freedoms*[56] was also argued. One of the significant issues in the *Multani* case was whether there is any duty on the religious adherent to adopt a less stringent standard. In that case, there was evidence that other Sikhs wore plastic or wooden replicas. The Supreme Court found that Multani sincerely believed that only a real kirpan met the requirements of his religion and upheld his right to wear that kirpan. In addressing the school's concern about weapons, the court found no evidence that Sikhs used the ceremonial kirpan for violent purposes. In Ontario, an earlier Divisional Court decision, *Peel Board of Education v Ontario Human Rights Commission*[57] upheld an Ontario human rights tribunal decision affirming the right of a Sikh teaching assistant to wear the kirpan on the job at school.

The Muslim hijab seems to have become a lightening rod for debate about "reasonable accommodation." It has been high profile in Quebec, with schoolgirls wearing hijabs barred from

---

53 *Re Hothi and R* (1985), 33 Man R (2d) 180 (QB), aff'd (1985), 35 Man R (2d) 159 (CA), leave to appeal to SCC refused (1986), 43 Man R (2d) 240.

54 "Calgary Concert Cancellation Prompts Kirpan Review" *CBC* (6 October 2009), online: www.cbc.ca/news/canada/calgary/story/2009/10/06/calgary-kirpan-concert-council.html.

55 *Multani*, above note 23.

56 RSQ c C-12.

57 *Peel Board of Education v Ontario Human Rights Commission* (1991), 3 OR (3d) 531 (Div Ct).

participating in sports competitions like soccer and tae kwon do. A woman wearing a niqab was asked to leave a government sponsored French class. In March 2010, the Quebec government introduced legislation that will ban the niqab for women who provide or require government services.[58] These issues have also arisen in other parts of the country; a woman wearing a niqab was refused entry onto a city bus in Halifax, for example.[59]

Several Muslim women were fired from the United Parcel Service (UPS) in 2005 because the employer alleged that their long skirts were hazardous when climbing ladders to retrieve packages.[60] Their complaint to the Canadian Human Rights Tribunal settled. In Ontario, a Muslim woman alleged that she was discriminated against in her employment both on the basis of her hijab and her loose, modest clothing. Her employer commented regularly that her manner of dress was "unprofessional" but a human rights tribunal found that it was a matter of personal taste.[61] Finally, a Quebec lifeguard filed a complaint against the YMCA after she was fired for wearing a "burqini," a full-body swimsuit that meets Muslim modesty requirements.[62] The YMCA alleged that it was a matter of safety as panicked swimmers might grab the loose fabric.

---

58 Bill 94, *An Act to establish guidelines governing accommodation requests within the Administration and certain institutions*, 1st Sess, 39th Leg, Quebec, 2010.

59 "Halifax Bus Driver Hassles Muslim Woman over Headdress: Eyewitness," CBC News (13 March 2009), online: CBC News www.cbc.ca/canada/nova-scotia/story/2009/03/13/ns-bus-muslim.html#ixzz0f4Fpm4zX.

60 See the report of a settlement in Paola Loriggio, "8 Muslim Women Settle Skirt Dispute with UPS" *The Toronto Star* (18 November 2008) A18.

61 *Saadi v Audmax Inc.*, [2009] OHRTD No 994.

62 Andy Blatchford, "Lifeguard Can't Wear Hijab, Files Rights Complaint" *The Toronto Star* (7 August 2008), online: www.thestar.com/news/canada/article/474250--lifeguard-can-t-wear-hijab-files-rights-complaint.

After reviewing the cases, one can see that there is a clear requirement to accommodate religious dress requirements under the *Code* except when they present proven safety risks.

c) Conscientious Objection

A third area where complaints have been made is that of conscientious objection to certain activities in relation to employment. There have been a number of cases as well as issues that have been settled where employees with conscientious objection to certain types of work have been accommodated.

A Newfoundland hospital suspended a Pentecostal clerk for two days because she refused to sell tickets to a social event at which liquor would be served. A board of inquiry found this discriminatory on the basis of religion because Pentecostals are strict teetotallers. The board found that she should have been accommodated.[63]

The Stouffville General Hospital required all obstetrics nurses to assist with abortions. Those who had religious objections were required to apply for transfers to other departments.[64] This case settled prior to a hearing with the hospital agreeing to change its policies to accommodate those nurses who conscientiously object to participating in abortions.

A Shoppers Drug Mart required a Jehovah's Witness to arrange a display of poinsettias during the Christmas season. Jehovah's Witnesses do not observe Christmas. A British Columbia Board of Inquiry found this to be a violation of the BC *Human Rights Code*[65] and required Shoppers Drug Mart to compensate

---

63 *Warford v Carbonear General Hospital* (1988), 9 CHRR D/947 (Nfld Comm of Inquiry).

64 One of the nurses consulted the author as to possible courses of action. The nurses made a complaint to the OHRC.

65 RSBC 1996, c 210.

the employee.[66]

An Ontario labour arbitrator ruled that the requirement that employees use a biometric scanner as part of a security system violated their religious beliefs. The complainants were all from a particular Pentecostal Church and believed that the measurements taken and associated number assigned by the scanner could be the "mark of the Beast" referenced in the Book of Revelations of the Bible, Chapter 13. The complainants had been disciplined and then fired for their refusals to use the new identification mechanism. The tribunal found that the three employees with religious objections should have been accommodated.[67]

One exception to the general rule that religious objections should be accommodated is union dues. An individual seeking exemption from paying union dues must be able to link their religion to their objection. An exemption was granted in *Niagara South (Board of Education Of)(Geyer and Hall)*[68] where the employees proved that public policy positions taken by the union violated their religious beliefs. Both complainants identified as Bible-believing Christians. They took issue with the union's support of abortion but were fundamentally opposed as well to the attitude the union took to the employer, which they argued was in opposition to the Christian requirement to respect or honour one's employer. However, in two other cases involving union dues, the Ontario Labour Relations Board did not find sufficient connection between objection to paying union dues and religious beliefs.[69]

---

66 *Jones v CHE Pharmacy Inc et al*, 2001 BCHRT 1.

67 *407 ETR Concession Co v National Automobile, Aerospace, Transportation and General Workers Union of Canada, CAW-Canada, Local 414 (Black Grievance)* (2007), 158 LAC (4th) 289.

68 *Niagara South (Board of Education Of) (Geyer and Hall)*, [1985] OLRB Rep July 1057.

69 *Carter v National Automobile, Aerospace and Agricultural Implement Workers Union of Canada, (CAW-Canada) and its Local 27*, [1987] OLRB

A current issue before the courts involves whether and to what extent religious objections to same-sex marriage must be accommodated. In Ontario, the *Code* was amended to make it clear that religious officials may refuse to solemnize, or otherwise be associated with, same-sex marriages if it violates their religious beliefs.[70] However, this does not address whether civil officials who solemnize marriages or even issue marriage licences, can or should be accommodated if their religious beliefs would be violated by participating in any way with a marriage between two persons of the same sex.[71] In Saskatchewan, a same-sex couple brought a complaint against Orville Nichols, a civil marriage commissioner, after he refused to marry them. The Saskatchewan Court of Queen's Bench ruled against Nichols: "In his capacity as a marriage commissioner, however, he is holding himself out to the public as a government official. In that capacity, his personal religious beliefs do not matter."[72] (see Wray, this volume, for a full discussion of the Saskatchewan decision).

d) The Interface between the *Charter* and the *Code* — Conflicting Rights

The issue involving accommodation of officials who have conscientious objections to same-sex marriage can be seen as an issue of competing rights. A number of hard cases have arisen that raise conflicting or competing rights. Many of the above-noted cases can be considered issues of competing rights. For example,

---

Rep March 343; *Butler v The York University Faculty Ass'n*, [1981] OLRB Rep September 1319.

70 *Code*, above note 2, s 18.1.

71 The Saskatchewan government referred two possible amendments to *The Marriage Act, 1995*, SS 1995, c M-4.1 to the Saskatchewan Court of Appeal. The hearing was on 13–14 May 2010, court no 1800.

72 *Nichols v MJ*, 2009 SKQB 299 at para 76 [*Nichols*]. BJ Wray's contribution to this volume for a full discussion of the Saskatchewan decision at Chapter 11.

the right of an individual to accommodation of their religious practices versus the rights of employers to run the business as they see fit, or the freedom to practice one's religion coming into conflict with equality rights of another individual or group.

Most of the cases of competing rights that have arisen under provincial human rights legislation involve a claim of discrimination on an enumerated ground on the one hand and a competing claim for religious freedom, or some other protected freedom, under the *Charter*. Courts have developed a framework using the *Oakes* test under the *Charter*, which requires the following:

1) an objective of pressing and substantial concern; and
2) proportionality between the objective and the remedy, which requires that
   a) there be a rational connection between the remedy and the objective
   b) the remedy minimally impair the protected freedom under the *Charter*
   c) there be proportionality between the objective and the remedy (salutary and deleterious effects)

Most issues of competing rights are resolved through this framework.

The Supreme Court of Canada established the approach for addressing competing rights within the provincial human rights code framework in *Ross v New Brunswick School District No 15*.[73] In that case, a Jewish parent made a complaint against the school board on the basis that a teacher, Malcolm Ross, created an anti-Semitic environment within the school system because of his out-of-classroom activism. Ross authored several books and appeared in the local media denying the Holocaust. There was evidence of growing anti-Semitism in the schools, including the appearance of swastikas. A board of inquiry found that the school board discriminated against Jews by failing to discipline

---

73 *Ross v New Brunswick School District No 15*, [1996] 1 SCR 825 [*Ross*].

Ross. It ordered that Ross be removed from the classroom and required that his employment be terminated if he published further anti-Semitic literature. Ross applied for judicial review of this order. The Supreme Court of Canada found that the board was correct in its determination on the discriminatory environment in the schools, and that the school board had a responsibility to ensure a welcoming environment for all. However, it found that the board's order violated Ross's freedom of religion and freedom of expression. The Court used the *Oakes* test to balance between the rights of students to a welcoming environment and Ross's right to freedom of religion and expression. Part of the board's order, namely the requirement that Ross not publish further anti-Semitic literature, did not meet the minimal impairment test. The Court therefore severed that part of the order.

The Ontario Divisional Court followed the same approach in *Brillinger v Brockie*.[74] The director of The Gay and Lesbian Archives made a complaint of discrimination on the basis of sexual orientation after a Toronto printer, Scott Brockie, refused to provide printing services on the basis of his religious beliefs. Brockie argued that he did not refuse services because Brillinger was gay, but that the Archives promoted "the homosexual 'lifestyle.'"[75] A Board of Inquiry found that Brockie had discriminated against Brillinger and ordered that Brockie provide printing services. On appeal, the Ontario Divisional Court noted, "The conflict of dignities presented by this appeal requires a balancing of individual religious rights and individual rights to protection from discrimination in the marketplace based on an analysis of the *Code* and of the Charter."[76] The court acknowledged that the board's order infringed Brockie's section 2(a) rights to freedom of religion. It engaged in a section 1 analysis and determined that the board's order was too broad. The court amended the

74 *Brillinger v Brockie* (2002), 161 OAC 324 (Div Ct) [*Brockie*].

75 *Ibid* at para 15.

76 *Ibid* at para 20.

order such that Brockie was not required to print material that offended his religious beliefs but he was required to print non-offensive material such as stationary.

Returning to the issue of the conscience rights of marriage commissioners, this issue of competing rights is actually more clear than either *Ross* or *Brockie*. If the marriage commissioners are employees of the government, their conscience must be respected to the point of undue hardship.[77] The challenge the courts have faced is that in some provinces, marriage commissioners are not employees but independent contractors who are licensed by the state to solemnize marriages. They are paid by the couple getting married. The Saskatchewan Court of Queen's Bench upheld the Human Rights Tribunal Ruling that the marriage commissioner "acts as government while acting as a marriage commissioner . . . ."[78] Following this ruling, the Saskatchewan government proposed two possible amendments to the Saskatchewan *Marriage Act*[79] that would allow marriage commissioners, or those appointed before the definition of marriage was changed, to exercise a right of conscience with respect to solemnizing marriages. The Lieutenant Governor of Saskatchewan sent a reference to the Saskatchewan Court of Appeal to determine if the amendments would be constitutional. The Court of Appeal determined that neither of the amendments would be constitutional. The majority judgment ruled on the basis that the amendments would violate the section 15 rights of same-sex couples to equality. While the amendments had a pressing and substantial objective, the protection of the conscience rights of marriage commissioners in accordance with section 2(a) of the *Charter*, they did

77 Bruce Ryder makes this point in "State Neutrality and Freedom of Conscience and Religion" (2005), 29 Sup Ct L Rev (2d) 169 at 191. But see Bruce MacDougall, "Refusing to Officiate at Same-Sex Civil Marriages" (2006) 69 Sask L Rev 351.

78 *Nichols*, above note 72 at para 24.

79 Above note 71.

not meet the minimal impairment test.[80]

It is not clear why an independent contractor takes on this delegation merely by being licensed to solemnize marriages and thereby loses all rights to conscientiously object. Nichols had exercised his discretion in the past to refuse to solemnize marriages where he believed the marriage was a sham, or a publicity stunt, or abusive. Absent clear government guidelines, it is not clear that in the function of "acting as government" a marriage commissioner has the ability to exercise any such discretion. Those who officiate at civil marriages in Ontario are not under a similar regime; indeed, they are government employees. Therefore, it appears that the provincial government would be under an obligation to accommodate conscientious objection.

The Supreme Court of Canada developed a different approach to competing rights in the case of *Trinity Western University v British Columbia College of Teachers*.[81] Rather than use the *Oakes* test framework, the majority adopted a "proper delineation of rights" approach. Trinity Western University is a private, Christian university whose charter exempts it from BC human rights legislation. The British Columbia College of Teachers refused the university's application for accreditation of its teacher training program on the basis that it was against the public interest because the university had policies that were discriminatory against gays and lesbians. These policies were based on the religious beliefs espoused by the institution. The majority ruled that there was no evidence that the religious beliefs evident in the policies resulted in discriminatory behaviour by the graduate teachers.[82] When the rights were properly delineated, students at the uni-

80 *Re Marriage Commissioners Appointed under The Marriage Act*, 2011 SKCA 3.

81 *Trinity Western University v British Columbia College of Teachers*, 2001 SCC 31, [2001] 1 SCR 772 [*Trinity Western*].

82 For a discussion on the distinction between belief and conduct see Chapter 13 by Iain Benson in this volume.

versity were free to hold their religious beliefs and students in the schools where graduate teachers taught had the right to non-discriminatory teachers. Approval of the program would not violate either of these rights so the College of Teachers was ordered to approve the program. This approach has not been used in other cases so it appears a rare case when the rights can be delineated so as to remove the conflict prior to applying the *Oakes* test.

Another complex issue is raised in *Ontario Human Rights Commission v Christian Horizons*.[83] Christian Horizons is the largest private provider of residential services to mentally handicapped adults in Ontario. As its name implies, it is a Christian organization and requires staff to sign a statement of faith and lifestyle policy. The complainant, Connie Heintz, signed both these documents when she started working at Christian Horizons. However, several years later, she began a lesbian relationship, which contravened the lifestyle policy. After a period of discord, she quit her job but made a human rights complaint. A human rights tribunal[84] found that Christian Horizons does not fit within the exemption for religious organizations found in section 24(1) of the *Code*, which reads:

> 24. (1) The right under section 5 to equal treatment with respect to employment is not infringed where,
>
> a. a religious, philanthropic, educational, fraternal or social institution or organization that is primarily engaged in serving the interests of persons identified by their race, ancestry, place of origin, colour, ethnic origin, creed, sex, age, marital status or disability employs only, or gives preference in employment to, persons similarly identified if the qualification is a reasonable and *bona fide* qualification because of the nature of the employment.

---

83 *Ontario Human Rights Commission v Christian Horizons*, 2010 ONSC 2105 (Div Ct) [*Christian Horizons*].

84 *Heintz v Christian Horizons* (2008), 63 CHRR D/12, 2008 HRTO 22.

The Tribunal ruled that Christian Horizons does not serve "persons similarly identified" because it provides services to mentally handicapped adults regardless of their religious affiliation.

The Ontario Divisional Court overturned the HRTO on the issue of whether Christian Horizons fits within the section 24(1) exemption. The court said that the HRTO was wrong to take an objective approach; "In doing so, it failed to respect the religious character of Christian Horizons' activities and the purpose of s. 24(1)(a) as to protect group rights of association."[85] This recognition of group rights is quite significant. Very few cases in Canada have recognized group rights. However, section 24(1)(a) also requires a *bona fide* qualification analysis and Christian Horizons was not able to prove that the particular position Connie Heintz fulfilled required that she be an evangelical Christian.

The recognition that religious organizations have a group right of association is very significant in terms of the conflict of rights. Religion is frequently practiced communally, not only in houses of worship but also in a wide variety of organizations from development agencies, to summer camps to homeless shelters. Had the HRTO decision stood, it would mean that all religious organizations that serve the public, as opposed to just their own religious community, would be treated as secular organizations. This would mean that they would not be permitted to continue their religious character as they could not hire preferentially from their own religious community.

The concern from those arguing against group rights is that they can be used as a cover for discriminatory behaviour. That is, if a group of individuals wishes to engage in discriminatory behaviour, they could form an organization and falsely claim that they have a religious belief that requires discriminatory behaviour. However, the courts have required that religious beliefs and practice be "sincerely held."[86] While courts have been reluctant

---

85 *Christian Horizons*, above note 84 at para 73.

86 See, for example, *Amselem*, above note 17.

to interfere in matters of religious doctrine, they will ensure that any organization claiming to be religious in nature is *bona fides*. As well, the additional requirement that the nature of a particular position also be proven to require a candidate affiliated with the religion means that the group right is not absolute. This provides a mechanism to resolve the competing rights of an individual claiming discrimination against a religious organization with a group right.

In the *Christian Horizons* case, the Divisional Court specifically rejected a public/private distinction, limiting its rights when its activity creates a relationship with the broader public.[87] Christianity is an outreach religion, meaning that it seeks to serve the broader community. Christians seek to follow the parable of the Good Samaritan, where a man was blessed because he cared for someone from a despised foreign country who was in need. It would therefore be profoundly problematic to insist that Christian religious organizations be restricted in their ability to engage with the public.

Issues of competing or conflicting rights are, no doubt, the most challenging to resolve, particularly where religion is involved. Religions provide a comprehensive code that applies to all aspects of life.[88] This makes it difficult for courts to impose limitations on the practice or application of religious perspectives because someone has raised their rights; the courts must necessarily interfere with a comprehensive code. In addition, religious beliefs are deeply held and profoundly influential in adherents' lives. Religious beliefs derive from centuries old writings and traditions.

---

87 *Christian Horizons*, above note 84 at paras 44–46.

88 Even Chief Justice McLachlin has recognized this in "Freedom of Religion and the Rule of Law: A Canadian Perspective" in Douglas Farrow, ed, *Recognizing Religion in a Secular Society* (Montreal and Kingston: McGill-Queen's University Press, 2004) at 14–15.

e) Negative Perceptions of Religious Communities

Evangelical Christians have been very critical of human rights codes over the last several years, even to the point of campaigning that they be abolished. They have felt targeted by certain high-profile cases that were well publicized within that religious community. These cases include the *Brockie* case and the case concerning marriage commissioners who objected to solemnizing same-sex marriages, both discussed above. Other cases include a Knights of Columbus hall in British Columbia that was refused to a lesbian couple for their wedding reception[89] and bed and breakfast operators in Prince Edward Island [90] and British Columbia[91] who faced complaints of discrimination on the basis of sexual orientation. The bed and breakfasts both went out of business rather than face public censure for their religious beliefs about homosexuality. An Alberta case dealing with expression, the Stephen Boissoin case,[92] also involved religious views and the ruling against this youth pastor garnered a great deal of negative commentary in the evangelical Christian community.

There is a sense in the evangelical Christian community that they are being asked to do all the accommodating.[93] If someone is offended by a Christian poster, the Christian is asked to remove it. Yet the perception exists that religious practices are

---

89 *Smith and Chymyshyn v Knights of Columbus and others*, 2005 BCHRT 544.

90 This case was settled in 2001 and is referenced on the website of the Prince Edward Island Human Rights Commission, online: www.gov.pe.ca/humanrights/releases/may22-01.php3.

91 "Tribunal Hears Gay Rights Complaint against B.C. B&B" *CBC* (17 October 2011), online: www.cbc.ca/news/canada/british-columbia/story/2011/10/17/bc-rights-tribunal-gay-b-and-b.html. See also *Eadie and Thomas v Molnar and others*, 2010 BCHRT 69 where the bed and breakfast owners applied to have the complaint dismissed.

92 *Boissoin v Lund*, [2009] AJ No 1345 (QB).

93 *Ontario Public Service Employees Union v Ontario (Ministry of Community and Social Services)*, 2006 CanLII 37572 (Ont GSB).,

accommodated if they are non-Christian. At the same time, other religious communities, particularly Muslims in Ontario, feel that they are targeted and marginalized in Canadian society too.[94]

Perception is often not reality, however, as the Bouchard-Taylor Commission[95] report in Quebec acknowledged. That Commission was established in the face of concerns that accommodation was threatening the fabric of society. The perceived deluge of instances of accommodation was an overreaction and was based on misconceptions.

The *Code* is intended to provide mechanisms for parties to negotiate and work out compromises that work in their particular context. However, some, like Ezra Levant, argue that "the process is the penalty."[96] Merely having to face a complaint is punishment. This does not give rise to a cooperative approach conducive to negotiated resolution.[97]

F. Toward a Framework for Resolving Competing Rights

It is clear that a fair and transparent framework is needed to resolve competing rights, a framework that respects all rights that are in competition. With respect, I do not believe that the sec-

---

94 See, for example, "Islamic Congress Concerned Over Recent Rise in Islamophobia and Hate" *Media Communique* (4 August 2009), online: Canadian Islamic Congress www.canadianislamiccongress.com/mc/media_communique.php?id=1112.

95 Gérard Bouchard and Charles Taylor, *Building the Future: A Time for Reconciliation* (Quebec: Government of Quebec, 2008) at 13.

96 Ezra Levant, *Shake Down: How Our Government is Undermining Democracy in the Name of Human Rights* (Toronto: McLelland & Stewart, 2009).

97 For an in-depth critique of Levant's arguments as they relate to hate speech and the Canadian Human Rights Commission, see Richard Moon, Chapter 4 in this volume.

tion 1 framework alone sufficiently recognizes all rights involved. I have argued elsewhere[98] that the section 1 analysis is rigid and tends to leave the courts focusing only on one of the rights involved. Perhaps the delineation of rights approach in the *Trinity Western* case could be utilized as a first step before the courts turn to the section 1 analysis. This would allow the rights to be fully explored and an attempt made to resolve the conflict outside the rigidity of the section 1 analysis. It would also provide a foundation for the section 1 analysis, at least for the application of the final branch of the minimal impairment branch of the test: salutary and deleterious effects.

G. Conclusion

The *Code* provides a mechanism for the resolution of allegations of discrimination on the basis of creed. Court and tribunal decisions have established clear interpretations in several significant areas including the following general principles. Creed is to be interpreted generously and should include beliefs and practices that the believer follows sincerely. Every effort should be made to allow flexibility for religious adherents, to ensure that they can observe religious holy days, Sabbaths, dress, and dietary requirements. Employees should not be required to perform work that violates their religious beliefs. However, health and safety requirements and undue hardship to employers should be taken into account.

While these core principles appear quite clear, when the right not to be discriminated against conflicts with the rights and freedoms of others, the process to resolve the issue and maximize the ability of everyone to enjoy their freedoms without discrimination becomes difficult. Coming back to the analogy we started with, rather than mixing and enhancing one another, those claim-

---

98 Janet Epp Buckingham, "Caesar and God: Limits to Religious Freedom in Canada and South Africa" (2001) 15 Sup Ct L Rev 461.

ing their rights and freedoms separate and polarize. The perception is that if one side wins, the other loses. The oil and vinegar become like oil and water, incapable of emulsifying. The courts have clearly wrestled with developing a framework that allows the competing rights to both be respected. Perhaps modifying the framework for resolving competing rights by delineating the rights prior to applying the *Oakes* test would ensure that courts fully recognize and respect all rights that are in conflict.

Chapter 4

The Attack on Human Rights Commissions

Richard Moon*

A. Introduction

In the fall of 2008 I prepared a report for the Canadian Human Rights Commission (CHRC)[1] in which I recommended the repeal of section 13 of the *Canadian Human Rights Act*[2] — the provision that restricts Internet hate speech. As I was writing the report, I became aware of what can only be described as a disinformation campaign against human rights commissions (HRCs). I am sure it comes as no surprise to anyone that there are Internet blogs that post things about the CHRC that are false and malicious. The problem is that the claims made in these blogs have seeped into mainstream discourse — they have been taken up by members of Parliament, they have been adopted in editorials in the *National Post* and columns in *The Globe and Mail* and *Maclean's* magazine and in a host of other publications,

---

* A longer version of this paper was published in the *Saskatchewan Law Review*: Richard Moon, "The Attack on Human Rights Commissions and the Corruption of Public Discourse" (2010) 73 Sask L Rev 93 [Moon, 2010]. The House of Commons voted to repeal s. 13 in June 2012, after this paper was written.

1 Richard Moon, "Report to the Canadian Human Rights Commission Concerning Section 13 of the *Canadian Human Rights Act* and the Regulation of Hate Speech on the Internet" (CHRC, 2008).

2 RSC 1985, c H-6 [*CHRA*].

and they have been repeated on radio and television current affairs programming. They have created in the larger public, or at least a significant element of the public, a "feeling" that there is a fundamental problem with HRCs, and in particular the Canadian Commission, that needs to be addressed.

There is a serious debate to be had about the regulation of hate speech by HRCs. But the debate is difficult and complex and there are many reasonable positions one can take on the issue. I do not agree with those who argue that the CHRC should be involved in the regulation of Internet hate speech, but I do not doubt their good faith in taking this position. The most vociferous and indeed the most media-amplified critics of the CHRC are not interested in this debate. It is easier, and it seems more effective, to exaggerate the case — to invent injustices, and engage in personal attacks. This approach has several related strategic advantages: (1) The case against the CHRC becomes clear-cut. All complexity is washed away. There are no longer competing interests or trade-offs that need to be addressed. (2) The attack on hate speech regulation, when based on the corruption and incompetence of the Commission, undermines the entire human rights commission process and not just the regulation of hate speech. (3) The attack on HRCs can be made without having to defend unpopular ideological positions. The regulation of hate speech can be attacked without having to rely explicitly on a libertarian free speech position — the claim that speech should never be subject to limits. And a broader challenge to anti-discrimination law can be made without having to defend the view that the market is a just and efficient mechanism for the distribution of goods that should not be subject to any form of regulation. (4) And, of course, it appears that this style of attack (personal and extreme) gets attention and is an effective means of self-promotion.

Why this style of attack is effective I will consider in a moment. First I want to look at three claims made by the critics and recycled in the mainstream media: (1) that the CHRC has a 100 percent conviction rate for section 13 cases; (2) that the CHRC has engaged in corrupt behaviour; and (3) that HRCs make unreasonable, even bizarre, decisions.

The techniques used by the critics are sadly familiar. They include: (1) identifying one or two commission or tribunal decisions which seem unreasonable in their outcome, and presenting them as if they are representative of the larger body of decisions; (2) when describing a particular case, highlighting certain facts or findings and omitting mention of others to give a misleading picture of the case; (3) relying on dubious sources and reporting their claims as if they are true and uncontested; (4) using terms in a way that is intended to mislead the audience, (i.e. making a claim that with some strain on the language may be "true" but which on an ordinary reading — the reading encouraged by the speaker — is false); (5) making blatantly false factual claims; and, finally, (6) engaging in personal attacks against those with opposing views, in order to undermine their credibility.

B. The CHRC Has a 100 Percent Conviction Rate

Ezra Levant, Mark Steyn, and others have frequently asserted that the CHRC has a 100 percent conviction rate. Here is how Levant put it in a *National Post* op-ed: "The CHRC already has a 100% conviction rate for censorship prosecutions — no one in 32 years has ever beat the rap. That's not hard to believe when you learn that truth, fair comment and honest belief are not legal defences in human rights hearings — the commissions operate more like kangaroo courts than real courts that way."[3] Levant, in his book *Shakedown*, asserts that "no one had ever beaten a hate speech accusation . . . at the Canadian Human Rights Commission."[4] The claim has also been made in a *National Post*

---

3 Ezra Levant, "Appetite for Censorship" *National Post* (16 June 2009) A16.

4 Ezra Levant, *Shakedown: How Our Government is Undermining Democracy in the Name of Human Rights* (Toronto: McClelland & Stewart,

editorial: "The CHRC, too, has a frighteningly undemocratic 100% conviction rate on hate speech cases."[5]

This claim is a little like Bill Clinton's statement: "I did not have sexual relations with that woman, Miss Lewinsky." It is intended to be misread. It is possible to interpret the 100 percent conviction rate claim as true, but in its "true" meaning it is entirely uninteresting and in no way a criticism of the CHRC. The ordinary reading of the claim is that the CHRC has found that section 13 has been violated in every complaint it has received (every "accusation"). The impression given is that the issue is fully decided by the CHRC, that it both investigates and adjudicates complaints and that once a complaint is made — once a respondent is drawn into the process — the outcome, "conviction," is inevitable. This was the claim made in a *Windsor Star* editorial: ". . . the problem is that the CHRC is essentially the investigator, prosecutor and judge of complaints of racism and hate speech."[6]

To show how this claim is deceptive I need to say a little bit about the CHRC process and the relationship between the CHRC and the Canadian Human Rights Tribunal (CHRT). Under the *CHRA* an individual or group may file a complaint with the CHRC, if they have "reasonable grounds for believing that a person is engaging or has engaged in a discriminatory practice"[7] contrary to the Act. The CHRC is bound to investigate any complaint that falls within its jurisdiction and is not excluded as trivial, frivolous, vexatious, or made in bad faith. The investigation of a complaint must be conducted in accordance with the principles of procedural fairness. This requires that the respondent be informed of the complaint made against her and given the opportunity to respond to it. A report is prepared by the investigation officer,

---

2009) at 146 [*Shakedown*].

5 "Muzzling the Human Rights Debate" *National Post* (18 June 2009) A20.

6 "The Code and Rights; Two Tiers We Don't Need" *The Windsor Star* (18 July 2009) A6.

7 *CHRA*, above note 2, s 40(1).

which is then submitted to the commissioners. The commissioners may ask the CHRT to institute an inquiry into the complaint if they conclude that "having regard to all the circumstances of the complaint, an inquiry . . . is warranted"[8] or they "shall dismiss the complaint"[9] if they conclude that an inquiry is not warranted. The CHRT is an entirely separate and independent body that adjudicates complaints under the *CHRA* that are referred to it by the CHRC. If the complaint is referred to the CHRT for adjudication, the CHRC may appear in order to represent the "public interest"; however carriage of the case lies with the complainant. The CHRC has appeared in all but one of the section 13 cases that have been decided by the CHRT. The CHRC does not adjudicate the complaint, and it does not determine the appropriate remedy. Instead it serves as a kind of filter for section 13 (and other *CHRA*) complaints.

Section 13 complaints represent a very small part of the CHRC's workload. Between January 2001 and September 2008 the CHRC received seventy-three section 13 complaints, which represented about 2 percent of the total number of complaints received by the CHRC (this number includes only those complaints that were not excluded prior to investigation as trivial or vexatious). In the fall of 2008, when I was writing my report, fifty-eight of the seventy-three complaints received by the CHRC had been resolved: thirty-two (about half) were dismissed after investigation by the CHRC and did not go to adjudication; ten were resolved through mediation at the CHRT prior to adjudication; and only sixteen were adjudicated. The CHRT found a breach of section 13 in 100 percent of the sixteen cases that it adjudicated — less than one-third of the complaints that were received and investigated by the CHRC.

It is true that all section 13 complaints adjudicated by the

8 *Ibid*, s 44(3)(a)(i).

9 *Ibid*, s 44(3)(b).

Tribunal have been upheld — at least until recently. The Tribunal then has a 100 percent conviction rate. ("Conviction" is not the right term since the standard remedy given by the Tribunal is a cease and desist order, but this is a relatively minor distortion.) It is also true that the Commission was represented, and argued that section 13 had been breached, in all but one of the Tribunal adjudications. The CHRC then has a 100 percent "conviction" rate as an advocate before the CHRT, but since so few section 13 complaints are sent to the CHRT that is not so remarkable. The CHRC dismissed approximately half of the investigated complaints because in its view the speech was not sufficiently extreme to breach section 13. Ironically the 100 percent "conviction" rate by the CHRT could be used to support the very different claim that the CHRC is filtering out too many section 13 complaints, preventing some complaints that might have succeeded at adjudication from even being considered by the Tribunal.

When Levant made the 100 percent conviction rate claim on the CBC radio program *The Sunday Edition*, the host Michael Enright said to Levant that he thought that "*Maclean's* beat it this year." To this Levant answered, "No they weren't charged federally, they beat it in BC. But no, the federal one, 100 percent conviction rate."[10] This was a misleading response to Enright's question. A complaint had been made to the CHRC against Steyn and *Maclean's*, which the Commission investigated but decided not to refer to the Tribunal for adjudication. Anyone listening to Levant would have filled in the gap and assumed that there had been no federal complaint against *Maclean's*. Levant frequently blurs the distinction between investigation by the CHRC and adjudication by the CHRT. For example, in an interview on CTV's *Powerplay*, he referred to the *Catholic Insight* case as a CHRC prosecution, even though the complaint was dismissed after investigation and did not go to the Tribunal for adjudication.

10 *The Sunday Edition*, CBC Radio (31 May 2009).

Levant asserted that "They [the CHRC] prosecuted a Catholic priest in Toronto."[11] He also uses the term "acquittal" to describe the dismissal of a complaint by the CHRC prior to adjudication before the Tribunal. Levant has also on a number of occasions referred to the Tribunal as the "Commission." For example, on the CBC radio program *The Sunday Edition* Levant referred to an order of the CHRT as "a human rights commission order."[12] If we followed Levant and viewed the CHRC investigation process as a prosecution then the CHRC's "conviction" rate would be no greater than 50 percent.

There are, of course, real and significant problems with the process that the CHRC is by law required to follow. I have made the point in my report that free speech interests are affected every time an investigation occurs — particularly since the investigation engages the parties and takes eight to ten months to conclude. This is a problem because the CHRC is required to investigate a complaint unless it is trivial, vexatious, frivolous, or made in bad faith. The CHRC therefore is bound to investigate some complaints that are unlikely to proceed to adjudication. Moreover, HRCs may be reluctant to exclude a complaint prior to investigation on the grounds that it is trivial, because such a finding may be seen as downplaying the genuine feelings of hurt or injury experienced by minority group members and will preclude the possibility of a facilitated resolution of the "dispute." Because section 13 is located in a law that seeks to advance the goal of social equality through education and conciliation, the CHRC may be inclined to err on the side of inclusion when deciding whether a complaint should be rejected prior to investigation on the grounds that it is trivial. These problems, however, are obscured by the misleading 100 percent conviction rate claim.

---

11 *Powerplay*, CTV (12 June 2009).

12 See above note 10.

C. Human Rights Commissions and Tribunals Make Bad Decisions

In his book *Shakedown,* Levant describes a handful of human rights code cases, dealing with issues other than hate speech, in which a provincial tribunal makes a decision that seems patently unreasonable. According to Levant the "craziest" of all the human rights decisions is the judgment of the BCHRT in *Datt*.[13] On the CBC's *The Current*, Levant said this about the case: "A woman didn't want to wash her hands and she sued McDonald's in human rights tribunal and won. She allegedly has this human right not to have to wash her hands at McDonald's."[14] On smaller radio programs his claims became even stronger:

> One day she said, "I don't like to wash my hands so much" . . . . Nothing was wrong, she just didn't want to wash her hands . . . . There was no name for this mystery illness . . . . [It was decided by the HRT that] she had the human right not to wash her hands . . . . McDonald's was ordered never to enforce its hand-washing policy on people with this hand-washing problem again . . . . That's just gross."[15]

In a blog entry on the case Levant informs us that: "[T]he British Columbia Human Rights Tribunal ruled that one of the employees there [at McDonald's] has a human right not to wash her hands when working in their kitchen" and the Tribunal "invent[ed] a human right for a worker to go to the bathroom and then handle meat without washing her hands in between . . . ."[16] The case also gets passing mention from columnist Rex Murphy

---

13 *Datt v McDonald's Restaurants (No 3)*, 2007 BCHRT 324 [*Datt*].

14 *The Current*, CBC Radio (28 April 2009).

15 CFRA Ottawa (25 April 2009).

16 Ezra Levant, "The Human Right for McDonald's Employees not to Wash Their Hands" (15 April 2008), online: Ezra Levant http://ezralevant.com/2008/04/the-human-right-for-mcdonalds.html.

in *The Globe and Mail*, who refers to the trivial "rights" recognized by HRCs "Like the right not to wash one's hands while working in a fast-food restaurant."[17] The impression one gets from Levant's account of the case is of a tribunal that is entirely out of touch with reality, and indifferent to important health and safety concerns.

Of course anyone who combs through the thousands of human rights cases that have been decided over the years is bound to discover decisions that seem wrong or unfair. This would be the case with any decision maker, including the courts. With that said, however, let me tell you what Levant leaves out of his account of this case. Ms. Datt had worked for McDonald's for twenty-three years until she developed severe dermatitis as a consequence of her frequent hand-washing. There seemed to be no dispute that frequent hand-washing had caused her to suffer severe dermatitis. The Tribunal, following *O'Malley v Simpson-Sears Ltd.*,[18] and other decisions of the Supreme Court of Canada, noted that once it had been established that Ms. Datt suffered from a disability, the burden shifted to McDonald's to establish that "her disability was not capable of being accommodated in the workplace without incurring undue hardship."[19] The Tribunal decision does not question the importance of hand-washing. The Tribunal member says: "I accept that the goal of preventing the contamination of food is why McDonald's established its hand-washing policy. This goal cannot be understated and it accords with common sense in the handling and preparation of food. However, there were duties that Ms. Datt could have performed that did not require her to handle food."[20] The problem, said the Tribunal, was that McDonald's did not seem to have considered in any serious way whether there were other tasks that Ms. Datt might perform

17 Rex Murphy, "Real Rights and Rights Commissions" *The Globe and Mail* (14 November 2008) A25 ["Real rights"].

18 *O'Malley v Simpsons-Sears* (1985), 7 CHRR D/3102 (SCC).

19 *Datt*, above note 13 at para 157.

20 *Ibid* at para 239.

that would not involve the handling of food and require hand-washing with the same frequency.[21] The Tribunal concluded:

> I am at a loss to understand why McDonald's did not take more steps to try to accommodate Ms. Datt, a 23-year committed

21 *Ibid* at paras 239–40. The following is the full-text of the relevant paras:

> [239] The Food Premises Regulations, referred to by McDonald's, does not contain a specific time, or even how often a person should wash their hands. The requirement is that hands be washed as often as necessary to prevent the contamination of food. As I said earlier, I accept that the goal of preventing the contamination of food is why McDonald's established its hand-washing policy. This goal cannot be understated and it accords with common sense in the handling and preparation of food. However, there were duties that Ms. Datt could have performed that did not require her to handle food. For example, there was the position of Swing Manager that had supervisory duties. These duties did not require that she handle food, unless she was required to help out when there was a shortage of staff. In these types of circumstances, Ms. Datt would be required to wash her hands but it is not clear to me if that would have been "frequent" or if the requirement would have caused her difficulty. This was not assessed in the context of the actual duties to be performed.
>
> [240] Further, there was no evidence about the relationship between food contamination and hand-washing frequency. For example, there was no evidence to address whether the goal could have been met with hourly or half-hourly hand-washing or some other timed hand-washing frequency that Ms. Datt might have been able to meet. There was no evidence of the actual risk to the public if Ms. Datt, the only employee who had some form of hand-washing restriction, was provided with modified duties or a modified way of working. A workplace policy that necessarily restricts McDonald's duty to accommodate a disabled employee might have to be varied in appropriate circumstances, with the appropriate mechanism in place to meet food safety requirements. As stated in *Meiorin*, the standard itself must allow for individual accommodation. (para 68)

> employee. Ms. Datt was not entitled to a "perfect" solution, but she was entitled to a fulsome consideration of her restrictions and how those restrictions intersected with the hand-washing policies and the jobs that were available. Without having done so, neither Ms. Datt nor McDonald's was in a position to know what the outcome of a return to work, with accommodations, might have been. It may be that, at the end of the day, Ms. Datt could not have been accommodated at McDonald's because she simply could not meet its hand-washing policies doing any job or combination of jobs, but based on the evidence before me, I find that McDonald's failed to take all the necessary steps to make this final determination.[22]

You can disagree with the decision — although that may only be possible if you believe that employers have no duty to accommodate employees with disabilities — but the result is not shocking in the way Levant suggests. If that is among the most egregious injustices that he is able to mine from the thousands of human rights decisions, then human rights bodies must be doing far better than I might have guessed. In this and other cases discussed in *Shakedown*, Levant gives an entirely distorted account of what occurred.

D. The CHRC and Its Staff Are Corrupt

Critics of the CHRC use the term "corruption" very loosely. Sometimes they use it interchangeably with incompetence to refer to what they regard as the Commission's unjustified interference with free speech or its failure to respect due process. However, the critics' general claims of "corruption" are sometimes bolstered by more specific claims of corrupt behaviour. The most significant of these is that Commission staff have joined neo-Nazi groups

22 *Ibid* at paras 249–50.

and made numerous anti-Semitic or racist postings.[23]

Levant tells us that "trial transcripts reveal that the staff of the CHRC's anti-hate squad, in their bid to entrap alleged hate-mongers, actually have become one of Canada's largest sources of hate speech"[24]; ". . . Canada's largest 'hate group' as measured by the number of anti-Semitic, anti-gay, anti-black, and pro-Nazi comments published on the Internet . . . [is] none other than the taxpayers' own Canadian Human Rights Commission"[25]; and "Their goal is to goad Canadian citizens into replying with their own hateful comments — which the human rights investigators can then prosecute as human rights abuses."[26] Conservative MP Russ Hiebert in an op-ed in the *National Post* makes a related claim: "Recent hearings such as the Marc Lemire case, have revealed that that current CHRC investigator Dean Steacy and former CHRC investigator Richard Warman regularly posted neo-Nazi diatribes under assumed names on white supremacist web-sites."[27]

When the Commission investigates a complaint about Internet postings, it must confirm that such postings were actually made and it must confirm or determine the identity of the person responsible for the postings. In order to do this the Commission's investigators sometimes go onto racist websites. In some cases the complaint relates to postings in a chatroom, or other location, that is accessible only to those who "join," although

---

23 In Moon, 2010, above note * I demonstrate the falsity of the critics' other claims of corrupt behaviour, including the claim that a CHRC investigator tapped into a private computer system in order to access a neo-Nazi website.

24 *Shakedown*, above note 4 at 31.

25 Ezra Levant, "Neo-Nazi Organization Infiltrates Ottawa Rememberance Day Ceremony" (10 November 2008), online: Ezra Levant http://ezralevant.com/2008/11/neonazi-activists-infiltrate-o.html.

26 *Shakedown*, above note 4 at 31.

27 Russ Hiebert, "The CHRC Is Ethically Challenged" *National Post* (29 July 2009) A19.

anyone who wishes to may join. However, there is no evidence to support the suggestions that CHRC investigator Dean Steacy has made racist postings on the *Stormfront* site (the website in question) or any other site. Indeed in Marc Lemire's submissions to the Tribunal in *Warman v Lemire* it was conceded that "There is no evidence he [Steacy] posted any racist material . . . ."[28] Even though Levant's accusations refer to the CHRC, the actual focus of his claims about racist postings is Richard Warman, who has been the complainant in virtually all of the successful section 13 complaints (i.e. almost all the complaints upheld by the Tribunal). Warman was at one time an employee of the Commission (from 2002–04), but he did not investigate section 13 complaints for the Commission. Levant says that Warman "worked at the CHRC as an anti-hate investigator."[29] But that is just not true. Warman did, however, initiate complaints, as a private citizen, while he was employed by the CHRC; although most of his complaints were filed after he left the Commission. Levant, however, attributes all of Warman's actions and postings to the CHRC. When Levant asserts that "CHRC investigators have admitted under oath to writing on Nazi websites that Jews are 'scum,' gays are a 'cancer' and white police should be loyal to their race, to list just a sample,"[30] he is referring to postings that have been attributed

---

28 Submissions of Marc Lemire in *Warman v Lemire*, [2009] CHRD 26 at 400. The sentence continues ". . . but he did attempt to engage Lemire in conversation about a complaint Lemire had laid under s. 13." The suggestion is that this was done to determine whether a complaint made by Lemire was vexatious.

29 *Shakedown*, above note 4 at 32.

30 Ezra Levant, "Levant Responds" *National Post* (18 July 2009) A19. See also his blog posting Ezra Levant, "Jennifer Lynch, Nazi Sympathizer?" (18 July 2009), online: Ezra Levant http://ezralevant.com/2009/07/jennifer-lynch-nazi-sympathize.html:

> What Lynch's staff did was join Stormfront as members. So when they go to the site, they log in with their membership names and

to Warman after he left the employ of the CHRC in March 2004.

About Warman, Levant says, "He would write bigoted comments on the Internet — disparaging Jews, blacks, gays, even fat people. He would engage other online Nazis in conversation. And whenever he encountered other Canadians doing the same thing, he would get them to reveal their identity to him — and then he'd slap them with a personal Section 13 human rights complaint."[31] I do not want to embark on the distasteful task of parsing the online exchanges that occurred on neo-Nazi websites. I will say simply that some of the statements attributed to Warman are reformulated by Levant and taken out of context.[32] Warman says that he engaged with individuals, who made racist postings, in order to determine their identities and to determine whether they were "acting in concert" with others.[33] Nothing said in response to Warman's postings has been the subject of a section 13 complaint and so Levant's claim about entrapment has no basis. The

---

> passwords. They do that for one reason alone: so they can participate in the site, not merely be passive observers. Her use of the phrase "log on" is designed to blur the fact that they were in fact logging in as signed-up Nazi members. It was as active participants that they wrote their hundred of bigoted remarks . . . . Jewish scum! Gay cancer! That's what they wrote. That's not investigation. That's bigotry. That's entrapment. And that's standard operating procedure in Lynch's little Nazi nest.

31 *Shakedown*, above note 4 at 100. Levant and others have claimed that Warman wrote racist and disparaging remarks about Senator Anne Cools. Levant's source for this claim is an extreme right wing website, which has been fighting a rearguard action against Warman. Warman denies that he made such a statement. Levant reports the claim as fact.

32 It appears that other statements attributed to Warman did not originate with him. They were made by others, but because Warman used the "reply with history" function in his exchanges, his postings repeated the more odious messages to which he was responding.

33 Section 13 of the *CHRA* prohibits "a person or a group of persons acting in concert" to communicate hate.

important point, though, is that none of these postings, however they are described, emanated from the CHRC or its section 13 investigators.

Again Levant's false or misleading claims about CHRC corruption fail to address the real problems with the current section 13 process. In my report I raised questions about the appropriateness of relying on private citizens to initiate and pursue section 13 complaints. There are a variety of reasons why this is problematic, although the main one is simply that it puts too much of a burden on the private complainant. Hate speech is most often directed at a receptive, or at least interested, audience and is only known to the complainant because he has looked for it or stumbled across it. Hate speech necessarily targets a group rather than an individual. The complainant makes the section 13 complaint on behalf of the group or society in general. She may not even be a member of the group targeted by the speech but has simply taken the initiative to bring a complaint. It is not accidental, then, that particular individuals have played a leading role in the initiation of complaints. Without the initiative of these individuals, section 13 might have no operation at all. The complainant carries responsibility for the complaint throughout the process, at both the investigation and adjudication stages.[34] In addition to the burden of time and money that a complainant must bear, particularly if the complaint proceeds to adjudication before the CHRT, a complainant may be subjected to threats of violence.[35] We should not expect complainants to bear such a burden. Moreover, searching neo-Nazi websites for hate speech, and engaging with individuals on those sites to determine their

---

34 As noted earlier, while the CHRC has the legislative authority to initiate complaints under s 13, it has generally not acted on this. The CHRC is not required to appear at the CHRT adjudication, but may do so as representative of the public interest.

35 Richard Warman has been the subject of several death threats posted on white supremacist websites.

identity, involves ethical challenges that should not be dealt with by private citizens. Hate speech harms the group and the community. It is a public wrong. The state, not private citizens, should be responsible for the enforcement of the law.

E. The State of Public Discourse

Many of the claims made by Levant, Steyn, and other critics of the CHRC are false or misleading. But how have these critics been able to make these false or deceptive claims go so far? Levant's claims are not just posted on his blog. They are in his book, which is published by a major Canadian publisher. They are repeated by him, almost always without challenge, in radio and television interviews. They are parroted by politicians and in newspaper editorials and columns. And, although this is more difficult to gauge, they appear to be taken up by Canadians, who watch or read the mainstream media.

The propaganda campaign against HRCs fits within the dominant model of contemporary political discourse, which is often referred to as "spin." Spin, described most generously, involves putting a positive gloss on an event or statement, or describing the actions of one's opponent in a negative light. More realistically described by Brooks Jackson and Kathleen Hall Jamieson, in their book, *unSpun*: "Spin is a polite word for deception. Spinners mislead by means that range from subtle omissions to outright lies. Spin paints a false picture of reality by bending facts, mischaracterizing the words of others, ignoring or denying crucial evidence, or just 'spinning a yarn' — by making things up."[36] Political spin inverts the relationship between fact and opinion, with the former often following the latter. To the political spinner, facts are just supports or props for a position. "Facts" may be selected, massaged, and even invented to advance a larger

36 Brooks Jackson & Kathleen Hall Jamieson, *unSpun: Finding Facts in a World of Disinformation* (New York: Random House, 2007) at vii.

"truth" or simply the self-interest of the speaker.

"Spin" is political speech in the model of commercial advertising. Commercial advertising has come to dominate public discourse not just in the sense that so much of that discourse is composed of ads — that we see ads everywhere — but also in the way in which these ads have become the general model for public expression — for how political and other public actors convey their views and seek to persuade others. Political speech, in the commercial model, seeks an emotional or visceral response, eschews complexity and nuance, and devalues factual accuracy. The dominance of public discourse by the advertising model has made it increasingly difficult for us to envision political speech that seeks to persuade citizens of the wisdom of a particular policy rather than simply to shape or manipulate the concerns and feelings of political consumers.

The Internet has been the breeding ground for many of the false claims made about the CHRC. The audience for the blogs of Levant and other CHRC critics, while not insubstantial, is still relatively small and generally confined to like-minded individuals, who are receptive to the claims made. But when the content of these blogs passes into the mainstream media, not only does it reach a larger and more politically diverse audience, it acquires greater credibility.

Why have mainstream media outlets been willing to provide a platform for these false and misleading claims? There are several reasons for the media's failing. The most obvious is that media reporters and interviewers have limited time and resources, making it difficult for them to fact-check — to confirm or correct the claims made. And, of course, the more these claims are repeated in the media, the less it seems necessary to check their accuracy. But there are other more significant factors that seem to support non-critical reporting of these claims — and similarly ungrounded claims about other public issues.

The first is the desire by most mainstream media outlets, in their role as reporter of news, to appear neutral or balanced in their reporting, particularly on matters of public controversy — to avoid taking a position (or appearing to take a position) on a public issue. In seeking to avoid the appearance of bias, newspapers and broadcasters, at least in their news coverage, often present different positions without commenting on their merits. The problem is that the positions reported may not have any factual grounding or may be based on factual claims that are contested. If the media simply report the factual assertions of one side without ensuring that they are accurate, or if they report competing factual claims with no comment on the accuracy of the claims, then the audience will at worst be misled and at best be denied enough information to make a reasoned judgment. Levant appeared on at least three CBC national radio programs — *The Sunday Edition, Cross-Country Check-Up,* and *The Current*. Each program allowed him to repeat his false claims with little or no challenge and so gave them validation. When Levant asserts in an interview that the CHRC has a 100 percent conviction rate and is not challenged by the interviewer, the audience might reasonably assume that his claim is true.

When the media treats factual claims the same way it treats opinions, and simply channels them to the audience, how is the audience to know whether the claims made are true? The audience has no other meaningful access to the facts. Even when the audience hears competing versions of the facts, how are they to decide between them if the media does not arbitrate or even comment on these factual "disputes"? Because there is often no common factual ground, it is left to the members of the audience simply to choose their position, based on "gut instinct" or ideological predisposition. Not surprisingly individuals tend to adopt the factual claims that fit with the views they currently hold and to discount or reject those that do not. If I am already wary of "big government" or resentful of "political correctness," I will be more receptive to the claims of Levant and Steyn. On the other hand,

I am more likely to discount their claims if I believe that government has a role in protecting minority groups from discrimination.

Indeed, this has been a significant problem in the "global-warming debate" where the requirement of balance is understood to mean that whenever the audience hears from those who say that the empirical evidence shows that global warming is occurring, that it is caused at least in part by human activity, and that it will have serious consequences for human life, it must also hear from those who are "skeptical" of the evidence, "of the science." When considering an issue such as global warming, most of us are unable to assess the scientific evidence. Instead we simply rely on the conclusions or assertions of experts. But the "balanced" reporting in the media informs us that there are experts on both sides of the issue. We may then try to assess the credentials of the experts and adopt the position that is supported by the most credible experts. Or we may do what tobacco companies once hoped and oil companies now hope, when they generate "expert" opinions that are contrary to mainstream scientific thinking. We may simply adopt the position that fits with our existing values or lifestyle. In such cases we adopt a position on the issue not as a judgment but as a preference.

The second factor, contributing to the media's uncritical reporting of the false claims about the CHRC, is the increasing prominence of columnists, who engage in advocacy rather than analysis and are concerned less with factual accuracy and more with simply provoking a reaction in their readers. Most mainstream print publications, although seeking to be impartial in their news reporting, publish opinion columns. Most of these columns offer a careful, factually grounded, analysis of current affairs, drawing on the knowledge and experience of the columnist. However, in recent years there has been a proliferation of columns, modelled on television commentary, that are designed to be provocative — to attract readers who strongly agree or disagree with the positions taken by the columnist. The authors of these advocacy columns are prepared to address a remarkably wide range of issues about which they have little or no background knowledge. Their object is advocacy rather than accuracy, and so they make simple and dramatic claims, often with little factual support. Indeed, they often seem to show the same indifference to factual accuracy as political spinners. Mark Steyn's column in *Maclean's* magazine is an obvious example. He seems to have no hesitation re-shaping the facts to fit the conclusion he wishes to reach. Rex Murphy, in the columns he has written for *The Globe and Mail* dealing with HRCs, has taken his information straight from Levant's blog. On one occasion Murphy wrote a column about how outrageous it was that the Chief Commissioner of the CHRC would lay a wreath at the war memorial in Ottawa, when she obviously had no grasp of the freedoms for which Canadian soldiers had fought.[37] Only two days earlier Levant had written about the very same thing, although in less grandiloquent terms.[38] Murphy has also repeated several of Levant's false claims, including the claim that the BCHRT has recognized a "right *not* to wash one's hands while working in a fast-food restaurant."[39] He has it seems made no effort to confirm the accuracy of any of Levant's claims. The emergence of this type of opinion column is part of the gradual reshaping of the print news media in the image of the entertainment-oriented current affairs programming that appears on television.

A third factor contributing to the problem of factual distortion is the tendency of the television (and increasingly radio and newspapers) to avoid complex analysis and to sensationalize issues. Television, as a visual medium, does better with spectacle, and with claims that are simple, direct, and dramatic.[40] Television

37 "Real rights," above note 17.

38 Ezra Levant, "Desecration" (12 November 2008), online: Ezra Levant http://ezralevant.com/2008/11/desecration.html

39 "Real rights," above note 17.

40 Neil Postman, *Amusing Ourselves to Death: Public Discourse in the Age*

current affairs programming often focuses on extreme positions. Accusations of corruption, deceit, or patent injustice play much better on television than do more nuanced arguments or moderate or conciliatory positions. Issues are generally presented as if they have only two sides, each of which is simple, straightforward, and diametrically opposed to the other. Even when both sides of an issue are represented, they do not engage with each other, at least not in any way that might contribute to audience understanding, or to the discovery of common ground. The two sides generally make different factual assertions or assumptions. Because the competing positions are so far apart and rest on completely different versions of the facts, the audience cannot learn from each but must choose one over the other. The audience is rarely given enough information and often lacks the background knowledge necessary to evaluate the claims made. When news is presented as entertainment, it becomes part of the spin process rather than its corrective.

F. Conclusion

We live in a world of spin and we know it. It is not uncommon to hear someone say that all public figures lie. This is often said with a degree of resignation that we cannot expect things to be any different. Indeed, the dominance of the advertising model of expression, or "spin," makes it difficult for us to even envision another form of public discourse — one characterized by sincerity and honesty, rather than simply their images, and intended to persuade citizens with arguments and facts, rather than simply impact consumers at a visceral or emotional level. General cynicism along with a withdrawal from politics is the most obvious response to the dominance of spin. But just as often the response is selective skepticism. The factual assertions made by critics of HRCs appeal to a constituency that is suspicious of government

---

of Show Business (New York: Penguin Books, 1986).

power. This group is ready to accept these false or misleading claims, apparently without skepticism, or at least with indifference to their accuracy, because they represent a larger "truth." Once you accept that everyone spins then it seems the facts are no longer at issue, only the preferred ideology.

In the end the debate about HRCs, like so much public debate, involves no real engagement between competing positions, and no real opportunity for the audience to judge whether or not the current law is good policy. The complexity of the issue is avoided or suppressed. The merits of the case, either for or against hate speech regulation by HRCs, are lost in a sea of exaggerations and fabrications. It is left to the audience, if it is paying attention, to make a choice, not based on reasoned judgment, but on their existing views, on their ideological predispositions — either suspicion of government regulation or belief in the importance of human rights protection. While the critics of the CHRC have been successful in spreading their views, all they can hope for is a marginal win in a polarized debate. This is the most spin can accomplish. It will not advance democratic engagement or meaningful discussion of public policy, and it cannot bring about consensus or compromise or even respectful disagreement based on an awareness of the costs and benefits of the different responses. Spin encourages the fragmentation of the civic audience into insular ideological communities that are unable to engage with each other.[41] The costs of spin are even more fundamental than this though. Spin degrades public discourse, so that we no longer expect to be told the truth and are no longer able to evaluate positions based on the accuracy of their claims or assumptions.

41 Kathleen Hall Jamieson & Joseph N Cappella, *Echo Chamber* (New York: Oxford University Press, 2008).

Chapter 5

Societal Perspectives in Competing Rights Policy: Law Reform Agencies and Consulting with Communities

Patricia Hughes*

A. Introduction

Rights are not only legal entities. Although rights may be abstract on paper, rights claims embody deeply held views about one's place in the world. They reflect or may indeed arise in response to a challenge to one's self-identity or because one perceives one's status, social or economic, to be threatened. This subtext underlying rights and rights claims means that unless we hear directly from the people affected, it is very difficult to develop effective and responsive ways to resolve tensions between or among rights. Those who experience a denial of their rights have a unique perspective on why that is the case and what needs to be done to remedy the situation. These views may not determine the outcome, but they are crucial to it. Yet, their claims often affect the rights — or interests — of others and the remedy they seek will sometimes curtail — or appear to curtail — these latter rights or interests.[1] Any determination of rights claims must

* The views expressed in this paper are those of the author alone and should not be read to represent the views of the LCO or of anyone associated with the LCO other than the author.

1 I use the term "interests," as well as "rights," for two reasons. The term "rights" denotes an interest that has acquired legal sanction, while other interests, which nevertheless may be significant, have not yet done so. The use of the term "rights" has both positive and negative connotations: it is important, for example, to say "people have the right to be

address the resulting conflicts or tensions.

This paper is about the value of including communities in the process of developing policy relating to rights, and about how agencies that develop policy discover societal perspectives. In developing policy the inclusion of "rights claimants" (or "societal perspectives") is less structured than in a legal proceeding, for example, and may occur because of political expectations or ethical mores rather than a legal requirement and may not follow a pre-determined pattern or set of rules. These perspectives are gathered through consultations with relevant community groups.

While the development of policy usually includes consultations with a range of different "stakeholders," I am limiting my consideration here to community-based groups. For my purposes, I assume that the views of, for example, banking or industrial interests, or similar well-established stakeholders relevant to the development of a particular policy, will be taken into account and that these interests will have a more or less direct or indirect influence on resulting policy. The issue I consider here, then, is the way in which agencies developing policy about rights ascertain the perspectives of community-based groups.

Community consultation is no longer the uni-dimensional activity it once was, at least in certain contexts, when academics and other researchers met with those they had decided to study. Now there are various degrees of "inclusion," "involvement," or "participation" by community members or so-called "stakeholders" that can occur, and thus different levels of influence community members or stakeholders expect. Consultation with community-based groups has been the subject of new research approaches developed over the past two decades in social research conducted by academics and research agencies. Inclusion

---

treated with respect, to be secure, to have religious and expressive freedom and to receive equal (not necessarily the same) treatment," yet the concept of "rights" has also acquired an adversarial tone that results in pitching rights against each other, thus the phrase "competing rights."

research, (participatory) action research, and community-based participatory research (CBPR) are all riffs on this shift premised on a distinctive relationship between the academics and social research agency researchers and communities. Here I draw on the insights of these approaches to illuminate the process of consultation designed to identify societal perspectives by bodies responsible for developing policy around rights. This discussion reveals the distinctive nature of this work and explores some of the challenges facing these bodies as they try to ensure that they hear from communities in the process of developing policy.

I use the law reform agency context as a frame for considering how an "unaligned" body (a body that is not intended to represent a particular interest), with a mandate related to increasing access to justice, can engage in this participatory research world and can obtain the kind of information it requires to take into account societal perspectives. As a concrete example, I further focus the discussion by citing the example of the consultation policy and practice of the Law Commission of Ontario (LCO).[2] A law reform agency will develop a policy underpinning to its recommendations that is in part based on what it learns from the various interests with which it consults. Its recommendations will often have to take into account societal perspectives that appear at first glance, at least, to "compete" with each other.

B. Approaches to Community-Based Consultation

There are several approaches to engaging in research premised on the involvement of community groups in the research practice that is intended to produce evidence to support particular policies. Broadly, these approaches reject research approaches that assume that research is neutral and objective or that "use"

2 My appreciation to Margaret Hageman, then the LCO's Community Outreach Coordinator, for prompting a discussion about the application of community-based research to the LCO's work.

members of groups simply to obtain data (that is, as study subjects) to benefit non-community research. In participatory action research, the "starting point . . . is people's needs and interests, not just an idea or hypothesis a researcher or academic has."[3] Put another way, these approaches "include local experience and skills as valuable knowledge contributions to research design and outcomes."[4]

While sometimes treated as interchangeable with community-based research (CBR), action research places greater stress on the research and action resulting from it than on the community involvement. Thus action research may limit the participation of community members to that of being "informants," although community participation is likely to take a more active form.[5] CBR, on the other hand, is defined with reference to a fuller understanding of participation and involvement.[6]

Thus in action research, participants' involvement can range from being informants to interpreting data (commenting on the meaning of the data), to planning (this might involve raising the participants' roles or in using the data to bring about change) to making decisions to implementing the data (effectively, being

---

3 Ontario Women's Health Network, *Inclusion Research Handbook* (Toronto: OWHN, 2009) at 111 [*Inclusion Research Handbook*].

4 Karen Edwards, Carrielynn Lund, & Nancy Gibson, "Ethical Validity: Expecting the Unexpected in Community-based Research" (2008) 6:3 Pimatisiwin: A Journal of Aboriginal and Indigenous Community Health 17 at 18 ["Ethical Validity"].

5 One proponent of action research, for example, defines it this way: it "is a flexible spiral process which allows action . . . and research . . . to be achieved at the same time . . . . People affected by the change are *usually* involved in the action research . . . ." [emphasis added]. Bob Dick, *Action research: Action and Research* (2002), online: www.aral.com.au/resources/aandr.html. Reflection is integral to the process.

6 CBR has been applied in the health field and definitions and principles reflect that development.

co-researchers).[7] Proponents of action research recognize that it is not always possible to have everyone involved at the same level throughout the project. Participants may act as facilitators because they know the community better or, no doubt linked to the first, because members of the community are more likely to respond to them or for reasons of language.[8] Action research notably and explicitly integrates the concept of critical reflection in its process, meaning that later stages of the research benefit from the lessons learned from earlier stages.[9]

CBR (using the methodology of CBPR) "is guided by the core principles of collaboration and partnership where research brings together community and academic expertise to explore and create opportunities for social action and social change."[10] CBPR has been defined as

> . . . [a] collaborative approach to research that equitably involves all partners in the research process and recognizes the unique strengths that each brings. CBR begins with a research topic of importance to the community with the aim of combining knowledge and action for social change to improve community health and eliminate health disparities.[11]

---

7 Bob Dick, *Participative Processes* (1997), online: www.aral.com.au/resources/partproc.html.

8 *Ibid.*

9 Bob Dick, *A Beginner's Guide to Action Research* (2002), online: www.aral.com.au/resources/guide.html.

10 Brenda Roche, "New Directions in Community-Based Research" (Wellesley Institute, 2008) at 2, online: Wellesley Institute www.wellesleyinstitute.com/wp-content/uploads/2011/11/newdirectionsincbr.pdf ["New Directions"].

11 *Ibid* at 4. This is the Kellogg Health Scholars Program definition: see online: Kellogg Health Scholars www.kellogghealthscholars.org. Although the focus of the Ontario Women's Health Network (OWHN) is health, this could apply to other areas. Also see the School of Public Health, University of Washington, "Community-Based Research Principles," online:

In CBPR, community members are involved from the earliest stages: CBPR "[b]egins with and builds on strengths and resources within the community" and "[i]nvolves a long-term process and commitment."[12] They determine or at least confirm the research topic, share in the resources (financial or expertise, for example), and contribute their own expertise. The process "recognizes and addresses power imbalances between researchers and community members" and is "driven by values, including: empowerment, supportive relationships, social change, learning as an ongoing process and respect for diversity."[13] The project should benefit the community in a way that has been defined by the community.[14] An important component is capacity-building in the community: there is, in this sense, an exchange of knowledge and expertise, with the community members learning about how to do research and develop policy and the academics learning about what the community members' experience is like "on the ground." The term "inclusion research" (a particular aspect of CBR and also incorporating the basic conception of action research of "moving research to action") highlights the development of "peer researchers" from the community itself to carry out the interviewing, for example.

Inclusion research trains members of relevant communities, often marginalized, to be co-researchers, with the objective "to unite researchers from the population 'under study' with

---

http://sph.washinton.edu/research/community.asp; Centre for Community Based Research, "What is Community Based Research?" online: Centre for Community Based Research www.communitybasedresearch.ca/Page/View/CBR_definition.html ["What is Community Based Research?"]

12 "New Directions," above note 10 at 3.

13 "What is Community Based Research?" Above note 11.

14 Atlantic Centre of Excellence for Women's Health, "Community-Based Research Ethics" (2000) 5 Moving Towards Women's Health 1, online: www.acewh.dal.ca/eng/reports/moving5.pdf.

professionals in order to collectively define research questions, facilitate focus groups, collect and analyze data and advocate for social change."[15] Thus "the line between the person doing the research and the people being researched is blurred."[16] Inclusion researchers are fully involved in the research, in "confirming methodology," serving as members of advisory groups, recruiting others to participate, recording discussions, developing and implementing dissemination, "participating in advocacy activities," and "[p]roviding input on the development of Inclusion Research tools and resources."[17]

The benefits of inclusion research include, among others, "[e]nabl[ing] marginalized groups to name their issues and priorities, while participating in effecting change."[18] It is more likely that with the experience of marginalized people ("women who are marginalized by such factors as colour, nationality, immigration status, disability, sexual orientation or the intersection of these identities"[19]), the project will develop practical recommendations that are grounded in "a more diverse and comprehensive source of knowledge."[20] Of particular importance is that the inclusion researchers benefit in ways other than having their views communicated: they receive training and income and develop new relationships and confidence, among other benefits. The organization conducting inclusion research is likely to have greater credibility in the community and increased possibility "to move research to action," as well as increasing accountability.[21]

The ethical values underlying participatory action research requires that the agreement between or among partners to

15 *Inclusion Research Handbook*, above note 3 at 14.

16 *Ibid*.

17 *Ibid* at 15.

18 *Ibid* at 16.

19 *Ibid* at 17.

20 *Ibid*.

21 *Ibid* at 18.

the research share ownership of the data and thus the right to publish.[22] If the results of research are particularly sensitive or community leadership changes, the community may prevent dissemination of the research.

These approaches emphasize the need to make the consultations or meetings with community members accessible: ensuring the time and location is appropriate (if in the evening, well-lit access, or wheelchair accessible), providing child or elder care, offering translation (including American Sign Language), providing tokens or other travel assistance, providing culturally appropriate refreshments, and providing plain language documents.[23] (These acknowledgements of the reality of community members lives are crucial to CBR and related approaches; however, they are also increasingly part of more traditional research approaches.)

C. Law Reform Agencies and Consultation

1) General Comments on Community Consultation

For philosophical, resource, or project selection reasons, some law reform commissions rely primarily on written submissions to consultation or discussion papers based on caselaw, the relevant literature and conversations with a few experts. Others who do engage in more pro-active in-person consultations may limit them mainly to the legal profession or similar groups.

For some law reform agencies, however, broad consultation has become an integral part of how they develop the policy underpinnings of analysis and recommendations. For example, the Australian Law Reform Commission (ALRC) is committed to extensive and effective project consultation. As the current presi-

---

22 "Ethical Validity," above note 4 at 25.

23 *Inclusion Research Handbook*, above note 3 at 112.

dent (then commissioner) explains:

> The ALRC also has a major obligation of consultation — not only in each Terms of Reference but also under the provisions of the *Australian Law Reform Commission Act 1996* (Cth), as the ALRC "may inform itself in any way it thinks fit" for the purposes of reviewing or considering anything that is the subject of an inquiry. The ALRC has really taken consultation to heart and widespread community consultation is a genuine commitment. As Professor Weisbrot [then the President] has commented:
>
>> This commitment to community involvement is part of the ALRC's DNA. We don't do public consultation just to tick that box; we do it because we know it significantly improves the quality, the grass roots applicability, and (not surprisingly) the public acceptability of our recommendations.
>
> In addition to receiving written submissions in response to each consultation document, the ALRC also maintains an active program of direct consultation with stakeholders and other interested parties throughout every inquiry. The nature and extent of community consultation is determined by the subject matter of the reference. While some areas may be seen to be narrow and technical, and of interest mainly to experts — like admiralty, or marine insurance — other ALRC inquiries involve a significant level of interest and involvement from the general public and the media — like privacy. Further, while the ALRC is based in Sydney, it is a national body and so consultations are usually conducted across Australia during each inquiry.[24] [footnotes omitted]

Generally speaking, law reform agencies tend to meet with

---

24 Rosalind Croucher, "Law Reforming — the whys, wherefores and whereto's" (Address delivered at the Legal Studies Teachers Conference, Sydney, Australia, 24 August 2007), online: ALRC www.alrc.gov.au/speeches/RC/2007/20070824.pdf.

individuals and groups in order to obtain information or data that will inform their research and recommendations. An agency may continue contact with the groups by sending updates (or it may not), but the intention is not to develop an on-going relationship. CBR goes beyond this kind of contact. The expectations created by this kind of research may result in pressure for other bodies engaged in incorporating societal perspectives into their work to adopt the practices of CBR and similar approaches. However meritorious these practices in the context of academic or social agency research or whatever their drawbacks in operation, discussed below, the issue for law reform agencies is not how desirable they are in the abstract, but how well the assumptions, principles, and practices of action research and CBR conform to the mandate of a law reform agency and similar bodies with a responsibility to consider societal perspectives in their work.

Consultations may initially help define the project or scope of the project (as in the case of the LCO's family law project, discussed below), but are primarily to obtain feedback and input from diverse communities and interests on consultation papers the law reform agency prepares. Consultations could be held to obtain input on how the agencies does its work — or indeed, carries out consultations. Generally speaking, however, consultations are a fundamental part of the research process, whether the agency actually thinks of them as research, along with academic and legal research, or thinks of them as informing the research, and ultimately the recommendations.

Thus the main purpose of consultations for a law reform body is to gather information and views about a particular subject or, in other words, to learn about societal perspectives on the subject. There are other important benefits to the consultation process, as well as this main one, benefits that go far beyond the particular project or subject matter. The consultation process is a statement about who should be involved in policy development, even if indirectly (and one might argue, filtered through the law reform bodies' retelling). While law reform commissions are not responsible for changing the law or policy, they do, to an extent, have an influence, specific or otherwise, meaning that groups that have contributed to the projects have at least an indirect impact. These groups are part of the debate around the project issues. In some cases, they might be part of a more public forum or conference, or at least the ideas they generate or experiences they recount might be.

Commentators have pointed out that consultation in a law commission project might help correct errors; these might be factual errors in a consultation document or errors in understanding a group's point of view, for example. Initial consultation may also reveal that the commission has omitted an issue crucial to understanding the full implications of the matter it is studying. Consultation may build support for a final report and the commission's recommendations and may promote use of the report in lobbying efforts by interested groups. When consultation is used appropriately with groups representing different views of an issue, their involvement in the process may assist in giving the recommendations widespread legitimacy and acceptance, even if not agreement, and, it has been suggested, might promote "public ventilation of issues" to help develop consensus or at least "defuse lingering tensions" around issues.[25]

Others see consultation as not only relevant for the law commission's own work, but also as a process that contributes to the development of civil society and of democracy, precisely because

---

25 For a discussion of the benefits mentioned in this paragraph and other benefits of consultation, see David Weisbrot, "What's the Value of a Full Time Standing Law Reform Commission? (You mean besides independence, quality scholarship, extensive public consultation, corporate memory, cost effectiveness...?)" (Address delivered at the Australian Law Reform Agencies Conference, Darwin, Australia, 10 June 2002), online: ALRC www.alrc.gov.au/speeches/DW/2002/20020620.pdf .

it involves citizens in the law reform process.[26] One observer argues that consultation is not just a question of expressing views on a consultation paper; rather, it has the wider goal of involving citizens more broadly in the law reform process and in accepting the *idea* of contributing to law reform and promoting civic engagement. Thus one purpose of consultation,

> . . . is to give people whose views have typically been suppressed or ignored an opportunity to be treated with dignity and to have their concerns taken seriously. Law reform commissions should make special efforts to engage with groups which have historically faced barriers to participation in civil society. These may be barriers based on gender, disability, language and culture, as well as barriers created by historical injustice.
>
> . . .
>
> The law reform approach which [this observer] favour[s] addresses disengagement and public distrust by putting community discussion and debate at the centre of policy making. It is based on the idea that all groups in the community have the right to engage in debate and have their concerns taken seriously. A process based on the principle of deliberative democracy may be valuable, even if its main outcome is to expose areas of disagreement. Encouraging public debate on controversial legal and moral issues helps to build public trust in government and the institutions of democracy.[27]

---

26 See, for example, Marcia Neave, "The Ethics of Law Reform" (Address delivered at the Centre for Applied Philosophy and Public Ethics, University of Melbourne, Australia, 11 August 2004), online: VLRC www.lawreform.vic.gov.au/wps/wcm/connect/Law+Reform/Home/Newsroom/Speeches/LAWREFORM+-+Ethics+of+Law+Reform+speech.

27 *Ibid.*

There are various ways consultation can occur, but not all will be effective in achieving the different objectives identified above. The New Zealand Law Commission invites comments on particular issues under their feature "Have Your Say" and it also has a Twitter account.[28] The LCO invites general comments, as well as specific project-related feedback, online.[29] Online consultation processes allow a different kind of consultation: they are open to anyone with computer literacy (or anyone who can attain it with some help) and permit far less formal expression of opinion than the written submissions that constituted a major part of the feedback to a law commission paper in the past. Because commissions post consultation papers (and other documents) online, the potential audience with relatively easy access to the consultation paper is broader than it used to be. Yet it can be argued that they cannot substitute for in-person engagement that often elicits the deeply held views and values — and sometimes fears — to which I referred at the beginning of this paper.

D. The LCO's Outreach and Consultation Processes

The LCO was launched in September 2007 with a mandate to make recommendations to make the law more effective, relevant, and accessible, to simplify and clarify the law, and to see how technology might be used to increase access to justice. It also has a mandate to stimulate critical debate about law. It was created by an agreement to which the Law Foundation of Ontario, the Ministry of the Attorney General, the Dean of Osgoode Hall Law School, the Law Society of Upper Canada (all of whom provide funding to the LCO), and the other Ontario law deans are parties.[30] LCO projects may be narrowly focused on legislative

28 New Zealand Law Commission, online: www.lawcom.govt.nz.

29 LCO, "Tell Us What You Think," online: www.lco-cdo.org/en/content/how-you-can-help.

30 Law Commission of Ontario, Foundation Agreement 2012, online:

reform or may address the law in the context of social and other issues ("socially oriented projects").[31]

The LCO's "Foundation Agreement" states that it "shall . . . foster links with communities, groups and agencies."[32] In bringing "societal perspectives" to bear in its research, analysis, and recommendations, the LCO has made a commitment to seek the views of those affected by its projects, whether professional, community-based, government, or others, with the greatest applicability to the socially-oriented projects.[33] Inevitably, there are different views, not only about recommendations, but also about analysis or even what should be studied. The LCO engages with communities in a number of ways; the two most relevant here are outreach and project-related consultation.

The purpose of outreach is to make initial contact with groups to let them know about the LCO and to learn about the groups and their law reform needs. While the purpose is not to discuss the particular projects, inevitably these projects are discussed and the group's relevant experiences expressed. In some cases,

---

www.lco-cdo.org/en/lco-foundation-agreement-2012 ["Foundation Agreement"].

31 See a description of current and completed projects at Law Commission of Ontario, online: LCO www.lco-cdo.org/en/content/our-projects.

32 "Foundation Agreement," above note 30, s 2(2)(b).

33 While any project, even the most technical, could involve extensive community-based consultation, the socially oriented projects are usually more broadly defined and involve the daily lives of large groups of people. Furthermore, the LCO selects projects for many reasons and the technical, more legislatively focused projects are often selected not only because they respond to the need to update or clarify the law, but because they require fewer resources to complete. An example is the LCO's joint and several liability under the *Ontario Business Corporations Act* project: Law Commission of Ontario, *Joint and Several Liability under the Ontario Business Corporations Act: Final Report*, online: www.lco-cdo.org/en/content/joint-several-liability.

these initial meetings do provide a good basis for follow-up consultation related to specific projects. For example, a visit to Thunder Bay in October 2009 included a presentation to the Thunder Bay Law Association and a meeting with the Regional Senior Judge of the Superior Court of Justice, discussion with several workers at the Kinne-Awaya Legal Clinic, the Ontario Native Women's Association, and area legal aid offices, and two meetings with representatives of various groups, including injured workers, disability advocates, a women's centre, the John Howard Society, and social workers. Subsequently, one individual from Thunder Bay submitted a project proposal, while the LCO consulted a number of groups in on-going projects. An initial outreach meeting with ARCH Disability Law Centre, the legal clinic that addresses the needs of persons with disabilities, led to partnering with ARCH in the LCO's consultations on its project relating to persons with disabilities. The range of outreach meetings is illustrated by the following non-exhaustive examples: the African-Canadian Legal Clinic board of directors, the executive director and workers at the Metro Toronto Chinese and Southeast Asian Legal Clinic, the National Anti-Poverty Organization, Maytree, the Ontario Centre for Engineering and Public Policy, Windsor Women Working for Immigrant Women, the Council on Aging in Kingston, the Public Accountants Council, and the Social Planning Council, among others.

These visits play an important role in communicating through action the agency's interest in making connections with the community outside the realm of existing projects and may also be a source for new projects. Outreach does not raise the same issues about the relationship between the agency and the community that actual consultation does. Nevertheless, it can be the "first impression" a group develops about the agency and its approach to community-based groups.

More pertinent here, however, are the consultations specifically related to LCO projects. In addition to formal written submissions, emails, or web-based comments, the LCO also arranges focus groups and individual and group interviews, in person, over the telephone, and online. For some projects, the consultation may be primarily with legal and other professional groups. As already indicated, for the socially oriented projects in particular, the consultation is far broader in scope.

The LCO considers consultation as part of its research process. Academic research is crucial to developing an understanding of any particular project area, whether undertaken by in-house lawyers or commissioned researchers. It is also important to hear about people's actual experience with the law. Academic and more popular articles may provide this perspective; however, the LCO has concluded that whenever feasible it should hear directly from people themselves as a way to enrich the work of others. The creation of project advisory groups also is a vehicle for consultation that can extend beyond the actual members as they in turn consult with their "constituencies."

Examples of project-related consultations show how different the process might otherwise be, depending on the project. In the project on the "Modernization of the *Provincial Offences Act*"[34] consultation has been primarily with the professional actors in the *POA* system, including judges, justices of the peace, prosecutors, court services administrators, and municipal lawyers and paralegals, among others. The LCO also released an "experiences" document, inviting those who had been through the system to make comment, although this elicited no response (it was posted on the LCO's website, however it was not otherwise widely distributed).[35] The project has also sought to take into account Aboriginal experiences with the *POA* with some limited consulta-

---

34 Law Commission of Ontario, "Modernization of the *Provincial Offences Act*," online: LCO www.lco-cdo.org/en/content/provincial-offences-act. See also *Provincial Offences Act*, RSO 1990, c P.33 [*POA*].

35 Law Commission of Ontario, online: www.lco-cdo.org/en/provincial-offences-experiences-document.

tion in this area. This project has not involved extensive community consultation in the sense intended by this paper, however.

Prior to the approval by the board of governors of a project in family law,[36] the LCO held a roundtable which brought together about thirty-five people from all areas of family law (practitioners, judges, community workers and advocates, academics, government policy makers, and others) to help identify the most important candidates for reform in family law, resulting after additional consultation in a project in family law. The family law project consultation focused on users of and workers in the family law system, through individual interviews and focus groups. In some cases, community organizations facilitated the consultation, allowing the LCO to hear from people whom it would likely otherwise not have heard.

The project relating to persons with disabilities[37] has had the most extensive consultation, with seventeen focus groups in five different Ontario centres, as well as individual interviews. There were separate focus groups for persons with disabilities and for representatives from service and advocacy organizations. There were separate meetings with Aboriginal elders, organized with the assistance of local organizations. Although there was a bilingual group, efforts to organize a French-language group, including seeking the assistance of a francophone organization, were not successful (why this was so will be one issue for the self-reflection post-completion of the consultations). Disability-related organizations arranged focus group meetings for the LCO. The LCO also has retained an Aboriginal consultant to undertake interviews in First Nations communities; at the time of writing, the LCO is waiting for approval from the Chiefs and Band Councils of these communities. The LCO staff engaged in the

36 Law Commission of Ontario, "Family Law Reform," online: LCO www.lco-cdo.org/en/content/family-law-reform.

37 Law Commission of Ontario, "Persons with Disabilities," online: LCO www.lco-cdo.org/en/content/persons-disabilities.

consultations reflected throughout the meetings and made modifications as seemed appropriate. A more thorough overall reflection occurred after the completion of the consultations with the intention of benefitting future consultations.

Given the nature of the project, accommodation was of particular importance to these consultations; however, it is available for all consultations. Refreshments were provided for all focus groups and travel costs, childcare, and honoraria for non-organizational participants. The head of the project sought the advice of disability-related organizations in framing the questions for the focus groups. In addition (as with the *POA* and family law projects), there is an advisory group, comprised in this case of representatives from community groups, particular communities, government, and others.

E. The Challenges of Community-Based Consultations

There are important lessons to be drawn from CBR for organizations that seek to take into account "societal perspectives" when developing policy about rights claims, or more broadly about social issue recommendations. These lessons must be contextualized against a mandate that requires independence by the agency from the groups whose views it takes into account and which it will likely have to reconcile with perspectives expressed by others.

Regardless of the appropriateness for law reform agencies or similar bodies, there has been some question about the extent to which the principles of CBR are or can be respected or observed in community-academic or research agency research. Often the community-based organizations are "cast into supporting roles for research" rather than being involved as full collaborators.[38] Others have pointed out that "engagement of communities as research partners can complicate ethical issues where cultural

38 "New Directions," above note 10 at 10.

differences, political factionalism, community research fatigue, fear of stigmatization, and other conditions may mitigate against readiness to participate in research."[39]

There are also concerns over having peer researchers carry out the interviews. In reality, it has been suggested that community members do not learn enough "to conduct research to a professional standard."[40] Additionally, "peer researchers" may engage more in the technical or prosaic aspects of the research than in the conceptual elements of the project. Furthermore, because of the emphasis on community participation, over more traditional and recognized ways of collecting data, the research may be vulnerable to criticism.

Roche has suggested that CRB be somewhat reconfigured, not in its fundamentals, but in some of its practices. Instead of building community capacity to undertake research, she would focus on "mobilization of community towards social change."[41] She recommends "re-assert[ing] the role of research in CBR," both established and innovative methods. Roche maintains that developing a research infrastructure, including an ethics process, linking CBR with other related projects in a broader context, and developing standards of practice would also make it more effective.[42]

To what extent can a body like a law reform agency meet the expectations of communities with the experiences or expectations of inclusion research or CBR? A fundamental question with respect to the capacity of law reform agencies to engage in CBR and similar research approaches is the degree to which the research (in all respects) must be "consistent with the goals of all

---

39 "Ethical Validity," above note 4 at 17. The focus of the article is on research with Aboriginal communities and their particular dynamics.

40 "New Directions," above note 10 at 11.

41 *Ibid* at 16–19

42 *Ibid*.

partners."[43] While the source of a law reform agency project may be "the community" — that is a particular segment of the community — the agency must have the capacity to undertake the project independently of the community, even while the community and other communities may be involved in various ways in the project. Its particular relationship to the law reform process and credibility with various constituencies rely on it. Any law reform agency's recommendations must take into account the concerns and views of other actors and may be affected by factors such as feasibility; in some cases, the community from which the project arose may be disappointed in the recommendations which may be counter to their own wishes. A requirement that all participants share ownership of the data, for example, consistent with the concept of a true and equitable partnership, is not feasible for a law reform agency which cannot confuse its mandate to advance access to justice for a particular group in a project with its broader obligation to consider a range of interests and the fact that the CBR is only part of the input into its recommendations.

An important aspect of these CBR approaches is community capacity-building. This is rarely something that can be done by a law reform agency in a sustained way. As Edwards, *et al*, point out, and as many researchers have discovered, research fatigue sets in when a community has been asked too often to participate. With diverse and uncoordinated projects, capacity building in the community (such as the development of new research skills) is not sustainable, long-lasting, or necessarily transferable to another project. As a response to this concern, while a law reform agency may in the appropriate case, work with other groups of researchers, depending on the agency's own role, this may give rise to other problems related to the objectives of the research, the treatment of results, and other aspects of the project. A law

43 "Ethical Validity," above note 4 at 20. The authors argue that where this is no longer the case, the project will have to be reconsidered or even discontinued.

reform agency may have to recognize, however, that its ability to include a community's views and experiences in its analysis and recommendations may require that it satisfy a community's own research advisory committee. Depending on the community's expectations, doing so may be consistent with the agency's mandate or not.[44] In these cases, the agency will have to decide whether it is appropriate to undertake the project by obtaining data in other, perhaps less satisfying, ways.

Even more traditional "consultation" is not without its difficulties and risks (which it shares with CBR as coming with the territory of consultation). Members of community groups have had their fill of participating, of sharing their experiences, only to see no tangible change. Commissions cannot guarantee results; they cannot control what is done with their reports. While community participation may improve the work being done, may receive public play, and may even result in change, the initial decision to become involved requires a leap of faith to some extent. Added to research fatigue and lack of impact, is participants' sense of being treated as subjects of study rather than authors of their own lives. Yet CBR, while designed to address the problems of traditional research, has now resulted in communities realizing they do not have the resources to engage in CBR, even when provided with some resources to do so. Of significance, too, is the commission paradigm: while having room for a certain amount of collaboration, it does not permit law reform agencies to become conflated with or to abdicate their role to others.

As many commentators have noted, there is also the question of "managing expectations." Initial outreach of the kind the LCO carries out results in contact with many groups with whom it is not feasible to do later project-related in-person consultation, especially in the short-term. It is important not to make assumptions about where people's interests lie, since groups

---

44 *Ibid* at 25.

may have at least a peripheral unexpected interest in projects. Nevertheless, groups who do not have an interest in a particular project may not see an immediate value to the commission. It is important to maintain contact and to provide the opportunity to participate in projects and activities of interest to the group, even if in a peripheral way.

When organizations or individuals propose law reform projects that are accepted by the LCO's board of governors, the community involved must understand that the LCO's shaping of the project, or the recommendations it makes, may not necessarily accord with how they would address the issue or with the changes they would propose. Although, certainly, the LCO listens seriously to what the community itself says causes problems and what is needed to remedy the situation, in the end law reform agencies must make their recommendations based on information gathered from many sources and take into account a wide range of factors. They do not make recommendations on the basis of hearing from one community, even the community most affected by the project, even if, the community members all agree. It must be remembered that projects are not always initially identified by the community most affected (assuming that there is "a" community that is most affected). It is therefore important that participants realize that, while treated seriously, their views may not be accepted, in whole or even in part. There are likely to be opposing views. Sometimes these can be reconciled, but sometimes they will not be. A community's preferred remedies may not be feasible or, indeed, acceptable when set against principles governing the agency's work. Law reform agencies are not advocates for any particular group, although their mandate is, as is the LCO's, roughly speaking, to increase access to justice. These realities of law reform work make the application of the ethics of shared identification of the project, ownership of the data, and dissemination of the results inappropriate for law reform agencies or similar organizations.

F. Conclusion

This paper is premised on the assumption that it is a "good thing" to include the views and experiences of affected groups (that is, societal perspectives) in the development of policy, obtained, to the extent possible, directly from them. The involvement of community groups in research has evolved considerably over the past two decades and much current work assumes an equivalency between community and academic participants in various ways. These approaches may not be appropriate for law reform agencies that are not engaged in carrying out research with one community or that have to take the views of a number of stakeholders into account in formulating recommendations. There are many ways in which respect for community members can be evidenced, however, even if the usual expectations in CBR — about design of the project or ownership of data, for example — are incompatible with the mandate of a law reform agency.

In some cases, this may limit access to important information. In other cases, it is possible to develop different protocols. Even where that is accepted, however, other issues have to be addressed, including how best to involve communities that are differently positioned in the conversation (and would one include all groups that might have an interest, regardless of how their views accord with widely accepted societal norms around equality, for example) and how to ensure that expectations about the impact of their involvement are clear.

The objectives, processes, and challenges around consultation with community groups carried out by the LCO are not unlike the objectives, processes, and challenges that would arise out of attempts to resolve "competing" rights claims or attempts to develop a protocol for the resolution of "competing" rights claims in other contexts, including those for whom the end goal is policy development. The development of policy, as the development of law commission recommendations, is almost always more complex than responding to one group's concerns. Even if a particular community's interests are the impetus for the policy, there may well be conflicting claims within the community itself, interests of other groups with the right to make claims, and societal interests "outside" the group that must be taken into account. Without as full an exploration of societal perspectives as possible, it will not be possible to advance policy that reflects these different interests nor to shape the policy in a way that seeks, even if not always successfully, to reconcile the different interests at stake.

Chapter 6

Competing Human Rights Claims during Tribunal Procedures

Gary Yee*

A. Introduction

In such a diverse society as Ontario, what are the competing rights issues faced by adjudicative tribunals that try to be responsive to the diversity of the parties and still operate wholly within the rule of law with an impartial and fair process? This short paper will seek to examine the intersection of human rights and the general procedural rights of natural justice and fairness in adjudicative tribunals.

In dealing with this relatively new subject, the expectation must not be raised that there are simple answers. As such, this paper seeks to lay the foundation for the discussion and set out some of the major areas for consideration, rather than to provide clear solutions in such a multi-faceted area.

B. Tribunals, Natural Justice, and Fairness

Before discussing competing rights issues in tribunals, I will provide a foundation for the discussion by briefly setting out the nature of tribunals, and the principles of natural justice and procedural fairness (with apologies to the tribunal and administrative law experts amongst us).

* The views expressed in this paper may be personal views that are not necessarily those of the Tribunal.

Adjudicative tribunals have a unique place in our system of justice and government — pulled by the demands and benefits of each of these institutions, and trying to find a place in the nebulous space between them. Tribunals may be described as "creatures of statute." They have only the jurisdiction or powers that are granted to them by legislation. In some cases, adjudicative tribunals are created by government to do something that the courts could do — such as review a government decision — but in a more efficient, accessible, and flexible manner than the courts. In other cases, adjudicative tribunals are created to make decisions that a government department would otherwise make, but a tribunal could do it in a more independent, participatory, and perhaps politically acceptable manner. In all cases, tribunals may be seen to have advantages related to being specialized, diverse, responsive, and efficient.

Although a hallmark of tribunals is the great variety we find amongst different tribunals, one commonality is the core business or product of tribunals — this is the resolution of the applications or appeals that are brought before it. Resolving cases is typically done through oral hearings and decisions, although the trend has certainly been towards various different types of proceedings, including more alternative dispute resolution (ADR).

In carrying out these core activities, the tribunal is faced with many limits and rules that are set out in various statutes or regulations. In addition to all this legislation, there is the common law as it relates to both the substance of the tribunal's subject matter and — more importantly for the issue of competing rights — the common law as it relates to the principles of natural justice and procedural fairness. It is this latter area where we find the most fruitful discussion about competing rights in a general sense.

There has not been a great deal of discussion or literature devoted to the intersection of human rights and natural justice, especially when it comes to general procedural rights in a tribunal. In addressing this area, we must acknowledge that the competition in this case is between a human right and the right of a party to natural justice and procedural fairness. In that sense, this is not the kind of pure conflict between two human rights (for example, religious freedom and gender equality) that may engage difficult choices involving a hierarchy of rights and other value-laden considerations. Nonetheless, controversy will be no stranger to any discussion about the need to balance one of the human rights with other laws or values in society.

A party's right to natural justice and procedural fairness before a public decision maker is one of the key components of administrative law. Administrative law is a form of public law — it is about the exercise of government powers and the remedies that persons have when they are affected by those powers. In a society where everyone relies upon the government to enforce or advance their rights, the area of administrative law acquires great significance. Administrative law comes into play every time a government department or a tribunal is set up to decide someone's benefits under legislation or to resolve disputes between the "rights" of two parties (for example, landlords and tenants; employers and unions; neighbours; human rights violators and victims; etc.).

As the role of government has expanded and as more and more administrative agencies make important decisions, the courts have developed certain rules to protect the parties that are affected. Through court cases and related legislation (such as the *Statutory Powers Procedure Act*[1]), parties have acquired rights that are described as the principles of natural justice and rules of procedural fairness.

Natural justice basically involves the right to be heard and the right to an impartial decision maker. The right to be heard includes the right to know the case against you and the opportunity to respond to that case by presenting evidence and making

---

1 RSO 1990, c S.22.

arguments. This is very flexible and it depends upon such factors as the nature of the tribunal or government department, the governing legislation, the decision that is being made and its impact on the party, and so forth.

Procedural rights may relate to: adequate notice (of hearing, of particulars, or of evidence); disclosure (of particulars or evidence); the form of hearing (oral, electronic, or written); a hearing before the decision maker (she who hears must decide, and only she who hears may decide); conduct of the hearing (right to counsel, right to cross-examine, right to call witnesses); and reasons for the tribunal's decision

The second branch of natural justice is the right to an impartial decision maker, which is basically the rule against bias. An adjudicator is disqualified if there is actual bias or a reasonable apprehension of bias. This may include a conflict of interest, prejudgment, or a lack of independence. The accepted legal test to determine impartiality refers to whether there is a reasonable apprehension of bias held by a reasonable and informed person.

The focus of this paper will be on adjudicative tribunals — that is, tribunals whose predominant responsibility is to adjudicate rights and to resolve disputes involving individuals, as opposed to administrative or regulatory agencies that may have an adjudication component to their work but whose main function involves policy making and perhaps investigations and recommendations as well.[2]

C. The Role of Public Opinion and Societal Pressures

Adjudicative tribunals, like courts, depend upon independence and impartiality for their credibility or legitimacy. Judges are pro-

---

2 For a comprehensive and enlightening discussion of the terminology and concepts related to the diversity of tribunals and agencies, see Ron Ellis, "Executive Branch Justice – Canada's 'Official Courts'" (PhD Dissertation, York University, Osgoode Hall Law School, 2009) [unpublished].

vided lifetime security of tenure and protection from political interference so that they may make decisions without bending to public pressure. While tribunal members in most jurisdictions do not have a similar security of tenure, they are also expected to act without undue influence. There is much academic debate and public policy debate over how much independence there is when tribunal members are appointed or reappointed by the Cabinet for fixed terms.[3] But the clear trend has been towards a truly merit-based system of appointments and reappointments.[4]

Regardless of legislative protections or government practices, there is certainly an expectation by the public — as well as a legal obligation imposed by the courts — that tribunal members act independently from government and be impartial when dealing with the parties, which in many cases would include a branch of the government. It is the tribunal's adjudicative independence that is essential to its identity; without it the tribunal would be just like any other part of the government, and its members just like any other public servants.

At the same time, tribunals are easy targets when they make what may be unpopular decisions, and they may face criticism — usually unfounded or unfair — that they are out of touch with societal values.[5] The reality of tribunals and their members is that they are pulled in many directions. The public — and this includes the media — often does not understand the nature of the restrictions faced by the tribunal's obligation to comply with the legislation and with natural justice.

Tribunal members often do not receive the kind of instant respect and credibility that judges benefit from. It is much easier for critics to cast aspersions of inexperience, arbitrariness,

3 *Ibid.*

4 This is being reflected in legislation in some jurisdictions, including Ontario with its recent *Adjudicative Tribunals Accountability, Governance and Appointments Act, 2009*, SO 2009, c 33, Sch 5, s 14 [*ATAGAA*].

5 See Richard Moon's contribution to this volume at Chapter 4.

improper influence, or bias upon tribunal members than it is upon judges. For courts, those kinds of criticisms or controversies rarely lead to calls for a judge to be removed and certainly not for the courts to be abolished. For tribunals, the members and the tribunal itself are much more vulnerable to those threats — whether they come from groups, the media, or politicians.

Because the role and identity of tribunals is often a hybrid one, we end up wanting tribunals to be sensitive to public opinions or government policies but still to act independently from public opinion or government policy. There is a dissonance between these expectations and demands that is rarely openly identified or addressed.

The process for resolving competing human rights may play out in several arenas in a healthy democracy. In each of these arenas, there will be different ways for public opinion to have its impact. For example, free speech is the expectation and reality at the community level and through various forms of media, including, of course, the Internet. At the political and government level, politicians and public servants may engage in public consultation or make statements or decisions that attempt to resolve competing rights. Some of these activities may eventually culminate in official government policies, resource allocation decisions, or legislation.

Prevailing societal values and public opinion may be powerful and effective factors in how competing rights get resolved in these democratic arenas. Of course, there is always a danger in submitting human rights to the test of a popular vote or referendum, but public officials and political leaders with courage and integrity will try to do the right thing. The democratic process will ultimately play itself out; sometimes this will be messy and sometimes this will be unfair (at least in the eyes of those on the losing end).

When it comes to courts or adjudicative tribunals making decisions about individual entitlements or settling disputes between individuals, we want to have independence from government direction and also from public pressure. We recognize the danger of permitting judicial decision makers to be lobbied or influenced by persons or forces that are outside of the transparent and impartial process of the tribunal or court. Part of the recognition of this danger — even by those with power — is the fact that the same kind of influence that may benefit them in one case could be used against them in another case if a more powerful lobby group arose or if the media turned the other way or if the government of the day changed. While courts and adjudicative tribunals are an essential part of democracy, this does not mean that they operate democratically in the sense of free speech, open access, a vote by the public, etc. With protections for adjudicative independence, courts and tribunals are well-placed to resolve competing rights issues in a manner that has more integrity and principle than the potential tyranny of the majority.

We may expect or want judges and tribunal members to be responsive to society but that should not be equated with having these adjudicators be swayed by popular opinion about the specific cases that may be before them. There are many appropriate ways in which tribunals can be more responsive to societal values — these would be systemic ways that fully respect the impartiality and adjudicative independence of tribunals.

One approach is to ensure that the tribunal has members and staff who reflect society, and who have a background and understanding that is relevant to the area. Having tribunal personnel who are qualified and expert in a narrow sense will not be enough when trying to achieve legitimacy in dealing with value-laden issues of human rights and inclusiveness. A broader view acknowledges that a tribunal's quality and expertise increases if the tribunal's personnel is diverse, and their life experiences can help to promote an understanding of the issues and parties that are dealt with by the tribunal.

Another way for tribunals to be responsive to societal values is to engage in stakeholder consultations, public education, and media relations.[6] It may not be surprising to know that tribunals traditionally shun publicity. This is manifested in the often-repeated fear of not making the front-page news and thereby causing the responsible minister to answer questions about the tribunal. At the same time, there is a trend towards tribunals becoming more transparent and open about their processes, and taking deliberate actions with respect to media and community outreach. These external activities, if done effectively, can have an impact on the overall reputation of the tribunal, on how well-informed the counsel and parties are, and on developing and implementing changes to practices and policies.

It is especially important for tribunals that deal in controversial areas or in highly polarized settings to have a proactive communications and stakeholder-relations strategy. These tribunals are seen as fair game in the media and political arena. Since tribunals are so limited in how they can respond to case-specific criticisms, the best strategy will involve actions that enhance general reputation and foster supporters in the media, legal groups, community groups, and the government or political realm. Of course, all of this must be done within the limits of a tribunal's unique needs to always maintain its integrity as an impartial and independent decision maker.

---

6 In Ontario's new *ATAGAA*, above note 4, there is a requirement for tribunals to establish a consultation policy, which "must describe whether and how the tribunal will consult with the public when it is considering changes to its rules or policies, including consultation with any persons, entities or groups of persons or entities whose interests, in the opinion of the tribunal's chair, would be affected by those changes" (see s 4). For a discussion of the ethical issues that arise when legal agencies attempt to engage in "stakeholder" consultations, see Patricia Hughes in this volume at Chapter 5.

D. Focus on Procedural Issues, Not Substantive Issues

In discussing specific issues about tribunals dealing with competing rights, a discussion about substantive decisions by tribunals will not be very instructive because it would tend to be too subject-matter specific. Indeed, not many tribunals have true discretion in their substantive decisions to weigh competing public interests or competing rights. This would be more common in tribunals on the regulatory end of the tribunal spectrum — such as those dealing with public safety, land use, telecommunications regulation, and so forth.

On the other hand, in Ontario (and other provinces), parties may challenge the application of a law by saying that it is discriminatory under the *Human Rights Code* — and that statute takes primacy over other provincial legislation.[7] In those cases, the tribunal must explicitly consider the issue of human rights and, in some cases, competing human rights. While there is undoubtedly some interesting discussion that can occur in this area related to the tribunal's substantive decision making, it may be fairly subject-matter specific. The focus of this paper is not on challenges under the *Code*, but rather on human rights in general and how that conflicts with or influences the procedural rights of parties. This is consistent with the focus of administrative law, which is on the procedural rights of the parties.

The discussion of rights becomes more interesting and relevant when we focus on process because that is also the area where tribunals have a great deal more discretion. It is only with the presence of discretion in the true sense that competing rights issues can become very significant. And it is only when the decision maker has broad discretion that the impact of societal values or public opinion becomes an interesting issue.

---

7 See s 47(2) of the *Human Rights Code*, RSO 1990, c H.19 [*Code*]. And see *Tranchemontagne v. Ontario (Director, Disability Support Program)*, [2006] 1 SCR 513.

In an area with little discretion, the law may lead to a result that is seen as harsh or unfair because tribunals are legally obliged to find the facts and to apply the law to those facts. The decision maker may have little choice in these situations — it is not a matter of whether he is insensitive or mean-spirited; it may simply be that the tribunal has no discretion and that it is simply upholding the law.

In contrast, procedural matters are rich in discretion. The rules of natural justice and procedural fairness are notoriously general and elusive. There is no single organized source with numbered paragraphs such as would be found in an Act or regulation. Instead, you must read many long court decisions, some of which may conflict with each other, all of which are open to interpretation, and most of which are specific to the particular case's fact situation.

The problem of the imprecision in this area of law is compounded by the fact that it is these issues of natural justice and fairness that apply the most to the immediacy of the conduct of the hearing. This is when tribunal members are put on the spot — dealing with objections about evidence, adjournment requests and other procedural motions, or deciding when and how to intervene to control a hearing. This is when the tribunal member must rely on the common law, and not so much on the enabling legislation. And this is when competing human rights may become more relevant, sometimes explicitly but sometimes in a more hidden or indirect way.

There are several common situations involving adjudicative discretion where human rights may intersect or overlap with procedural rights: adjournment requests; extension of time deadlines for filing materials or forms; accommodation requests for persons with a disability; reconsideration requests. As illustrations, one can consider what a tribunal should do in the following situations:

1) A party with anxiety disorder has a panic attack during a hearing and wants to stop, but the other side will be prejudiced by any further delay, and asks that the hearing continue after a short break.
2) A party asks for an extension of time to file an application for a postponement of the hearing date because his depression caused him to lack the motivation and energy to get someone to help him in a timely manner.
3) A party asks for an interpreter even though she understands English adequately, but would be more comfortable in a stressful situation to have some assistance.
4) A party starts using racially offensive words in his testimony and submissions.
5) A party enters the hearing room with her face covered by a veil that shows only her eyes and the tribunal member sometimes finds it difficult to understand her because she speaks very softly and the veil makes it even more difficult to hear her; also, her credibility is the key issue in the hearing.

These examples raise issues such as how to accommodate for disabilities and for diversity, what are the rights of one party when faced with a request by the other party that is based upon their human rights, and how does the tribunal deal with the intersection between human rights and procedural fairness when these two rights may conflict. It is not easy to answer the questions that arise from these above examples.

This is an area that is complex and developing. There is potential to develop practices and guidelines to address some of these areas specifically or to put forward some general principles and directions. But as with all areas of natural justice and procedural fairness, the multitude and diversity of tribunals and their specific circumstances will make it very challenging to provide any truly practical assistance. At this stage of dealing with these issues, it marks progress to at least begin to identify the problems, discuss the framework and concepts, and move towards a principled approach that respects both the human rights of a tribunal's parties and the natural justice procedural rights that are at the core of a tribunal's identity.

Part II

Principles and Applications

Chapter 7
Sidewalk Stories: Sites of Encounter and Coexistence

Shauna Van Praagh

A. Introduction: The Sidewalk Moment

Imagine a sidewalk in a major cosmopolitan Canadian city. As you walk along, with your list of errands in hand, you see someone heading towards you. You do not know the person, you know nothing of where she comes from or where she is going, and she does not know you. You step to the right, as does she, and you pass each other — having avoided eye contact and collision. You have shared the sidewalk, you have acknowledged each other, you have followed well-known norms of conduct, and nothing about your purpose, direction, or trajectory has been affected by the moment of encounter. This is coexistence in the absence of conflict, controversy, or even conversation.

We have all had sidewalk moments like this. And yet, of course, some sidewalk moments do not share these simple characteristics. Sometimes we do indeed notice each other in more detail, perhaps assisted by a particularly curious and outspoken child. Sometimes we both move in the same direction at the same time, and are forced into an awkward readjustment in order to avoid bumping into each other. Perhaps it is an encounter of two runners in a city park who share a "good morning" as they move past each other. Perhaps it is a sidewalk moment in a city or neighbourhood you do not know, turned into a lesson on local customary behaviour. Perhaps the other person signals, implicitly or explicitly, a preference that you walk in the road instead. Perhaps you find the other person inappropriate in her dress, or her iPod-created obliviousness, or her inability to control her dog on a leash. In all of these examples, there is more than silent coexistence. The risks of collision and competition for the space are present; so are the potential promises of conversation and concern.

Confronted by the range of possible sidewalk encounters and their particular dynamics — shaped by the identities of the sidewalk users, the nature and norms of the neighbourhood, and the character of the sidewalk itself — we might imagine various ways to govern the coexistence of sidewalk users. We might focus on the possibility of conflict, and then create general principles or specific rules to resolve conflicts that do arise. We might imagine ways to communicate or teach norms of conduct such that controversy is avoided. We might also observe the encounters and collect stories in order to construct a narrative or conversation surrounding sidewalk moments.

These possible responses, and the models of governance they embody, are reflected in any discussion of "competing rights." The notion of competition implies conflict or battle, with a need to declare a winner — or at least to provide a process such that the declaration in any particular case is accepted. Charters or codes are obvious structures for grounding the principles relevant to resolving the competition. Specific legislation may be even more effective at targeting particular kinds of conflict. Educational processes and policies emphasize the need for effective forums and tools for anticipating and resolving competition.

These are all sites that typically provide the kind of "framework" referred to in the name of the 2010 policy dialogue organized by the Ontario Human Rights Commission and the York Centre for Public Policy and Law. In the search for a template response to anticipated conflicts between rights holders and rights claims, we might hope to adopt a particular set of interpretive rules in applying the freedoms guaranteed by human rights codes or charters. We might call for new rules or principles clearly setting out the parameters of particular rights, or we might articulate lessons that illustrate appropriate ways to negotiate potential strife. The search for a framework is understandable in its aim to achieve the apparent comfort of a fixed, clear model, to be developed and applied in a consistent and just way.

This paper questions that quest for comfort and certainty, and its reliance on competition-resolving structures. While it acknowledges the significance of explicit human-rights-protecting structures, it adopts a pluralist sensibility and approach to law and governance. Thus, rather than offering a model for imposing law's roles and responsibilities upon difficult social interactions, the paper accepts a mix of voices, jurisdictions, practices, and norms that constantly create and recreate the ways in which individuals and communities coexist. Thus, in addition to the approaches identified above (codes, legislation, education), this paper suggests that the collection of stories and behaviours is an equally significant approach to direct both conflicts (that we often expect rights discourse to resolve) and day-to-day peaceful negotiations over coexistence as sidewalk users.

Rather than imagining rules that govern the "sidewalk moment" of rights holders who stop as they approach each other and challenge each other to a duel, the approach I suggest is committed to a careful observation of the interactions — of rights, interests, identities, narratives, and real people — in the limited space that a sidewalk provides. Thus, actual practices can provide a reliable and helpful map of the kinds of governance choices and instruments that are effective and responsive. Social policy may be constructed "on the ground," both figuratively and literally. The sidewalk moment helps us engage in that construction project.

B. Stories and Social Policy: Variations on the Sidewalk Theme

1) Redefining the Sidewalk

The metaphor of the sidewalk moment reminds us that some basic rules or minimal ordering are required to govern the interaction of two pedestrians going in opposite directions. The norm that might tell us to move to one particular side in order to avoid collision gives us only a skeletal picture of human relations and interactions. The sidewalk itself in this image is a neutral background against which two similar users balance each other out. The picture is slightly more interesting if there is some imbalance between the two pedestrians — imagine one an elderly person in a wheelchair, and the other a young, adult, able-bodied jogger — posing the question of who yields to whom.

But this is an analysis of competing rights without the complex richness of actual sidewalks in real neighbourhoods. Once we add in that complexity, the rights picture too becomes multi-textured. That is, sidewalks are not only public spaces alongside roads, used by pedestrians to get from one place to another. Sidewalks are places to sell things, to sleep, to put out a hat for money, to train a dog, to play hopscotch, to colour a chalk picture, to negotiate a business deal, to operate a snow removal truck, to sell lemonade, or to learn how to ride a bicycle. They are collective sites of many intersecting interactions.

The neighbourhood of Outremont, in Montreal, Quebec, offers a rich example of this coexisting collection of meanings and practices. Each Saturday morning, the sidewalk is both a public path for some people and an extension of their homes for others. Religious fiction allows the Hasidic Jewish residents of Outremont to treat all space demarcated by wires or strings overhead as domestic or private.[1] From a practical point of view, this means that baby carriages can be pushed down the sidewalk on the Sabbath, their owners reassured by the overhead wires that the ground is deemed domestic for religious reasons. Thus, the shared sidewalk is not only a potential site for the encounter of a deeply religious pedestrian and her non-religious neighbour. It is also literally a fusion of definitions: a religious community definition of the sidewalk as private, and a secular state definition of the sidewalk as public. One definition is visibly inscribed, through wires high above the pedestrians' heads. The other is necessarily invisible, marked by the mix of users and uses of the space.

Ten years ago, an objection to the "*eruv*" being juxtaposed on Outremont neighbourhoods resulted in the dismantling of the wires by the municipal government. But, in a 2001 Quebec Superior Court case *Rosenberg v Outremont*,[2] the Hasidic communities were successful in arguing that such action amounted to a violation of freedom of religion and they succeeded in reinstating the *eruv*. Thus, the literal line placed by the Hasidim around their communities to facilitate religious observance coexists with the figurative line drawn by the municipality around the entire neighbourhood, filling it in with public space.[3]

No individual Hasidic Jews argued that the *eruv* is crucial to their ability to believe and practice their religion; rather, the *eruv*

---

1 Shauna Van Praagh, "The Chutzpah of Chasidism" (1996) 11:2 CJLS 193; Julie Chateauvert and Francis Dupuis-Deri, *Identités mosaïques* (Montréal: Boreal, 2004); Pierre Anctil, Ira Robinson, and Gérard Bouchard, *Juifs et canadiens français dans la société québécoise* (Montréal: Septentrion, 1999).

2 *Rosenberg v Outremont (City)*, [2001] QJ No 2858 [*Rosenberg*].

3 Davina Cooper, "Talmudic Territory? Space, Law, and Modernist Discourse" (1996) 23:4 JL & Soc'y 529; Julie Elizabeth Gagnon, "Cohabitation interculturelle, pratique religieuse et espace urbain: quelques réflexions à partir du cas des communautés hassidiques juives d'Outremont/Mile End" (2002) 3:1 Cahiers du Grés 39.

simply makes observance easier or more convenient and, importantly, does not interfere with the freedom of non-Hasidic citizens of the municipality. As the judgment points out,

> From a practical point of view, without an *eruv*, an Orthodox Jew is effectively housebound on the Sabbath and religious holidays if he or she wishes to or is required to take anything out of the house and bring it on to other property. This prevents, for example, such commonplace activity as pushing a stroller with young children, carrying medication or bringing food to a neighbour's home.[4]

In effect, then, the judgment denying the municipality of Outremont the power to dismantle the *eruv* wires demarcating "domestic space" for the purposes of Sabbath observance, invites local Hasidic Jews to share the sidewalk in a meaningful way.

The *eruv* story is effective for three principal reasons. First, it teaches us that stories of encounter — or of competing rights — have to be placed in context in order to be meaningful. It is futile to imagine telling two sidewalk users how to behave vis-à-vis each other if we do not know where they are and who they are at the moment of encounter. Second, it reminds us that the well-worn dichotomy of public and private requires particular sensitivity and attention. Not only can it be turned on its head, such that private interactions depend on public structures, and public norms can sometimes be best seen through a private lens, but it denies important overlap. Thus, approaches to "competing rights" are drawn from both public law and private law; citizens assert their interests through public engagement and private pressure; and private choice may be meaningless without a level of public facilitation.

Third, the *eruv* brings together two seemingly disparate actors and institutional sites of governance. The role and responsibility of the municipal authorities illustrate state authority. At the same

4 *Rosenberg*, above note 2 at para 7.

time, the extension of the domestic sphere invites us through the front door of a Hasidic Jewish home writ large. We expect to turn to the municipality as the site of jurisdiction over a sidewalk; after all, there must be rules on snow clearance, spring-cleaning, and general maintenance. But the possibility of a Hasidic Jewish mother carrying her baby on that sidewalk on a Saturday comes from the normative authority situated in her home: the authority that allows her to do what would otherwise be deemed prohibited work. The governance of the sidewalk is simultaneously top-down, in the form of state law, and bottom-up, in the form of religion-derived family custom.

2) Governing the Sidewalk

Stories and examples of state desire to define space and modes of behaviour in those spaces are not hard to find. The *Canadian Charter of Rights and Freedoms*[5] is one such story, as are all provincial human rights codes or charters. When individuals bring claims of discrimination or the infringement of their fundamental rights, against either state or non-state actors, they rely on an explicitly articulated commitment to individual freedoms.

Major Supreme Court judgments in two cases from Montreal, from neighbourhoods not far from Outremont, illustrate that reliance. In *Syndicat Northcrest v Amselem*,[6] one person insisted that his religious beliefs were protected to the extent of overriding the agreement he had made as a property owner in a condominium community. His right to follow his faith in erecting an individual *sukkah* for the ten days of the Jewish holiday of *Sukkot* was guaranteed by the freedom of religion articulated in Quebec's *Charter of Human Rights and Freedoms*.[7] Likewise, in

5 Part I of *The Constitution Act, 1982*, being schedule B to the *Canada Act 1982* (UK), 1982, c 11 [*Charter*].

6 *Syndicat Northcrest v Amselem*, [2004] 2 SCR 551 [*Amselem*].

7 RSQ c C-12 [Quebec *Charter*].

Multani v Commission scolaire Marguerite-Bourgeoys,[8] one individual student argued that his Sikh faith required him to carry a ceremonial dagger, apparently contrary to the school's rules governing the student body. His success underscored the priority given to personal conviction and belief, as protected by the Quebec and Canadian *Charters*.

In emphasizing individual belief over communal agreement (*Amselem*) or codes of behaviour (*Multani*), justification for these particular judgments, and others like them, is grounded in the interpretation of human rights charters. The individual, whose freedom has been violated, can walk down any sidewalk, head held high, once those in his path have been told to step aside in the name of human rights protection.

As one state authority orders one sidewalk user to yield to the other, however, another state authority may try to impose a different, or even opposing, rule. Thus, one way to react to these two judgments is to celebrate the Supreme Court of Canada's respect for the religious individual, whether the Orthodox Jewish man in *Amselem* or the Sikh student in *Multani*. Another is to worry that these individuals — confident in their victory — might metaphorically push other sidewalk users into the street. This was precisely the concern, explicitly raised in the wake of these specific judgments, and their strong acknowledgement of individual freedom of religious belief and practice, that triggered the Quebec government's creation, in 2007, of the *Bouchard-Taylor Commission*.[9]

---

8 *Multani c Commission scolaire Marguerite-Bourgeoys*, [2006] 1 SCR 256 [*Multani*].

9 Quebec Government Order in Council 95-2007 (8 February 2007) Concerning the establishment of the Consultation Commission on Accommodation Practices Related to Cultural Differences, reproduced as Appendix A in Gérard Boucher & Charles Taylor, *Building the Future – A Time for Reconciliation* (Quebec: Bibliothèque et Archives nationales du Québec, 2008) [Bouchard-Taylor Report] at 275–76, online:

The preoccupation with governing the shared sidewalk, or Quebec society more generally, is reflected in the part of the Commission's mandate explicitly directed to the appropriate balance between the rights of the majority and the rights of minorities.[10] Thus, after the opening section that underscores Quebec's fundamental commitments to gender equality, separation of church and state, primacy of the French language, human rights, justice and the rule of law, and the protection of minorities, the preamble to the mandate states:

> Whereas certain accommodation practices related to cultural differences might call into question the fair balance between the rights of the majority and the rights of minorities;
>
> . . .
>
> It is hereby decreed . . .
>
> That a consultation commission on accommodation practices related to cultural differences be established;
>
> . . .
>
> That the commission be given the mandate to:
>
> . . .
>
> formulate recommendations to the government aimed at ensuring that accommodation practices related to cultural differences conform to Québec's values as a pluralistic, democratic, egalitarian society.[11]

The Commission was thus clearly asked to grapple with the "just balance" between majority and minorities, between individual rights holders and the communities in which they live and learn, between recognition of specific identity and flourishing of

---

http://collections.banq.qc.ca/ark:/52327/bs1565996.

10 *Ibid.*

11 *Ibid.*

societal values. At the same time that the Commission was created, the municipal government of the small village of Hérouxville in rural Quebec expressed concern over that balance in a strikingly transparent way. Pointing specifically at the Quebec and Canadian *Charters* as the source of unreasonable accommodation of certain immigrant cultures, the village introduced a municipal "Code de vie."[12] In it were spelled out the rules governing dress, behaviour, and even diet in contemporary Hérouxville. At the same time that it was widely ridiculed for its unsophisticated and simplistic legislative project, Hérouxville did reflect a broad desire to set out a clear framework for the potentially competing interests and rights of all citizens.

By placing side-by-side the mandate of a Commission tasked with considering the place of minority cultures within broader Quebec society, and the objectives of a village government determined to communicate and maintain its communal way of life, it is clear that different state actors compete in their attempts to define and govern space and behaviour. Both instances are examples of skepticism towards interpretation by courts and tribunals of state instruments of human rights protection. Both react to state governance of "competing rights" by questioning its language, structures, and application. The Commission turned to, among others, experts in law to help it understand the substance and process of human rights protection. The politicians of Hérouxville turned to their own power to legislate to articulate particular rules of behaviour for sidewalk users in their jurisdiction.

The "Code de vie" proposed in Hérouxville literally addressed questions of who could walk where, how, why, and with whom. Significantly, the "Code de vie" specified that individuals covering their heads and faces were not welcome in the village, an intended reference to Muslim women. The visit of a busload of Muslim

---

12 Municipalité de Hérouxville, "Normes de vie," (Hérouxville, 2007), online: Municipalité de Hérouxville http://municipalite.herouxville.qc.ca/normes.pdf ["Code de vie"].

women from Montreal to Hérouxville, arms full of baked treats, gave the Hérouxville residents a much-needed reality check. But the clumsy attempts to articulate a broad answer to the question of "Qui sommes-nous?" through a specific exclusion of particular religious people from the sidewalks are worth closer attention. Most noticeably, the reaction to accommodation perceived as overly generous to religious minorities takes the form of explicit exclusion of religious women whose mode of dress identifies them as such. That is, the easiest target is the most visible, and the prime example seems to be the Muslim woman who covers her head, her face, or her body.

It is not just a small municipality in rural Quebec that expresses its discomfort with broad social dynamics by banning obviously religious women from public space. In July 2010, the lower house of French parliament voted overwhelmingly in favour of a bill that makes it illegal to wear the niqab or the burqa in any public space. Women who break the law may be fined 150 euros and men who force their wives to wear the burqa could face fines of up to 30,000 euros and a one-year term of imprisonment. The French Senate ratified the ban in September 2010 and the law went into force throughout France in April 2011.[13]

Closer to Hérouxville, and to the aftermath of the Commission's report, the Quebec provincial government tabled a bill in the spring of 2010 meant to establish guidelines for responding to individual complaints of discrimination and related claims for accommodation. The proposed law, which failed to proceed past the discussion stage by the end of the legislative session, did two things. First, it played the role of confirming the background of the "sidewalk moment": the Quebec *Charter* provides the overarching framework, and is to be interpreted in a way that avoids excessively burdensome exceptions to general rules. Second,

13 "Women in face veils detained as France enforces ban" *BBC News* (13 July 2010), online: www.bbc.co.uk/news/world-europe-13031397.

it introduced a new and specific rule related to encounters on the "sidewalk": employees and clients of provincial public institutions and services (educational, health, and administrative) are expected to interact with each other with faces uncovered, and any individual exception to the rule must be justified in terms of safety, communication, or identification. Welcomed by many as a clear instance of governance responding to the preoccupations and public policy of Quebec society, the bill just as clearly targeted Muslim women who cover their faces and bodies, thus turning them into prime symbols of gender inequality combined with an excessive expression of faith.[14]

The call — both metaphorical and literal — for a clearing of the sidewalks of explicitly or excessively religious women in Quebec and in France is often supported in the name of gender equality. Indeed, the Quebec Council on the Status of Women has argued for a modification of the Quebec *Charter* such that freedom of religion would be explicitly subordinated to the right to gender equality.[15] Accordingly, religious norms or rules regarding modesty would clearly yield to secular rules requiring the visibility of the individual faces of all participants in public society. The proposed Bill in Quebec did not go this far, and indeed anticipated appropriate exceptions to the uncovered face rule in the absence of compelling reasons related to safety, communication, or identification. And yet, although it refused to adopt the rigid formula requiring the lifting of the veil in the name of equality, it introduced the risk of simplistic, insensitive, and unnecessary exclusion of the small number of female Muslim Quebecers who

---

14 Shauna Van Praagh, "Niqab Bill Is a Statement of Shared Values" *Ottawa Citizen* (3 April 2010) B.7; Bill: Projet de loi no 94, 2010: Loi établissant les balises encadrant les demandes d'accommodement dans l'Administration gouvernementale et dans certains établissements.

15 Le Conseil du Statut de la Femme, *Résumé: avis du conseil du statut de la femme: à l'égalité entre les femmes et les homes et liberté religieuse* (Québec: Gouvernement du Québec, 2007).

wear the niqab or burqa.

In Supreme Court jurisprudence, official commissions, legislative proposals, or the Quebec *Charter* modification suggested by the Quebec Council on the Status of Women, the framework of human rights codes or charters is central. Whether perceived and focused on as problem or solution, a human rights framework defines the parameters of the discussion in every context. Thus, even those who disagree vehemently with the interpretation and application of that framework firmly believe that its restructuring will point the way to the correct resolution of rights claims and disputes. The issues are characterized as challenges of competing rights, and the remedy is the imposition of clear hierarchy. In particular, if strong religious freedom is understood as a threat to gender equality, then the answer is to turn equality into a trump. As religious individual meets woman on the sidewalk, the religious individual would always give way and walk in the street.

3) Confrontation on the Sidewalk

Such an encounter characterizes the patch of Montreal sidewalk that links two now-famous neighbours: the YMCA and the Satmar Hasidic synagogue.[16] Satmar Hasidic Jews pray at the synagogue and use it as a community centre and yeshiva. Next door, YMCA members swim, exercise, work out with weights, and participate in children's programs. When representatives from the synagogue offered to pay to frost the YMCA's windows in order to stop Hasidic boys from spending time looking across the alley into the exercise room where women were dressed in spandex, the YMCA accepted their proposal. In doing so, it failed to take into account the views of its own community and clients. After much reaction, debate, and heated discussion in 2007, the frosted windows disappeared, the Hasidic boys — one presumes

16 Agnes Gruda, "Les réacs ont la cote" *La Presse* (28 March 2007).

— were placed under stricter surveillance, and the neighbourly equilibrium was restored.

The sidewalk site for this back-and-forth can be interpreted as a battle between gender equality and religious ideology. The women of the YMCA might embody equality, freedom, and the future; the men of the synagogue religious authority, isolation, and the past. But the story and the sidewalk need not be presented in this way. No explicit conflict on the sidewalk ever took place; each neighbour, and its members, displayed respect for the other. The initial negotiation of neighbourly coexistence was simply reworked, as more voices were heard and perspectives added. Rather than a clear-cut victory of one neighbour over another, of one right over another, this is a story of shared space marked by dynamic diversity or fluid hybridity.[17]

This alternative perspective on the story — one according to which the contours of coexistence are shifting rather than sharp — holds out more potential for recognizing the missing people in the picture. Whether in the Quebec Council on the Status of Women's recommendation for a trumping right of gender equality or in a simplistic characterization of the YMCA and synagogue as a conflict between gender and religion, religious women are absent. That is, all individuals of faith appear to be men, and all women appear to be faith-free. The notion that a choice needs to be made between equality and religious freedom in human rights law, or between the generic woman and the religious man on the sidewalk, does not seem to make real space for women as members of religious communities.

The story of the Jewish divorce or *get* serves as a good illustration of the interactions of religious women with Canadian public policy. According to Jewish law, a marriage remains in effect until a *get* is given by the husband and accepted by the wife. Without this religious divorce, the couple remains married even if a civil

---

17 Sherry Simon, *Hybridité culturelle* (Montreal: Ile de la tortue, 1999).

divorce has been finalized. The recent Supreme Court of Canada judgment in *Bruker v Marcovitz*[18] sent a strong message that a husband's refusal to uphold a promise to provide a *get* cannot be justified on the basis of his individual freedom of religion. That decision — essentially a ruling on the scope of contractual obligation in a divorce context — goes hand-in-hand with earlier amendments to the *Divorce Act*[19] provoked by the narrative of religious Jewish women themselves.[20]

The example of the *get* illustrates the mutual coexistence and influence of targeted legislation, judicial interpretation of the private law in relation to a human rights code, and evolution within religious law, norms, and behaviour themselves. All are linked, such that the protection of women from husbands who try to blackmail them by threatening not to provide the *get* comes from multiple directions. It would be a mistake to think that either explicit legislation or the judgment in *Bruker* is solely responsible, necessary, or sufficient in responding to the needs, voices, and claims of religious women in the context of family law. Thus, the Supreme Court decision, while significant, is not a simple victory for gender equality as it pushes aside freedom of religion. Instead, it can and should be read as a story of women of faith working through the meaning of equality within the framework of their religious lives and communities.

On this reading, no easy choice is made between one freedom — that of religion — and another — that of equality. The possibility of aiming for meaningful equality while maintaining not only respect for but also membership in communities of faith is held out. What might be perceived as a conflict of rights that calls out for clear resolution is instead accepted as a mix of interests

---

18 *Bruker v Marcovitz*, [2007] SCJ No 54 [*Bruker*].

19 RSC 1985, c 3 (2d Supp).

20 Rosalie Jukier & Shauna Van Praagh, "Civil Law and Religion in the Supreme Court of Canada: What Should We Get Out of *Bruker v Marcovitz*?" (2008) 43 Sup Ct L Rev 381.

and identities that coexist in many varied ways. In other words, going for an actual walk through the neighbourhood, and getting a sense of the mélange of activities that fill the buildings and sidewalk, holds real potential for interacting with women of faith.

4) Reimagining Sidewalk Space

In Philip Roth's short story, "Eli, the Fanatic," a lawyer sends a letter to the principal of the town's yeshiva in which he expresses concern over the appearance in the town of a man dressed all in black, complete with sidecurls and a black hat.[21] He writes, "This is, after all, the twentieth century, and we do not think it too much to ask that the members of our community dress in a manner appropriate to the time and place." In response, the principal replies, "The suit the gentleman wears is all he's got."[22] There is no other way in which the man can present himself.

The sentiment of the town, articulated by the lawyer, is familiar. It is the challenge of change, of diversity, of incorporation of practices that seem caught in a time warp unable to adapt to today. It is not only a metaphorical concern, but an actual one in Outremont, where the Hasidic men indeed have only black suits to wear, and the common refrain of their non-Hasidic neighbours goes as follows: they refuse to share the sidewalks, they prefer to walk in the street rather than have to cross paths with others. The challenge — for those who believe in a shared neighbourhood and a true mix of its residents — is to get them back on the sidewalks, like everyone else, where they have to share the space no matter how uncomfortable.

But the paradigmatic image of the problematic outsider has changed in much of the discourse on social diversity and citizenship. The new subject of concern is the religious woman, cloaked

21 Phillip Roth, "Eli, the Fanatic" in *Goodbye, Columbus* (New York: Vintage, 1959).

22 *Ibid* at 261–62.

(whether literally or figuratively) in the vestments of her faith. She is seen as a victim of religious norms governing gender dynamics and roles, someone caught in traditions that need to change. Often it sounds like it is the responsibility of the state to somehow save her, to help her take off the cloak and find herself. And yet, to paraphrase Roth's fictional narrative, "the suit the woman wears is all she's got."

Not acknowledging that reality and denying a religious woman the right to wear the vestments of her faith in public risks pushing her right off the sidewalk, either into oncoming traffic with no protection or visibility in the "public" thoroughfare or back into her "private" home with the blinds closed and the curtains drawn.[23] This is precisely the potential consequence of legislation that demands a particular way of presenting oneself to the world. If such a presentation is too difficult or even impossible for some reason — whether personal, family-related, community-driven, or faith-based — then women who dress differently will simply disappear.

Instead it may be possible to find ways to accompany a religious woman on the sidewalk, to converse with her even if part of her face is covered, to acknowledge that she may take up a lot of space with her double baby carriage. Above, we saw how the *eruv* turns the sidewalk into both public space and an extension of the home. Perhaps encouraging that extension, such that the private is opened up rather than kept closed, means that the religious woman's footprints can be traced in the fresh snow along with those of her neighbours. She might just modify her trajectory with the baby carriage and even become comfortable talking to the other children playing with her own at the sandbox in the neighbourhood park. Instead of telling her she cannot come outside as she is, we develop our side-by-side existence until we

---

23 For a more general discussion of religious views and the public sphere, see Iain Benson's contribution to this volume at Chapter 13.

each feel "at home" inside and out.

In a collection of essays written in Yiddish and now published in French and English, a Hasidic woman in Outremont writes of her daily life, the challenges of bringing up twelve children, and the tiny moments that constitute her relationships and responsibilities.[24] As she says, she lives with her curtains closed to the outside world. But she is prepared, through her writing, to extend an invitation into her home: to her friends in Yiddish, and to her next-door neighbours and fellow citizens in French and in English. By sharing her own space, space usually closed-off as private or domestic, she offers an opportunity to all of us to recognize the complex ways in which religious women organize and experience their overlapping membership in their communities of faith and in the broader community at large.

An invitation into a religious woman's home is much harder to come by than a confident handle on how to approach "competing rights." Yet, I would suggest that it has the potential to be turned into a much more meaningful story, one that sheds light on how claims of rights violations can be both understood and effectively addressed. A real mix of narratives and experiences serves as the multi-textured sidewalk space in which individuals and communities observe, acknowledge, and talk with each other. Sometimes, conflicts do occur and require resolution, yet it is futile to search for a constitutional or legislated or policy template that simply provides the answer and sidesteps complicated conversation. Each conflict, like each story of encounter on the sidewalk, will carry its own context and characters and consequences.

---

24 Malka Zipora, *Lekhaim! Chroniques de la vie hassidique à Montréal* (Montreal: Les éditions du passage, 2006); Malka Zipora, *Rather Laugh than Cry: Stories from a Hassidic Household* (Montreal: Véhicule Press, 2007).

C. Conclusion

Codes, charters, and constitutions are structures that frame our institutions and guide our collective character and well-being, but they coexist with daily dialogue and interaction in which we engage as neighbours and citizens. That is, while state instruments and institutions embody a "desire" to define and govern shared space, the "capacity" to actually oversee and govern the sidewalks belongs to the users. Another way to express this relationship between desire, on the one hand, and capacity, on the other, is to refer to "best practices." By observing, absorbing, assessing, and emulating the practices that best foster meaningful and satisfactory interactions, we develop the language and principles and rules that best sustain and promote mutually respectful everyday life. All sidewalk users are thus important subjects in the always-evolving study, articulation, and propagation of the norms of sidewalk conduct.

Attempting to address the competition between rights in an abstract way assumes that charters set out basic background rules that resolve any imagined or real conflict. If we recognize instead the complexity of that background through the multiple meanings of the shared sidewalk, we begin to realize how many sites of encounter exist, whether formal or informal, easy to see or quietly hidden; we refine our ability to draw upon those sites for enriched understanding and governance of both the users and uses of our many sidewalks.

Chapter 8

Framing Competing Human Rights Claims: The Promise of Shared Social Citizenship

Lorne Foster and Lesley Jacobs

A. Introduction

The practice of human rights in diverse societies like Canada has become more complex because diversity breeds competing human rights claims. With increased diversity comes the ordeal of more visible conflicts between different beliefs about how people should best lead their lives and what sorts of accommodations should be made for persons with different beliefs out of respect for human dignity and mutual recognition. Competing human rights claims are one reflection of this ordeal.

The institutions at the core of the Canadian human rights system — the courts and human rights commissions — are currently struggling to respond to the challenges presented by competing human rights claims in Canada. These challenges are multi-dimensional, involving deep philosophical questions about the nature of human rights, juridical questions about how cases involving competing human rights should be judged and decided, and policy questions about how in principle and practice issues involving competing human rights should be framed and approached in Canadian society.

This paper argues that the development of social policy for addressing competing human rights claims should be built on recognition that, even in a society like Canada that is characterized by a high degree of diversity, when persons press competing human rights claims, they are doing so in the context of shared social citizenship. This shared citizenship is significant in two respects. First of all, it captures the point that human rights claims are a social construction, not something that is ahistorical, abstract, or universal. In other words, human rights claims are community-specific. Secondly, shared citizenship provides some common ground for balancing competing human rights between parties in a dispute. This common ground — what we owe to each other as social citizens — offers to human rights commissions in Canada, like the Ontario Human Rights Commission (OHRC), direction for the development of a social policy framework that addresses competing human rights claims.

B. Social Constructionist Engagement with Human Rights

This paper assumes a *social constructionist* engagement with human rights. Social constructionism is a sociological theory of knowledge that considers how social phenomena develop in social contexts; and seeks to explore rigourously the nuances, contingencies, contestations, and meanings that are part and parcel of the social construction of reality. Within constructionist thought, rights are considered as a construct or "artifact" that is dependent on contingent variables of our social selves. There is now a substantive body of literature examining various aspects of the social practice of human rights. Here, rights are not simply given as divine will, or as transhistorical being, or as universal ontology — but are considered products of human social interaction with all its imbalances and imperfections. From this perspective, human rights are invariably the product of the balance of power between normatively oriented social actors in social-historical context.

The idea of the "universality" of rights, argued Malcolm

Waters, "is itself a human construct."[1] The social constructionist approach examines what actors actually do with human rights in everyday life, in institutional settings, and in other specific fields of political contestation. In developing a framework for understanding the social construction of rights, research has begun a move toward foreclosing on the age-old philosophical and ontological status debates, and focusing on the investigation of their meaning, use, and mobilization. Moreover, by declaring an interest in the "indeterminacy" of rights, social constructionist research is well-placed to investigate the shifting dynamics of rights disputes, or *competing human rights claims*, which are becoming increasing prevalent in our transnational and diverse world. By investigating the social relationships, practices, and struggles that mobilize right claims and rights talk, and animate rights disputes, the social constructionist approach can "bracket" the prevailing dominant discourses and provide a more dynamic and textured understanding of rights.

From a social constructionist perspective, human rights claims should be seen as the product of a particular place and time, and in this respect historically and socially contingent. This observation is significant in a number of ways. First, rights are not simply inalienable or natural; and they are not necessarily beneficial for the right holder to exercise. Second, human rights were invented in the modern age both as a product of the exercise of a particular type of political power and as a response to a particular form of power.[2] Contrary to Lockean political philosophy, "rights" and "freedom" were not in existence before "power," but rather are the distinctive products of the "new mode of life" that is modern global capitalism.[3] They have a paradoxical nature in that they allow us to challenge inequalities whilst

1 Malcolm Waters, "Human Rights and the Universalisation of Interests: Towards a Social Constructionist Approach" (1996) 30:3 Sociology 593.

2 Lynn Hunt, *Inventing Human Rights* (New York: WW Norton, 2007).

3 Anthony Woodiwiss, *Human Rights* (New York: Routledge, 2005) at 32.

contributing to the production of social divisions. Third, although human rights typically find expression in law, they have a life in society outside the law and do not rely solely on the juridical sphere to dictate their meaning. For this reason, the doctrine of human rights can go beyond law and form a fundamental moral basis for regulating contemporary social order.

C. Social Citizenship and Human Rights Claims

Although in diverse societies there is a high degree of fragmentation and potential for conflict, members of these societies share a common citizenship.[4] Citizenship means, for our purposes, "the collection of public claims and duties bestowed on people by the political order."[5] Social citizenship is at base a form of community membership, as opposed to a legal status bestowed by the state. (On this definition even undocumented immigrants or unsuccessful refugee applicants are social citizens.) From a social constructivist perspective, the public claims and duties that define citizenship are not changeless but rather socially contingent. In countries like Canada, the public is more than just the state; there is no doubt that the public nature of the claims and duties of citizenship regulate the relations between citizens. In other words, shared citizenship defines in part what we owe each other.

Human rights in a society that values and aspires to diversity should be, in our view, a constitutive component of full citizenship and standing on human rights claims is an expression of that shared citizenship. In a social constructionist ideal world, social actors go through human rights discourses to get to citizenship. In this ideal world, the mutual recognition of others as

---

4 Will Kymlicka, *Multicultural Citizenship* (Oxford: Oxford University Press, 1995).

5 Lawrence Mead, "Citizenship and Social Policy: T.H. Marshall and Poverty" (1997) 14:2 Social Philosophy and Policy 197 at 198.

human rights bearers is a function of shared citizenship, which shifts the terms of debate from the problems of balancing or reconciling competing human rights claims to their democratic citizenship potential. Here, competitive practice and conflicting rights claims at the individual and collective level are conceived as disciplinary threads in weaving the social fabric of a fulsome and expanded "social citizenship." This social ideal is an emergent reality that extends the meaning of citizenship rights beyond conventional notions of legal and political equality to encompass rights of inclusion. These social citizenship rights of inclusion refer to guarantees of equal opportunity, equity, and non-discrimination for socially disadvantaged groups — such as women, Aboriginal peoples, and other people of colour — to participate fully in the public as well as economic life and to expect a reasonable level of respect and recognition from others. In this ideal social constructivist world, the task of state and institutional social actors, the courts, and human rights commissions is to increase the access points to justice. Shared citizenship provides, in other words, the context for these actors to advance competing human rights claims against each other and the state.

This idea that shared citizenship frames competing human rights claims differs from how too often parties in these disputes as well as the media and other interpretative communities frame competing human rights. Rather than identifying shared citizenship, these conflicts are framed often in terms of the rights of "others." "Others" are precisely not people with whom we share anything other than perhaps a common humanity. This language of the rights of others is exemplified in the cases of the human rights claims of refugees or recent immigrants.[6] And the most oft-cited examples of disputes involving competing human rights claims in Canada revolve around immigrants or refugees with

---

6 Seyla Benhabib, *The Rights of Others: Aliens, Residents and Citizens* (Cambridge, UK: Cambridge University Press, 2004).

their "foreign" cultural practices. Framed in terms of the rights of others, there is unfortunately little promise of striking a fair balance between competing human rights claims, for there is no common ground. Framing these disputes instead as ones involving parties who share a social citizenship means that there is some common ground between them, for citizenship defines in part what the parties owe each other. What do these parties owe each other? At minimum, they owe each other mutual respect and recognition, which is in most cases enough to sway the parties to join a process where the competing human rights claims are balanced against each other.

The modern concept of citizenship, as we noted, entails recognition of a full and inclusive membership in society. The extent of this membership is the outcome of political contestation. Following World War II, the British sociologist TH Marshall offered an important analysis of citizenship that concerns the content of mutual recognition and empowerment and how they may be realized in the context of market-based inequalities. Marshall divided citizenship into three elements: civil, political, and social. Civil rights include "liberty of person, freedom of speech, thought and faith, the right to own property . . . and the right to justice."[7] Political rights for Marshall included the right to vote and the right to run for political office. The institutions he associated most closely with these first two elements were the courts and Parliament.[8] But Marshall was also concerned with social rights — "the right to a modicum of economic welfare and security . . . according to the standards prevailing in society"[9] — and he viewed the welfare state as the institutional mechanism for the distribution of these rights. Through the welfare state, provisions are made for public education, universal health care, and public housing and income

7 TH Marshall, "Citizenship and Social Class" in TH Marshall & Tom Bottomore, *Citizenship and Social Class* (London: Pluto Press, 1991) at 8.

8 *Ibid.*

9 *Ibid.*

security programs. Thus, social rights make possible a fuller expression of citizenship for those groups who would be disadvantaged in terms of resources and power and, hence, would suffer most acutely from insecurities generated by a market economy. Without the provision of social rights, gross inequalities would undermine the equality of political and civil rights inherent in the idea of citizenship.[10]

Marshall's argument for social citizenship can be read as a dynamic account of the social-historical development of citizenship in Western society, and as a relentless struggle between the extension of political equality and social rights on the one hand, and the capitalist market and social class on the other hand.[11] In this account, civil citizenship becomes the arena for this struggle with each side trying to limit the reach of the other by defining the scope of civil rights in terms favourable to its side. And this struggle is then deflected back into the political arena. That is, Marshall provides a picture of a dynamic struggle in which the proponents of the market are continually seeking to reign in the spread of social rights by redefining civil protections in individualist terms while seeking to confine political equality to the sphere of the state. The proponents of social citizenship, by contrast, are seeking to expand not just a steadily higher level of social services, rendering money income less relevant, but more significantly, to forge within civil society a sphere of "citizenship" that complements political citizenship in the state. Thus the struggle for social rights against the market and social class becomes a struggle for the very definition of civil society itself.[12]

---

10 Ruth Lister, *Citizenship: Feminist Perspectives* (London: MacMillian Press, 1997).

11 Peter Breiner, "Is Social Citizenship Really Outdated? TH Marshall Revisited" (Paper delivered at the annual meeting of the Western Political Science Association, Albuquerque, New Mexico, 25 May 2009), online: All Academic www.allacademic.com/meta/p97572_index.html.

12 *Ibid.*

In Marshall's view, through this historical struggle of equity-seeking groups the meaning of citizenship rights in capitalist societies have been expanded beyond formal legal and political equality to encompass social equality rights, including the right to a minimum level of economic security and social welfare assured by the state. Here is contained Marshall's notion of an emergent universal dictate that all members of the political community ought to have a fundamental claim to certain social services and programs such as food security, health care, education, unemployment insurance, environmental safety, and so on. The degree of universality of these reforms is the degree to which the concept has been realized. Social citizenship implies an equality of status in the social realm, in the same way that contemporary or prevailing versions of citizenship denote equality in the political realm: just as there is universal enfranchisement, there ought to be universal entitlement to certain social security guarantees Within civil society and the contemporary global order.

The dynamic vision we are advancing sees shared social citizenship being extended from a form of membership that is a response to the challenges of class inequality in a capitalist economy to one that addresses the challenges of increased diversity in Canadian society. Human rights institutions grounded on shared citizenship are invaluable for the recognition, protection, and promotion of rights of inclusion and developing policy for balancing competing human rights claims that arise from that diversity.

D. The New Mandate of the Ontario Human Rights Commission

Comprehending the history of human rights protection in Ontario from the perspective of a theoretical argument about the linkages between social citizenship and the emerging importance of rights of inclusion provides a fruitful vocabulary for situating the new role of the OHRC. In more concrete terms, our approach to competing human rights claims can be shown to fit well with the new mandate of the OHRC given by the *Human Rights Code Amendment Act, 2006*.[13] The new mandate requires the Commission to bridge the gap between public policy and justice administration. Thereby, the Commission is now responsible for developing public policy as well as addressing tension and conflict in the province, in order to bring people and communities together to help resolve differences. This new mandate bestows the unique capacity to address multi-faceted social issues with a broad range of processes — those both rule and policy-based, and those left to discretionary decision makers.

Under the mandate of the new Act, the Commission has the role of monitoring the state of human rights and reporting directly to the people of Ontario. It has been given the power to

- expand its work in promoting a culture of human rights in the province,
- conduct public inquiries,
- initiate applications (formerly called "complaints"),
- intervene in proceedings at the Human Rights Tribunal of Ontario (HRTO), and
- focus on engaging in proactive measures to prevent discrimination using public education, policy development, research, and analysis.

The interpretive principles governing Ontario's *Human Rights Code*[14] have been left to the courts. But the new mandate shifts the institutional focus of the OHRC from a more legalistic to a more social-policy approach. In the words of the Attorney General of Ontario,

---

13 SO 2006, c 30.

14 RSO 1990, c H.19 [*Code*].

> The Ontario Human Rights Commission works to promote, protect and advance human rights. Its main focus is to address the root causes of discrimination. Activities include research and monitoring, policy development, and education and training. The Commission also conducts human rights inquiries and may initiate human rights applications or intervene in important cases before the Tribunal. Through outreach, cooperation and partnership the Commission aims to advance Ontario's human rights culture.[15]

In the old human rights structure, the issues of Commission gate-keeping and delay certainly reveal the limitations of the system. The challenge for the new Commission is affecting social policy by bringing people and communities together to help resolve differences, while being at risk of becoming an object of the tension and conflict they seek to resolve. Yet it must be said that, as sophisticated articulations of constitutionally-protected rights emanate from the courts and laypersons perceive a broad spectrum of wrong treatment as at least potentially actionable discrimination or harassment, the commission system cannot be expected to bear the full weight of responsibility for achieving anti-discrimination social goals. Rosanna Langer (2006) has argued that government-sponsored anti-discrimination enforcement must be situated within a broader set of common practices such as municipal accessibility plans (for example, those stipulated under the *Ontarians with Disabilities Act, 2001*[16]), progressive employment legislation, in-house corporate and employer anti-discrimination and anti-harassment "best practices," and community-based educational initiatives.[17] A healthy network

15 Ministry of the Attorney General, "Human Rights in Ontario" (Toronto: Ministry of the Attorney General, 2008), online: Ministry of the Attorney General www.attorneygeneral.jus.gov.on.ca/english/news/2008/20080630-ohrc-brochure-en.pdf.

16 SO 2001, c 32.

17 Rosanna Langer, "Publics and Counter-Publics: Exploring the Contested

of anti-discrimination practices is the best insurance of a vital normative fabric of human rights protections.

Meanwhile, the pragmatism of seeking social policy solutions, as opposed to judicial ones, fits comfortably within the new mandate of the OHRC. Its new flexibility can also mean increasing the range and repertoire of remedies for fulfilling social justice goals. This includes, and also opens up, the possibility of incorporating Alternative Dispute Resolution (ADR) and "win-win approaches," rights-based mediation, and the collaborative problem-solving techniques that integrate practical experience with theoretical knowledge. ADR, for example, has experienced increasing acceptance and utilization primarily because of a perception of greater flexibility, costs below those of traditional litigation, and speedy resolution of disputes. In recent years there has been more discussion about taking a systems approach in order to offer different kinds of options to people who are in conflict, and to foster appropriate and effective dispute resolution. Some cases and some complaints are viewed to be appropriate for formal grievance or for the courts or for the police or for a tribunal, and the like. Other conflicts could be settled by the parties if they had enough support and coaching, and yet other cases need third-party mediation or arbitration. Thus ADR usually means a method that is not the courts, and involves processes and techniques that act as a means for disagreeing parties to come to an agreement short of litigation. ADR considers all the possible responsible options for conflict resolution that are relevant for a given issue.

Ultimately, the social justice mandate of the OHRC is configured by the assurance of neutral (non-advocate, non-adversarial) communicative interactions, which open up the possibility for

---

Nature of the Public Interest In Domestic Human Rights Administration" (Paper presented at Symposium Proceedings: "Values, Ethics and the Public Sector: How to Serve the Public Interest?" Saint Paul University Ethics Centre, Ottawa, Canada, 2006).

contextual problem-solving for the mutual empowerment of human rights bearers. In this world, access to justice ought not to require formal processes for its assurance. The ideal OHRC would be responsible for engaging the public interest goals in anti-discrimination beyond a formulaic rigidity of law, by broadening the constellation of remedies and preventing the premature legalization of individual and social harms.

E. Reframing the Competing Human Rights Debate

Under section 29 of the *Code*, the OHRC has been designated the broad responsibility to promote, protect, and advance respect for human rights in Ontario, to protect the public interest, and to eliminate discriminatory practices. In addition, within this wide mandate, section 30 authorizes the OHRC to prepare, approve, and publish human rights policies to provide guidance on interpreting its provisions. These powers to both promote a culture of human rights and develop anti-discrimination policy do not "beef-up" the province's human rights administration system so much as simplify its focus; making it less cumbersome organizationally than the old enforcement and compliance model, and potentially more responsive in addressing an increasingly diverse population and more complex rights scenarios. The new discrimination prevention model provides the necessary administrative space from which to undertake more robust and progressive intervention into the ever-increasing intricacies of modern rights claims and the growing intractability of rights conflicts and disputes.

In a discrimination prevention model, the OHRC can assume a role as the instrument of the positive state, facilitating the realization of human potential by developing human rights policies that provide cutting-edge and innovative interpretations of human rights law, opening up possibilities for expanding the protections of the *Code* in order to address new and emerging human rights issues and trends, incorporating international understandings of human rights, and breaking down social and economic barriers to the exercise of positive freedom. In this regard, the discrimination prevention model should be understood as an authorization to deal in areas of new and more inclusive citizenship. The OHRC's role in dealing with "tension and conflict" and bringing people and communities together to help resolve differences recommends a foundation for mutual recognition and empowerment of human rights claimants, consistent with the remedial objectives of the *Code*. This model has to have the capacity to effectively address human rights scenarios and disputes by building on a pattern of practices, and creating the necessary social space for parties with rights claims and disputes to engage in interpersonal responsiveness and constructive interaction. In a discrimination prevention model, the norm of human rights administration shifts to a more inclusive and respectful approach to marginalized and historically disadvantaged persons, with the goal to give people a voice and diminish any power imbalances.

How does the idea of shared social citizenship in a diverse society help us to make sense of the OHRC's new mandate? For Marshall and social constructionist thought, citizenship is a dynamic phenomenon that flexes the dimensions of political, social, and civil life. In a human rights context, it is a logical extension of inclusive citizenship for legal rights to be reinforced and further developed in civil society through self-reflective social policy initiatives that create opportunities for empowerment and recognition. The discrimination prevention model affords the opportunity for the new Commission to use its mandate to promote rights of inclusion in diverse Ontario by resolving human rights claims and disputes in a manner that is respectful, efficient, transparent, and more in-line with anti-oppression principles and transformative approaches than the former process. More than simply enforcing the provisions of the *Code*, the OHRC is now mandated as a positive state actor to expose the dimensions of power embedded in historical-social and political contexts and to make more room for power considerations when balancing competing human rights claims.

F. Implications for a Social Policy Framework

It has been suggested above that one of the most fundamental insights of a social constructivist approach to human rights is an appreciation of the context in which competing human rights claims are made. In particular, in Ontario shared citizenship in an advanced capitalist global society provides the context and the means for differently situated persons to advance competing human rights claims. These competing human rights claims do not reflect natural inequalities nor innate differences and conflicts between persons. They reflect instead power dynamics and socially constructed differences among people. But the fact that this conflict and competition is embedded in human rights discourse expresses the social fact that these individuals also share a social citizenship, and this shared citizenship can be a resource for developing social policy that frames competing human rights claims.

This approach helps us to identify three important elements that should be considered in the development of a policy framework for the OHRC. The first element revolves around the centrality of the access-to-justice agenda in its new mandate. Social constructivism highlights the political and economic differences and ideological supports that have created the social cleavages which rouse human rights movements in the first place. The OHRC, as an institution committed to human rights in Ontario, must in any balancing-rights policy recognize the full continuum of social life, from competition to conflict, and the dimensions of power, including their intrusion into the political and economic and ideological structures of society. Human rights discourse, in the absence of a clear focus and understanding of differential access to power and resources, loses sight of the principle of equality of citizenship. In other words, the policy framework must have integrated within it a component of access to justice.

The second element provides direction for the educational component of the policy framework. It is important that the educational component be organized around the significance of shared citizenship as a resource for mitigating conflict and being proactive in ensuring that conflict does not escalate. Seeing different claimants as fellow citizens and viewing those citizens in a way that is empathetic holds much greater promise than an adversarial process where there are only winners and losers.

The third element requires accommodating for the social contingency of particular competitions between human rights claims. The challenge of a modern human rights system is to craft social policy in a way that recognizes the overriding importance of human rights protections and that is flexible enough and fluid enough to allow for changing power dynamics within our society, as well as evolving knowledge and new insights about human rights and discrimination.

Chapter 9

Reaching Equilibrium between Conflicting Rights

Errol P. Mendes

A. Contextual Equilibrium Versus Conflicting Rights under the *Canadian Charter of Rights and Freedoms*[1]

One of the most overlooked quotes from the Supreme Court of Canada is the landmark ruling of Dickson CJC on the overarching values to be kept in mind in interpreting the *Charter*, including section 1, in *R v Oakes*.[2] He stated that the key values of the *Charter* can be found in the phrase "free and democratic society" and it should also be used as the "ultimate standard" for interpretation of section 1. Chief Justice Dickson articulated this ultimate standard in the following terms:

> Inclusion of these words as the final standard of justification for limits on rights and freedoms refers the Court to the very purpose for which the *Charter* was originally entrenched in the Constitution: Canadian society is to be free and democratic. The Court must be guided by the values and principles essential to a free and democratic society which I believe embody, to name but a few, respect for the inherent dignity of the human person,

---

1 *Canadian Charter of Rights and Freedoms,* Part I of the *Constitution Act, 1982*, being Schedule B to the *Canada Act 1982* (UK) 1982, c 11 [*Charter*].

2 *R v Oakes*, [1986] 1 SCR 103 [*Oakes*].

> commitment to social justice and equality, accommodation of a wide variety of beliefs, respect for cultural and group identity, and faith in social and political institutions which enhance the participation of individuals and groups in society. The underlying values and principles of a free and democratic society are the genesis of the rights and freedoms guaranteed by the *Charter* and the ultimate standard against which a limit on a right or freedom must be shown, despite its effect, to be reasonable and demonstrably justified.[3]

While these values will inevitably conflict in theory, what the Court in *Oakes* and in subsequent decision have strived to do is to "hunch" out a jurisprudential framework of what I call "contextual equilibrium" in concrete cases where these values may conflict. In some of the leading decisions on the *Charter* the conflict has been between two sets of rights, but in other cases between rights and the other values not exhaustively listed by Dickson CJC in his statement on what are the foundational societal values of a free and democratic society. In both cases, but especially in the latter case, the focus will immediately turn to the proportionality analysis in section 1 of the *Charter*. This analysis will focus primarily on the situation where the values underlying two sets of rights may appear to be in conflict.

Because these values, even though they may conflict in theory, are the fundamental values of the *Charter*, they are supposed to guide not only the development of the common law, but also the interpretation of statutory law in Canada, including quasi-constitutional human rights legislation, such as Ontario's *Human Rights Code*.[4]

Justice Frank Iacobucci, one of the most influential justices on the Supreme Court to shape the evolution of the *Charter*, has proposed that rather than addressing conflict of rights, there should

3 *Ibid* at para 64.

4 *Human Rights Code*, RSO 1990, c H.19 [*Code*].

be a focus on *reconciling* rights.[5] This is crucial because the Supreme Court has insisted that there is no hierarchy of rights to be inferred from the jurisprudence of the *Charter* and that no one right should be privileged at the expense of another. This critical ruling by the Supreme Court was firmly stated by Lamer CJC in *Dagenais v Canadian Broadcasting Corporation*:

> A hierarchical approach to rights, which places some over others, must be avoided, both when interpreting the *Charter* and when developing the common law. When the protected rights of two individuals come into conflict, as can occur in the case of publication bans, *Charter* principles require a balance to be achieved that fully respects the importance of both sets of rights.[6]

The way in which Iaccobucci J and most *Charter* decisions have attempted to avoid the emergence of a hierarchy of rights is through the fundamental appreciation of rights in context. Before this can be illustrated, Iaccobucci J points out that the reconciliation of rights must be distinguished from balancing rights under section 1. While Section 1 analysis deals with putting the onus on the government to justify the violation of a *Charter* right, Iaccobucci J argues that the reconciliation of rights focuses on the values of different *Charter* rights in dealing with the problem before the Court. This requires an examination of the underlying interests at stake in the context in which the *Charter* rights are being asserted.[7]

While Iaccobucci J may wish to call this reconciliation of rights, it is suggested that what is really occuring is an attempt to

---

5 Frank Iacobucci, "Reconciling Rights: The Supreme Court of Canada's Approach to Competing *Charter* Rights" (2003) 20 Sup Ct L Rev 137 ["Reconciling Rights"].

6 *Dagenais v Canadian Broadcasting Corporation*, [1994] 3 SCR 835 at 877 [*Dagenais*].

7 "Reconciling Rights," above note 5 at 144.

put rights that seem to conflict into an equilibrium depending on what particular interests are at stake in any particular fact situation. This is also a key objective of the balancing test under section 1 of the *Oakes* test. For that reason, I do not agree with the learned justice that there is much difference between the framework involved in the balancing of rights and that of reconciling rights. They both involve what I call searching for the "contextual equilibrium" of rights that may at first seem to be in conflict.

The examination of the Supreme Court's modification of the common law on publication bans in *Dagenais*[8] is a classic case of reconciling rights as opposed to balancing rights according to Iaccobucci J. In *Dagenais*, Lamer CJC, in modifying the common law rules on such bans, ruled that it was inappropriate to always favour the fair trial rights protected by section 11(d) of the *Charter* over the rights of free expression protected by section 2(b) of the *Charter*. Chief Justice Lamer asserted that the common law rule "must be adapted so as to require a consideration both of the objectives of a publication ban, and the proportionality of the ban to its effect on protected *Charter* rights."[9] The modified rule may be stated as follows:

> a) Such a ban is necessary in order to prevent a real and substantial risk to the fairness of the trial, because reasonably available alternative measures will not prevent the risk; and
>
> b) The salutary effects of the publication ban outweigh the deleterious effects to the free expression of those affected by the ban.[10]

The values of both rights were taken into account on the facts of the case and the Court established the contextual equilibrium of both rights, but while the section 11(d) rights are very important

---

8 *Dagenais*, above note 6.

9 *Ibid* at 839.

10 *Ibid* at 878.

the ban was far too broad on the facts as it prohibited the broadcasting of the *Boys of St. Vincent* series throughout Canada as well as reporting on the ban itself. Other alternative measures were available that would impinge less on the freedom of expression right such as changing the venue or sequestering jurors.

While Iaccobucci J calls this an exercise in reconciling rights, it still amounts to finding the contextual equilibrium between rights that is also one of the key objectives of the balancing tests under section 1 of the *Oakes* test. Justice Iaccobucci insists that the difference between rights balancing and rights reconciliation is that the former connotes assigning primacy to one right over another right or interest under the section 1 analysis. In contrast the learned judge argues that reconciliation of rights is the exercise that courts engage in when they define the content and scope of rights in relation to one another.[11]

What is surprising is that Iacobucci J also points to what I consider perhaps the paradigm of reconciling rights or what I term "contextual equilibrium" as the application of the traditional balancing test, namely the decision on *R v Keegstra*.[12] It is also suggested that the approach taken by the Supreme Court in interpreting the two-stage approach to rights interpretation under the *Charter* assists in understanding how to reach the point of contextual equilibrium where rights may seem to be in conflict. In *Keegstra*, as in other landmark freedom of expression cases, the Court held that all expressive content (except those manifested in violent form) is, in principle, protected under section 2(b) of the *Charter*.

This principle is a good starting point for any factual situation where the right of free expression may be in conflict with other rights. While the willful promotion of hate propaganda is therefore protected by the *Charter*, it is through the section 1 lens

---

11 "Reconciling Rights," above note 5 at 142.

12 *R v Keegstra*, [1990] 3 SCR 697 [*Keegstra*].

that we have to look at putting the right of free expression into contextual equilibrium with other rights that may seem to be in conflict. It was in the context that the Court ultimately ruled that the equality rights of minorities and the protection and promotion of Canadians' multicultural heritage were in the societal interest under section 27 of the *Charter*; the harmful effects of hate propaganda on society, including combating racial and ethnic tension along with potential violence, and international obligations against racial discrimination and hate propaganda would contribute to upholding the constitutionality of section 319(2) of the *Criminal Code*.[13]

What could be the lesson of this approach to what seemed like a conflict of some of the most fundamental rights and values articulated by Dickson J in his interpretation of a free and democratic society? I suggest the key part of the attempt to find a contextual equilibrium of the rights and interests involved in the *Keegstra* fact situation was articulated in this crucial statement by Dickson CJC for the majority:

> One must ask whether the expression prohibited by s. 319(2) is tenuously connected to the values underlying s. 2(b) so as to make the restriction "easier to justify than other infringements . . . ."
>
> From the outset, I wish to make clear that in my opinion the expression prohibited by s. 319(2) is not closely linked to the rationale underlying s. 2(b). Examining the values identified in *Ford* and *Irwin Toy* as fundamental to the protection of free expression, arguments can be made for the proposition that each of these values is diminished by the suppression of hate propaganda. While none of these arguments is spurious, I am of the opinion that expression intended to promote the hatred of identifiable groups is of limited importance when measured against free expression values.

---

13 RSC 1985, c C-46.

. . . .

> As I have said already, I am of the opinion that hate propaganda contributes little to the aspirations of Canadians or Canada in either the quest for truth, the promotion of individual self-development or the protection and fostering of a vibrant democracy where the participation of all individuals is accepted and encouraged. While I cannot conclude that hate propaganda deserves only marginal protection under the s. 1 analysis, I can take cognizance of the fact that limitations upon hate propaganda are directed at a special category of expression which strays some distance from the spirit of s. 2(b), and hence conclude that "restrictions on expression of this kind might be easier to justify than other infringements of s. 2(b)" (*Royal College*, *supra*, at p. 247).[14]

The strong dissent in *Keegstra* by McLachlin J (as she then was) focused on how, in primarily principled argumentation, the general prohibition against hate propaganda in section 319(2) of the *Criminal Code* was overbroad, too vague, and subjective and therefore failed under each part of the *Oakes* test.[15] In contrast, the main thrust of the majority's decision as articulated by Dickson CJC seemed focused on seeking a contextual equilibrium in concrete situations where the individual right of free expression in the particular context of the facts in *Keegstra* conflict with the group rights of the targeted minorities to equality. In order to find that equilibrium, Dickson CJC sought to locate the core of the rights being asserted and then ascertain, based on the facts of the particular context in *Keegstra*, whether those core values of the rights asserted were indeed at play or were really peripheral in the actual factual context. Then the rights whose core values were not at play would have to be placed in a just equilibrium

---

14 *Keegstra*, above note 12 at 766.

15 For an analysis and critique of McLachlin J's dissent see Lorraine Weinrib, "Hate Promotion in a Free and Democratic Society: *R v Keegstra*" (1991) 36 McGill LJ 1416 at 1446.

with rights whose core values were at play.

This approach can be termed balancing rights, reconciling rights, or, my preferred term, "contextual equilibrium" in concrete factual situations. In *Trinity Western University v College of Teachers (British Columbia)*[16] the Court faced one of the most controversial of the so-called "conflict of rights" contexts. As is well-known, here the Court had to reconcile, balance, or find a contextual equilibrium between the religious freedoms of individuals choosing to attend an evangelical institution and the equality concerns of potential discrimination against students in the BC school system. The Court ruled that the *Charter* did not apply but went on to make the point that there was not really a conflict of rights *on the particular facts involved*. Instead the majority ruled that any potential conflict between religious freedoms and equality rights should be resolved through the proper delineation of the rights and values involved. On the particular facts of the case a delineation of the rights involved did not indicate a conflict of rights. While not applying a section 1 analysis, the majority seemed to introduce a balancing type of analysis by stating that neither of the rights that were involved were absolute and that the proper place to draw the line is generally between belief and conduct. In the context of the facts in the case, the freedom to hold beliefs was held to be (as it should always be) broader than the freedom to act on them. Therefore given that there was no concrete evidence that training teachers at Trinity Western fosters discrimination in the public schools of BC, the freedom of individuals to adhere to certain religious beliefs while at the institution had to be respected.

The Court did warn however, that if there was evidence of acting on those beliefs, the context would shift dramatically. If a teacher in the public school system engages in discriminatory conduct, that teacher can be subject to disciplinary proceedings

16 [2001] 1 SCR 772 [*Trinity Western*].

before the BC College of Teachers. Implied in this ruling is the fact that if evidence of discrimination did take place, the core values of the equality rights of students would be at play, while the freedom of religion right of the teacher to discriminate would be peripheral and therefore be legitimately circumscribed. This more concrete context would produce a contextual equilibrium of the rights involved, just as in *Keegstra* decision. It is suggested that whether one terms this hunching out of a framework to deal with seeming conflicts of rights is called balancing, reconciliation, or contextual equilibrium, it is manifest in a wide range of cases.

These cases include not only the area of publication bans, as in the *Dagenais* case, but also in related cases involving not only rights seemingly in conflict, but also rights conflicting with legitimate societal values such as in *R v Mentuck*,[17] other religious freedom cases such as *B(R) v Children's Aid Society of Metropolitan Toronto*,[18] *Sydicat Northcrest v Amselem*,[19] *Multani v Commission scolaire Marguerite-Bourgeoys*,[20] and *Reference re Same-Sex Marriage*.[21] In the last decision, the Court stressed that a contextual framework of actual facts is critical to find an appropriate equilibrium between rights that may seem to conflict. When the federal government referred the draft of Bill C-38, *An Act respecting certain aspects of legal capacity for marriage for civil purposes*,[22] it had hoped the Court would provide a framework to resolve the several levels of potential conflicts (for example, between freedom of religion and sexual orientation equality rights and over the amendment of the common law to include same-sex marriage and the rights of religious officials to refuse to be involved in the solemnization of same-sex marriages). The

17 [2001] 3 SCR 442.

18 [1995] 1 SCR 315.

19 [2004] 2 SCR 551 [*Amselem*].

20 [2006] 1 SCR 256 [*Multani*].

21 [2004] 3 SCR 698 [*Same-Sex Marriage*].

22 1st Sess, 38th Parl, 2004–05 (Royal Assent, 30 June 2005).

Court rightly resisted giving a comprehensive approach to the reconciling of seeming conflicting rights absent a concrete contextual factual framework.

What the Court did rule on, was the foundational principle behind any contextual framework by stating that the mere recognition of the equality rights of one group does not violate the rights of another group. Extending the right of same-sex couples to marry did not, of itself, conflict with any other *Charter* right. In a critical part of the decision, the Supreme Court almost defined what I have termed contextual equilibrium of conflicting rights when it stated that "[c]onflicts of rights do not imply conflict with the *Charter*; rather the resolution of such conflicts generally occurs within the ambit of the *Charter* itself by way of internal balancing and delineation."[23] I would add that such balancing and delineation can only take place within the context of concrete facts as opposed to a general statement of principles. The Supreme Court agreed by stating that it would not rule on whether the proposed legislation would result in an impermissible conflict of rights absent an actual factual context.[24]

However, the Court did affirm that the freedom of religion is a broad one that is jealously guarded under the *Charter* and includes, as in the *Trinity Western* decision, the right to implement religious beliefs through practice and the performance of religious rights. The decisions in *Amselem* and *Multani* have confirmed that this freedom extends to individuals within the religious group so that sincerely held beliefs as to religious practices will be protected under the *Charter*, even if not generally practiced by others in the religious association.

A counter-argument to the above thesis of contextual equilibrium of rights is that in many contexts, especially in religious freedom cases, the real conflict is between collective rights and

---

23 *Same-Sex Marriage*, above note 21 at para 52.

24 *Ibid* at para 51.

individual rights to equality and non-discrimination. It could then be argued that it is very difficult, if not impossible, to find a contextual equilibrium when collective and individual rights collide. The Supreme Court of Canada does not seem to agree. In the *Ford v Quebec (Attorney General)*[25] the Court held, *inter alia*, that sections 58 and 69 of the *Charter of the French Language*[26] infringed the freedom of expression as protected both by Quebec's *Charter of Human Rights and Freedoms*[27] and section 2(b) of the *Charter*. In its section 1 analysis, the Court acknowledged that Bill 101 was a response to a pressing and substantial concern and that there was a rational connection between protecting the French language and assuring that the reality of Quebec society is communicated through the "*visage linguistique*." This was an acknowledgement by the Court that there was a primordial collective linguistic right of the francophone majority at play. The Court ultimately ruled that Bill 101 had failed the proportionality part of the *Oakes* test for not realizing that there was an alternative solution to put both the freedom of expression and the collective linguistic rights of the francophone majority into a contextual equilibrium:

> Whereas requiring the predominant display of the French language, even in marked predominance, would be proportional to the goal of promoting and maintaining a French "*visage linguistique*" in Quebec and therefore justified under the Quebec *Charter* and the Canadian *Charter*, requiring the exclusive use of French has not been so justified. French could be required in addition to any other language or it could be required to have greater visibility than that accorded to other languages.[28]

---

25 *Ford v Quebec (Attorney General)*, [1988] 2 SCR 712 [*Ford*].

26 RSQ c C-11, s 1 [Bill 101].

27 RSQ c C-12.

28 *Ford*, above note 25 at para 73.

I have argued elsewhere that many, if not most of the rights under the *Charter* can be regarded as collective rights in the sense that they can be experienced in the context of group activities such as freedom of religion, association, assembly, expression, and the rights to liberty and security of the person.[29] In some contexts one could regard the claiming of individual rights as a way of advancing the rights of a collectivity. Indeed the claim by individuals that Bill 101 violated their individual freedom of expression was also a claim that the collective freedom of expression rights of the English speaking minority in Quebec was being violated.

What is often termed collective rights is part of humanity's desire to "self-collect" to belong in community.[30] This is such an essential part of existence that without the ability to fulfill it, we cannot be fully human. The fact of human existence requires that we experience the world as much through community as through individual personhood. Rights are part of the world we experience both as individuals and in community and that is what makes them inalienable and deserving of protection. Contextual equilibrium requires societies that claim to be free and democratic to do justice to both sets of rights in concrete situations.[31]

In this sense, "contextual equilibrium" moves away from the implication in the term "conflicting rights" that when such conflict occurs one right must trump over another. Contextual equilibrium instead can be analogized to a radar screen where in any factual context the centre of the screen is the core values underlying each of the contested rights. It is suggested that in the vast majority of cases where there is a conflict of rights, one set of rights is closer to the core values underlying that right than the

---

29 Errol P Mendes, "Two Solitudes, Freedom of Expression and Collective Linguistic Rights in Canada, A Case Study of the *Ford* Decision" (1991) 1 NJCL 283.

30 *Ibid*.

31 *Ibid*.

other one, which may be on the periphery. In the case of the prohibition of the vilest forms of hate propaganda, for example, the equality and security of the person rights of the targeted groups are closer to the core values of those rights than the freedom of expression rights of the hate monger. The core values of freedom of expression, as enunciated by Dickson CJC in the *Keegstra* decision, are quite distant from the actual contextual free expression of a hate monger.

B. Contextual Equilibrium Versus Conflicting Rights under Ontario's *Human Rights Code*

In a paper prepared for the Ontario Human Rights Commission (OHRC) in August 2005 titled "Balancing Conflicting Rights: Towards an Analytical Framework" the unnamed author proposes an intriguing and creative framework for balancing conflicting rights.[32] The OHRC paper first highlights what is termed "two main paradigms" for balancing conflicting rights. The two are termed "principled" and "pragmatic" balancing. The two are regarded not as binary opposites but as necessarily intertwined in the analysis of any conflicting rights case. I will suggest below that both paradigms are an integral part of what I call the "contextual equilibrium of rights" that may seem in conflict and may, in fact, be an integral part of one paradigm.

The principled balancing paradigm is stated to focus on the values underlying the *Code* and the *Charter* and delineates the rights in such a way as to avoid conflict. The pragmatic approach looks to provisions in the *Code*, such as the exception sections of the *Code* and the duty to accommodate, to allow two conflicting rights to be managed within a particular context. The OHRC

---

32 Ontario Human Rights Commission, "Balancing Conflicting Rights: Towards an Analytical Framework" (OHRC, August 2005), online: OHRC www.ohrc.on.ca/sites/default/files/attachments/Balancing_conflicting_rights%3A_Towards_an_analytical_framework.pdf [OHRC paper].

paper first suggests that it is imperative that only actual conflicts of rights are approached as balancing tasks under either or both paradigms. I suggest that the determination of whether there is an actual conflict or not is part of the first step of ascertaining the contextual equilibrium of rights that may only seem to be in conflict. Indeed the *Trinity Western* decision of the Supreme Court described above is a classic example of this first step of the search for contextual equilibrium.

The Nova Scotia Board of Inquiry decision in *Berry v Manor Inn* regarding a women's right to breastfeed in public is another example.[33] This and other oft-cited examples of two different claims for reasonable accommodation illustrated by the author of the OHRC paper are usually not rights conflicts but an inquiry into whether the specific needs of each rights claimer can be met within the parameters set by the *Code*.

C. The Principled Balancing Approach: The Preamble to the *Code* and Interpretative Principles

It is suggested in the OHRC paper that the values in the preamble to the *Code* and how the courts have interpreted them bring into focus the need to balance individual and group rights along with community development and well-being in any claims brought under the *Code*.[34] As discussed above, Dickson CJC's elaboration

---

33 *Berry v Manor Inn* (1980), 1 CHRR D/152.

34 OHRC paper, above note 32 at 7. The author lists the four key principles of the *Code* that are elicited from the Preamble as follows:

1. Recognition of the dignity and worth of every person;
2. Provision of equal rights and opportunities without discrimination that is contrary to the law;
3. Creation of a climate of understanding and mutual respect, so that;
4. Each person feels a part of the community and able to contribute fully to the development and well being of the community and the Province.

of the values of a free and democratic society under the *Charter* reinforces the principled position that individual and group rights are inextricably linked in the realm of human existence. For that reason, I would contest the claim that where the legislated exceptions in the *Code* are protective of certain collective rights, they should always be interpreted in a manner which predetermines the outcome in favour of any asserted individual right against discrimination, no matter how marginal. Where these exceptions are intended to protect fundamental collective rights, the provisions in the exceptions may well be an attempt to lay out a principled framework for contextual equilibrium between the individual rights to be free of discrimination and the collective rights encapsulated in the enumerated exceptions. Indeed the fundamental purpose of the *Code* is the removal of discrimination, but this can also include unprincipled discrimination against the collective exercise of individual rights protected not only by the *Code*, but also by the *Charter*, which is now the supreme law of the land. Given the adamant rulings of the Supreme Court that there is no hierarchy of rights in the *Charter*, it should be assumed that there is also no principle in the *Code* that would give an automatic priority to any individual right to be free from discrimination against a fundamental collective right encapsulated in one of the exceptions in an actual factual context.

The principled approach outlined in the OHRC paper is, I suggest, another way of describing the core values of the rights in the *Code* that identifies the centre of the contextual equilibrium radar screen.

It is interesting how similar these fundamental values of the *Code* are to the values enunciated by Dickson CJC as underlying the *Charter*; see *Oakes*, above note 2 at para 64.

D. The Exception Sections

The OHRC paper suggests that there are several exception sections that operate as defences and that respondents must meet the criteria to prove that they are entitled to the exception. The most critical ones are found in sections 18, 20(3), and 24 of the *Code*. Tribunals and courts have rightly stated that these exceptions should be narrowly construed,[35] while the enumerated rights to non-discrimination must be broadly construed. The OHRC paper acknowledges that these exceptions attempt to balance freedom of association (often in the religious context) with the broader right to be free from discrimination protected under the *Code* and indeed under the section 15 equality guarantee of the *Charter*. The Supreme Court of Canada in *Caldwell v Saint Thomas Aquinas High School*[36] also confirmed that such exception sections confer and protect rights, in particular the right to associate. In a crucial part of the decision McIntyre J made the following ruling:

> To begin with it must be recognized that we are here facing a situation where there is a clear conflict between two sound legal positions. There is an assertion by each party of a clear legal right and the two rights, if each is to be accepted with no modification or limitation, are incompatible . . . .
>
> There can be no serious question that Roman Catholic schools, having their special nature, have functioned and continue to function lawfully in the Province. On the other hand, the law

---

35 See, for example, *Gibbs v Battleford & District Co-Operative Ltd* (1996), 27 CHRR D/87 (SCC).

36 *Caldwell v Saint Thomas Aquinas High School*, [1984] 2 SCR 603 [*Caldwell*]. A similar approach to finding the contextual equilibrium can be discerned in another Supreme Court decision in *Brossard (Town) v Quebec (Commission des droits de la personne)*, [1988] 2 SCR 279 [*Brossard*].

> of the land has conferred rights regarding employment which have come into conflict with the rights of the respondent in the operation of its denominational school . . . .
>
> It seems evident to me that the Legislature of British Columbia, recognizing the historically acquired position of the denominational school and the desirability of preserving it, in enacting a Human Rights Code which goes far to eliminate differences and distinctions in society, included s. 22 as a protection for the denominational school or other institution in like case. It is therefore my opinion that the courts should not in construing s. 22 consider it merely as a limiting section deserving of a narrow construction. This section, while indeed imposing a limitation on rights in cases where it applies, also confers and protects rights. I agree with Seaton JA in the Court of Appeal where he expressed this thought in these words:
>
>> This is the only section in the Act that specifically preserves the right to associate. Without it the denominational schools that have always been accepted as a right of each denomination in a free society, would be eliminated. In a negative sense s. 22 is a limitation on the rights referred to in other parts of the Code. But in another sense it is a protection of the right to associate. Other sections ban religious discrimination; this section permits the promotion of the religion.[37]

I suggest that what courts and tribunals have done in rulings on the narrow interpretation of the exception sections is to give advance warning that contextual equilibrium requires that such collective assertions of freedom of association, religion, or other forms of collective rights *do not overreach* in attempting to "self-collect" in community with others similarly identified. Such an examination of whether there is overreaching will include the test

---

37 *Caldwell*, *ibid* at 625–26.

of *bona fide* — what are the true, core, or primary interests of the collectivity and, after the Supreme Court's ruling in the *Meiorin Grievance*,[38] the impossibility of accommodation without the imposing of undue hardship.

Without commenting on the correctness of the HRTO's decisions in the context of the most controversial of the exceptions, namely the special employment exception in section 24(1) of the *Code*, the allegations of overreaching of the collective right to freedom of association and religion was at the heart of the dispute that lead to the decisions in *Brockie*,[39] *Parks*,[40] and in the more recent *Heintz*.[41] This last case perhaps best illustrated the complex task of tribunals and courts in finding the contextual equilibrium in situations where conflicts of rights are being asserted.

In March 1995, Connie Heintz, a devout Christian was employed as a support worker in a group home by Christian Horizons in Waterloo, Ontario. Support workers in the group residence for developmentally disabled individuals carry on non-managerial tasks such as cooking, cleaning, laundry, and assisting in the daily routines of the residents such as meals, toileting, and outings or appointments.

Christian Horizons is an Evangelical Christian not-for-profit corporation which operates close to 200 group homes in Ontario, serving over 1,400 group home residents and employing approximately 2,500 staff. These homes are substantially funded

---

38 *British Columbia (Public Service Employee Relations Commission) v BCGSEU*, [1999] 3 SCR 3 [*Meiorin Grievance*].

39 *Ontario Human Rights Commission v Brockie*, [2002] OJ No 2375 (SCJ) [*Brockie*].

40 *Parks v Christian Horizons* (1992), 16 CHRR D/40 (Ont Board of Inquiry). This author constituted the Board in the case [*Parks*].

41 *Heintz v Christian Horizons*, 2008 HRTO 22 [*Heintz*], aff'd in part in *Ontario Human Rights Commission v Christian Horizons*, 2010 ONSC 2105 [*OHRC v Christian Horizons*].

to the amount of approximately $75 million by the Ontario Ministry of Community and Social Services. All employees of Christian Horizons are required to adopt a "Doctrinal Statement" and a "Lifestyle and Morality Statement" that prohibits homosexual relationships, with the latter being a part of their contract of employment. Employees are also required to sign the statements as part of their contract of employment. Christian Horizon regards homosexuality as contrary to biblical scriptures and immoral.

After a few years of work for Christian Horizons in the Waterloo group home, Ms. Heintz came to an understanding that she was a lesbian and entered into a same-sex relationship and subsequently revealed it to her colleagues and supervisor. After being accused herself of harassment by a co-worker and a threat from her supervisor that she would be terminated if she did not improve her performance in accordance with the Lifestyle and Morality Statement, Ms. Heintz resigned after taking a medical leave. She had also been offered counselling to return to compliance with the Statement, whatever that meant.

Before the HRTO, Heintz complained that she had been discriminated in her job contrary to section 5 of the *Code,* which prohibits, *inter alia* discrimination in employment on the basis of sexual orientation, and had been exposed to a poisoned work environment.

Christian Horizons, in response, raised the "special employment" exemption in section 24(1)(a) of the *Code* which provides:

> 24. (1) The right under section 5 to equal treatment with respect to employment is not infringed where,
>
> (a) a religious, philanthropic, educational, fraternal or social institution or organization that is primarily engaged in serving the interests of persons identified by their race, ancestry, place of origin, colour, ethnic origin, creed, sex, age, marital status or disability employs only, or gives preference in employment to, persons similarly identified if the

> qualification is a reasonable and bona fide qualification because of the nature of the employment

The HRTO held that Christian Horizons could not claim the exemption because it was not primarily engaged in serving the interests of Evangelical Christians who are "similarly identified," which in the view of the HRTO were those who subscribed to its Christian teachings and the Lifestyle and Morality Statement. The Tribunal ruled that Christian Horizons was primarily engaged in providing for the interests of individuals who have developmental disabilities, regardless of their creed. The Tribunal rejected the decision of a previous Board in *Parks*[42] that Christian Horizons could have two primary functions — that of serving its Evangelical community and also serving the developmentally disabled. The Tribunal in *Parks* had reached this conclusion because to decide otherwise would have been tantamount to preventing any *bona fide* religious qualifications imposed on the leadership of the organization, thus imperiling the continued existence of the group. The HRTO in *Heintz* rejected this conclusion and held that even if Christian Horizons was primarily engaged in serving the interests of persons of the same creed, the Lifestyle and Morality Statement qualification was not reasonable and *bona fide* given the nature of the employment duties of Ms. Heintz. The Tribunal came to this conclusion following the Supreme Court of Canada jurisprudence in the *Meiorin Grievance*[43] and the earlier decision in *Ontario (Human Rights Commission) v Etobicoke*,[44] on the nature of a *bona fide* occupational qualification. Such jurisprudence had required that a *bona fide* occupational qualification be imposed honestly and in good faith and belief that the qualification is required for the adequate performance of the employment

42 *Parks*, above note 40.

43 *Meiorin Grievance*, above note 38.

44 *Ontario (Human Rights Commission) v Etobicoke*, [1982] 1 SCR 202 [*Etobicoke*].

duties and not for ulterior or extraneous reasons that defeat the objective of the *Code*. There is also an objective criterion to the *bona fide* occupational qualification: it must be reasonably necessary for the efficient and economical performance of the job that does not endanger fellow employees and the general public.

While the HRTO held that Christian Horizons had sincerely and honestly believed that the Lifestyle and Morality Statements were necessary for the performance of Ms. Heintz's employment, it was not a qualification that was appropriate or reasonably necessary for the performance of her duties according to the objective test for the *bona fide* occupational qualification. The primary role of a support worker, like Ms. Heintz, at Christian Horizons' group homes is not to help residents to prosetelize the Christian way of life or to convert residents. As such Christian Horizons qualification could not pass the objective test.

While some residents were from Christian family backgrounds and some families sought the group homes because of the Christian environment, there was no evidence that the residents as a whole come from the Christian background or seek the services from the organization for the religious education and environment. The HRTO concluded that the primary purpose of Christian Horizons is to provide residential services for individuals with developmental disabilities.

Having dismissed the claim that the organization was covered by the section 24 exemption, the HRTO ruled that Christian Horizons had discriminated against Ms. Heintz on the grounds of sexual orientation, taking into account other relevant evidence. This included various activities of co-workers that included rumours and false allegations related to the complainant's sexual orientation that constituted a poisoned work environment. The HRTO added that Christian Horizons even used these activies to negatively reflect on the performance review of Ms. Heintz instead of taking action to counter the poisoned work environment, which was a requirement even if the section 24 exemption applied. In light of these violations of the *Code*, the Tribunal ordered Christian Horizons to pay Ms. Heintz $23,000 as general damages as well as eighteen months of special damages for lost wages and benefits.

Christian Horizons appealed the decision to the Ontario Divisional Court and on 14 May 2010 the court allowed the appeal in part. The court parted company with the HRTO on its interpreation of the second requirement in section 24(1)(a) relating to the requirement that Christian Horizons must prove that it is a "religious . . . organization that is primarily engaged in serving the interests of persons identified by their . . . creed, or gives preference in employment to persons similarly identified." The court, in part motivated by the French version of section 24(1)(a), which refers in the English equivalent to "the principle objective of the religious organization," held that "the proper approach to the interpretation of the section is to focus on the subjective purpose of the group."[45] The English version, in contrast, focused on the interests being served without reference to the objective or purpose of the organization, which would of necessity have a subjective element. Relying on the French version of the *Code* for this interpretation, the court overuled the HRTO decision that Christian Horizons could not be regarded as primarily serving Christian interests and come within the exemption of section 24(1)(a).

The logic of the court was that if the HRTO was correct, Christian organizations like the respondent which serve individuals regardless of their religious beliefs could not require adherence to its religious beliefs, even for senior officers comprising the directing mind of the organization. There could not have been a legislative intention to effectively make religious organizations cease offering their services in such a situation or to only provide their critical services to members of their own faith group when their religious beliefs direct them to serve all the needy without

45 *OHRC v Christian Horizons*, above note 41 at para 56.

discrimination. This reasoning of the Divisional Court is similar to the logic that led to the decision of the Board in the *Parks* decision.[46]

Critically, the court also ruled that the HRTO had failed to consider what would be the effect of its ruling "on the rights and freedoms of members of religious organizations, despite the guarantee of freedom of religion in s. 2(a) of the *Charter*."[47] In a crucial ruling that cited the *Caldwell*[48] and *Brossard*[49] decisions of the Supreme Court of Canada and the freedom of religion guarantee in the *Charter*, the Divisional Court moved to find a contextual equilibrium between the rights of religious groups engaged in servicing the public and the equality rights of individuals working for such groups. The court stated:

> Subsection 24(1)(a) seeks to balance the rights of certain groups against equality rights. An approach to s. 24(1)(a) that takes into account, in the determination of the primary activity of a religious organization, the perspective and purpose of the organization is consistent with the guarantee of freedom of religion. At the same time, the BFOQ requirement found in s. 24(1)(a) upholds the important *Charter* protection for equality rights.[50]

The court therefore ruled that the HRTO erred in approaching the second element in section 24(1)(a) from an objective standpoint. In doing so it had failed to respect the religious nature of Christian Horizons' activities and indeed the purpose of the section in protecting the group's right of association. The Tribunal had to first examine whether the particular activity is seen by the group as a fundamentally religious activity. This must be followed

46 *Parks*, above note 40.

47 *OHRC v Christian Horizons*, above note 41 at para 70.

48 *Caldwell*, above note 36.

49 *Brossard*, above note 36.

50 *OHRC v Christian Horizons*, above note 41 at para 71.

by an assessment of whether the activity furthers the religious purposes of the group and its members. If it does, the organization does fall within the exemption in section 24(1)(a) and the *bona fide* occupation qualification then has to be examined.[51] The court then held that given the finding of fact by the Tribunal, it was clear to the court that Christian Horizons was indeed carrying out a Christian mission and would not be assisting the disabled residents of the group homes but for the religious calling of those involved. Even Ms. Heintz had stated that the goal of the group homes was "to show Christ to the individuals in the home in all things."[52]

The court concluded that "Christian Horizons is, in fact, primarily engaged in serving the interests of persons identified by their creed, with resultant benefits to individuals with developmental disabilities who live in their group homes and the families of those residents."[53] Therefore, Christian Horizons came within this part of the exemption in section 24(1)(a) of the *Code*.[54]

This conclusion is not too dissimilar from the decision reached in *Parks* that the main objectives of the organization were to serve both the Christian mission and also to serve the interests of the developmentally disabled. However, the court agreed with the HRTO that the organization had failed to show that the prohibition against homosexual lifestyles was a *bona fide* occupational qualification for support workers such as Ms. Heintz. Relying on the Supreme Court decisions in the *Etobicoke*[55] and *Brossard*[56] cases, also cited by the HRTO, the court emphasized that it is the context and nature of the employees' duties in determining

51 *Ibid* at para 73.

52 *Ibid* at para 75–76.

53 *Ibid* at para 77.

54 For further discussion of this issue as it relates to creed see Epp Buckingham at Chapter 3 in this volume.

55 *Etobicoke*, above note 44.

56 *Brossard*, above note 36.

whether a requirement could qualify as a *bona fide* occupational qualification and that that the qualification should be interpreted restrictively as it takes away rights which otherwise benefit from a liberal interpretation. These decisions of the Supreme Court, cited by both the Tribunal and the Divisional Court, laid down the fundamental principle that the employer must clearly demonstrate that the *bona fide* occupational qualification was reasonably necessary to assure the efficient and economical performance of the job without endangering the employee, his fellow employees, and the general public.

In addition the Divisional Court cited the Supreme Court's decision in the *Caldwell*[57] case that it will be only in rare circumstances that religious conformance would satisfy the test of *bona fide* occupational qualification. The court stated that such a requirement had to be tied directly and specifically to the execution and performance of the employees' duties, otherwise it would deprive section 24(1) of the *Code* of any meaning. The court therefore concluded that there was nothing in the context or nature of Ms. Heintz's duties, such as cooking, cleaning, doing the laundry, assisting with the daily eating and bathing duties of the residents, and taking them for appointments and outings required a prohibition of same-sex relationships. There was indeed nothing in the way in which Ms. Heintz carried out her duties that prevented her from being capable of performing her duties. The evidence also indicated that Ms. Heintz did not refuse to participate in the Christian enviroment activities in the group home including hymn singing, Bible reading, and prayer activities. From an objective perspective therefore there was nothing to make the prohibition of same-sex relationships a *bona fide* qualification for the duties that Ms. Heintz performed.

Support workers like Ms. Heintz were also not expected to prosetelyze the lifestyle and morals of Christian Horizons to the

---

57 *Caldwell*, above note 36.

residents in the group home. The court approved the Tribunal's reference to other religious organizations like the Salvation Army which did not require all job functions to adhere to its religious or moral beliefs, limiting it only to those in leadership positions. The court upheld the HRTO's ruling on the poisoned work environment at the Christian Horizon's home. For these reasons, described above, the court upheld the HRTO's ruling that the discrimination against Ms. Heintz on the grounds of sexual orientation was not covered by the section 24(1)(a) exemption. The damage award given by the HRTO was also upheld. However, the court did set aside the HRTO's order to cease applying the Lifestyle and Morality Statement as a condition of employment and instead narrowed it to the statement ceasing the prohibition of same-sex relationships for support workers. In addition, the court direct Christian Horizons to develop a policy and training program that targets discrimination on the ground of sexual orientation. The broader anti-discrimination and anti-harassment training and policy order of the Tribunal was also set aside as the complaint was focused on discrimination on the grounds of sexual orientation.

The decision by the Divisional Court is the latest example that the human rights jurisprudence of the courts and tribunals are focusing on identifying the contextual equilibrium of rights that may appear to be in conflict, but are really situations where one set of rights are at the centre of the values enunciated by the relevant human rights legislation and the *Charter*.

E. Section 18.1: The Solemnization of Marriage by Religious Officials

The best statutory attempt to entrench the concept of the contextual equilibrium of rights may well be the Ontario legislature's attempt to reconcile what may seem like conflicting rights in the amendment to the *Code* in section 18.1, relating to the solemnization of marriage by religious officials after the legalization of same-sex marriage at the federal level.

Section 18.1 states:

> 1) The rights under Part 1 to equal treatment with respect to services and facilities are not infringed where a person registered under section 20 of the *Marriage Act* refuses to solemnize a marriage, to allow a sacred place to be used for solemnizing a marriage or for an event related to the solemnization of a marriage, or to otherwise assist in the solemnization of a marriage, if to solemnize the marriage, allow the sacred place to be used or otherwise assist would be contrary to,
>
> 2) (a) the person's religious beliefs; or
> (b) the doctrines, rites, usages or customs of the religious body to which the person belongs.

The clear objective of the amendment was to allow religious officials to exercise their freedom of religion by not forcing them to solemnize marriages contrary to their religious beliefs. However, the amendment is carefully drafted to apply only to those religious officials registered under section 20 of the *Marriage Act*[58] and in relation to services and facilities. It should not apply to civil marriage officials or other non-religious officials and is applicable only to activities related to the solemnization of marriage. No doubt there will be remaining ambiguities, which will trigger the need for contextual equilibrium if disputes arise as to the range of events the religious official can refuse to participate and the definition of what constitutes a "sacred place." However, the amendment proactively forces Ontario residents to understand that seemingly conflicting rights must be viewed in context and that rights claimants should not overreach. Civil marriage commissioners would be overreaching if they were to claim the protection of section 18.1, while managers of buildings owned

58 RSO 1990, c M.3.

by religious associations that offer rental services to the public would be hard-pressed to come within the protection of section 18.1.

F. Conclusion

This analysis has attempted to demonstrate that if we are to take seriously the repeated rulings of the Supreme Court that there is no hierarchy of rights under the *Charter* or under the provincial human rights legislation in Canada, there has to be both a principled and pragmatic way of achieving what I am calling a contextual equilibrium of seemingly conflicting rights in an actual factual context. What is often in dispute in situations that are termed "conflicting rights" is the assertion by one side that seeks protection of the inherent dignity of the individual in a factual context that a group has overreached in promoting its claim to a collective right to freedom of association, religion, or expression. At the same time the group that is asserting that right is concerned that their cherished beliefs, practices, rites, or, in the case of linguistic minorities, language rights will be ultimately threatened by what they assert is a peripheral intrusion against their claimed right. What should always be kept in mind is that Canada is a free and democratic society which values, in the words of Dickson CJC that opened this article, "the inherent dignity of the human person, commitment to social justice and equality, accommodation of a wide variety of beliefs, respect for cultural and group identity, and faith in social and political institutions which enhance the participation of individuals and groups in society."[59]

The task then of the judge or human rights tribunal member is to ascertain the contextual equilibrium between these fundamental values of Canadian society which can do justice in a manner that does not constitute such an intrusion on asserted rights that the fundamental values and principles underlying both the

59 *Oakes*, above note 2 at para 64.

Charter and the relevant human rights legislation are seriously impaired. In most cases, this involves identification of which of the rights asserted in the factual context represent the core values of the right in general and merit it being situated at the centre of the contextual equilibrium rights radar. Once that is decided, adjudicating what are termed "conflicting rights" becomes less of a zero-sum game and more of a commitment to finding the contextual equilibrium of rights in a free and democratic society. Sometimes it may require the wisdom of Solomon to do justice in these circumstances, but justice demands it.

Chapter 10

The Reconciliation of Legal Rights

Patricia Hughes*

A. Introduction

Over the past quarter century "rights," on the whole, have been reinforced in Canada by the *Canadian Charter of Rights and Freedoms*[1] although they have been the subject of human rights legislation for far longer. The international emergence of rights along with the now numerous human rights instruments, have established an atmosphere in which individual — and sometimes group — rights dominate the discourse, encouraging the "pitting" of rights against each other or against broader societal concerns. For example, each guarantee under the *Charter* stands alone, although as part of a document that as a whole reflects identifiable values. Inevitably there have been and will continue to be occasions when the benefit claimed by a complainant under one section has the potential for detrimental impact on the rights of someone else, on other values inherent in the *Charter*, or on societal requirements, as recognized by the balancing required under section 1 of the *Charter*. Similarly, assertions of rights

* The views expressed in this paper are those of the author alone and should not be read to represent the views of the LCO or of anyone associated with the LCO other than the author.

1 *Canadian Charter of Rights and Freedoms*, Part I of the *Constitution Act, 1982*, being Schedule B to the *Canada Act 1982* (UK) 1982, c 11 [*Charter*].

under human rights legislation may be met with the defence that permitting the claim will deny others their rights; human rights legislation does not always provide a built-in balancing mechanism.[2]

When thinking generally about how rights interrelate (and not merely under particular documents), there are at least two primary ways to address so-called "competing" rights claims. One is to treat each of the claims in isolation and attempt to gauge how much each has been infringed and then weigh them against each other. This approach treats rights as having hard edges and is not widely accepted. The other is to consider how to reconcile or balance the claims. Since balancing may have the connotation of one right trumping another, I prefer the term "reconcile."[3] This approach sees rights as having softer contours that seep into each other because different rights find their meaning in the same overall understanding of the relevant legal document or in the overriding values of society. Different rights may even raise similar claims or at least relate to the same interest (freedom of religion and religious equality, for example).

I make three further preliminary points. The first is that rather

---

2 On "competing" rights under human rights legislation, particularly the Ontario *Human Rights Code*, RSO 1990, c H.19, see Ontario Human Rights Commission, "Balancing Conflicting Rights: Towards an Analytical Framework" (OHRC, August 2005), online: OHRC www.ohrc.on.ca/sites/default/files/attachments/Balancing_conflicting_rights%3A_Towards_an_analytical_framework.pdf.

3 Reconciliation has been used by the Supreme Court of Canada in addressing *Charter* claims, as well as in many other contexts. For a discussion of the former, see Frank Iacobucci, "Reconciling Rights: The Supreme Court of Canada's Approach to Competing *Charter* Rights" (2003) 20 Sup Ct L Rev 137. The notion of "reconciliation" is also reflected in the view that rights should be viewed as relational: see Jennifer Nedelsky, "Reconceiving Rights as Relationship" in Jonathan Hart and Richard W Bauman, eds, *Explorations in Difference: Law, Culture, and Politics* (Toronto: University of Toronto Press, 1996) at 67.

than "competing" rights, a phrase that sets the stage for an adversarial process, I will primarily use the term "rights in tension." The second is that while the reconciliation approach will often result in recognition of both rights, even if not in the form originally claimed, there will be times that this is not possible because one right claimed is too antithetical to the other right or to societal values and interests. In these cases, the label "competing" right might seem more appropriate at the end of the process. The third is that I use the term "interests," as well as "rights." "Rights" denotes legal recognition in some form, whether in an international or domestic rights according document, while "interests" may not have been legally recognized, but do have a moral or other kind of status.

B. The Philosophical Premise and the Process

Rights are contextual. They represent recognition of the complexity of human interaction and activity which is both individualistic and communal. All societies involve the need — and desire — for human beings to function alone and all societies are based on communal engagement, but the balance between individuality and communality differs from society to society. Nevertheless, many individual rights, while accruing to the individual, recognize the significance of interaction with others, albeit on a different level than will likely occur in a society where the communal good is stressed more strongly. Tully uses the terms "critical freedom" and "belonging" to identify the sometimes conflicting needs most human beings and cultures experience.[4] Thus one might view the underlying premise of "accommodating" religious views, for example, as one that acknowledges religious expression as a form of individual autonomy and as a means of community adherence.

When individuals (or groups) make rights claims, either in chal-

4 James Tully, *Strange Multiplicity: Constitutionalism in an Age of Diversity* (Cambridge: Cambridge University Press, 2002) at 199.

lenge or defence, they do not do so as an intellectual or academic exercise. The denial of their rights may have practical consequence (such as exclusion from receipt of an economic benefit), but they may also or equally see it as denying their sense of self, risking destruction of their community, or displacing them from their rightful place in society. The subtext of rights, even if never made explicit, will play a role in how claimants view attempts to reconcile rights in tension.

Rights claims may go beyond the individual, and often do. A single rights claim may be symptomatic of a feeling of exclusion at a fundamental level. It may really be a way to gain broader "cultural recognition" for ways of being and acting that are "new" to an established society or have previously been excluded. Tully sees in "the politics of cultural recognition" the potential to transform constitutionalism if "the constitution [is] seen as a form of activity, an intercultural dialogue in which the culturally diverse sovereign citizens of contemporary societies negotiate agreements on their forms of association over time in accordance with the three conventions of mutual recognition, consent and cultural continuity."[5] I do not intend to enter into this rather larger discussion here, but I do suggest that when we think about rights claims and how to address them, we acknowledge that in many instances they are part of a larger enterprise that requires us to grapple with how to negotiate shifts in the constitutional framework.

My comments are premised on characterizing Canada as secular, civic, and pluralist. I can explain these terms only briefly here. By "secular," I mean that Canadian political and other major institutions (other than religious institutions themselves) are non-religious, that decisions are made on bases other than recourse to a "god" or deity or religious doctrine, that one is not expected to belong to a particular faith, or, equally importantly (although perhaps not yet equally so), that one is not expected

5 *Ibid* at 30.

to express any particular faith in order to hold an "important" position in society. A secular society is thus one "in which faith, even for the staunchest believer, is one human possibility among others," compared to a society "in which it was virtually impossible not to believe in God."[6] There are those who would argue that religion has been excised from the public square.[7] Yet for an atheist, the more subtle reminders of religious observance (prayers or religious services at major events, the invocation of "God" in the preamble to the *Charter*, the privileged position accorded freedom of religion and religious accommodation, the reality that political leaders attend church — nearly always "church") might suggest that the change has not been complete. Nevertheless, Canada is best described as a secular society, although it has not yet embraced this identity as enthusiastically as has France, for example.

The term "civic nationalism" distinguishes the contemporary national basis of Canada from an older understanding of a nationhood based on ethnicity. It is the shared political and other institutions that comprise Canada as a nation state. Accordingly, it can accommodate the views and practices of diverse peoples from different parts of the world.

"Pluralism" refers to the coexistence of different cultural and other entities within Canada, as well as to some extent different "sovereign" orders (such as varying degrees of First Nations "sovereignty"). Pluralism implies a "welcome" multiplicity of cultural,

---

6 Charles Taylor, *A Secular Age* (Cambridge, MA: Belknap Press, 2007) at 3.

7 See, for example, Paul Horwitz, "The Sources and Limits of Freedom of Religion in a Liberal Democracy: Section 2(a) and Beyond" (1996) 54 UT Fac L Rev 1; David Brown, "Freedom from or Freedom for?: Religion as a Case Study in Defining the Content of *Charter* Rights" (2000) 33 UBC L Rev 551; and MH Ogilvie, "Overcoming 'The Culture of Disbelief,'" CCR Discussion Paper #2 (Montreal: Cardus Centre for Cultural Renewal, 2006), online: Centre for Cultural Renewal www.cardus.ca/columns/2704.

religious, ethnic, and social groups. It also implies that in many cases, there is no "right" way to do something.

These simplistic comments on Canada as a secular and pluralist society based on a civic nationalism are sufficient to explain why "competing rights" or "rights in tension" play such a major role today. Although a secular society, Canada is not a non-religious society or an atheistic society; on the contrary, it welcomes (albeit to differing degrees) "new" religions or religions from other countries with little or no tradition in Canada. In other words, it is characterized by religious pluralism. Similarly, pluralism is based on giving "space" to divergent views of various kinds, including religious views. In order to constitute a "nation," the civic virtues or values on which Canada is based have increasingly been defined with reference to autonomy, difference, and freedom, values which are consistent with pluralism and with secularism or lack of official religion or political ideology; at the same time, however, there are some implicit limits within them.

For my purposes, the main value which might limit the full recognition of some religious and political beliefs, for example, is equality. At least this is the case if equality is not defined in relative terms (equality is what each group says it is for them), but in some overriding sense. The question then becomes how much "toleration" — the capacity to stretch without fully losing its shape — does Canadian society have?[8] The question for Canada is whether it should be a "monoculture-based system," as Taieb describes both the United States and France, "refusing the competition between the laws enacted by the state and the laws produced by communities and their collective narratives[9] or whether

8 I speak generally of "Canada," recognizing there are significant differences between Quebec and the "rest of Canada," between the territories and the provinces, and among the provinces and regions.

9 Julien Taieb, "Freedom of Religion: From France to the United States, a National Conflict of Law" (2004) 4:3 Global Jurist Advances, online: Bepress www.bepress.com/gj/advances/vol4/iss3/art1.

it should countenance "multiple normative orders," that is, "take cognizance of, and even, give way to, social [or religious] norms that develop independently of officially endorsed rules?"[10] While we may think we know the answer to this question, that answer (that Canada is based on multiple normative orders) is always open for reconsideration. This very large question is beyond the scope of this paper, yet it sets the backdrop for any legal framework that seeks to address competing rights or rights in tension.

The process of reconciling rights in tension requires two major interrelated inquiries:

> (1) To what extent does one right or interest interfere with the enjoyment of the other right? The more one right infringes the others, the less likely it is that a rights claim can be recognized in its existing form.[11]
>
> (2) To what extent are the rights or interests consistent with or apparently antithetical to broad societal values or interests? The greater the dissonance between the effect of the claim and the societal value, the less likely it is that a rights claim will be recognized, *especially when it denies the rights of others*.

To be clear, not conforming to significant societal values or interests is not reason enough to deny a rights claim. Underlying the notion of a pluralist society is that diverse viewpoints and actions are part of the fabric of the society.

I suggest that a reconciliation approach reflects a pluralist view of Canadian society in which there is recognition of the complexity of interests and claims, which is characterized by a system of values transcending individual rights and which provides a way

---

10 Denise G Réaume, "The Legal Enforcement of Social Norms: Techniques and Principles" in Alan C Cairns *et al*, eds, *Citizenship, Diversity and Pluralism: Canadian and Comparative Studies* (Montreal: McGill-Queen's University Press, 1999) at 177.

11 There may be more than two rights involved; however, for simplicity, I will assume that only two rights are at issue.

by which all citizens can access these rights.[12] In this sense, reconciliation becomes part of the process by which diverse cultures negotiate not only entry into the existing system, but in doing so, *may* change the shape of the system. In other words, reconciliation of rights in tension becomes an aspect of "the politics of cultural recognition," to use Tully's phrase. At the same time, my comments are premised on limits to change that overlay the way in which rights are reconciled; for example, recognition of religious claims should not result in Canada's becoming a theocracy (or reasonable facsimile thereof) or recognition of claims rooted in ethnicity should not transform Canada into a country characterized by ethnic nationalism.

C. Illustrations[13]

One of the more complex and contemporary examples of rights tension is that of freedom of religion and equality (which itself includes religious equality). These are both significant Canadian values and, to the extent that rights may be said to be "competing," provide a number of illustrations.[14] To illustrate the model or process I have proposed I refer to claims based on religion and equality. One might just as easily use many other examples, including claims based on expression, religion, and equality, as well as those involving security interests.

What is the backdrop against which the tension between equality and religious rights or interests plays out? A country defining itself as both secular and pluralist faces two major challenges with respect to how it treats religion. The first is how to protect the private exercise of religious beliefs and the extent to

12 I use the term "citizen" broadly rather than as a legal citizen.

13 My purpose here is to raise the kinds of considerations that are relevant to the framework I propose here, not to reach a solution.

14 As do freedom of expression and equality, and freedom of expression and freedom of religion.

which it will allow or facilitate the public exercise of religious beliefs. The second issue raises the legitimacy of the state's condonation of religious practices that may be contrary to or inconsistent with other widespread values such as equality, or requirements such as the need for security. These two challenges are, of course, interrelated in so far as the public exercise of religious beliefs may be contrary to how people should be treated in conformity with other constitutional guarantees. The state's acquiescence in the operation of principles held by private groups that appear contrary to mainstream values may raise some opposition, but generally speaking these groups operate within a scope of tolerance, although recent developments (discussed below) do challenge that statement. The strength of that tolerance is put to the test, however, when the same groups seek positive endorsement by the state of their internal practices or when they want to influence the mainstream society's approach to certain issues.

Taking this backdrop into account might produce different results in different contexts. I use three examples: the facts in *Trinity Western University v British Columbia College of Teachers*,[15] the assertion of a provocation defence in a murder case, and the controversies around women who wear the burqa (or niqab) in Canada.

1) Religious Claims and Equality of the LGBT Community: Private or Public?

Trinity Western[16] squarely raised the tension between religious

---

15 [2001] 1 SCR 772 [*Trinity Western*].

16 Trinity Western's teacher training program had been affiliated with Simon Fraser University. It then sought the approval of the BC College of Teachers (BCCT) for full responsibility for its teachers program. Trinity Western required teachers, students, and others at the University to sign a code setting out community standards that included a requirement to refrain from homosexual (and other "biblically condemned") conduct on

rights and the equality rights of "homosexuals." In its decision, the Supreme Court of Canada focused on the equality concerns of students in the classroom, concerns that the majority described as shared by society generally. Ultimately, the Court held that equality rights were not infringed because apparently the code was not translated into action (discrimination in the classroom, in word or deed). Thus to the extent homosexuals were harmed, it is that they would probably not feel welcome at Trinity Western. This analysis does not consider that state tolerance of discriminatory codes might harm those whose conduct is said to be "sinful." However tolerated in a private context, once the state is involved in approving the organization to participate in the socialization of children, the state's commitment to certain values comes into play.

Trinity Western invokes the equality interest of "homosexuals"[17] in being presented as "legitimate" members of Canadian society. Thus a requirement in a state sanctioned (albeit passively) document that compels people to agree with the view, based in religious belief, that members of the homosexual community do not have that status needs to be assessed against the right to be portrayed as equal to other members of society. It also must be assessed against societal values that acknowledge that homosexuals are full members of society. In other words, equality "rights" not only accrue to individuals, but are also a mark of society's values.

The approach in *Trinity Western* might be contrasted with the

---

the basis that it is a sin. The BCCT refused approval because it considered the code discriminatory. The BC Supreme Court granted an order in the nature of mandamus. The Court of Appeal held that there was no reasonable foundation for the BCCT's finding of discrimination. The Supreme Court of Canada dismissed the appeal.

17 The community standards referred only to "homosexual behaviour," although one might assume that it would have been expanded to cover the conduct of the entire LGBT community.

Court's comment in *Butler* where it was recognized that women feel degraded "as 'victims' of the message of obscenity"[18] or with the majority's comment in *Keegstra* that clearly stated, "[i]t is indisputable that the emotional damage caused by words may be of grave psychological and social consequence."[19] One might have concluded that the religious-based claim at issue in *Trinity Western* could have been better framed as whether the right, on the basis of religious belief, to harm members of a group by assumptions and words about their moral worth could be reconciled with the equality right not to be the subject of words that might cause "damage . . . of grave psychological and social consequence." This broader inquiry acknowledges that the assertion of a group's inequality in a publicly condoned or passively acknowledged statement is more than just a belief. It is easy to see the point if "homosexual" is replaced by "black person" or even "women." Put another way, the assertion has consequences, just as actions have consequences. This does not require people to change their beliefs, although admittedly it does show that the beliefs are not in accordance with important societal values, nor does it require people to engage in homosexual behaviour, to have homosexuals as friends, or to approve of their son marrying a gay man or their daughter a lesbian.[20]

In *Reference re Same-Sex Marriage*, the Court gave short shrift to the argument that recognizing same-sex marriages interfered with the equality rights of religious groups opposed to same-sex marriage and opposite-sex married couples, concluding that "[t]he mere recognition of the equality rights of one group cannot, in itself, constitute a violation of the rights of another. The promotion of *Charter* rights and values enriches our society as a whole and the furtherance of those rights cannot undermine the very

18 *R v Butler*, [1992] 1 SCR 452 at para 117 [*Butler*].

19 *R v Keegstra*, [1990] 3 SCR 697 at para 60 [*Keegstra*].

20 Query whether this analysis would apply to the teaching of certain doctrines in publicly supported Catholic schools.

principles the *Charter* was meant to foster."[21] The legal recognition of same-sex marriage gave rise to another example: whether it is consistent with the *Charter* to permit officials licensed to perform civil marriages to refuse to marry same-sex couples.[22]

This example illustrates the importance of determining whether a claim (refusal to perform same-sex marriages) is premised on denying the equality of others, that is, that the basis for the claim reflects beliefs that some people are not equal. Here the religious claim is not merely for recognition of a particular belief that does not affect those outside the community, but is based on denial of some people to benefit from a state sanctioned practice (some of whom might be members of the same community). While it is unlikely that a same-sex couple would choose to be

---

21 [2004] 3 SCR 698 at para 46. The Court pointed out that there were no submissions explaining how same-sex marriage contravened equality rights and that the Court was unable to "surmise" how it could.

22 The Saskatchewan Attorney General referred amendments to the *Marriage Act, 1995*, SS 1995, c M-4.1, that would permit marriage commissioners to refuse to perform same-sex marriages if contrary to their religious beliefs, to the Saskatchewan Court of Appeal for its opinion with respect to the constitutionality of the provisions. Under the statute, the only way to have a non-religious marriage solemnized was by a marriage commissioner. The Court of Appeal held that the refusal of a marriage commissioner to perform a same-sex marriage would be offensive to gays and lesbians and might lead to a situation where it would be difficult to find a commissioner prepared to perform the marriage. There was thus a contravention of section 15 of the *Charter*, above note 1. The court also held that if they were required to solemnize marriages against their religious beliefs, commissioners' freedom of religion under section 2(a) of the *Charter* would be infringed. In balancing these two infringements under section 1, the majority concluded that permitting public officials to discriminate, even on the basis of their freedom of religion, was not justifiable. The minority agreed in the result, but analyzed the section 1 process differently: *Saskatchewan (Marriage Act, Marriage Commissioners) (Re)*, 2011 SKCA 3.

married by someone with these views, it nevertheless is the case that their desire to be married is not *premised* on forcing others to renounce their religious views, while the refusal of someone to marry them on the basis of religious views is premised on the denial of their equality rights. This is a nuanced distinction, but it is not an irrelevant one in thinking about how to reconcile apparently opposing rights in cases where reconciliation is difficult to achieve.

In this case, is it sufficient that a same-sex couple seeking to marry could undoubtedly find someone willing to marry them in a state-sanctioned civil ceremony? One may be tempted to say "yes," that in this case the denial of the right to be married by a particular person is less of an infringement than is the compulsion to marry a couple whose actions contravene one's religious beliefs. Yet the issue goes beyond this. In a religious context, religious beliefs are paramount. Thus Catholic priests are not required to marry same-sex couples in a religious ceremony. When someone has been given authority by the state to preside over a marriage ceremony, the nature of the ceremony and the obligation may be thought to change to one that reflects the society's commitment to certain values. This is, however, perhaps a more difficult case than is the recognition of same-sex marriage.

2) Religious Claims and Gender Equality: Provocation

The tension between rights claims does not arise only in constitutional cases. The "answer" to my next example may seem obvious, yet it echoes the justifications given recently for so-called "honour killings" in Canada[23] and makes clear that claims for

---

23 For a discussion of the killing of Aqsa Parvez by her father and brother (who pled guilty to second degree murder), see Kate Allen & Joe Friesen, "Father, Brother Plead Guilty to So-called 'Honour Killing'" *The Globe and Mail* (15–16 June 2010), online: *The Globe and Mail*

"cultural recognition" have limits. In this case the limit is obvious, but it raises the question of what, short of this, would be the outer edge of recognition.[24]

In *R v Humaid*,[25] Humaid admitted that he had killed his wife (he stabbed her in the neck nineteen times, as well as stabbed her in her heart), but argued provocation. His wife, he said, had made comments to him that made him believe that she had been unfaithful to him. He relied on expert testimony at trial that in Islam, infidelity, particularly by women, is "a very serious vio-

---

www.theglobeandmail.com/news/national/toronto/father-brother-plead-guilty-in-death-of-ontario-teen/article1605082. For a review of other incidences in Canada and of practices elsewhere, see Tobi Cohen, "'Honour killings' on the Rise in Canada: Expert" *Vancouver Sun*, online: *Vancouver Sun* www.vancouversun.com/life/Honour+killings+rise+Canada+Expert/3165638/story.html; Jim Wilkes, "Ottawa condemns honour killings" *The Toronto Star* (13 July 2010), online: *The Toronto Star* www.thestar.com/news/canada/article/835153--ottawa-condemns-honour-killings. The Minister for the Status of Women mused about adding a prohibition against "honour killings" in the *Criminal Code*, RSC 1985, c C-45; as subsequently pointed out, however, prohibitions against murder already encompass these killings.

24 As with a number of issues (including women wearing the burqa, an issue I discuss below), these killings are often attributed to Islamic religious beliefs. There is much dispute about this, however, and the better view seems to be that they reflect cultural expectations, rather than religious ones, although the cultural expectations have developed in Muslim countries that have particular views about the role and place of women. Having said that, it is also true that violence against women is not limited to these communities; what may be different is how widespread the view that the violence is legitimate is today (although it is not hard to recall when members of the Canadian Parliament laughed when the issue of violence against women was raised there), how it might be officially sanctioned, and what the cultural motivations for "honour killings" in Canada are.

25 *R v Humaid* (2006), 81 OR (3d) 456 (CA).

lation of the family's honour and worthy of harsh punishment by the male members of the family."[26] Although he did not have to decide it, Doherty JA, for the Court of Appeal, commented on what he saw as "the nub of the problem" raised by the argument that Humaid's "religious and cultural beliefs should have been factored into the 'ordinary person' test" relevant to the provocation defence. While these beliefs will be considered when the insult at issue is targeted at the accused's beliefs, in this case, the insult was not *targeted* at Humaid's beliefs; rather the argument is that it be given increased gravity *because of* his beliefs. Doherty JA addresses the issue squarely at paragraph 93 when he refers to women's right to equality:

> . . . The difficult problem, as I see it, is that the alleged beliefs which give the insult added gravity are premised on the notion that women are inferior to men and that violence against women is in some circumstances accepted, if not encouraged. These beliefs are antithetical to fundamental Canadian values, including gender equality. It is arguable that as a matter of criminal law policy, the "ordinary person" cannot be fixed with beliefs that are irreconcilable with fundamental Canadian values. Criminal law may simply not accept that a belief system which is contrary to those fundamental values should somehow provide the basis for a partial defence to murder.

In this case, the analysis is not difficult. The restriction on Humaid is denial of the right to carry his belief into action. It might be said more accurately, instead, that what Humaid is being denied is his "right" to have cultural/religious influences on him recognized to absolve him (to some degree, to reduce murder to manslaughter) of the crime. To do so would give legitimacy to values or beliefs that undermine the capacity of the society to protect the rights of the victim.

26 *Ibid* at para 67.

3) The Intersection of Religion and Equality: The Burqa

My last example is one that is posing serious challenges in Canada, as well as in other countries, today. For that reason, it is my most extensively discussed illustration. This is the issue of when and where women should be "permitted" to wear a burqa.[27] In Canada, the issue has arisen with respect to voting and to being a witness,[28] as well as other contexts. The rights or interests at

---

27 I am using the word "burqa" to apply to full loose clothing that covers the body, including the face, without making a distinction between a garment or combination of garments that leaves an opening for the eyes (but covers the head, including the forehead and the face from the nose to below the chin) and one that has a mesh portion that covers the eyes. The concerns raised about what women wear relate to the covering of the face, although I think it fair to say that to the extent that people are disturbed by this full body covering, they are even more disturbed when the eyes are also effectively covered. The issues raised here are not raised by a head scarf or combination of long garment and headscarf that leaves the face completely open.

28 After the initial completion of this paper, the Ontario Court of Appeal released a decision articulating a complex process for "reconciling" the witness's freedom of religion and the accused's right to make a full answer and defence in the context of whether a complainant/witness in a sexual assault case may wear her niqab when she gives testimony: *R v NS*, 2010 ONCA 670. The process the court sets out involves three steps: (1) determining whether the "constitutional values underlying both claims are in fact engaged in the specific circumstances"; (2) a fact specific assessment of whether the wearing of the niqab would interfere with cross-examination more than minimally or insignificantly (the accused must establish any claim that the interference affects something other than demeanour, for example); and (3) efforts to reconcile taking into account context (such as the stage of the proceeding or the role of the witness) or mitigating measures or compromises (such as the material used for the niqab or possibly removing all men except the accused from the courtroom and using a female counsel or judge). These are

stake here are those of religion, gender equality of women, societal interests such as security, and the integrity of the election process or assumptions about appropriate court procedures. For instance, this mix of interests is complicated since, for example, the women wearing burqas are claimed to have both religious and gender equality interests, depending on perspective. Furthermore, the equality interest might mean that women should be permitted to wear what they wish or that women cannot be permitted to wear clothes that graphically represent their oppression.

There are additional complications. For some, the justification for the burqa is that it is required by Islam; however, it is also argued that it is not a religious requirement, but a cultural one in certain countries (that also happen to be Muslim) that has developed separately from religion, but in which religion may be used to enforce the requirement. Some women who wear a burqa wear it from choice because they feel closer to "God" in doing so; others wear it from choice because they feel it frees them from the gaze of men. Younger women may wear it because of pressure from their families, while others wear it despite familial pressure *not* to wear it. There is significant disagreement among Muslims (between men and women and among men and among women) about not only whether women should wear the burqa, but also whether they should be permitted to wear it.[29] Even among

---

just a few factors described by the court in an attempt to ensure that both claimants' rights are protected as much as possible (others include whether the case is being tried by judge alone or judge and jury). If the judge concludes that the witness's wearing the niqab would impair the cross-examination by the accused and thus the right to a fair trial, the former must give way to the latter. The court remitted the case back to the preliminary inquiry judge whose initial decision had been that the witness could not wear her niqab.

29 See, for example, "Muslim Group Moves to Ban Burqa" *The Globe and Mail* (7 October 2009), online: *The Globe and Mail* www.theglobeandmail.com/news/national/muslim-group-moves-to-ban-burka/

Islamic adherents who believe women should wear "hijab" or modest clothing in public, some believe that there are circumstances when women can expose their face, including when women are prohibited from covering their faces.[30]

We have gone some distance today in Canada in allowing freedom of dress. The history of expanding notions of acceptable attire around headwear suggests it is complicated by assumptions around gender, ethnicity, and religion. While women were "required" by social mores to wear hats in church and men were not supposed to do so, Sikh men had to fight to wear a turban in the RCMP (where other members of the force were wearing a hat as part of their uniform). Women wore veils at funerals and wear them as brides. Yet while we debate the freedom to wear a covering that appears to insulate a woman from the society around the wearer, we have to acknowledge that there are some ironies in our treatment of dress. Women who are "too" scantily attired or women who are "too" covered up are equally subject to criticism (or their clothes are), although for different reasons.

What is it, then, that troubles us about the burqa? The burqa is a graphic representation of the "other." The wearer is unknown and unknowable. In the UK, judges have discretion to decide whether lawyers and legal advisors and others are able to wear the niqab (full face covering) in court; factors with respect to legal advisors include that their client agrees and they can be understood in relevant parts of the courtroom.[31] On the other hand, in France, legislation banning the wearing of the burqa in

---

article1316126.

30 "Saudi Clerics Say Women in France Exempted from Veils" *Toronto Star* (25 July2010), online: *Toronto Star* www.thestar.com/news/world/article/840044--saudi-clerics-say-women-in-france-exempted-from-veils.

31 Judicial Studies Board, Equal Treatment Bench Book (February 2007), online: www.judiciary.gov.uk/publications-and-reports/judicial-college/Pre+2011/equal-treatment-bench-book.

public places has been passed.[32] The legislation prohibits the wearing of the burqa in public places, including the street, and makes women liable for a fine and citizenship classes if she refuses to remove her veil when required by police.[33] The legislation also makes it illegal to compel a woman to wear a burqa. In Quebec, proposed legislation making it permissible to refuse public services to a woman wearing a burqa (niqab) and prohibiting those providing the service from wearing it, attracted the approval of the Prime Minister of Canada, Stephen Harper, and the Leader of the Official Opposition, Michael Ignatieff.[34]

---

32 CNN Wire Staff, "Burqa Ban Passes French Lower House Overwhelmingly" CNN (13 July 2010), online: CNN www.cnn.com/2010/WORLD/europe/07/13/france.burqa.ban/index.html; Hillary Stemple, "France Parliament Approves Burqa Ban" *Jurist* (13 July 2010), online: *Jurist* http://jurist.law.pitt.edu/paperchase/2010/07/france-parliament-approves-burqa-ban.php; "Syria Bans Full Islamic Veils at Universities" *The Globe and Mail* (19 July 2010), online: *The Globe and Mail* www.theglobeandmail.com/news/world/syria-bans-full-islamic-face-veils-at-universities/article1645185.

33 Some see a distinction between banning the burqa from public buildings and banning it from the street. Thus one Frenchman, a Muslim, is prepared to pay the fine of women convicted of wearing it in the street, but not in a public building. See "Fighting a Burka Ban with a Bucketful of Euros" *The Globe and Mail* (14 July 2010), online: *The Globe and Mail* www.theglobeandmail.com/news/opinions/editorials/fighting-a-burka-ban-with-a-bucketful-of-euros/article1640347. He believes that a ban in public buildings is consistent with a secular France.

34 "No Veil or No Service from Public Institutions, New Bill Urges Quebeckers" *The Globe and Mail* (25 March 2010), online: *The Globe and Mail* www.theglobeandmail.com/news/national/quebec/no-veil-or-no-service-from-public-institutions-new-bill-urges-quebeckers/article1511365; Jane Taber, "Ignatieff Backs Quebec Veil Ban" *The Globe and Mail* (26 March 2010), online: *The Globe and Mail* www.theglobeandmail.com/news/politics/ottawa-notebook/ignatieff-backs-quebec-veil-ban/article1513537. The Bill focuses on exposing the face and continues to permit the display

The burqa symbolizes the oppression of women that appears fundamental to some strands of Islam. Yet it is women who are at the centre of the debate and the prohibitions. Women will be the ones penalized under legislation such as that in France and it is women who, under the proposed legislation in Quebec, will risk not receiving benefits they are otherwise entitled to and may even, in some cases, remove themselves (or be forced to stay away) from public places. The women who wear the burqa in France will do so publicly and it will be easy to prove their offence; those who compel them to wear it will do so privately and it will be difficult to prove *their* offence.

Apart from the notion that the burqa is a statement about the need for women to hide themselves away (even though they are in public spaces and acting as public actors), something offensive to liberal equality principles, the covering of the face, leaving only the eyes visible, is a reminder of the covered faces of militants hoisting their guns into the air or the covered face of bank robbers as they storm the bank safe. In Western society, the covered face, apart from being covered as protection from physical danger such as cold weather, represents the desire to be secretive, in fun or in earnest. In a world where we are more and more open to public scrutiny, whether we wish to be or not, the woman wearing a burqa is able to maintain her privacy, even

---

of (other) religious clothing or wearing of religious symbols. For Bill 94, *An Act to establish guidelines governing accommodation requests within the Administration and certain institutions*, 1st Sess, 39th Leg, Quebec, 2010 online: Quebec National Assembly www.assnat.qc.ca/en/travaux-parlementaires/projets-loi/projets-loi-39-1.html. Section 6 of Bill 94 provides: "The practice whereby a personnel member of the Administration or an institution and a person to whom services are being provided by the Administration or the institution show their face during the delivery of services is a general practice. If an accommodation involves an adaptation of that practice and reasons of security, communication or identification warrant it, the accommodation must be denied."

while she sees everything others see. It cannot be ignored, too, that the burqa carries a connotation of other beliefs that might be contrary or threatening to mainstream Canadian norms. This is, I suggest, the subtext behind efforts to regulate where and when women may wear the burqa.

With this in mind, when women choose to wear the burqa, the issue becomes whether there are interests that justify the limitation on women's religious freedom (if this is why they wear the burqa) or gender equality (that they have chosen to wear the burqa for one reason or another).[35] What are the interests in "conflict" or in tension with wearing the burqa and is there really a tension with this interest? For some the burqa is a message about the unequal treatment of women, regardless of context, while others limit their objections to particular contexts. For example, the burqa is said to be a risk to the integrity of the voting system (although no woman in Canada has ever tried to vote wearing a burqa) or of the natural justice requirement to allow a defendant to face her accuser. To the extent that wearing the burqa is justified on religious grounds, it is difficult, given Supreme Court of Canada jurisprudence, to go behind the affirmant's declaration that this is an important aspect of her religious beliefs.[36] One

35 This is an important aspect of this debate since some commentators do not accept that women would ever make this choice, but that it is always a decision imposed on women by men. We cannot ignore, either, that "choice" is a complex term. There is a view that women wearing the burqa would not if they "knew better," an echo of the "false consciousness" discussions of the women's movement in years past or of the women who thought women should not have the vote.

36 *Syndicat Northcrest v Amselem*, [2004] 2 SCR 551. Writing for the majority, Iacobucci J explained at para 43: "claimants seeking to invoke freedom of religion should not need to prove the objective validity of their beliefs in that their beliefs are objectively recognized as valid by other members of the same religion, nor is such an inquiry appropriate for courts to make . . . ." He summarized at para 46:

might consider, on the one hand, whether it is preferable to ask first whether a particular practice is required by the religion or whether the religion provides an exemption for certain circumstances than to be forced to accept that the choice is between a religious practice and denying it.[37] On the other hand, it is also legitimate to ask whether the reason for forcing a woman to reveal her face is actually one that is justified; if identity is the concern, we may ask whether it is possible to arrange for another woman to confirm the identity of a woman wearing a burqa. In other words, this example illustrates just how complex these issues can be, how much a "subtext" informs the thinking, and how flexible and iterative the process of reaching a resolution needs to be.

D. Conclusion

Rights do not exist in isolation, nor, in most cases, do those who make rights claims. They live in a society in which the rights of others and the broader interests of society as a whole may be affected by their claims. Yet they, too, are part of the society, a

---

our Court's past decisions and the basic principles underlying freedom of religion support the view that freedom of religion consists of the freedom to undertake practices and harbour beliefs, having a nexus with religion, in which an individual demonstrates he or she sincerely believes or is sincerely undertaking in order to connect with the divine or as a function of his or her spiritual faith, irrespective of whether a particular practice or belief is required by official religious dogma or is in conformity with the position of religious officials.

37 This approach would be likely rejected by those who believe that the courts are not capable of addressing "irrational" beliefs through a lens of rationality and those who do not accept the "authority" of particular branches of a religion. Thus the Saudi clerics' "liberalism" on the matter of whether women must wear veils in the face of a prohibition otherwise might not be accepted by all Muslims.

society that shifts its shape somewhat each time there is a successful recognition of cultural diversity. Conceptualizing different rights claims as "competing rights" sets the stage for an interpretation that results in the triumph of one right over another. Thinking about them as "rights in tension" permits a more nuanced assessment of how rights interrelate with each other and with broader societal interests. Situations may still arise in which rights cannot be reconciled, in which "compromise" is asking too much of the claimants or of those whom the claim is affecting, or in which the claim constitutes too much of a challenge to societal interests. Society may change its shape, but it should not be shapeless. It does mean, however, that rights analysis should be more reflective of societal dynamics – or of what those dynamics ought to be in a civic, secular, pluralist society.

Chapter 11
Balancing Conflicting Rights: Towards an Analytical Framework

B.J. Wray*

A. Introduction

This paper was initially drafted for the Ontario Human Rights Commission (OHRC) in the summer of 2005 as part of their process of developing a formal policy on balancing conflicting rights. In the intervening years, there have been a number of notable developments in the jurisprudence on conflicting rights and I have updated this paper accordingly. Since the legalization of same-sex marriage in June 2005[1] some of the most prominent conflicts of rights have occurred in the context of balancing freedom of religion and sexuality equality rights. In Saskatchewan, for example, the Court of Appeal was called upon by the provincial government to review the constitutionality of proposed provincial legislation which would have exempted civil marriage commissioners from officiating at weddings that run counter to their religious beliefs.[2] In Ontario, the Superior Court recently grappled with an exception provision in Ontario's *Human Rights Code*[3] that

* The opinions expressed in this paper are those of the author alone and do not represent the views or opinions of the Department of Justice.

1 *Civil Marriage Act*, SC 2005, c 33.

2 *In the Matter of Marriage Commissioners Appointed Under* The Marriage Act, *1995, SS 1995, c M-4.1*. 2011 SKCA 3 [*Reference re Marriage Commissioners*].

3 RSO 1990, c H.19 [*Code*].

involved balancing the rights of a religious organization with the sexuality equality rights of one of its employees.[4] These developments provide the background for this paper and, not surprisingly, several of the scenarios outlined below are drawn from the litigation of these two particular conflicting rights.

The purpose of this paper is to provide an analytical framework for balancing conflicting rights, especially in the context of the *Code*. It is not meant to be an academic exploration of the theories or philosophies that inform the balancing process. Nor is it meant to be a treatise on how, precisely, one ought to implement a balancing process. Rather, this paper was developed as a practical exploration of the tools one may use when faced with two (or more) conflicting rights. Section B foregrounds the issues raised in conflicts of rights cases through a discussion of the legalization of same-sex marriage and the rights conflicts that have ensued. Section C outlines criteria for identifying when there is *no* conflict of rights. Section D surveys approaches to balancing conflicting rights that have been taken in the Canadian context. A number of balancing tools emerge from an examination of three main sources: caselaw, the preamble and exception sections of the *Code*, and previous policy work in this area. Section E applies these tools to balance conflicting rights in the contexts of employment and services. Throughout the paper, specific examples are used to illustrate how the balancing process may work within and across a range of protected grounds.

Two main paradigms for balancing conflicting rights are highlighted below: pragmatic balancing and principled balancing. These models represent distinct approaches to the issue of balancing. The implications of these distinctions, in terms of how the tensions between conflicting rights are resolved by each model, are explored through specific employment and service ex-

---

4 *Ontario Human Rights Commission v. Christian Horizons*, 2010 ONSC 2105 [*Christian Horizons*].

amples. Each model tends to foreground certain balancing tools over others.

For instance, pragmatic balancing focuses on the need to carefully weigh competing interests in such a way that the resolution of these interests reflects a compromise position. Consequently, pragmatic balancing looks to tools such as the exception sections of the *Code* and the duty to accommodate as factors that allow two conflicting rights to be managed within a particular context. On the other hand, principled balancing often foregrounds factors such as the values underlying the *Code* and the *Canadian Charter of Rights and Freedoms*,[5] and delineates the scope of each right in such a way as to avoid conflict as much as possible. Whereas pragmatic balancing will always proceed in a case-by-case manner, principled balancing may put forward overriding concerns that will apply across all cases and all contexts.

Although it is the aim of this paper to tease apart these two distinct theoretical approaches to balancing, in practice they necessarily coexist. This will become particularly evident in the caselaw section of this paper where the tools associated with both pragmatic and principled balancing are often employed within a single judicial decision. Courts generally must grapple with both types of balancing in their assessment of a rights conflict because principles and pragmatic outcomes are both at stake. Indeed, the Supreme Court noted this in *Sydicat Northcrest v. Amselem*: "This appeal requires the Court to deal with the interrelationship between fundamental rights both at a conceptual level and for a practical outcome."[6] This paper explores how the conceptual or principled tools for balancing are translated into practical or pragmatic outcomes in conflicts of rights cases. It is important to identify the separate strands of balancing in order

---

5 *Canadian Charter of Rights and Freedoms,* Part I of the *Constitution Act, 1982*, being Schedule B to the *Canada Act 1982* (UK) 1982, c 11 [*Charter*].

6 *Syndicat Northcrest v Amselem*, [2004] 2 SCR 551 at para 1 [*Amselem*].

to gain a better understanding of the actual factors that influence the balancing process in these difficult cases. This kind of close analysis also reveals the visions of equality that drive each balancing paradigm.

This paper should be understood as a starting point that may be used as a resource for approaching further policy work on balancing conflicting rights. It will highlight the conceptual toolbox that is employed by judges, lawyers, and policy makers as they undertake the complex task of balancing conflicting rights. Establishing a formulaic balancing test is not the goal of this paper. There is no "correct" model for solving conflicts of rights issues. However, it is important to articulate the general factors that inform the task of balancing and to apply these factors in specific hypotheticals. The set of balancing tools presented in this paper is necessarily incomplete and, undoubtedly, future caselaw and legislation will supplement these basic tools. It is also important to note that the usage of these tools will vary depending on the balancing approach that is taken, as well as the right at stake.

B. Background

Many of the passionate and often heated debates that have occurred in the wake of the legalization of same-sex marriage in Canada showcase the difficulties that accompany the balancing of conflicting rights. From the outset, the *Civil Marriage Act* raised concerns about how best to ensure a balance between freedom of religion and sexuality equality rights. Opponents of same-sex marriage worried that freedom of religion would be trumped by sexuality equality rights, and they argued for stronger legislative guarantees that would protect the beliefs and practices of religious officials and institutions. On the other hand, proponents of same-sex marriage generally agreed that freedom of religion must be respected, but differed in their assessments of how far the protections of the *Charter* should extend.

In many instances, the conflict between competing rights is settled through a delineation of the scope of the right at stake. It seems clear, for example, that freedom of religion and religious equality rights will allow religious officials to solemnize only those marriages that they believe adhere to the doctrines or tenets of their religion. This type of activity would fall squarely within established cultural and legal understandings of freedom of religion. The need for balancing arises only when the edges of two rights bump up against one another. *Actual* conflicts occur in the murky area of overlapping interests.

In the context of same-sex marriage, many difficult conflicting rights questions reside in this murky territory on the borders of rights. Should, for instance, the religious beliefs of civil marriage commissioners be accommodated in the workplace? Should religious organizations maintain their charitable tax status if they refuse to perform same-sex marriages? Should groups who are affiliated with religious organizations be given the protection of freedom of religion guarantees in, for example, the rental of their facilities for same-sex marriage celebrations? Should a religious organization be permitted to refuse to accept the valid civil marriage of any employee on the grounds that its own view of marriage is different?

In order to answer these questions, adjudicators must undertake a complex balancing of the rights at stake. The debate surrounding same-sex marriage is simply the latest instalment in an ongoing struggle to craft a paradigm for balancing conflicting rights in the human rights context. Over the years, the OHRC has dealt with competing rights claims across virtually all of the protected grounds under the *Code*. The OHRC is sensitive to the need to find an appropriate balance between the different rights protected in the *Code* and the *Charter*. Previous briefing notes and policy documents produced by the OHRC have outlined the tools used by tribunals and courts in the balancing of rights. Most recently, the OHRC has posted an online document outlining the process for reconciling competing rights that courts ought to follow.[7] These documents provide a useful starting point for a more detailed inquiry into the benefits and limitations attached to the balancing approaches taken up in previous cases.

C. Identifying When There Is *No* Conflict of Rights

Many disputes in which there appears to be a conflict of rights will be revealed, upon closer examination, to be situations in which the resolution of the dispute does not engage a formal balancing process. It is important that only *actual* conflicts of rights are approached as balancing tasks. This section of the paper will briefly outline factors for assessing the extent to which the balancing of competing rights is the real issue at stake. In particular, before proceeding to the task of balancing, careful consideration must be given to four key questions:

1) Are the rights claims characterized appropriately?
2) Are valid, legally recognized rights at stake?
3) Are the needs of both parties truly in conflict?
4) Are the rights more than trivially interfered with?

A "no" response to any one of these questions will mean that wading into the murky territory of balancing conflicting rights is not required. Instead, the competing claims will be dismissed as inappropriate, invalid, or insubstantial, or, alternatively, conflict management is likely to occur through informal accommodation.

The Supreme Court has distinguished the task of "reconciling" from the task of "balancing" competing rights claims. Reconciling implies harmonizing apparently contradictory things to render them compatible, while balancing suggests that one right will

7 Ontario Human Rights Commission, "Process for Reconciling Competing Rights Claims," online: OHRC www.ohrc.on.ca/en/reconciling-rights [OHRC, "Process for Reconciling Competing Rights Claims"].

ultimately outweigh another.[8] The questions above are more in line with the reconciling process than with the balancing process in that they are meant to end the conflict by properly characterizing the rights and adjusting, where reasonable, the measures that are sought in order to respect and fulfill the asserted rights.[9] These questions should help identify to what extent there is an irreconcilable conflict of rights that must then be further assessed through the balancing tools outlined in Section D.

In any apparent conflict of rights case the appropriateness of

---

8 Frank Iacobucci, "Reconciling Rights: The Supreme Court of Canada's Approach to Competing *Charter* Claims" (2003) 20 Sup Ct L Rev 137; *Reference re Same-Sex Marriage*, [2004] 3 SCR 698 at para 50 [*Reference re Same-Sex Marriage*]; OHRC, "Process for Reconciling Competing Rights Claims," above note 7 at 3.

9 The reconciliation process was recently articulated in *R v NS*, 2010 ONCA 670. In this case, NS alleged that she was sexually assaulted by her uncle when she was a young girl. NS is a Muslim who wears the hijab and a niqab when in public or in the presence of males who are not direct members of her family. At the preliminary inquiry, the accused sought an order requiring NS to remove the niqab covering her face when testifying. The preliminary inquiry judge allowed the order. The matter made its way to the Ontario Court of Appeal where Doherty JA, for a unanimous court, laid out the approach to be taken to reconciling the rights in this case. The court appears to favour a pragmatic approach when dealing with conflicting rights. They rely heavily on a contextual, fact-driven analysis to determine (1) whether two valid rights claims are actually engaged; (2) whether the interference with the rights are more than minimal or insignificant; and (3) to what extent "constructive compromises" may be made that would give effect to each of the rights as much as possible (see, in particular, paras 70–89). The court recognized that efforts to reconcile the rights may ultimately fail. If this occurs, the court suggests that a principled balancing must be engaged — "the threat of convicting an innocent person strikes at the heart of the principles of fundamental justice" — in which underlying *Charter* values and the nature of the proceedings will determine the outcome (para 89).

the claim must be considered. Utilizing a conflict of rights analysis as a defence is common, however, the number of cases in which there may be an actual conflict will be much rarer. The use of a conflict of rights defence may be a mischaracterization of the issues. In order to test this characterization, it is important to ask whether or not the dispute actually engages two equally valid rights claims. As the OHRC has pointed out, the courts should first determine the rights that are being asserted and whether the measures sought actually fall within the boundaries of the rights delineated within the particular context.[10] The conflict may be framed as one of competing rights, but this framing is only appropriate if the claims are actually linked to protected grounds under the *Code* or *Charter*.

For instance, it is a long-established principle in human rights law that customer preference cannot be used to justify a discriminatory act.[11] Customer preference, however, may be the driving force behind complaints that, on their face, seem to engage a conflict of rights. One way of testing whether or not this is the case is to carefully delineate the rights at stake. A particularly cogent example of framing customer preference within the language of competing rights may be seen in objections to breastfeeding in public spaces. Organizations and individuals objecting to this practice have frequently asserted that they have a "right" to request that a woman cover herself, move to a private area, and so forth. This right has sometimes been grounded in a freedom of expression claim as a way of legitimizing these requests as a valid human rights issue.

At first glance, then, there appears to be a conflict between freedom of expression and freedom from discrimination based on sex. But a careful consideration of whether or not the rights claims are appropriately characterized tells a different story.

10 OHRC, "Process for Reconciling Competing Rights Claims," above note 7 at 1.

11 *Berry v Manor Inn*, [1980] NSHRBID No 4 at para 18 [*Berry*].

Court and tribunal decisions have clearly established a woman's right to breastfeed in public.[12] Importantly, these decisions have concluded that actions which prevent a woman from breastfeeding in public are discriminatory. These precedents mean that in the absence of a compelling, equally valid discrimination claim, a woman has an unqualified right to breastfeed in public. The freedom of expression claim is not a valid counter-claim because there is no established positive legal right to individual preference. That is, you may air your personal preferences about a woman breastfeeding in public, but you may not use those preferences to compel a woman to stop an activity that is already recognized as an established equality right. In this instance, what amounts to a community standards test for discrimination masquerades as a freedom of expression claim.[13] Once this guise is exposed and the actual driving force of the complaint is revealed, there is no need to engage in the task of balancing.

There may be other cases, however, in which the first two questions concerning characterization and validity are answered affirmatively. In these situations, the conflict between competing rights will move to the third level of assessment: Are the needs of both parties truly in conflict? As the OHRC notes, "[r]ights may also be reconciled by making reasonable adjustments to the circumstances related to the exercise of the asserted rights. This could be in the nature of a human rights accommodation process and analysis that canvasses various options through witness testimony and submissions by the parties."[14] At this stage of analysis, it is important to focus on the *specific* needs of each party in order to determine whether or not informal accommodation is possible. If it is possible, then there is no need to use the

---

12 See, for example, *Quebec et Giguere v Montreal (Ville)*, [2003] JTDPQ No 9.

13 *Berry*, above note 11.

14 OHRC, "Process for Reconciling Competing Rights Claims," above note 7 at 5.

more formalized balancing tools.

By way of illustration, consider the following scenario: An individual with a disability uses a service dog in order to perform her work duties as a teacher, but a student in the classroom has her disability (allergies) triggered by the presence of the service dog. The *Code* requires employers to accommodate the needs of employees with disabilities, and it also requires service providers to accommodate the needs of customers with disabilities. The *Code* does not prioritize these needs or requirements — one is as important as the other. However, it is possible that these competing rights claims may be resolved by a precise assessment of the needs of both parties. The employer/service provider would first need to determine the accommodation needs of both the employee and the customer as accurately as possible to determine whether the needs of the two parties are necessarily in conflict. For example, in what ways is the service dog assisting the employee in the classroom? Are there other ways in which that support could be provided without the service dog? The Commission's *Policy on Disability and Duty to Accommodate* notes that "if there is a choice between two accommodations which are equally responsive to the person's needs in a dignified manner, then those responsible are entitled to select the one that is less expensive or that is less disruptive to the organization."[15] The needs of the student should be similarly evaluated. If the accommodation needs are directly in conflict, then the employer/service provider should explore solutions for accommodating both. In this case, there may be other instructors/sessions with whom the student can study.

Before moving on to a formal balancing process, the final question to ask involves a consideration of the extent to which the asserted rights are infringed. The OHRC notes that, "[i]f there

15 Ontario Human Rights Commission, *Policy and Guidelines on Disability and the Duty to Accommodate* (OHRC, 2000) at 15, online: OHRC www.ohrc.on.ca/en/resources/Policies/PolicyDisAccom2/pdf.

appears to be conflict between rights following any reasonable adjustments, a court should determine whether there is sufficient interference, beyond the trivial, with the rights in question. If the interference with a right is not substantial, it is not likely to receive protection. There would be no conflict unless there is an actual burden, or intrusion, on a right."[16] The fourth question examines the burdens placed on each of the rights to discern if they are more than a trivial or minimal. One of the rights may be merely inconvenienced but not actually in conflict with the other right.

The Supreme Court considered the degree of interference with protected rights in their decision in *Amselem* mentioned above. In this case, certain Jewish residents of a Montreal condominium complex erected *sukkahs* (a small enclosed temporary hut or booth) on their balconies in observance of the religious festival of *Sukkot*. Other residents objected to the *sukkahs* and claimed that they negatively affected their aesthetic, economic, and security interests in their property. Writing for the majority, Iacobucci J refused to engage in the formal balancing process required by section 1 of the *Charter* because the impact of freedom of religion in this case was substantial, while the impact on the right to peaceful enjoyment and free disposition of the property was, at best, minimal.[17] The potential conflict of rights in *Amselem* was diffused by the majority's recognition that one of the rights in conflict in that case was actually not burdened, or at least was so minimally burdened, by the other right and that it would be inappropriate to characterize the situation as one of balancing conflicting rights.[18]

While the first two stages of assessment focus on determining

---

16 OHRC, "Process for Reconciling Competing Rights Claims," above note 7 at 5.

17 *Amselem*, above note 6 at paras 57–64.

18 For a more detailed discussion of *Amselem* see Shauna Van Praagh's contribution to this volume at Chapter 7.

the appropriateness and validity of the claims, the third stage of assessment focuses on the specific needs raised by conflicting rights in order to narrow the scope of the conflict. The fourth stage then inquires into the degree to which each right is interfered with and avoids the need for balancing conflicting rights when one of the rights incurs a merely trivial impact. When the precise location of conflict is identified, it may be possible to meet the needs of both parties concurrently without resorting to the complicated process of balancing these equally valid competing claims. Only after these initial four questions have each been answered affirmatively will it be necessary to employ the balancing tools outlined in Section D.

D. The Balancing Tools

This section of the paper surveys the balancing tools found in the *Code* and relevant caselaw. Documents such as OHRC briefing notes and policy papers provide invaluable commentary on these tools and their insights are woven into the following discussion. The goal of this section is to identify the resources for balancing conflicting rights that will be utilized in the scenarios discussed in Section E. Rather than evaluate the benefits and limitations of each of these tools, this section is primarily concerned with assembling a conceptual toolbox whose contents represent the full spectrum of balancing tactics.

1) Balancing within the Provisions of the *Code*

The structure of the *Code* itself provides valuable balancing tools. A principled approach to balancing may focus on the values embodied in the preamble and in the established statutory interpretive framework, while a pragmatic approach may foreground the relevant exception sections of the *Code* (sections 18; 18.1; 20(3); and 24). This part of the paper examines each of these aspects of the *Code* in order to identify the specific balancing tools they contain.

a) The Preamble

The preamble to the *Code* offers initial guidance for balancing conflicting rights in that it embodies the values underlying the *Code* and human rights legislation in general. These values make up the general framework in which balancing occurs. Four key principles emerge from the preamble:

1) recognition of the dignity and worth of every person;
2) provision of equal rights and opportunities without discrimination that is contrary to law;
3) creation of a climate of understanding and mutual respect, so that;
4) each person feels a part of the community and is able to contribute fully to the development and well-being of the community and the Province.

Inherent in these values is a balancing of individual and group rights. The preamble puts forth a vision of relational rights in which the equality of each person exists alongside community development and well-being. The dual focus of the preamble on individual equality and creating a community-based climate of mutual respect sets in motion a consideration of the importance of both of these elements. These values are not conceived of as hierarchical but, instead, are described as mutually constitutive. That is, individual equality is fostered through the creation of a climate of mutual respect and, conversely, community is fostered through the recognition of the inherent dignity and worth of each individual. The preamble makes clear that the purpose of human rights legislation is not simply to obtain concrete redress for violations of equality rights, but also to foster an inclusive climate of mutual respect.

b) Interpretive Principles

From the outset, the *Code* grapples with the complicated relationship between conflicting rights and seems to anticipate that individual equality may sometimes be at odds with creating a climate of mutual respect. While the preamble sets out the general aims of the *Code*, it has been left to the courts to craft the interpretive principles governing the *Code*. These interpretive principles also act as valuable tools that may guide the process of balancing. Indeed, the issue of balancing may be an issue of statutory interpretation.[19] For the purposes of this paper, three broad interpretive principles are noteworthy.

Firstly, the *Code* should receive an interpretation that advances the overarching aims set out in the preamble,[20] and a key aim is the removal of discrimination. As has already been mentioned, the preamble envisions a balancing process in which individual and group rights coexist.

Secondly, the right against discrimination in the *Code* is subject to any defence provided in the *Code* to those who discriminate. The exception sections provide for such defences but must be viewed as exceptions to the general rule of non-discrimination. The Supreme Court has held that while rights in human rights legislation should receive a broad interpretation, defences to the exercises of those rights should be interpreted narrowly.[21] The exception sections, though, provide a balancing mechanism so that the many competing interests of society can be accommodated.[22] The interpretive principles governing the exception sections are explored in more detail below in Section D(1)(c).

---

19 *Christian Horizons*, above note 4.

20 *Ontario (Human Rights Commission) v Simpsons-Sears Ltd*, [1985] SCJ No 74 at para 12.

21 *Dickason v University of Alberta*, [1992] SCJ No 76 at paras 17 and 95 [*Dickason*].

22 *Ibid*.

Thirdly, the *Code* must be interpreted in a manner consistent with the interpretation of the *Charter*. Specifically, the interpretation of section 15 of the *Charter* should inform the interpretation of human rights codes across Canada.[23] Also, the meaning of a right should be determined by an analysis of its purpose and the interests it was meant to protect, and the context in which the right is asserted must be considered.[24] It must be borne in mind, however, that there is an important difference between human rights legislation and the constitutional rights protected in the *Charter*: "Human rights legislation is aimed at regulating the actions of private individuals. The Charter's goal is to regulate and, on occasion, to constrain the actions of the state."[25] The relationship between the *Code* and the *Charter* is discussed at length in the caselaw section of this paper below.

c) The Exception Sections

The *Code* contains several exception sections that, when asserted by a respondent, operate as defences.[26] In many conflicts of rights cases, the interpretation of these sections is hotly contested. At issue is whether or not the respondent meets the criteria outlined in the relevant exception section and the onus is on the respondent to prove that she is entitled to the exception. To determine this, the adjudicator is in part guided by the established interpretive principles for exception sections. Generally, exceptions to the basic provisions and underlying values of the *Code* should be narrowly construed, while rights themselves should be broadly construed.[27] It is important to recognize, how-

---

23 *Quebec (Commission des droits de la personne & des droits de la jeunesse) v Montreal (City)*, [2000] SCJ No 24 at paras 26–41.

24 *Ibid*; *Christian Horizons*, above note 4 at paras 68–72.

25 *Dickason*, above note 21.

26 *Gibbs v Battlefords & District Co-Operative Ltd*, [1996] SCJ No 55.

27 *Ibid*; see also *Dickason*, above note 21.

ever, that the exception sections serve a dual purpose: "they both confer rights on some persons and limit the rights of others in situations where the section applies."[28]

The exception sections of the *Code* that most often emerge in conflicts of rights cases are sections 18, 20(3), and 24. The more recently enacted section 18.1 may also figure in conflicts of rights cases in the future.[29] The eligibility criteria contained in each of these sections delimits to whom and in what circumstances these exceptions will apply. What follows is a brief discussion of each exception section that outlines the parameters of the eligibility criteria. These sections of the *Code* mediate between conflicting rights by providing adjudicators with balancing guidelines, but the proper scope of these sections must be ascertained before an exception may be factored into the balancing process.

i) Section 18: Special Interest Organizations

> The rights under Part I to equal treatment with respect to *services and facilities*, with or without accommodation, are not infringed where *membership or participation* in a religious, philanthropic, educational, fraternal or social institution or organization that is *primarily engaged* in serving the interests of persons identified by a prohibited ground of discrimination is restricted to persons who are *similarly identified*. [emphasis added][30]

The italicized sections highlight the key eligibility criteria that an organization must meet if it desires to use this section of the

---

28 *Christian Horizons*, above note 4 at para 60.

29 Section 18.1 of the *Code* was added by Bill 171, *An Act to amend various statues in respect of spousal relationships*, 1st Sess, 38th Leg, Ontario, 2005 (assented to 9 March 2005) [Bill 171].

30 *Code*, above note 3, s 18.

Code as a defence. Section 18 applies only to services and facilities that are restricted on the basis of membership or participation in an organization that primarily serves the interests of persons identified by a prohibited ground of discrimination. Additionally, in order to qualify for an exception under this section, membership and participation must be restricted to persons who are similarly identified with the primary service interests of the organization. For example, this provision accommodates religious freedoms by allowing religious institutions to discriminate in their admission policies on the basis of religion. Under section 18, a private Christian post-secondary school would be able to restrict its admissions to students who agree that homosexuality is a sin and undertake to refrain from homosexual practices.[31]

The interpretation of this section in the caselaw balances freedom of association with equality rights. Section 18, like each of the other exception sections, considers the relationship between the private and public spheres. The public's right to be treated without discrimination must be considered against a private organization's right to limit its membership to an identified group.[32] In one prominent example, refusal to admit a woman to membership in a men's organization was not considered a discriminatory denial of services because members of a group against which discrimination is prohibited may be excluded from social or cultural organizations which are *not* a public service.[33] The onus is on the party seeking the exemption to prove that it falls squarely within the criteria of the section.[34]

If an organization engages *primarily* in activities serving the interests of its members it will tend to receive the protection of

---

31 *Trinity Western University v British Columbia College of Teachers)*, [2001] SCJ No 32 [*Trinity Western*].

32 *Martinie v Italian Society of Port Arthur* (1995), 24 CHRR D/169 (Ont Board of Inquiry) [*Martinie*].

33 *Gould v Yukon Order of Pioneers*, [1996] SCJ No 29.

34 *Martinie*, above note 32.

this section even if the organization also includes some community participation in its activities. "Primarily" has been interpreted to mean "for the most part" rather than "solely." Some leeway has also been given to the interpretation of "similarly identified."[35] For instance, an Italian organization whose goals include a desire "to unite male members of Italian descent" can meet the requirement in section 18 that it restrict membership to persons similarly identified even though it admits males married to women of Italian descent. Such men are "similarly identified" for the purposes of section 18.[36] The courts have looked to the primary purpose of the organization or institution to determine whether it means to serve the interests of an identifiable group characterized by a common ground in the exemption provision.[37] Like section 24, section 18 "confer[s] a right to associate on certain groups so that they can join together to express their views and carry out their joint activities."[38]

ii) Section 18.1: Solemnization of Marriage by Religious Officials

> (1) The rights under Part I to equal treatment with respect to services and facilities are not infringed where a person registered under section 20 of the *Marriage Act* refuses to solemnize a marriage, to allow a sacred place to be used for solemnizing a marriage or for an event related to the solemnization of a marriage, or to otherwise assist in the solemnization of a marriage, if to solemnize the marriage, allow the sacred place to be used or otherwise assist would be contrary to,

---

35 *Ibid.*

36 *Ibid.*

37 *Christian Horizons*, above note 4 at paras 63–67.

38 *Ibid* at para 64.

(a) the person's religious beliefs; or
(b) the doctrines, rites, usages or customs of the religious body to which the person belongs.[39]

In the wake of the legalization of same-sex marriage, the Ontario government introduced Bill 171, *An Act to amend various statutes in respect of spousal relationships*.[40] Included in this legislation was an amendment to section 18 of the *Code* that added section 18.1. As indicated above, this new section addresses the issue of solemnization of marriage by religious officials and is a further attempt to balance conflicting rights within *Code* provisions. To date, there is no caselaw and, hence, no judicial interpretation of this section. However, it is possible to speculate on how the eligibility criteria will contribute to the balancing process. This section appears to apply only to religious officials (those registered under section 20 of the *Marriage Act*[41]) and their actions in relation to services and facilities. It is unlikely this section will apply to civil marriage commissioners or other non-religious officials. It is also unlikely this section will apply to activities beyond those associated with the solemnization of marriage. This interpretation of section 18.1 is consistent with the statement released by the Ontario Ministry of the Attorney General when Bill 171 was introduced: "The proposed bill also includes provisions to clarify that religious officials cannot be compelled to perform marriages or use their sacred places for the celebration of marriages that are inconsistent with their religious beliefs."[42]

While this amendment expressly protects religious officials

39 *Code*, above note 3, s 18.1.

40 See Bill 171, above note 29.

41 *Marriage Act*, RSO 1990, c M.3 [Ontario *Marriage Act*].

42 Ministry of the Attorney General, "Ontario to Amend Laws to Update Legal Definition of Spouse," News Release Communique (22 February 2005), online: Ministry of the Attorney General www.attorneygeneral.jus.gov.on.ca/english/news/2005/20050222-spousalDefinition.asp.

from solemnizing marriages that contravene their religious beliefs, the extent of these protections remains to be tested. At least two elements of section 18.1(1) will require further interpretation: the range of events associated with the solemnization of marriage that a religious official may reject; and, the proper scope of spaces included under the "sacred place" designation. The amendment provides some guidance on this latter issue in that it defines "sacred place" as including "a place of worship and any ancillary or accessory facilities" (section 18.1(3)). The meaning of "ancillary" and "accessory" will be contested, especially in a case in which a building owned by a religious organization is offered to the public at large as a rental space, but is denied to a same-sex couple wanting to rent it for their wedding reception.[43]

43 This scenario was at the heart of the dispute in *Smith and Chymyshyn v Knights of Columbus and others*, 2005 BCHRT 544 [*Knights of Columbus*]. Smith and Chymyshyn were a same-sex couple who rented, for their wedding reception, a hall that was run by the Knights of Columbus and owned by the Archdiocese of Vancouver. When the Knights found out the purpose of the rental, they cancelled the rental agreement. Smith and Chymyshyn filed a complaint with the BC Human Rights Tribunal alleging discrimination based on sexual orientation, contrary to the BC *Human Rights Code*, RSBC 1996, c 210 [BC *Code*]. The Tribunal found, *inter alia*, that the Knights had offered the hall as a rental space to the general public and had never rented only to those in the Catholic community or to members of the Knights and their families, or to those who share the Catholic Church's core religious beliefs. The Tribunal held that the Knights had discriminated on the basis of sexual orientation and did not meet the criteria of the exception section under the BC *Code*. The Tribunal accepted that if the complainants had wanted to be married in the parish church, the Church would have been within its constitutionally protected right to refuse to perform that marriage. This case illustrates that in defining "ancillary" or "accessory" spaces, a contextual analysis that is sensitive to the circumstances of each case will be required in order to determine the reach of a religious freedom defence to a conflict of rights.

Similarly, the range of events associated with the solemnization of marriage requires clarification. Will, for instance, a same-sex wedding anniversary or a same-sex wedding reception classify as "an event related to the solemnization of marriage"?

As an example of balancing conflicting rights, the defence offered by this section appears to reiterate the general principles of interpretation that accompany all of the exception sections of the *Code* in that it posits a narrow, rather than a broad exception. Section 18.1 reasonably circumscribes the exception to ensure full protection for religious officials while deliberately remaining silent on exceptions for civil marriage commissioners. This silence is likely to be interpreted as an implicit refusal to statutorily enshrine exceptions for these secular officials. However, employers in both the public and private sectors have a legal duty to accommodate the sincerely held religious convictions of employees up to the point of undue hardship. The issue of accommodation in the context of civil marriage commissioners will be explored in more detail in Section E as an illustration of how the balancing tools may be used to navigate conflicting rights.

Section 18.1 adheres to the balancing principles found in *Charter* decisions on freedom of religion. Precedents indicate that freedom of religion is to be interpreted broadly,[44] but that services normally offered to the public must be offered in a non-discriminatory manner.[45] In section 18.1, it appears that it will be possible for a religious official to assert this defence even where the denomination he belongs to does not have a position against same-sex marriage (a broad interpretation of freedom of religion). At the same time, however, it appears that only a religious official can assert this defence and that a church administrator cannot refuse rental of a sacred place and rely on the defence (an implicit recognition that individuals offering services to the

---

44 See *Trinity Western*, above note 31; *Christian Horizons*, above note 4.

45 *Ontario Human Rights Commission v Brockie*, [2002] OJ No 2375 (SCJ) [*Brockie*]; *Knights of Columbus*, above note 43.

public must provide equal treatment with respect to services and facilities).

iii) Subsection 20(3): Recreational Clubs

> The right under section 1 to equal treatment with respect to services and facilities is not infringed where a recreational club restricts or qualifies access to its services or facilities or gives preferences with respect to membership dues and other fees because of age, sex, marital status, or family status.[46]

While subsection 20(3) is not often employed as a defence, it offers another glimpse into the ways in which balancing conflicting rights occurs within the sections of the *Code* itself. This section appears to be based on assumptions regarding the irreconcilability of specific identity characteristics. Four grounds of discrimination (age, sex, marital status, and family status) are given exception status in this section. It is important to note the grounds that are not included: race, ancestry, place of origin, colour, ethnic origin, creed, sexual orientation, and disability. The four included grounds seem to represent those characteristics which are thought to contain actual or fundamental differences that deserve protection. The grounds which are not included seem to represent those characteristics which are thought to be socially or culturally imposed rather than actual. In other words, the actual differences between men and women are served by the existence of sex-specific recreational clubs, while a whites-only recreational club merely perpetuates stereotyping and discrimination based on race. The whites-only policy is not based on actual differences, but rather on the illusion of difference that is used to justify discriminatory practices.

Like section 18, subsection 20(3) attempts to balance freedom of association with equality rights. However, subsection

46 *Code*, above note 3, s 20(3).

20(3) is a one-sided, essentialist form of balancing in that it is the mere fact of identity that determines whether or not an organization is eligible for protection under this section. This section raises a number of interpretive issues that, in turn, will have consequences for the balancing of conflicting rights: What constitutes the definition of a "recreational club"? Should there be a *bona fide* and reasonable connection between the interests of the particular group and the basis upon which it discriminates? Should there be a connection between the interests of the group and the services or facilities that it offers that advance those interests? What if there is a difference between the "stated" and "practiced" interests of the group or if these interests change or diminish over time? Can a recreational group selectively discriminate?

The lack of caselaw on subsection 20(3) means there are few interpretive guidelines for this section. On its face, this section appears to protect recreational clubs from complaints that they treat women, among others, differently in terms of the service they provide to their customers. For instance, under the auspice of this section, a golf club may argue that it is permitted to give preference to male members in terms of tee times and access to the golf course. It is unlikely, though, that such a defence would withstand the scrutiny of *Charter* equality rights. Given that *Code* provisions must be interpreted according to the principles of *Charter* review, the defences offered by this section of the *Code* are on shaky ground.

To date, the OHRC has not developed a policy position on subsection 20(3), and the defences potentially permitted by this section are perhaps indicative of an underdeveloped approach to balancing. To allow exceptions that are based on the mere fact of identity is overly broad and does not honour the spirit of the law in the other exception sections of the *Code*. The rather arbitrary designation of certain identity characteristics as actual or fundamental does not resonate with the preamble's stated intention of creating a climate of mutual understanding and respect. The usefulness of this section in terms of understanding how to balance conflicting rights is that it highlights the dangers of an overly simplistic approach. Intending to provide a defence that respects certain forms of association, this section may inadvertently legitimize the very discrimination that the *Code* seeks to eradicate.

iv) Subsection 24(1): Special Employment

> The right under section 5 to equal treatment with respect to employment is not infringed where,
>
> (a) a religious, philanthropic, educational, fraternal or social institution or organization that is *primarily engaged in serving the interests of persons identified* by their race, ancestry, place of origin, colour, ethnic origin, creed, sex, age, marital status, or disability employs only, or gives preference in employment to, *persons similarly identified* if the qualification is a reasonable *and bona fide qualification* because of the nature of the employment. [emphasis added][47]

Many of the prominent conflicts of rights cases engage subsection 24(1) and, as a result, the interpretative principles associated with this section have emerged as significant balancing tools. The balancing process within this section begins with an assessment of whether or not the respondent meets the section's eligibility requirements. As with section 18, the respondent must be primarily engaged in serving an identifiable group and the preference in employment must be given to persons similarly identified. Additionally, subsection 24(1) requires the employer to prove that the preference in employment is a reasonable and *bona fide* qualification because of the nature of the employment. These criteria work to ensure a fair and proportionate balancing

47 *Code*, *ibid*, s 24(1).

of rights because they build-in several hurdles that employers must overcome if they wish to employ this defence.

In the recently decided *Christian Horizons*,[48] the Divisional Court conducted a detailed analysis of the special employment exception section. At issue in this case was whether Christian Horizons was entitled to a defence under the exception provision in the wake of a discrimination complaint filed by a former employee, Connie Heintz. Christian Horizons is an Evangelical Christian organization founded with the goal of ministering to individuals with developmental disabilities. As part of this mission, Christian Horizons operates over 180 residences for disabled individuals in Ontario.[49] All employees were required to adhere to the "Lifestyle and Morality Statement" developed by Christian Horizons as part of their employment contract. The statement included a rejection of a variety of sexual conduct, including "homosexual relationships."[50] Ms. Heintz was employed by Christian Horizons as a support worker in one of its community living residences. She signed the statement in 1995 and again in 1996. However, four years later, she realized she was a lesbian and entered into a same-sex relationship. When her employer found out, Ms. Heintz was offered counselling to restore her to a state of compliance with the statement.[51] Over the next few months, the relationship between Ms. Heintz and Christian Horizons deteriorated and Ms. Heintz resigned in the fall of 2000. She then filed a complaint with the OHRC alleging discrimination on the basis of her sexual orientation and that she had been exposed to a poisoned work environment.

At issue before the Human Rights Tribunal of Ontario (HRTO) was whether or not Christian Horizons could claim the benefit of paragraph 24(1)(a). Christian Horizon had the onus to prove that

48 *Christian Horizons*, above note 4.

49 *Ibid* at paras 4–5.

50 *Ibid* at para 6.

51 *Ibid* at para 8.

1) It is a religious organization;
2) It is primarily engaged in serving the interests of people identified by their creed and employs only people similarly identified; and
3) Religious adherence is a reasonable and *bona fide* qualification because of the nature of the employment.[52]

The HRTO found that the first requirement was satisfied. However, on the second requirement, the HRTO determined that Christian Horizons was primarily engaged in serving the interests of people with developmental disabilities rather than the interests of Evangelical Christians and, therefore, could not claim the exception provided by subsection 24(1). The HRTO also found that, in the alternative, Christian Horizons did not meet the third requirement because in adopting the qualification on employment imposed by the statement, no real effort was made to examine whether the requirement was reasonably necessary or whether the employment could be performed without the discriminatory restrictions.[53]

Christian Horizons appealed the HRTO's decision primarily on the basis that the Tribunal erred in its interpretation of paragraph 24(1)(a). The Divisional Court conducted a lengthy analysis of this exception section and found that the Tribunal erred in its interpretation of the second requirement of the section. At the heart of the appeal was the issue of whether or not Christian Horizons was "primarily engaged" in serving the interests of persons identified by their creed.[54] The court's assessment of this issue provides further guidance on how to balance conflicting rights under this section. In a nutshell, the court held that the second element in 24(1)(a) must not be approached from an objective standpoint but, rather, the "language and purpose of the provision require

52 *Ibid* at para 15.

53 *Ibid* at paras 16–17.

54 *Ibid* at para 27.

an analysis of the nature of the particular activity engaged in by the religious organization to determine whether it is seen by the group as fundamentally a religious activity."[55] According to the court, since the purpose of 24(1)(a) is both to protect the group rights of association and to respect the religious character of the organization's activities, an analysis of the second element under 24(1)(a) must foreground the organization's perspective. In this case, the court found that Christian Horizons operates its group homes for religious reasons and it would not be doing the work of assisting people with disabilities in a Christian home environment "but for the religious calling of those involved."[56]

A key aspect of the court's interpretation of the second element of 24(1)(a) is that an adjudicator must look to the *primary purpose of the organization* to determine whether it means to serve or promote the interests of an identifiable group characterized by a common ground in the exception provision.[57] This interpretation follows from the overall purpose of the exception provision which is to "confer a right to associate on certain groups so that they can join together to express their views and carry out their joint activities."[58] Following from *Amselem*, the court also opined that freedom of religion should be considered from the perspective of the religious minority whose rights are infringed.[59] The court rejected an interpretation of the provision that would have made the exception unavailable to religious organizations that are engaged in "public life."[60] The court noted that the words of paragraph 24(1)(a) make no reference to a public/private distinction and "it is inappropriate to read one in."[61]

---

55 *Ibid* at para 73.

56 *Ibid* at para 75.

57 *Ibid* at para 63.

58 *Ibid* at para 64.

59 *Ibid* at para 70.

60 *Ibid* at para 43.

61 *Ibid* at para 46.

On the third element of 24(1)(a), the court found that the HRTO applied the correct test and that Christian Horizons did not discharge its burden of showing that the qualification that its support workers adhere to the statement by not participating in same-sex relationships is reasonable and *bona fide* because of the nature of that employment. The court affirmed that the *bona fide* occupational qualification (BFOQ) exceptions in human rights legislation ought to be "interpreted restrictively since they take away rights which would otherwise benefit from a liberal interpretation."[62] The BFOQ test was developed by the Supreme Court in *Meiorin*.[63] Each stage of this test ensures that the interests of both parties are carefully weighed:

> First, the employer must show that it adopted the standard for a purpose rationally connected to the performance of the job . . . . Second, the employer must establish that it adopted the particular standard in an honest and good faith belief that it was necessary to the fulfilment of that legitimate work-related purpose. Third, the employer must establish that the standard is reasonably necessary to the accomplishment of that legitimate work-related purpose. To show that the standard is reasonably necessary, it must be demonstrated that it is impossible to accommodate individual employees sharing the characteristics of the claimant without imposing undue hardship upon the employer.[64]

The Supreme Court's formulation of the BFOQ test resonates with the aforementioned values articulated in the preamble of the *Code*. While on its face, the test is an example of pragmatic

---

62 *Ibid* at para 84.

63 *British Columbia (Public Service Employee Relations Commission) v British Columbia Government and Service Employees' Union (BCGSEU)*, [1999] SCJ No 46 at para. 54, paraphrased in headnote [Meiorin Grievance].

64 *Ibid*.

balancing in that it focuses on the duty to accommodate, the stringency of this duty is an example of how principled balancing converges with this pragmatic exercise. An employer has a duty to reasonably accommodate an employee and this duty is an extension of the overarching principle that an individual has a right to be free of discrimination. Conversely, an employer who meets *all* of the criteria attached to subsection 24(1) has the ability to justify preferential hiring practices.

In *Christian Horizons*, the court agreed with the Tribunal's finding that Christian Horizons satisfied the subjective element of the BFOQ test in that it sincerely believed that the qualification was necessary for the performance of the support worker job. The court also agreed with the Tribunal that Christian Horizons failed to satisfy the objective element of the BFOQ test. Christian Horizons did not provide the service of religious education and indoctrination and never turned its mind to a consideration of whether "the prohibition on same-sex relationships was necessary for the effective performance of the job of support worker in a home where there is no proselytizing and where residents are not required to be Evangelical Christians."[65]

The court commented on how paragraph 24(1)(a) seeks to balance the rights of certain groups against equality rights:

> An approach to s. 24(1)(a) that takes into account [in the analysis of the second element], in the determination of the primary activity of the religious organization, the perspective and purpose of the organization is consistent with the guarantee of freedom of religion. At the same time, the BFOQ requirement found in [the third element of] s. 24(1)(a) upholds the important *Charter* protection for equality rights.[66]

The Christian Horizons decision foregrounds the importance of perspective in assessing conflicting rights. On the one hand,

65 *Christian Horizons*, above note 4 at para 95.

66 *Ibid* at para 71.

the perspective of the religious organization ought to be paramount in assessing whether or not it meets the "primarily engaged" part of the exception section, while on the other hand, the BFOQ must be both subjectively and objectively appropriate. This focus on perspective is derived from the court's reading of the purpose of the section as primarily concerned with protecting the rights of association for certain organizations and from the well-established jurisprudence on the dual perspective required in the assessment of a BFOQ.

2) Balancing in the Caselaw

The balancing tools present within the *Code* itself are both informed by and taken up in judicial decisions on balancing conflicting rights. This section of the paper highlights three cases in which the complexity of balancing is explicitly addressed:[67] *Trinity Western*;[68] *Reference re Same-Sex Marriage*;[69] and *Brockie*.[70] In previous policy briefing notes and in the Commission's *Policy on*

---

67 These three cases have been selected because they illustrate three different approaches to balancing: principled; pragmatic; and a mixture of both. One notable case not discussed in this section is *Hall (Litigation guardian of) v Powers* (2002), 213 DLR (4th) 308 (Ont SCJ) [*Hall*]. The issues raised in *Hall* are almost identical to the ones dealt with in the three cases that are discussed. *Hall* involved an application for an interlocutory injunction restraining the Catholic District School Board from preventing Marc Hall's attendance at his high school prom with his boyfriend. The Court was called upon to balance Hall's s15 *Charter* right to be free from discrimination on the basis of his sexual orientation with the right to freedom of religion in s 2(a) of the *Charter* and the protection of denomination school rights in s 93(1) of the *The Constitution Act, 1867*, 30 & 31 Vict, c 3.

68 *Trinity Western*, above note 31.

69 *Reference re Same-Sex Marriage*, above note 8.

70 *Brockie*, above note 45.

Discrimination and Harassment because of Gender Orientation,[71] these cases have been examined in detail and their balancing strategies have been noted. The goal of this section of the paper is to evaluate how courts rely on *both* pragmatic and principled approaches to balancing. *Trinity Western* is perhaps the most fully integrated vision of pragmatic and principled balancing. The absence of a factual context means that the *Reference re Same-Sex Marriage* case is necessarily focused on a principled articulation of balancing. On the other hand, the Superior Court's decision in *Brockie* tends to privilege a pragmatic approach to balancing. Ultimately, the balancing tools forged in each decision expand the conceptual toolbox for balancing conflicting rights.

a) Trinity Western

Trinity Western University (TWU) is a private institution in British Columbia associated with the Evangelical Free Church of Canada. TWU established a teacher training program offering baccalaureate degrees in education upon completion of a five-year course, four years of which were spent at TWU, the fifth year under the aegis of Simon Fraser University. TWU applied to the BC College of Teachers (BCCT) for permission to assume full responsibility for a teacher education program. TWU offers education within a "Christian context" and requires students to sign a document outlining "community standards" containing a prohibition on homosexual behaviour. The BCCT refused to approve the application because it was contrary to the public interest for BCCT to approve a teacher education program offered by a private institution that appears to follow discriminatory practices.

As part of its disposition on this case, the Supreme Court

71 Ontario Human Rights Commission, *Policy on Discrimination and Harassment because of Gender Orientation* (OHRC, 2000), online: OHRC www.ohrc.on.ca/sites/default/files/attachments/Policy_on_discrimination_and_harassment_because_of_gender_identity.pdf.

had to consider how to balance two competing *Charter* guarantees: freedom of religion and sexual orientation equality rights. Although *Trinity Western* was decided within the context of the *Charter*, established interpretive principles require human rights codes to be applied in accordance with *Charter* values. Indeed, *Trinity Western* has become the paradigmatic example of balancing in many subsequent Human Rights Tribunal decisions, and the tools offered by *Trinity Western* have tended to dominate the OHRC's understanding of how to balance conflicting rights.

The Court's approach to balancing integrates both principled and pragmatic considerations. The overarching principle articulated in this case is that any potential conflict between rights should be resolved through properly defining the scope of the rights involved. This process is required because, in principle, there is no hierarchy of rights in the *Charter* or the *Code*: "Any potential conflict between religious freedoms and equality rights should be resolved through the proper delineation of the rights and values involved. Properly defining the scope of the rights avoids a conflict in this case. Neither freedom of religion nor the guarantee against discrimination based on sexual orientation is absolute."[72] A clear delineation of the extent and reach of each of the rights at stake may resolve the balancing issue at a very early stage in the task. That is, once the scope of the right is determined, both the complainant and respondent will have a better sense of whether or not their actions are legally protected.

In *Trinity Western*, the Court concluded that the distinction between beliefs and conduct could serve as the marker of the proper scope of freedom of religion; "The proper place to draw the line in cases like the one at bar is generally between belief and conduct. The freedom to hold beliefs is broader than the freedom to act on them."[73] So long as a discriminatory belief is

72 *Trinity Western*, above note 31 at para 29.

73 *Ibid* at para 36.

not translated into a discriminatory behaviour, individuals and institutions have the right to uphold those beliefs.[74] This distinction functions as a key tool in principled balancing but, crucially, determining the scope of the right is not accomplished within a vacuum. The scope of one right is, in part, assessed in relation to other rights and with respect to the particular factual context at hand: "The ultimate protection of any particular *Charter* right must be measured in relation to other rights and with a view to the underlying context in which the apparent conflict arises."[75] This comparative and contextual approach to rights protection opens the door for pragmatic tools to enter into the balancing equation.

The pragmatic balancing tools espoused in *Trinity Western* foreground the context of the rights claims.[76] First, evidentiary requirements loom large in pragmatic balancing. The Court emphasized that the mere anticipation of discriminatory behaviour is not enough to justify limits on rights. Absent concrete evidence that teachers trained at TWU fostered discrimination in the classroom, the freedom of individuals to adhere to certain religious beliefs should be respected. In essence, unless evidence indicated otherwise, teachers trained at TWU could keep their own personal beliefs in check when they began to teach in a public

---

74 Justice MacKinnon articulates this principle in *Hall*, above note 67 at para 31: "If individuals in Canada were permitted to simply assert their religious beliefs require them to discriminate against homosexuals without objective scrutiny, there would be no protection at all from discrimination for gays and lesbians in Canada because everyone who wished to discriminate against them could make that assertion."

75 *Amselem*, above note 6 at para 62.

76 Context-specific analysis plays a large role in the majority of balancing cases. Justice MacKinnon states in *Hall*, above note 67 at para 26, that, "the Prom in question is not part of a religious service (such as a mass), is not part of the religious education component of the Board's activity, is not held on school property, and is not educational in nature."

school. Second, the Court continued to adhere to a public/private distinction in determining the appropriate balance between competing rights. They did not take issue with the ability of TWU, as a private religious institution, to require its students to sign the community standards agreement. Although the Court did note that homosexual students would not be tempted to apply for admission there and could only sign this contract at great personal cost, the Court was of the view that the voluntary adoption of a code of conduct based on a person's own religious beliefs, in a private institution, was not in itself discriminatory. In *Trinity Western*, the emphasis on pre-existing evidence of discrimination and the distinction between private and public institutions provide two specific pragmatic approaches to balancing rights that uphold the larger principle of delineating the proper scope of the rights at stake.

b) *Reference re Same-Sex Marriage*

In response to provincial court decisions in British Columbia,[77] Ontario,[78] and Quebec[79] that changed the definition of marriage to include same-sex couples, the federal Liberal Government drafted Bill C-38, *An Act respecting certain aspects of legal capacity for marriage for civil purposes*.[80] Bill C-38 proposed to legalize same-sex marriage across Canada. One of the most pressing issues that arose in the provincial cases and in Bill C-38 was how to ensure that freedom of religion would be protected, especially in relation to the solemnization of marriage, while also recognizing that the conventional definition of marriage inher-

---

77 *EGALE Canada Inc v Canada (Attorney General)*, 2003 BCCA 251.

78 *Halpern et al v Canada (Attorney General) et al* (2003), 65 OR (3d) 161 (Ont CA).

79 *Catholic Civil Rights League v Hendricks* (2004) 238 DLR (4th) 577 (Que CA).

80 1st Sess, 38th Parl, 2005 (Royal assent 20 July 2005) [Bill C-38].

ently violated the equality rights of same-sex couples.

Mindful of the complexities involved in balancing two equally valid rights claims, the Liberal Government referred a draft of Bill C-38 to the Supreme Court for their guidance. Hoping the Court would provide a methodology for working out the tensions between freedom of religion and sexuality equality rights, the Government asked the Court if the freedom of religion guaranteed by section 2(a) of the *Charter* protects religious officials from being compelled to perform a marriage between two persons of the same sex that is contrary to their religious beliefs. The Court's answer to this question provides a further articulation of the principled approach to balancing and also reasserts that absent a factual context, the pragmatic application of these principles is impossible.

The most important principled balancing tool that arises in this case is that in order for a conflict of rights to occur, an *actual intrusion* of one right onto the other is necessary. According to the Court, "The mere recognition of equality rights of one group cannot, in itself, constitute a violation of the rights of another. The promotion of *Charter* rights and values enriches our society as a whole and the furtherance of those rights cannot undermine the very principles the *Charter* was meant to foster."[81] Equality rights, then, coexist in a relationship that is consistent with the values of mutual understanding and respect underlying both the *Charter* and the *Code*.[82] This principle encapsulates the

---

81 *Reference re Same-Sex Marriage*, above note 8 at para 46.

82 Justice MacKinnon expressed this principle in *Hall*, above note 67 at para 60:

> It is one of the distinguishing strengths of Canada as a nation that we value tolerance and respect for others. All of us have fundamental rights including expression, association and religion. Sometimes, as in this case, our individual rights bump into those of our neighbours and our institutions. When that occurs we, as individuals and institutions, must acknowledge the duties that accompany our

aforementioned third step in identifying when there is no conflict of rights; a conflict does not exist unless *actual* burdens on rights occur. Extending the right to marry to same-sex couples does not, in itself, conflict with any *Charter* rights that others may have. As the OHRC's factum to the Court states, "Exclusion is discriminatory, inclusion is not. An individual denied access may complain of discrimination; an individual wishing to deny access may complain, but not of discrimination."[83]

In *Reference re Same-Sex Marriage*, the Court affirmed that freedom of religion is an expansive right that is "broad and jealously guarded in our *Charter* jurisprudence."[84] This principle also applies to human rights codes: "human rights codes must be interpreted and applied in a manner that respects the broad protection granted to religious freedom under the *Charter*."[85] The Court decisively concluded that any compulsion on religious officials to perform same-sex marriages "would almost certainly run afoul of the *Charter* guarantee of freedom of religion, given the expansive protection afforded to religion by s. 2(a) of the *Charter*."[86] As in *Trinity Western*, the reasoning driving this conclusion stems from the Court's delineation of the scope of freedom of religion. Included in this right is the right to manifest religious beliefs through religious practice, and the performance of religious rights — such as the solemnization of marriage — is a

---

> rights. Mr. Hall has a duty to accord to others who do not share his orientation the respect that they, with their religious values and beliefs, are due. Conversely, for the reasons I have given, the Principle and the Board have a duty to accord Mr. Hall the respect that he is due as he attends the Prom with his date, his classmates and their dates.

83 *Reference re Same-Sex Marriage*, above note 8 (Factum of the Intervenor Ontario Human Rights Commission at para 35) [OHRC Factum].

84 *Ibid*, above note 8 at para 53.

85 *Ibid* at para 55.

86 *Ibid* at para 56.

fundamental aspect of religious practice. When the scope of the right is made clear, the potential for conflicting rights claims is significantly decreased.[87]

The Court suggested that tools found within the *Charter* itself will play a large role in balancing any potential conflicts of rights: "Conflicts of rights do not imply conflict with the *Charter*; rather the resolution of such conflicts generally occurs within the ambit of the *Charter* itself by way of internal balancing and delineation."[88] This statement resonates with the previous discussion in this paper of the importance of the internal balancing provisions within the *Code*. While section 1 is the primary site of internal balancing in the *Charter*, the exception sections of the *Code* offer pragmatic balancing solutions with similar justificatory criteria as is found in section 1 jurisprudence.

But aside from these statements of principles and recognition of existing balancing tools, the Court was wary of providing a more detailed analysis of whether or not the proposed legislation would create "an impermissible collision of rights."[89] This wariness stems from a refusal to examine a potential conflict of rights in a purely abstract form. When there is no factual context it would be "improper" to assess how balancing may take place: "*Charter* decisions should not and must not be made in a factual vacuum. To attempt to do so would trivialize the *Charter* and inevitably result in ill-considered opinions."[90] This passage serves as a valuable reminder that the balancing of conflicting rights

---

87 The relational nature of *Charter* rights is addressed in *Amselem*, above note 6 at para 62. The Court states: "Conduct which would potentially cause harm to or interference with the rights of others would not automatically be protected. The ultimate protection of any particular *Charter* right must be measured in relation to other rights and with a view to the underlying context in which the apparent conflict arises."

88 *Reference re Same-Sex Marriage*, above note 8 at para 52.

89 *Ibid* at para 50.

90 *Ibid* at para 51.

must *always* consider the factual context in which the conflict occurs. It is also a reminder that a generic formula is inappropriate when dealing with the balancing of conflicting of rights. Both a principled and a pragmatic approach to balancing provide valuable tools, but they are tools only. Neither approach should be understood as providing a determinative balancing test.

c) *Brockie*

Ray Brillinger, in his capacity as president of the Canadian Lesbian and Gay Archives (CLGA), attended the offices of Imaging Excellence Inc (Imaging), a commercial printing company owned and operated by Scott Brockie, to ask Imaging to print blank letterhead and envelopes for CLGA's general correspondence and some business cards for its officers. The copy presented to Imaging contained the CLGA's new logo and noted that it represented interests of "gays" and "lesbians" but said nothing of CLGA's objects, activities, or membership. Brockie refused to provide the requested printing services. Brillinger and the CLGA brought a complaint based on discrimination based on sexual orientation. In response, Brockie focused his defence on freedom of religion and asserted that providing printing services to homosexual organizations would be in direct opposition to his religious beliefs.

The Ontario Board of Inquiry held that Brockie's denial of service contravened the sexual orientation protections of the *Code* and that it was reasonable to limit Brockie's freedom of religion in order to prevent harm to members of the lesbian and gay community and their organizations by the denial of services because of their sexual orientation. Brockie appealed to the Ontario Superior Court which upheld the Board's original decision, but amended it to add an explicit recognition of Brockie's freedom of religion. In coming to the conclusion that this was a necessary addition, the court took a pragmatic approach to balancing conflicting rights that builds on the *Trinity Western* principle of separating beliefs and conduct.

The court noted that the freedom to act on religious beliefs is circumscribed when it interferes with the rights of others. By examining the "core" of the freedom, it is possible to determine which activities engage the protections of the *Code* and the *Charter*. Those activities at the "periphery" of the freedom will be less likely to be protected: "The further the activity is from the core elements of the freedom, the more likely the activity is to impact on others and the less deserving the activity is of protection. Service of the public in a commercial service must be considered at the periphery of activities protected by freedom of religion."[91] The court's pragmatic balancing emerges out of this distinction between core and peripheral elements. Stating that the Board's order could have been less intrusive, the court's addition to the Board's order makes clear that "this order shall not require Mr. Brockie or Imaging Excellence to print material of a nature which could reasonably be considered to be in direct conflict with the core elements of his religious beliefs or creed."[92] The court worried that the original order was overbroad and could extend to other material with editorial content that is "repugnant to the fundamental religious tenets of the printer,"[93] such as "material that conveyed a message proselytizing and promoting the gay and lesbian lifestyle."[94]

While this form of pragmatic balancing is envisioned in both *Trinity Western* and the *Reference re Same-Sex Marriage*, the court in *Brockie* runs the risk of balancing conflicting rights within a factual vacuum. The court's addition to the Board's order is grounded in "a few hypothetical situations"[95] rather than in an *actual* evidentiary context. This type of speculation is precisely what the Supreme Court sought to avoid in the *Reference re Same-Sex*

---

91 *Brockie*, above note 45 at para 51.

92 *Ibid* at para 58.

93 *Ibid* at para 49.

94 *Ibid* at para 56.

95 *Ibid*.

Marriage because they understood that the task of balancing is not accomplished solely through a reliance on a principled articulation of the scope of the rights at stake, but that this process must necessarily be grounded in the specific scenario at hand. As the OHRC briefing note on this case makes clear, this aspect of *Brockie* has "the potential to open the door to future disputes about what actions could be considered to conflict with the core elements of religious beliefs. In particular, the notion that materials that 'proselytise' a gay and lesbian 'lifestyle' may be refused, leaves open the potential for future arguments that any number of activities strike at the core of religious beliefs."[96] *Brockie* is an example of overzealous balancing; the court's eagerness to imagine future hypothetical balancing scenarios oversteps the parameters created by the facts of the case. In short, the desire to engage in principled balancing must be tempered by the tools of pragmatic balancing.

3) A Summary of the Balancing Tools

This section of the paper provides, in point form, a summary of the balancing tools discussed above. The two approaches to balancing that this paper identifies (principled and pragmatic) provide the framework for sorting these tools into two conceptual toolboxes. However, as has been noted many times through this discussion, these two approaches will necessarily overlap in the adjudication of conflicting rights claims and in the text of the *Code* itself. Some of these tools may also be employed at the first instance to determine if there is actually no conflict of rights (Section C above) and, if that is the case, formal balancing would be unnecessary.

---

96 Ontario Human Rights Commission, Briefing Note, "Reconciling Rights: *Trinity Western*, *Marc Hall* and *Brillinger v. Brockie*" (3 July 2002). This document was provided by the Ontario Human Rights Commission.

Principled Balancing Tools	Pragmatic Balancing Tools
• Maintain the inherent dignity and worth of each individual. • Foster a climate of mutual understanding and respect. • No right is absolute. • Delineate the proper scope of the right. • There is no hierarchy of rights. • Freedom of belief is wider than the freedom to act on those beliefs. • Mere recognition of the equality rights of one group is not a violation of the rights of another group. • Contextual analysis is always required. • Only actual burdens on rights trigger conflicts. • Use a purposive interpretation of rights. • Exception sections are construed narrowly; rights are construed broadly.	• Equally valid competing rights? • Actual conflict? • Core or peripheral activities? • Evidence proves discrimination? • Public versus private entity? • Duty to accommodate? • Exception sections available? • Extent of infringement on each right?

E. Using the Tools

A number of conflicting rights scenarios and their potential resolutions have been presented throughout this paper in order to illustrate specific balancing tools. This section of the paper will utilize each of the tools noted above by working through one timely example of conflicting rights: same-sex marriage and civil marriage commissioners.[97] This example has been chosen not

97 As noted in the opening paragraph of this chapter, the issue of whether or not civil marriage commissioners may refuse to perform same-sex marriages on the basis of freedom of religion was recently before the Saskatchewan Court of Appeal (see *Reference re Marriage Commis-*

only for its currency, but also because it encompasses both the service and employment contexts. There are distinctively different ways to balance the conflicting rights in this scenario, and the outcome will be determined by the extent to which one is guided by either a principled or pragmatic approach or some combination of the two.

For the purposes of this scenario, let us assume that civil marriage commissioners are employed and authorized by the province to solemnize marriages. A same-sex couple decide to get married at Toronto City Hall. After filling out the requisite paperwork, licence in hand, they want to make an appointment for the solemnization. They are told that the only commissioner available that day is, because of deeply and sincerely held religious beliefs, unwilling to solemnize a same-sex marriage. The couple is told that they should return the following day when another commissioner will be able to perform their ceremony.

---

sioners, above note 2). In the wake of a lower court decision (*Nichols v MJ*, 2009 SKQB 299 [*Nichols*]) which ruled that the freedom of religion of civil marriage commissioners does not extend to permitting discrimination based on sexual orientation, the Saskatchewan Government proposed legislation that would expressly permit marriage commissioners to refuse to officiate at weddings that are not in accord with their deeply held religious beliefs. The Government asked the Court of Appeal to rule on the constitutionality of the proposed amendments. The full text of the proposed amendments is set out at paragraph 16 of *Reference re Marriage Commissioners*, above note 2. The Court of Appeal found that the proposed legislation violated the equality rights of gays and lesbians under s 15(1) of the *Charter*. A plurality of the court also found that the freedom of religion of marriage commissioners would be curtailed if they were required to perform same-sex marriages. A plurality of the court dealt with the balancing of these conflicting rights under section 1 of their *Charter* analysis, particularly at the minimal impairment and proportionality of effects stages of the analysis. Ultimately, the court found the proposed legislation unconstitutional.

The same-sex couple has brought a discriminatory service complaint before the OHRC and the marriage commissioners are vigorously defending their freedom of religion and the employer's duty to accommodate their beliefs.

The questions outlined in Section C of this paper provide the starting point for assessing this scenario. In order to identify if there is an *actual* conflict of rights, we must begin by asking whether or not the rights claims are characterized appropriately and whether or not they are valid, legally recognized rights. The same-sex couple grounds their claim in the right to be free from discrimination based on sexual orientation in a service context (section 1 of the *Code*).[98] Since they were explicitly refused service because they were a same-sex couple, a discrimination claim based on sexual orientation is the appropriate characterization of the issue. So, too, this is a valid, legally recognized right found in the text of the *Code* itself. The marriage commissioners base their claim on a right to be free from discrimination based on creed in the workplace (section 5(1) of the *Code*)[99] and the duty of an employer to reasonably accommodate religious beliefs (section 11(2) of the *Code*).[100] The commissioners argue that the

98 Section 1 of the *Code*, above note 3, states: "Every person has a right to equal treatment with respect to services, goods and facilities, without discrimination because of race, ancestry, place of origin, colour, ethnic origin, citizenship, creed, sex, sexual orientation, age, marital status, family status or disability."

99 Section 5 of the *Code*, *ibid*, states: "Every person has a right to equal treatment with respect to employment without discrimination because of race, ancestry, place or origin, colour, ethnic origin, citizenship, creed, sex, sexual orientation, age, record of offences, marital status, family status or disability."

100 Section 11(2) of the *Code*, *ibid*, states: "The Commission, the Tribunal or a court shall not find that a requirement, qualification or factor is reasonable and bona fide in the circumstances unless it is satisfied that the needs of the group of which the person is a member cannot be accom-

tenets of their religion do not permit them to solemnize same-sex marriages and that to do so would undermine their deeply and sincerely held religious beliefs. They want their beliefs accommodated in the same way that the celebration of religious holidays must be accommodated, short of undue hardship. Assuming the commissioners provide evidence of the requirements of their religious beliefs, they appear to have characterized their rights claim appropriately according to the legally recognized right to freedom from discrimination based on creed.

We may now move on to the third question of whether or not the needs of the parties are truly in conflict. In the service context, an argument could be made that the couple's "need" to get married is indeed being fulfilled, but just not within their preferred time frame. However, it is unlikely this argument will stand up to scrutiny because it amounts to adverse effects discrimination in that preferential treatment is inadvertently given to non-same-sex couples. In effect, to allow this argument would be to accord same-sex couples second-class citizenship. On the other hand, the "need" to adhere to one's religious beliefs is met within the service context because the commissioners simply refuse to solemnize these couples. The commissioners' religious need directly conflicts with the couple's solemnization need. The province, as the employer, *may* have a duty to accommodate the commissioners' needs, but it *absolutely* has a duty to provide services without discrimination. It appears that these two needs will not be easily reconciled and that they are truly in conflict.

The fourth initial question asks whether the rights are more than trivially interfered with. In this scenario it appears that both of the rights in conflict are more than trivially interfered with in that each right is fully compromised by the requirements of the other right. While the same-sex couple in question may be able to

---

modated without undue hardship on the person responsible for accommodating those needs, considering the cost, outside sources of funding, if any, and health and safety requirements, if any."

return on another day to be married by a more amenable commissioner, the conflict itself will continue to arise in future scenarios and the unequal access to services has not been remedied for either this couple or future couples. The marriage commissioner's religious beliefs are also fully compromised if she would be required to perform a marriage which does not accord with those beliefs. It may be likely that the marriage commissioner would resign rather than perform a same-sex marriage.

At this point in our assessment, we may begin to consider the balancing tools and the potentially different outcomes produced by using either a pragmatic or principled approach. In the service context, from a principled perspective, the denial of same-sex solemnization services violates the values underlying the *Code*. Specifically, the inherent dignity and worth of these individuals is undermined by this refusal. The failure to provide service to this couple is a denial of their equality rights. This, in fact, is the position that the OHRC has previously taken on this issue. In his letter to the Attorney General on this issue, the former Chief Commissioner stated: "The denial of service by a public official to a same sex couple is no less a violation of the *Code* and the *Charter* than a denial of this service to an interfaith or interracial couple."[101] Indeed, allowing marriage commissioners to pick and choose to whom they offer their services potentially opens the door to an endless number of refusals based on religious beliefs. For instance, a practising Catholic may refuse to solemnize the marriage of a previously divorced Catholic. A principled approach in the service context foregrounds the anti-discriminatory mandate of the *Code* as embodied in the preamble's call for "a climate of understanding and mutual respect for the dignity and worth of each person so that each person feels a part of the community." As the former Chief Commissioner reminded in his letter, "Inclusion

101 Letter from Keith Norton to The Honourable Michael J Bryant, Attorney General of Ontario (as he then was) (20 December 2004) at 2. This document was provided by the Ontario Human Rights Commission.

is an essential part of equality."[102]

A pragmatic approach to the service issue would undoubtedly begin by stating the principles and values above and then go on to look at this particular service context. Factors to consider include: the fact that civil marriage commissioners are designated under the *Marriage Act*;[103] the solemnization of marriage by civil officials is a public service;[104] civil marriage commissioners are the civil alternative for those who do not wish (or cannot obtain) a religious marriage; the couple meets the eligibility criteria for marriage, so there is an obligation to provide this service whether or not it conflicts with the views of an individual employee; there

---

102 *Ibid.*

103 Ontario *Marriage Act*, above note 41. In *Nichols*, above note 97, the court examined the function of civil marriage commissioners under Saskatchewan's *Marriage Act, 1995*, SS 1995, c M-4.1, and found that civil marriage commissioners were acting as government in that they were implementing a particular government scheme (the solemnization of civil marriage). The court further found that the fundamental role of the marriage commissioner is to solemnize marriages and, as such, is performing a governmental activity: "As a government actor, he is not permitted to consider his personal religious views when performing his public functions" (at para 55).

104 The Court of Appeal in the *Reference re Marriage Commissioners*, above note 2, confirmed that individuals acting as government (as is the case with public officials designated by legislation to perform certain functions) should be held to a higher standard than those acting in the private sphere because governmental actors have *Charter*-imposed duties of equal treatment and religious neutrality. In the words of Richards J: "Marriage commissioners do not act as private citizens when they discharge their official duties. Rather, they serve as agents of the Province and act on its behalf and its behalf only. Accordingly, a system that would make marriage services available according to the personal beliefs of commissioners is highly problematic. It would undercut the basic principle that governmental services must be provided on an impartial and non-discriminatory basis" (at para 98).

is clear evidence of discrimination against an identifiable, protected group; there is no exception section of the *Code* for the provision of services; caselaw has determined that the freedom to hold beliefs is greater than the freedom to act on those beliefs when it negatively impacts the equality rights of others, especially in a service context; caselaw also recognizes that providers of public services must be able to "check their personal views" at the door. Both a pragmatic and principled approach to balancing would agree that under the *Code* and the *Charter* there is no doubt that same-sex couples are entitled to equal service. The attitudes of individual employees must not be allowed to "poison" the environment for same-sex couples requesting civil solemnization services.

The analysis becomes more complicated when the employer-employee relationship is factored into this equation and the debate shifts to a consideration of the extent to which a duty to accommodate applies in this particular case. By way of example, in 2009, the government of Saskatchewan proposed legislation that would exempt civil marriage commissioners from performing marriages that do not accord with their religious beliefs. The government asked the Court of Appeal to review the constitutionality of their proposal. The legislation had two options: (1) an exemption provision for marriage commissioners who were appointed before 2004 when same-sex marriage was legalized; or (2) a blanket exemption provision for all civil marriage commissioners.[105] Both options were silent on the scope of the religious exception. That is, the legislation was not limited to refusals to perform same-sex marriages on the basis of religious beliefs but could, at least hypothetically, extend to other refusals based on religious grounds such as inter-religious marriages or interracial marriages.

105 *Reference re Marriage Commissioners*, above note 2 at para 16.

In *Reference re Marriage Commissioners*, the Saskatchewan Court of Appeal addressed the issue of accommodation at the minimal impairment stage of its section 1 *Charter* analysis. A plurality of the court found the objective of both versions of the proposed legislation to be "the accommodation of the s. 2(a) *Charter* freedoms of commissioners by relieving them of the obligation to perform marriage ceremonies in circumstances where doing so would be contrary to their religious beliefs."[106] In the spirit of pragmatic balancing, Richards J endorsed the practice of informal accommodation when assessing whether or not the proposed legislation minimally impaired the equality rights of gays and lesbians. Justice Richards expressly approved of the "single entry point" system for accessing civil marriage commissioners that is currently used in parts of Ontario, including Toronto. Under this system, when a couple seeks a marriage commissioner, they contact a central office rather than an individual commissioner. The central office then assigns a commissioner to the couple. This permits individual commissioners to be "accommodated 'behind the scenes' with the result that no couple would be denied services because of a consideration which would engage s. 15 of the *Charter*."[107]

Given this recent endorsement of informal accommodation by an appellate level court, we are likely to see an increased reliance on this pragmatic balancing tool in the service context. However, while it is easy enough to achieve this informal accommodation in a large urban centre such as Toronto where there are enough marriage commissioners to make equal access to marriage commissioners possible at all times, informal accommodation may not be possible in rural Ontario settings without disrupting equal access to the services of civil marriage commissioners. When the issue of accommodation is addressed through

---

106 *Ibid* at para 76.

107 *Ibid* at para 85.

a pragmatic analysis, the overarching consideration is thus the impact that such accommodation would have on the delivery of services.

Justice Richards in the *Reference re Marriage Commissioners* was very alive to this issue and carefully noted that the validity of any "single entry point" system "would need to be assessed in light of all of the relevant facts pertaining to it and with reference to the specific features of the proposed system."[108] In other words, it is not a foregone conclusion that "behind the scenes" accommodation will ensure the appropriate balancing of rights in all circumstances. Service providers, especially in the governmental context, must ensure that there is no risk of a same-sex couple being refused services because of their sexual orientation.

A recent op-ed piece for the Canadian Civil Liberties Association (CCLA) posed the following three scenarios to concretely illustrate the limits of accommodation:

> 1) if you're licensed as the only marriage commissioner within a 100 mile radius, performing all marriages in the vicinity will likely be considered to be a BFOR [*bona fide* occupational requirement], as accommodation would significantly impair the government's ability to provide a service to the public without discrimination;
>
> 2) if you're one of 200 commissioners in a city, performing same sex marriages may not be a BFOR, as accommodation could be accomplished without undue hardship — you'd really only need a bifurcated list or a single access entry point;
>
> 3) if your religious belief prevented you from marrying any couple not adhering to the True Faith (lets pretend it's Scientology, just for fun), it's probably impossible to reason-

108 *Ibid* at paras 43 and 89.

> ably accommodate that belief. The ability to solemnize the unions of, say, at least 75% of eligible couples would likely be considered a BFOR regardless of the circumstances, and inability to do so would thus warrant dismissal.[109]

The scenarios from the CCLA illustrate how a pragmatic analysis will tend, on a case-by-case basis, to focus on the "short of undue hardship" aspect of accommodation. If same-sex couples have equal access to the solemnization of marriage and the same calibre of service when employees' religious beliefs are accommodated, then balancing has been achieved. Recognizing that freedom of religion is not absolute, and hence the duty to accommodate religious beliefs is also not absolute, a pragmatic approach would seek to set limits on accommodation only when the rights of same-sex couples are infringed (directly or indirectly), or when a poisoned atmosphere is created by the accommodation of an employee's religious beliefs. A potential downside of this pragmatic approach is that it may rely on same-sex couples to "police" their equal access to services and report any discrepancies or inequities.[110]

---

109 Benjamin Oliphant, "Saskatchewan Marriage Commissioners: Is There a Duty to Accommodate Discrimination?" CCLA Rights Watch (31 May 2010), online: CCLA www.ccla.org/rightswatch/?p=1223.

110 One prominent example of a pragmatic approach to an employer's duty to accommodate in conflicting rights cases may be seen in the settlement reached in a complaint against Markham-Stouffville Hospital. Seven nurses objected to participating in abortion procedures due to their religious convictions. They filed a complaint with the OHRC claiming that their religious rights were violated when the hospital required them to participate in abortion procedures. Under the terms of the settlement, the hospital adopted a policy that allows staff with a religious objection to abortions to be excused from directly performing or participating in such procedures, except where the mother's life is in danger. In this situation, the religious convictions of the nurses are accommodated without affecting a patient's ability to access abortion

A principled approach to accommodation in this context will likely foreground the scope of freedom of religion. In order to delineate the scope, a comparison of religious officials to civil marriage officials may be useful. The Commission's factum to the Supreme Court on the *Reference re Same-Sex Marriage* notes that, "religious officials acting in an official religious capacity express their religiosity in the performance of their job functions. In contrast, secular service providers that hold personal religious beliefs cannot claim that the performance of their job functions is an expression of their deeply held religious beliefs."[111] Justice Smith's concurring opinion in the *Reference re Marriage Commissioners* echoes these views. Justice Smith found that, "[t]he performance of a civil marriage by a marriage commissioner under the [Saskatchewan marriage] *Act* is not a religious rite or practice. Nor does the requirement to do so limit or restrict religious belief."[112] Justice Smith further notes that "these marriage commissioners are not themselves compelled to engage in the sexual activity they consider objectionable. Their objection is that it is sinful for *others* to engage in such activity."[113] Accordingly, Smith J finds that the scope of freedom of religion does not extend to protecting a civil marriage commissioner's refusal to marry same-sex couples.

Additionally, within a principled analysis the *public* nature of the duties of civil marriage commissioners will influence the belief-action analysis with respect to the scope of freedom of religion: "The expectation that an individual perform certain job duties may not, at the end of the day, violate freedom of religion if, by virtue of that person's public office, such duties are

---

procedures. In the particular context of this case it is possible to ensure equal, unaffected access to a public service while concurrently protecting an expansive understanding of freedom of religion.

111 OHRC Factum, above note 83 at paras 15–16.

112 *Reference re Marriage Commissioners*, above note 2 at para 147.

113 *Ibid* at para 148.

essential, and if the failure to perform them violates the *Charter* rights of others."[114] Courts have more often than not concluded that freedom of religion is not a sufficient justification for conduct that discriminates against others in areas of public life to which human rights legislation applies. A principled analysis may not need to address the question of accommodation because this approach may find that the scope of freedom of religion, in terms of acting on one's beliefs when they conflict with another's equality rights, does not extend to public officials employed in a public service context.

A principled approach to balancing may also focus on *Code* values in order to determine whether or not a duty to accommodate exists in this particular scenario. Human rights tribunals and courts would need to ask "whether a need that appears to be inconsistent with the Code is less deserving of accommodation than a need that does not conflict with the values of the Code."[115] A duty to accommodate may not extend to situations in which discrimination against another group is the by-product of accommodating a particular belief. A principled approach to balancing would ask if it is desirable to protect a value that is antithetical to the *Code*.

The benefit of a principled approach in the civil marriage commissioner example is that it strictly adheres to the underlying values of human rights legislation and it relies on established interpretive principles for *Code* exception sections. Principled balancing is likely to provide the most certainty for all parties in that employees would have the scope of their religious beliefs in the workplace clearly delineated and employers would have "either/or" guidelines for the provision of services. But, the certainty that comes from an analysis grounded solely in principled balancing is also the greatest limitation of this approach. It may

114 OHRC Factum, above note 83 at para 16.

115 *Ibid* at para 17.

not be flexible enough to provide the very mutual respect and understanding that it espouses. It may also privilege ideals and overarching values at the expense of actual, real-world concerns.

On the other hand, flexibility characterizes pragmatic balancing. This approach focuses on specific contextual questions and is more attentive to the actual working conditions of the everyday. This approach generally embodies a compromise mentality that attempts to accommodate the needs and rights of all parties. But flexibility and compromises may come at the expense of underlying anti-discrimination values. Pragmatic balancing will tend to rely more heavily on the particular situations of individual actors to assess the extent to which compromise is possible. As noted above, this means that these individuals may be expected to regulate and monitor how well the compromise is actually working.

F. Conclusion

The civil marriage commissioner scenario highlights the different resolutions that principled and pragmatic balancing exercises may offer. It also illustrates the overlap of these two approaches and the wide range of balancing tools that may be employed in any given situation. The best approach appears to be one that mixes and matches these two styles of balancing. Indeed, it is crucial that these two approaches complement and inform each other. For that reason, these approaches should not be understood as binary opposites. Rather, pragmatic and principled balancing may be located on a continuum in which most balancing occurs in the middle ground where these approaches overlap. Finally, it is always appropriate to let the context at hand dictate which balancing tools will be employed. Otherwise, we run the risk of over-stepping what is actually required to resolve a particular conflict and, in doing so, place unnecessary constraints on future balancing scenarios. The different outcomes discussed in this scenario are not simply the product of pragmatic or principled balancing, they are also markers of different philosophical understandings of equality and rights.

Chapter 12

Sexual Orientation and Religion in Canada: Litigation and Beyond

Miriam Smith*

A. Introduction

Conflicts between religious rights and other *Charter*-based[1] equality rights involve deep-seated matters of highly personal individual beliefs. In Canada's perennial constitutional debates, politicians and citizens have argued over the ordering of conflicting constitutional principles, scholars in political and legal philosophy have puzzled over how to reconcile seemingly irreconcilable rights conflicts, and judges have been called upon to rule in disputes in which each side claims fundamental *Charter* values.

This paper explores one specific type of conflict among *Charter* values — the conflict between religious rights on the one hand and lesbian, gay, bisexual, and transgender (LGBT)[2] rights on the

---

* The discussion of the Surrey book banning is drawn in part from my previously published article: "Questioning Heteronormativity: Lesbian and Gay Challenges to Educational Practice in British Columbia, Canada," (October 2004) 3:2 Social Movement Studies 131 ["Questioning Heteronormativity"]. The research for that article was supported by a grant from the Social Sciences and Humanities Research Council of Canada.

1 *Canadian Charter of Rights and Freedoms,* Part I of the *Constitution Act, 1982,* being Schedule B to the *Canada Act 1982* (UK) 1982, c 11 [*Charter*].

2 The terminology of "lesbian and gay" is highly contested and fluid in the field of sexuality studies. Many younger people reject the terms "lesbian"

other. I present a description of some of the key cases that have occurred in Canada pitting sexual orientation rights against religious rights under the *Charter*, showing how these cases have most commonly been resolved in the most recent period. While the last fifteen years have seen a significant expansion of LGBT rights, there have also been significant tensions over the status of religious rights in relation to claims for protection from discrimination based on sexual orientation. Some of these issues have included the introduction of reading material depicting children with same-sex parents in elementary schools (the Surrey book banning in BC[3]); teacher training for public schools (*Trinity Western* case[4]); the debate over the recognition of same-sex relationships and same-sex marriage (1995–2005); the *Owens*,[5] *Boissoin*,[6] and *Whatcott*[7] cases on free speech; cases on employment discrimination (*Heintz*[8]) and discrimination in the provision of services (*Brockie*[9]) in Ontario; and the ongoing case of a Sas-

---

and "gay" and, instead, identify under the umbrella of "queer"; others find the term "queer" to be offensive and, instead, identify as lesbian or gay. Many lesbians identify with the women's movement and have not felt that their interests were well represented in gay politics. The terms "trans," transgender, and transsexual are used to refer to gender identity (which is not the same as sexual orientation).

3 *Chamberlain v Surrey School District*, [2000] BCJ No 1875 (CA) [*Chamberlain*, 2000] and *Chamberlain v Surrey School District*, [2002] 4 SCR 710 [*Chamberlain*, 2002].

4 *Trinity Western University v British Columbia College of Teachers*, [2001] SCJ No 32 [*Trinity Western*].

5 *Owens v Saskatchewan (Human Rights Commission)*, 2006 SKCA 41 [*Owens*].

6 *Boissoin v Lund*, 2009 ABQB 592 [*Boissoin*].

7 *Whatcott v Saskatchewan Human Rights Tribunal et al*, 2010 SKCA 26 [*Whatcott*].

8 *Heintz v Christian Horizons*, 2008 HRTO 22 [*Heintz*].

9 *Ontario (Human Rights Commission) v Brockie*, [2002] OJ No 2375 (SCJ) [*Brockie*].

katchewan marriage commissioner who has refused to perform same-sex marriages (*Nichols*[10]) (see Table 1). In each of these cases, Christian Evangelicals claimed that their freedom of religion had been infringed by the assertion of same-sex equality rights. Two of the cases concerned the moral status of homosexuality itself, especially in relation to the education system. Other cases concerned the status of same-sex relationships and the legal recognition of such relationships in provincial and federal jurisdictions. The *Owens*, *Boissoin*, and *Whatcott* cases concerned the publication of statements condemning homosexuality while the *Heintz* case concerned employment discrimination on the basis of sexual orientation and the *Brockie* case dealt with the refusal of service to a lesbian and gay organization by a printer.

This debate has more than two sides, however. In both the "religious" and "LGBT rights" camps, there are multiple voices with different stances across a range of current policy issues including education, free speech, and the administration of same-sex marriage. In Canada, religious opinion on same-sex marriage is divided, with some liberal denominations arguing in favour of same-sex marriage and even claiming that their freedom of religion requires that they be permitted to perform such ceremonies as legal marriages while, in contrast, there are Protestant Evangelical, Roman Catholic, orthodox Muslim, orthodox Jewish, and other religious groups that oppose same-sex marriage. Further, while Protestant Evangelicals have played an important role in litigation against LGBT rights, adherents of other religious traditions have pursued other political strategies to block the recognition of LGBT rights or have intervened in court cases. In the queer community, there are those who oppose the campaign for same-sex marriage as normalizing same-sex relationships and as undermining distinctive urban queer cultures,

---

10 *Nichols v MJ*, 2009 SKQB 299 [*Nichols*].

while other same-sex couples favour state recognition of same-sex relationships and define the issue as one of fundamental human rights.[11] LGBT adherents of different religious traditions have also sought recognition within their own religious communities, sometimes openly challenging homophobic religious beliefs and opening up debates over the moral status of homosexuality.[12] In the Anglican Church, this debate has brought the Church to the brink of schism. However, it is certainly not the only case in which LGBTs have challenged faith communities as similar debates have occurred in the Muslim and Jewish communities in different ways. In Toronto and other Canadian cities, there are significant local groups of queer Muslims as well as queer Jewish groups and queer-friendly Reform synagogues.[13] At the same time, the queer community is understandably emphatic in claiming equality under the law and in pointing out the harmful effects of discrimination on the LGBT communities.[14] Therefore, focussing on litigation does not tell us the whole story of the complexity of the encounter of religion and sexuality with regard to the wholescale changes in the recognition of LGBT citizenship that

---

11 Susan Boyd & Claire FL Young, "From Same-Sex to No Sex? Trends towards Recognition of Same-Sex Relationships in Canada" (2003) 1:3 Seattle Journal of Social Justice 757.

12 Jennifer Nedelsky & Roger Hutchinson, "Clashes of Principle and the Possibility of Dialogue: A Case Study of Same-Sex Marriage in the United Church in Canada," in Richard Moon, ed, *Law and Religious Pluralism in Canada* (Vancouver: University of British Columbia Press, 2008) at 41–64.

13 Miriam Smith, "Identités queer: Diaspora et organisation ethnoculturelle et transnationale des lesbiennes et des gais à Toronto" (Spring 2005) 53 Lien social et Politiques 81, translated by Maya Berbery, online: www.erudit.org/revue/lsp/2005/v/n53/011647ar.pdf.

14 Community-University Institute for Social Research, *The Cost of Homophobia: Literature Review on the Human Impact of Homophobia on Canada* (Saskatoon: University of Saskatchewan, 2003).

have taken place in Canada over the last fifteen years.

In the first part of this chapter, I briefly sketch out the political background of conflicts over religion and same-sex equality rights in Canada and discuss three recent examples of conflict between the equality rights of gays and lesbians and freedom of religion. I then go on to argue that the courts may not be the best venue for reconciling conflicts over sexuality and religion. In particular, I argue that the *Charter* has tended to draw out the dominant forms of religious conflict over sexuality, especially conflicts pitting Christian Evangelicals against LGBT citizens, while marginalizing other important debates within religious communities over the recognition of LGBT members and the moral status of same-sex relationships as well as the debates between and among LGBT people and adherents of other non-Christian religious traditions, including the Muslim, Jewish, and other faith communities. I argue that these other debates and tensions are vitally important to balancing religious freedom with the recognition of LGBT rights. The paper argues that consultative and deliberative processes should supplement *Charter* litigation as a means of ensuring that diverse views within the LGBT community (which includes adherents of religious faith) and within various religious communities, including Christian, Muslim, Jewish, and other groups, are heard. The chapter concludes by pointing out that provincial human rights commissions have an important role to play in engaging local communities, particularly because some of the issues in balancing freedom of religion with the *Charter* rights of LGBT citizens fall within the constitutional jurisdiction of provincial governments. A broader consultative process based on deliberative mechanisms provides a proactive way for governments to manage the tensions around religion and sexual orientation and to ensure that a broader range of voices is heard than those who are privileged through the process of *Charter*-based legal mobilization.

B. Religion and Same-Sex Rights in Canada

While Canadians are accustomed to hearing American Evangelicals proselytizing against homosexuality and same-sex marriage, it is important to recognize that Canada is different from the US when it comes to the role of religion in public life in general and the role of religion in relation to same-sex rights in particular. In Canada, there is no constitutional separation of church and state, as in the US, and various religious rights have been recognized in the Canadian constitution, most importantly, the rights of Catholic and Protestant schools in *The Constitution Act, 1867*.[15] The Evangelical Protestant community in Canada is smaller than in the US and the political and institutional conditions for the mobilization of Evangelical political opinion in Canada are much less favourable than in the US.[16] Furthermore, as Bean *et al* have argued, "American evangelical identity is shot through with nationalistic symbolism" while nationalism is weaker in the Canadian Evangelical tradition.[17] While accelerating immigration has diversified Canada's urban centres over the last ten years, racialized communities and minority religious groups are far from unified in their approach to same-sex rights. Some representatives of visible minorities such as the Council of Chinese Canadians were very strong supporters of the campaign for same-sex marriage, while other groups have intervened in same-sex marriage litiga-

---

15 (UK), 30 & 31 Vict, c 3, reprinted in RSC 1985, App II, No 5.

16 Miriam Smith, *Political Institutions and Lesbian and Gay Rights in the United States and Canada* (New York: Routledge, 2008) [*Political Institutions*]; Sam Reimer, *Evangelicals and the Continental Divide: The Conservative Protestant Subculture in Canada and the United States* (Montreal: McGill-Queen's University Press, 2003).

17 Lydia Bean, Jason Kaufman, & Marco Jesus Gonzalez, "Why Doesn't Canada Have an American-style Christian Right? A Comparative Framework for Analyzing the Political Effects of Evangelical Subcultural Identity" (2008) 33:4 Canadian Journal of Sociology 899 at 927.

tion to oppose the legal recognition of same-sex marriage.[18]

Similarly, in most religious traditions, there is currently debate about the recognition of homosexuality and the status of same-sex relationships. Some liberal Protestant churches such as the Metropolitan Community Church in Toronto (MCCT) argued that the *denial* of their right to perform state-sanctioned same-sex marriages *infringed* the *Charter* guarantee of freedom of religion,[19] the opposite position to that of the Evangelical Protestant churches. Within many religious traditions, queer people themselves have challenged traditional beliefs that homosexuality is morally wrong. In the Canadian context, lesbian, gay, bisexual, and transgender people within the main Protestant denominations (notably, the Anglican Church and the United Church), the Catholic Church, the Muslim and Jewish communities, and many other religious denominations have undertaken a struggle for recognition. Therefore, there is much diversity of religious opinion on homosexuality and same-sex relationships as well as diversity within the LGBT community on questions of religion and faith.

Despite these multiple diversities, *Charter* litigation in this area has overwhelmingly pitted Christian Evangelicals against LGBT citizens and organizations. LGBTs of faith have been relatively absent from litigation (with the important exception of MCCT's role in the same-sex marriage debate) as have the Jewish and Muslims communities. Further, among Christians, litigation has tended to spring from the Protestant Evangelical tradition, rather than from adherents of mainstream Protestantism

---

18 Krishna Rau, "Fighting Back Religion: Part III" *Xtra* (15 March 2007), online: *Xtra* www.xtra.ca/public/National/Fighting_back_religion_Part_III-2747.aspx. For an earlier discussion of ethnicity and sexual orientation, see Avvy Go & John Fisher, "Working Together across Our Differences: A Discussion Paper on Coalition-Building, Participatory Litigation and Strategic Litigation" (Ottawa: Court Challenges Program, 2009).

19 *Halpern v Canada (Attorney General)* (2003), 65 OR (3d) 161 (CA).

such as the Anglican Church or the United Church. Similarly, the Roman Catholic Church and its members have not been directly involved in litigation around sexual orientation issues. From the facts of the cases outlined in Table 1, it is clear that Evangelical Christians (themselves a diverse group) are involved in the litigation in every case, at least as far as is evident from the public record. Of the cases listed in Table 1, I will focus on three cases that exemplify different aspects of the debate over sexual orientation and religion: the Surrey book banning, the *Boissoin* speech case, and the *Nichols* marriage commissioner case.

1) Surrey Book Banning, 2002

In the mid-1990s, gay teachers in the public schools of the Vancouver suburbs of Surrey and Port Coquitlam challenged their school board's decision to ban gay and lesbian-positive reading material in the elementary school classroom.[20] At the same time, the British Columbia College of Teachers (BCCT), the body responsible for certifying teachers in BC, refused to certify a teacher-training program at a Christian Evangelical university, Trinity Western University (TWU), because student teachers at TWU were required to sign a statement condemning homosexuality as a condition of their education.[21] These challenges to existing practice in the BC education system were mounted by lesbian and gay teacher activists and their sympathizers in the school system and within the BC Teachers' Federation (BCTF), who refused to accept the dominant heterosexual definition of norms appropriate to public school teaching. Activist teachers put forth a counter-discourse which problematized the normalized status of heterosexuality, arguing that lesbian and gay parents, their partners, and their children should be represented in the school curriculum and that lesbian and gay youth should not be stigmatized through silence

20 *Chamberlain,* 2000, above note 3 and *Chamberlain,* 2002, above note 3.

21 *Trinity Western*, above note 4.

or exclusion about their sexuality. Both cases went before the courts and were litigated under the *Charter*.

The Surrey book banning challenged *heteronormativity*, or the assumption that heterosexuality is the norm from which lesbian, gay, and bisexual people "deviate." As many scholars have pointed out, the idea that the fear of homosexuals is "irrational" erases and overlooks the structured heterosexuality of social practices.[22] As homosexuality is different from the norm, it is implicitly stigmatized as deviant and, in such a context, the fear of what is stigmatized and different is "rational," rather than "irrational." In contrast, the concept of heteronormativity calls attention to the structured sources of social power which define the lesbian, gay man, or bisexual as deviating from the norm of heterosexuality. Heteronormative practices imply heterosexism — they imply that heterosexual families and relationships are natural, normal, and better than homosexual and lesbian relationships. Heteronormative practices oppress through silence and exclusion, while heterosexism refers to an overt valorization of heterosexuality over homosexuality.[23]

The case arose out of the activism of teachers within the BCTF who organized around a broad range of issues related to equality in the classroom, including anti-racism education, Aboriginal issues, and programs to counter homophobia in the schools. In 1997, the first motions on homophobia were passed at the BCTF Annual General Meeting which stated "that the BCTF create a program to eliminate homophobia and heterosexism within the BC public-school system."[24] The BCTF would assist with teacher training and run workshops on the issue as well as develop

---

22 Cecilia Kitzinger, *The Social Construction of Lesbianism* (London: Sage, 1987).

23 Elizabeth Peel, "Mundane Heterosexism: Understanding Incidents of the Everyday" (2001) 24:1 Women's Studies International Forum 541.

24 British Columbia Teachers' Federation, News Release, "Teachers Debate Program to Eliminate Homophobia" (5 March 1997).

curriculum materials which, in turn, would have be to be approved by the provincial ministry of education or the school boards themselves. The BCTF emphasized that students "need to be reassured that our schools offer them an open, healthy, and safe place for learning."[25] The BCTF's activism and its motion on homophobia were strongly opposed by the Evangelicals in BC. By the mid-nineties, Evangelicals had organized to obtain seats in local government and had succeeded in dominating elections to the school board in the Vancouver suburb of Surrey. The Surrey School Board was at loggerheads with the BCTF, objecting to presentations on anti-racism in the schools and banning Gay-Straight Alliances, the only school board to do so in BC.[26]

The group Gay and Lesbian Educators (GALE) was also an important part of the activist network. GALE's membership fluctuated over the course of the nineties; it was a small but broadly based group including teachers and school administrators from all levels of the education system. While GALE stated that its purpose was simply to "advocate for change in the education system which will result in a positive environment for lesbians, gays and bisexuals in education,"[27] it was clear that GALE was also intent on challenging the heteronormative structures of knowledge and practice in which students were socialized. For example, GALE emphasized the importance of making visible lesbian and gay people in the educational process by providing LGBT role models for youth and including information about lesbian and gay people in the curriculum. GALE recognized the importance of "stopping homophobic slurs, violence and intolerance toward glbtq people in educational settings."[28]

---

25 *Ibid.*

26 British Columbia Teachers' Federation, News Release, "BC Teachers' Federation Supports Petitioners in Surrey Book Banning Appeal" (20 June 2000).

27 GALE, *About GALE* (Vancouver: GALE, 2002).

28 *Ibid.*

Two teachers who had been active in GALE raised the issue of gay/lesbian-positive readings materials in the schools. James Chamberlain, an elementary school teacher in the Surrey School district, and Murray Warren, a teacher in the Coquitlam School Board, had both raised the issue in their respective districts.[29] In 1997, when Chamberlain introduced three gay/lesbian-positive books into his elementary school classroom, the issue came to a head. The Surrey School Board passed a motion to say that resources from GALE were not approved for use in the Surrey School District. Two weeks later, even though the Surrey School Board received a delegation from GALE, from the BC Civil Liberties Association, and several parents of students in the Surrey School Board, the board voted to ban three specific gay/lesbian-positive books as learning resources in the elementary schools of the Surrey School District. These books were *Asha's Mums*,[30] *Belinda's Bouquet*,[31] and *One Dad, Two Dads, Brown Dad, Blue Dads*,[32] all books which depicted the lives of young children with same-sex parents. Although these books could be held in the elementary school library according to the Surrey School Board resolution, they were prohibited from use in the classroom. The lesbian and gay community in education in BC read the Board's action as a reaction to the longstanding campaign by GALE, the BCTF, and by Chamberlain and Warren as activist teachers to raise the issues of homophobia and heterosexism in the Coquitlam and Surrey School Board schools.[33]

---

29 Peter Cook & Murray Warren, Interview by the author, 2002. [Cook and Warren].

30 Rosamund Elwin, Michele Paulse, & Dawn Lee, *Asha's Mums* (Toronto: Women's Press, 1990).

31 Lesléa Newman & Michael Willhoite, *Belinda's Bouquet* (Boston, MA: Alyson Wonderland, 1991).

32 Johnny Valentine & Melody Sarecky, *One Dad, Two Dads, Brown Dad, Blue Dads* (Los Angeles, CA: Alyson Wonderland, 2004).

33 Cook and Warren, above note 29; see also "Questioning Heteronormativ-

Following the ban, teachers, a parent, a student, and the author of one of the books banded together to bring a *Charter* challenge to the BC Supreme Court arguing that the ban was unconstitutional.[34] The challenge was supported by the BC Civil Liberties Association. In 1998, the Court agreed, declaring that banning these books from the elementary school classroom violated the equality rights of lesbian and gay students and parents and violated free expression. The Court overturned what had become known as "the Surrey book ban." The Surrey School Board appealed this decision to the BC Court of Appeal. On 20 September 2000, the BC Court of Appeal rendered an ambiguous ruling which permitted the books to be used in the classroom and in libraries at the professional discretion of teachers. At the same time, the BC Court of Appeal upheld the original ban by the Board by stating that the books did not have to form part of an approved list of "learning resources."[35] Seemingly, then, the court upheld the Surrey School Board's discretion to "decertify" gay/lesbian or GALE-recommended books as "learning resources" in the school, even while permitting particular teachers or librarians to use the books in the teaching of elementary school children.

The arguments of the case went beyond the simple demand for inclusion by raising the issue of heteronormativity and pointing to the costs for lesbians and gays themselves of the "enforced visibility" of exclusion and silencing. Chamberlain and his allies argued that treating lesbian and gay behaviour as if it is something that can only be tolerated in the private realm is oppressive because it erases lesbian and gay people from the school and from the family. This erasure is deeply stigmatizing for children with same-sex parents and creates another generation who view lesbian and gay life as deviant from the heterosexual norm. This issue was directly joined in the legal debate as Christian Evan-

ity," initial note.

34 *Chamberlain v School District #36 (Surrey)*, 1998 CanLII 6723 (BCSC).

35 See *Chamberlain*, 2000, above note 3.

gelicals claimed the protection of religious freedom, arguing that including the books in the classroom or as approved learning resources would send the message that homosexuality was condoned by or encouraged in the school system. Of course, this is the precise message that activist teachers wanted to send. By arguing that lesbian and gay-positive reading material should be introduced at the elementary level, activist teachers were seeking to challenge the socialization of the next generation and to normalize lesbian and gay life.[36]

The case was finally appealed to the Supreme Court of Canada where the Court ruled against the school board and in favour of Chamberlain and the activists from GALE in *Chamberlain*, 2002.[37] The majority and minority decisions in the 2002 Supreme Court ruling engage centrally with the role of religion in the schools. The majority ruling stated that, although the religious beliefs of parents deserved expression in the public sphere, they could not be used to deny recognition and respect to other members of the community while the minority opinion held that neither religion nor sexual orientation should be confined to the private sphere. Both rulings suggested a balancing of rights without suggesting a general principle by which such balancing could be carried out. Given that the books involved did not discuss or even refer to sexual relations in any way (as was age-appropriate for very young children), the question of distinguishing the identity of same-sex parents from their (sexual) conduct was not tenable. If religious beliefs about the immorality of homosexuality were to be privatized, then the rights of religious people would be jeopardized while, similarly, acceding to the demand that same-sex couples should not be visible in the schools, would privatize, stigmatize, and re-closet same-sex couples and their children. Hence, although the *Chamberlain*, 2002 case discussed

36 John Fisher, Executive Director, Egale, *Notes of the Hearing (Surrey Book Banning)* (Ottawa: Egale, 2002) [unpublished].

37 Above note 3.

the need to balance the rights of each group, it did not propose a means to recognize the expression of religious opposition to homosexuality in the schools.[38]

2) *Boissoin*

In 2002, Stephen Boissoin, a leader in the Concerned Christian Coalition, sent a letter to the editor of the local newspaper in the town of Red Deer, AB. Part of the letter read as follows:

> Our children are being victimized by repugnant and premeditated strategies, aimed at desensitizing and eventually recruiting our young into their camps. Think about it, children as young as five and six years of age are being subjected to psychologically and physiologically damaging pro-homosexual literature and guidance in the public school system; all under the fraudulent guise of equal rights. Your children are being warped into believing that same-sex families are acceptable; that men kissing men is appropriate. Your teenagers are being instructed on how to perform so-called safe same gender oral and anal sex and at the same time being told that it is normal, natural and even productive. Will your child be the next victim that tests homosexuality positive?
>
> Come on people, wake up! It's time to stand together and take whatever steps are necessary to reverse the wickedness that our lethargy has authorized to spawn. Where homosexuality flourishes, all manner of wickedness abounds . . . .
>
> Don't allow yourself to be deceived any longer. These activists are not morally upright citizens, concerned about the best interests of our society. They are perverse, self-centered and

38 See the discussion in Carl Stychin, "Faith in the Future: Sexuality, Religion and the Public Sphere" (2009) 29:4 Oxford J Legal Stud 729 ["Faith in the Future"].

> morally deprived individuals who are spreading their psychological disease into every area of our lives. Homosexual rights activists and those that defend them, are just as immoral as the pedophiles, drug dealers and pimps that plague our communities.
>
> The homosexual agenda is not gaining ground because it is morally backed. It is gaining ground simply because you, Mr. and Mrs. Heterosexual, do nothing to stop it. It is only a matter of time before some of these morally bankrupt individuals such as those involved with NAMBLA, the North American Man/Boy Lovers Association, will achieve their goal to have sexual relations with children and assert that it is a matter of free choice and claim that we are intolerant bigots not to accept it. If you are reading this and think that this is alarmist, then I simply ask you this: how bad do things have to become before you will get involved? It's time to start taking back what the enemy has taken from you. The safety and future of our children is at stake.[39]

Darren Lund, a professor at the University of Calgary, took Boissoin to the Alberta Human Rights and Citizenship Commission, arguing that Boissoin had violated section 3 of Alberta's human rights legislation, the *Alberta Human Rights Act*,[40] which prohibits speech that exposes people to contempt or hate. Lund explained that he was motivated by his concern that Boissoin's letter could cause gay-bashing. The Alberta Human Rights Commission ruled in favour of Lund in 2007.[41] In 2008, the Commission ruled on the remedy, fining Boissoin $5,000 and ordering him to cease from disparaging homosexuals or specifically disparaging Lund

---

39 Stephen Boissoin, "The Letter" (2009), online: stephenboissoin.com www.stephenboissoin.com/letter.html.

40 RSA 2000, c A-25.5 (formerly the *Human Rights, Citizenship and Multiculturalism Act*).

41 *Lund v Boissoin*, 2007 AHRC 11 (CanLII).

and his supporters.[42] He appealed and the case was heard by the Alberta Court of Queen's Bench, which ruled on the case in 2009, overturning the decision of the Alberta Human Rights Commission.[43]

This case raised pitted hate speech laws in provincial human rights codes against freedom of expression, especially the free expression of religious views. It was picked up by right-wing political commentators in the *National Post* and *Maclean's* and became a *cause célèbre* among right-wing bloggers, many of them based in the US where the *Boissoin* case became part of the anti-gay Christian Evangelical coverage.[44] However, beyond the predictable discussion of free speech, what was more interesting about the case was the fact that the lesbian and gay communities were far from united on the issue and the Canadian Civil Liberties Association intervened to argue for what it termed a principled approach to freedom of speech, conscience, and religion, even when the views expressed are "jarring, extreme, polemical, offensive and confrontational."[45]

---

42 *Lund v Boissoin*, 2008 AHRC 6 (CanLII).

43 *Boissoin*, above note 6.

44 Tim Bloedow, "Canadian Group Celebrates Stephen Boissoin's Victory over 'Hate Speech' Charge for Writing Letter against Homosexuality" (4 December 2009), online: Americans for Truth http://americans-fortruth.com/news/canadian-group-celebrates-stephen-boissoins-victory-over-hate-speech-charge-for-writing-letter-against-homosexuality.html; Colby Cosh, "The *Boissoin* case: Freedom Gains a Moral Victory" *Maclean's* (4 December 2009), online: *Maclean's* www2.macleans.ca/2009/12/04/the-boissoin-case-freedom-gains-a-moral-victory; Ezra Levant, "What Could Mark Steyn's Punishment Look Like? Look at Alberta" (6 June 2009), online: ezralevant.com http://ezralevant.com/2008/06/what-could-mark-steyns-punishm.html. For a further discussion of hate speech laws as they relate to freedom of expression see Richard Moon, Chapter 15 in this volume.

45 Canadian Civil Liberties Association, *Submission of the Intervener, Lund*

The queer community was divided over the *Boissoin* case because, although there was understandable agreement regarding the offence caused by the letter to the editor, there were diverse views in the community over the issue of censorship. Some lesbian and gay advocates and lawyers argued that the queer community should not support censorship in any form because state restrictions on free expression have historically been used against queer sexuality. Since the 1970s, for example, gay and lesbian bookstores such as Little Sisters in Vancouver have fought an ongoing legal battle with the Canada Border Service Agency (CBSA), which has routinely stopped many lesbian and gay publications at the border.[46] The issue of censorship of lesbian and gay reading materials continues to be a very live issue in queer communities. Among other recent incidents, a PG-rated film about a gay couple adopting a child, slated for an Ottawa film festival, was stopped at the border by the CBSA[47] The feminist community is also divided over the issue of free expression and pornography as some feminists, including some lesbian feminists, take what they would define as a pro-sex position and argue that pornography should not be overly restricted by the state; other feminists, including some lesbian feminists, argue that pornography is degrading to women and that it should be regulated by the state. In Canada, this debate was joined over the *R v Butler*[48] case on pornography in the 1990s and, subsequently, in a series

---

v Boissoin (CCLA, 2007), online: http://ccla.org/wordpress/wp-content/uploads/2008/09/2007-07-18-lund-v-boissoin-provincial-hate-speech-laws.pdf.

46 Janine Fuller & Stuart Blackley, *Restricted Entry: Censorship on Trial* (Vancouver: Press Gang, 1996).

47 Marcus McCann, "PG-rated Gay Film Seized en Route to Ottawa Film Fest" *Xtra* (21 November 2009), online: *Xtra* www.xtra.ca/public/National/PGrated_gay_film_seized_en_route_to_Ottawa_film_fest-7893.aspx.

48 [1992] 1 SCR 452.

of other debates over censorship.[49]

In the *Boissoin* case, Canada's flagship lesbian and gay publication, *Xtra*, came out against the Alberta Human Rights Commission's 2007 decision. Brenda Cossman, a law professor and member of the *Xtra* editorial collective, argued that "Boissoin's views are appalling. But, censoring them isn't the answer. Holding them up to the light of day is admittedly more time consuming, but in the long run, much more effective."[50] Similarly, Egale, Canada's lesbian and gay organization, also supported Boissoin's right to publish his views, emphasizing its opposition to government censorship which, in the past, had been used against the lesbian and gay community and its concern to counter Boissoin's views in the open.[51] Others in the queer community agreed with the views of Darren Lund that the expression and publication of views such as Boissoin's cause damage to vulnerable LGBTs and, in particular, to youth. The Alberta Court of Appeal agreed that free expression outweighed the argument about the damaging

49 Shannon Bell, Brenda Cossman, & Lise Gotell, *Bad Attitude/s on Trial: Pornography, Feminism, and the Butler Decision* (Toronto: University of Toronto Press, 1997).

50 Brenda Cossman, "Censorship Not the Solution to End Homophobia" *Xtra* (13 December 2007), online: *Xtra* www.xtra.ca/public/National/Censorship_not_the_solution_to_end_homophobia-4061.aspx.

51 Interestingly, Egale's position was characterized by the Alberta Court of Queen's Bench as "supporting the publication of the letter," *Boissoin*, above note 6 at para 92. The court also misspelled the name of Egale as an organization. In fact, Egale did not "support the publication of the letter" but merely stated that it defended Boissoin's *right* to voice his views. See Gilles Marchildon, "Freedom for All Means Freedom for Each" (3 November 2005), online: Egale www.egale.ca/index.asp?lang=E&menu=12&item=1245; see also, *Xtra* (Toronto), "Free Speech Triumphs as Anti-Gay Letter Ruled Legal" *Xtra* (4 December 2009), online: *Xtra* www.xtra.ca/blog/national/post/2009/12/04/Free-speech-triumphs-as-anti-gay-letter-ruled-legal.aspx.

effects of Boissoin's remarks. Nonetheless, the issue of speech, expression, and publication of homophobic views has continued to recur in other cases such as the case of *Owens* and the ongoing case of *Whatcott* (see Table 1).

3) *Nichols*

In 2005, following the legalization of same-sex civil marriage in Canada, Orville Nichols, a marriage commissioner in Saskatchewan, launched a human rights complaint arguing that his freedom of religion would be violated if he were asked to marry a same-sex couple. This complaint was dismissed by the Saskatchewan Human Rights Commission in 2006. At around the same time, a gay man ("MJ") applied to get married in Saskatchewan and Nichols refused to perform the marriage, stating that it was against his religious beliefs. MJ filed a human rights complaint against Nichols, which was adjudicated in MJ's favour by a Saskatchewan Human Rights Tribunal in 2007. Nichols was ordered to pay $2,500 and to perform marriages of same-sex couples when called upon to do so under his duties as marriage commissioner. Nichols in turn appealed the ruling of the Tribunal but lost his case in the Saskatchewan Court of Queen's Bench in July 2009. In explaining his religious beliefs, Nichols stated that the Bible taught him that "God hates homosexuals."[52]

In this case, Nichols's freedom of religion was pitted against his duties as a marriage commissioner performing civil marriage under Canadian law. The right to same-sex marriage would be

---

52 "Commissioner Who Refused to Marry Same-Sex Couple Loses Appeal" CBC News Online (23 July 2009), online: CBC News www.cbc.ca/canada/saskatchewan/story/2009/07/23/marriage-ruling.html; see also "Rights Tribunal Rebukes Marriage Commissioner in Same-Sex Ruling" CBC News Online (30 May 2008), online: CBC News www.cbc.ca/canada/saskatchewan/story/2008/05/30/sask-marriage-commissioner.html.

meaningless if access was restricted because of the refusal of marriage commissioners to perform the ceremony. As the determination of the capacity to marry is a federal power, federal jurisdiction would also be undermined if the provincial power over the administration of marriage was used to circumvent a federal law. Further, it is very clear that the state's recognition of marriage in Canada is a civil, not a religious matter and that the state takes no position on the religious recognition of marriage or on the performance of marriage ceremonies by churches, mosques, temples, or any religious organization. The 2005 *Civil Marriage Act* simply extends the possibility of legally recognized marriage to same-sex couples. At the time of the passage of the legislation, the government was perfectly clear about the fact that the performance of such marriages was not an interference with freedom of religion and wrote the following statement into the legislation: "nothing in this Act affects the guarantee of freedom of conscience and religion and, in particular, the freedom of members of religious groups to hold and declare their religious beliefs and the freedom of officials of religious groups to refuse to perform marriages that are not in accordance with their religious beliefs."[53] Further, the *Charter*'s protection for religious officials who refuse to marry same-sex couples on religious grounds was upheld by the Supreme Court of Canada in the reference case of 2004.[54]

Nonetheless, some have argued that individual marriage commissioners should be able to pass the duty of performing same-sex marriages on to other commissioners if they have a religious or conscientious objection.[55] This occurred in the *Nichols* case as he referred MJ to another commissioner who was able to perform the ceremony on the desired date. The Saskatchewan Human Rights Tribunal declined this compromise and clearly

53 *Civil Marriage Act*, SC 2005, c 33, preamble.

54 *Reference re Same-Sex Marriage*, [2004] 3 SCR 698.

55 See Janet Epp Buckingham, Chapter 3.

stated that public servants must conform to the law in the performance of their duties. As Nichols had accepted a statutory appointment as marriage commissioner, he was obligated to administer his duties in accordance with the laws of Saskatchewan and Canada, according to the Tribunal. This point was considered at length by the Saskatchewan Court of Queen's Bench, which concurred with the Tribunal.[56] This case has been appealed to the Saskatchewan Court of Appeal.

A number of compromises have been proposed in this case. When same-sex marriage was legalized in Saskatchewan in 2004, the NDP Government made it clear that marriage commissioners were expected to perform same-sex marriages. However, the recently elected Saskatchewan Party, led by Premier Brad Wall, has referred the marriage commissioner question to the Saskatchewan Court of Appeal. The government is considering legislation to exempt commissioners appointed prior to 2004 from performing same-sex marriages or exempting all commissioners from performing same-sex marriages in cases where their beliefs are at odds with performing same-sex marriages.[57] The court has specified the procedure to be followed for interveners in the appeal in this case and it is expected that a large group, coordinated in part by Egale, will assist in supporting the position of the Saskatchewan Human Rights Commission.[58] At the same time, a large group of religious interveners will also act on the other side of the question. Whether this will produce a solution that satisfies the diverse stakeholders remains to be seen.

---

56 *Nichols*, above note 10.

57 Canadian Press, "CBC News — Saskatchewan — Same Sex vs Religious Freedom Case in Sask Court" CBC News Online (13 May 2009), online: CBC News www.cbc.ca/canada/saskatchewan/story/2010/05/13/sask-gay-rights-marriage-commissioner-courts.html.

58 Gens Hellquist, "Saskatchewan Same-Sex Marriage Case Heats Up" *Xtra* (27 October 2009), online: *Xtra* www.xtra.ca/public/National/Saskatchewan_samesex_marriage_case_heats_up-7744.aspx.

These three cases provide a sampling of the types of arguments that have been most commonly raised by litigation over *Charter* values in the most recent period. While there have been important victories for LGBT litigants, it also seems clear that the right of free expression of religion is an important value that is not only taken seriously by the court, but also by some representatives of the queer community as well as by generally queer-friendly interveners such as the Canadian Civil Liberties Associations. Strikingly, all of the cases involving legal conflicts over religious values and sexual orientation in Canada in the most recent period (with the expectation of the same-sex marriage cases) have involved conservative Protestants. None of the individuals who have cited religious beliefs have identified themselves with any of the three largest Christian churches in Canada: the Roman Catholic Church, the United Church, or the Anglican Church. Despite the growing diversity of religions in Canada, none of the litigation so far has directly pitted the freedom of religion of any non-Christian individual or organization against the rights of LGBT people.

C. Balancing Rights: Beyond Litigation

Much discussion of the balancing of rights in Canada has centred on the courts and on litigation as the means by which this balancing of rights will occur. Nonetheless, as this survey of recent cases demonstrates, the cases that come to litigation do not necessarily reflect the diversity of tensions, conflicts, and opinions around sexual orientation and religion. Only certain types of conflicts are litigated. In some cases, there may be a lack of ground for a dispute that would be recognized in Canadian law while, in other cases, the parties to conflict may not have the economic, political, and legal resources to pursue a legal strategy. The debate over the Toronto District School Board's (TDSB) adoption of an equity policy for Toronto schools in 1998 is one example of a case in which tensions arose over the recognition of sexual orientation in the school curriculum without leading to litigation. Representatives of the Muslim, black, and South Asian parents and students had successfully pushed for the adoption of an expanded anti-racist policy for the TDSB, which was then critiqued by some members of the LGBT community for not dealing with sexual orientation, disability, and other issues.[59] This debate engaged parents from various faith traditions, including orthodox Muslim, Jewish, Sikh, and Hindu groups who did not believe that information on sexual orientation should be included in the school curriculum.[60] In contrast to the Surrey school board case, the Toronto debate did not lead to *Charter* litigation and, again in contrast to Surrey, Christian Evangelicals played a tangential role. This example illustrates the point that, by focusing on litigation, we may concentrate too much on extremes in the debate, we may marginalize the views of other faith communities beyond Evangelical Protestantism, and we may ignore cases in which settlements among diverse stakeholders have been successfully reached.

Moreover, litigation does not capture the diversity of views within faith communities and within the LGBT community. Litigation is an adversarial system in which there are winners and losers, each of which defines a position in jurisprudential terms. This approach does not necessarily reflect the potential for balance and compromise. In the case of the Surrey book banning, one side claimed the right to integrate gay-friendly literature into the elementary school classroom, while the other side claimed that such literature violated their religious beliefs. In jurisprudential terms, this case turned on the freedom of religion of some parents versus the equality rights of other parents. In the *Bois-*

59 See Jasmin Zine, "'Negotiating Equity': The Dynamics of Minority Community Engagement in Constructing Inclusive Educational Policy" (2001) 31:2 Cambridge Journal of Education 239 ["Negotiating Equity"].

60 *Ibid* at 264.

soin case, one side claimed the right to free speech to voice religious beliefs while the other side saw the same speech as constituting hate and encouraging denigration and damage to a minority group. In jurisprudential terms, the cases pitted free speech against equality rights. In the case of the marriage commissioner, one side claims freedom of religion while the other side claims equality rights. If the marriage commissioner exercises his freedom of religion as a public servant, this might lead to the violation of the legal right of same-sex couples to marry. Litigation presents the issues in two-sided terms, marginalizing the voices of complexity and compromise. Most importantly, the legal process structures the voice of citizens in very particular ways. Generally, citizens speak only in their role as plaintiffs, interveners, or through the indirect electoral accountability of the government, when the government is party to the litigation.

In contrast, a deliberative approach recognizes issues are by definition multifaceted and that they may be defined in terms of the voices of the stakeholders as well as the general public. From this perspective, the law itself is seen as mutable and solutions to interpretative conflicts over balancing religious rights and equality rights are not to be found solely in black-letter constitutional law. Although deliberation emphasizes the importance of active listening and participating, it is based on the political idea that there is more than one way to balance rights that come into conflict. Deliberation brings the stakeholders and policy makers into conversation with each other through mechanisms such as citizen juries, consultative fora, or citizens' assemblies.[61] When we are discussing issues that are deeply held reflections of personal identity and belief, a deliberative forum can provide the opportunity for deeply entrenched opponents to listen respect-

61 James S Fishkin & Robert C Luskin, "Experimenting with a Democratic Ideal: Deliberative Polling and Public Opinion" (2005) 40:3 Acta Politica 284; John Gastil, "Is Face-to-Face Citizen Deliberation a Luxury or a Necessity?" (2000) 17:4 Political Communication 357.

fully to each other and to walk in each other's shoes. When given the opportunity to enter into conversation on the basis of mutual respect, what may appear to be two sides of an issue may transform into many sides and, out of many sides, a compromise position may be found which, while it is not the first choice of either side, may be minimally acceptable. These solutions may be seen as more legitimate and just than remedies imposed by courts. Moreover, they may open up new policy options for governments who are considering how to manage diversity conflicts.[62]

Deliberation and citizen engagement call upon participants to recognize that, as stakeholders and policy makers, we come into contact with each other and that, no matter what our differences, we must agree on common rules. The role of government in this exercise is to provide the mechanisms through which the conversation can take place, to seriously consider the solutions that are devised among the stakeholders, and to provide the organizational and financial resources that may be needed for the deliberative process itself and for the implementation of new solutions. The debate over Toronto's equity policy provides an example of a case in which a more level playing field for resourcing the stakeholders might have led to a more balanced debate as some critics of the process felt that the interests of women and the disabled were marginalized in the process.[63] Table 2, below, illustrates some of the key differences between litigation and deliberation.

Deliberation may be organized in many different ways and deliberative exercises vary according to the nature and range of participants, the length of the deliberative process, the extent of its institutionalization, and the framing and resources of the participants. One of the most important questions is who partici-

62 See the discussion in Mark Warren, "What Should and Should Not Be Said: Deliberating Sensitive Issues" (2006) 37:2 Journal of Social Philosophy 165.

63 "Negotiating Equity," above note 59 at 466.

pates in the deliberation? Is the deliberative exercise organized for the mythical "ordinary" citizen? Or, is the exercise organized for stakeholder groups? Do individuals speak for themselves or do individuals speak on behalf of groups? Related to this is the question of how individuals or groups are selected to participate in the process. Some of the mechanisms, such as the citizen jury, are institutionalized means of bringing a sample of mythical "ordinary" citizens into the policy process to consider an issue of public policy. Other concepts, such as citizen engagement, seek to bring citizens together for consultation in particular policy areas.

For example, during Canada's constitutional debates of the early 1990s, the federal government organized citizens' forums in cities across Canada to hear citizens' views on constitutional change.[64] Recently, in Quebec, the province appointed a commission to hear the views of citizens on interculturalism and reasonable accommodation.[65] A number of jurisdictions in Canada have run citizen assemblies as a means of engaging citizens, especially on the issue of electoral reform.[66] Parliamentary committees may provide a venue for citizens to express their views on policy issues, especially when these travel across the country. A recent example of this kind of engagement occurred during the debate on same-sex marriage when the Standing Committee on Justice and Human Rights travelled across Canada to hear the views of citizens and groups on the issue. When major delibera-

---

64 Peter H Russell, *Constitutional Odyssey: Can Canadians Become a Sovereign People?* 3d ed (Toronto: University of Toronto Press, 2004).

65 Gérard Bouchard & Charles Taylor, *Fonder l'avenir—Le temps de la conciliation, Rapport abrégé* (Government of Quebec, 2008), online: www.accommodements.qc.ca/documentation/rapports/rapport-final-abrege-fr.pdf.

66 Mark Warren & Hilary Pearse, *Designing Deliberative Democracy: The British Columbia Citizens' Assembly* (New York: Cambridge University Press, 2008).

tion has been required, governments in Canada — both federally and provincially — have often appointed royal commissions or committees of inquiry into specific questions, which may hear from individuals or groups.

In contrast to participation from citizens as individuals, deliberative democracy can also be organized around collective actors, who speak on behalf of specific constituencies. These groups can be named as representatives on citizen juries or other forms of institutionalized deliberation. Government agencies may also hold consultative exercises with groups which are focused on particularly policy issues or pending decisions. In the traditional view of policy communities, organized groups were viewed as key players in networks that spanned the state/society divide in a particular policy area. While informal, these networks were characterized by ongoing patterns of interaction between government departments and agencies and specific groups which were recognized by governments and by other groups as stakeholders in the policy area. The concept of the policy community was premised on the notion that state-society interactions would take place under the radar of public debate. The shift to governance and partnership in the era of new public management, beginning in the 1980s, slowly altered this once-traditional concept of the policy community, as groups were often defined as partners with governments and agencies in delivering goods and services to communities and citizens. In this framework, groups are often integrated into policy frameworks which require them to benchmark and account for their activities, rather than to act as independent advocates of policy advice.[67] Moreover, *ad hoc* consultative exercises undertaken around particular policy questions may not be particularly public, transparent, or accountable, either to stakeholder constituencies or to the general public.

67 Susan Phillips, "SUFA and Citizen Engagement: Fake or Genuine Masterpiece?" (2001) 2:7 Policy Matters, online: www.irpp.org/pm/archive/pmvol2no7.pdf.

Another important aspect of deliberation is the extent to which it is an episodic mechanism, employed by governments (or their agencies) when an issue arises or whether it is institutionalized as a permanent feature of policy making. The deliberations of parliamentary committees are an institutionalized part of the legislative process in Canada; however, the extent to which committees exercise scrutiny over government action, their degree of independence from the government of the day, the extent of their resources, and their ability and willingness to call witnesses certainly vary depending on the committee, the government, and the legislature. Further, this form of deliberation can only be used when legislation is under consideration.

Political theorist Archon Fung has provided a parsimonious scheme to understand different types of deliberation. His schema considers a range of options along three different dimensions: who participates, how communication and decisions occur, and the link between deliberation and authoritative decisions (law-making and implementation).[68] Fung provides numerous examples of deliberative exercises from the US, many of them based in urban areas around issues such as policing, arguing that "[c]itizens can be the shock troops of democracy. Properly deployed, their local knowledge, wisdom, commitment, authority, even rectitude can address wicked failures of legitimacy, justice, and effectiveness."[69] Fung also makes clear, however, that successful deliberation consumes an incredible amount of time and energy from those who participate as well as requiring the commitment of government and agency officials to crafting rules and procedures for successful communication and decision making. Many of his examples are core issues of the implementation of public policy and public administration, rather than constitutional and jurisprudential questions such as the balance of religious

---

68 Archon Fung, "Varieties of Participation in Complex Governance" (2006) 66:1 Public Administration Review 66.

69 *Ibid* at 74.

freedom and equality rights, as we are dealing with here. Can the lessons of public administration be applied successfully to the conflicts between deeply held religious beliefs and equality rights?

I would argue that, in specific cases, stakeholder consultation using deliberative mechanisms can provide an alternative to the adversarial structure of litigation. In public policy controversies such as the debate over the marriage commissioners, a deliberative consultation held by human rights commissions can provide the means for different stakeholders to convey nuanced and diverse views on the issues. Similarly, such an exercise would facilitate participation by LGBTs of faith as well as by those from the Muslim, Jewish, Sikh, Buddhist, and Hindu communities. Rather than engaging in the racialization and stereotyping of Muslims as the "other" who oppose the putatively liberal and tolerant values of Western societies such as Canada, a consultative and deliberative forum would enable intercultural exchange and the expression of diverse views in a non-confrontational setting. Deliberation creates a civil space in which, unlike the disconnected postings of lone bloggers, adversaries must listen to each other's views and arguments in the same room. Deliberative exercises must be based on agreed upon rules of personal conduct and even predetermined limits on forms of speech such as blanket condemnation of all religions and religious people or statements that gay men and lesbians are seeking sexual access to children. Furthermore, the playing field must be level in terms of economic resources for deliberation. The economic costs of participation must be recognized, as well as the costs of developing deliberative expertise among stakeholders. Provincial human rights commissions are an important potential venue for consultative exercises given that many (although not all) of the key issues in the engagement between religion and sexual orientation fall under provincial jurisdiction.

Finally, deliberation over these kinds of issues must be based on recognition of the different power relations that underpin the resources and historical position of the stakeholders. Christianity has been the dominant religion in Canadian society since European settlement. While Canadian society has undergone substantial secularization over the last forty years, Christian churches in Canada command impressive economic and financial resources, institutional infrastructure, and direct access to politicians and government. Christian churches in Canada have enjoyed constitutional guarantees of publically funded religious education, as well as tax-exempt status that brings very substantial financial advantages. While Christian Evangelicals or Roman Catholics may feel beleaguered, they are much more powerful than Canadian lesbian and gay organizations which are poorly resourced and organizationally fragmented.[70] As a long-stigmatized minority group, some LGBT citizens may hardly have come to terms with their sexual identity (as was the situation for the plaintiff MJ in the *Nichols* case), while Christians enjoy a long-dominant social identity, which is well-integrated in Canadian communities. In the recent past, lesbians and gay men in Canada have been jailed, bullied, physically assaulted, and subjected to systematic discrimination in every area of life from the most intimate areas of sexuality, relationships, and parenting to the public arenas of politics and employment. Studies show that opposition to gay rights is still strong even in Canada and other countries in which LGBT people have strong protections in law.[71] Any deliberative exercise must take these inequalities in power

---

70 *Political Institutions*, above note 16.

71 Marc Hooghe, Ellen Claes, Allison Harell *et al*, "Anti-Gay Sentiment among Adolescents in Belgium and Canada: A Comparative Investigation into the Role of Gender and Religion" (2010) 57:3 Journal of Homosexuality 384. But see Amy Adamczyk, "Shaping Attitudes about Homosexuality: The Role of Religion and Cultural Context" (2009) 38:2 Social Science Research 338.

relations into account in its design of the elements of deliberation identified by Fung.

D. Conclusions

In recent years, there have been a number of important cases that have pitted religious rights against the equality rights of lesbian and gay citizens, as well as same-sex couples. This issue will likely heat up in the public debate when the marriage commissioner case is heard. Litigation and human rights complaints provide one venue for reconciling these conflicts. Deliberative democracy provides another option. While this may be undertaken through existing mechanisms such as legislative committee hearings or through the appointment of commissions such as Quebec's Bouchard-Taylor Commission, other forms of deliberative democracy may also prove useful, such as consultation organized through provincial human rights commissions. Rather than fora in which citizens come to give their views to government, issues of religion and sexuality might benefit from an engagement of stakeholders in which parties talk to each other with the goal of considering other points of view and even, on some issues, crafting compromise positions which avoid the all-or-nothing adversarial contest of the courtroom. However, such processes must take place within a framework that recognizes the traditionally marginalized minority position of LGBT people in Canadian society and that provides fairly for the resourcing of all parties who wish to participate in the process.

As Carl Stychin has recently commented, this type of balancing of religious rights with the rights of LGBT citizens "is pluralism at the coalface, in which purity is foregone, solutions may not be pleasing to participants, and agreements are contingent and partial. Nevertheless, I believe that this is a model of society that allows people to live together, if not in harmony, then at least in civility."[72] Deliberation and consultation provide an alternative approach to the assertion of rights through the confrontation of litigation. While adjudication plays a fundamental role in the balancing of constitutional rights, the deliberative participation of citizens and their community representatives in the policy making process constitutes an alternative mechanism that has the potential to elicit the full range of diverse voices and positions at stake in these debates. As such, it may provide a useful complement to the process of *Charter*-based litigation.

72 "Faith in the Future," above note 38 at 755.

Table 1: Selected Cases on Religion and Sexual Orientation in Canada, 1998–2009

Year	Case	Issue	Outcome
1998	*Vriend v Alberta*, [1998] 1 SCR 493	Inclusion of sexual orientation in Alberta human rights legislation; gay man (Vriend) alleging employment discrimination in a Christian Reformed college has his case heard by provincial human rights tribunal.	Victory for Vriend.
2000	*Chamberlain v Surrey School District*, [2002] 4 SCR 710	Inclusion of gay-positive reading material in elementary school curriculum. Some trustees objecting to gay-positive books were active in the Christian Heritage Party in BC.[1]	Victory for gay teachers (Chamberlain).
2001	*Trinity Western University v British Columbia College of Teachers*, [2001] SCJ No 32	Inclusion of anti-homosexual morals statement in teacher training for BC schools at Trinity Western University.	Victory for Trinity Western, although Court made it clear that discriminatory treatment of students could not be constitutionally tolerated.
2002	*Ontario Human Rights Commission v Brockie*, [2002] OJ No 2375 (SCJ)	Printer (Brockie) refused to print materials for Canadian Lesbian and Gay Archives. Brockie identified as Evangelical Christian.	Defeat for Brockie as he was forced to pay damages. However, the court found that conflicting rights had to be balanced and this process was context-dependent.
2005	*Corren and Corren v BC (Ministry of Education)* (No 2), 2005 BCHRT 497	Gay activist plaintiffs claimed lack of gay-friendly curriculum in BC schools constituted discrimination based on sexual orientation. Opposed by Evangelicals.	Victory for the Correns. Led to signing of Corren Agreement which mandates the teaching of social justice studies in BC schools. However, the agreement is still under challenge.[2]

Year	Case	Issue	Outcome
2006	*Owens v Saskatchewan (Human Rights Commission)*, 2006 SKCA 41	Several members of the gay community complained to the provincial human rights commission after Owens published an advertisement condemning homosexuality in the newspaper. This is Owen's appeal from 2002 Court of Queen's Bench ruling. Owens is identified as Evangelical.[3]	Victory for Owens.
2008	*Heintz v Christian Horizons*, 2008 HRTO 22	Heintz alleged employment discrimination based on sexual orientation against her employer Christian Horizons, a Christian non-profit. Heard by HRTO.	Victory for Heintz.
2009	*Nichols v MJ*, 2009 SKQB 299	Religious accommodation of marriage commissioners who do not wish to perform same-sex marriages. Nichols identified as Baptist.	Defeat for Nichols (under appeal).
2009	*Boissoin v Lund*, 2009 ABQB 592	Expression and publication of religious opinion that homosexuality is evil. Boissoin identifies as former Protestant pastor.	Victory for Boissoin.
2010	*Whatcott v Saskatchewan Human Rights Tribunal et al*, 2010 SKCA 26	Expression and circulation of religious opinion that homosexuality is immoral and that lesbians and gay men should be subjected to discrimination. Fines and a gag order imposed on Whatcott by Saskatchewan Human Rights Tribunal under hate speech provisions were struck down.	Victory for Whatcott (under appeal).

1 Chris MacKenzie, *Pro-Family Politics and Fringe Parties in Canada* (Vancouver: University of British Columbia Press, 2005).
2 Marci McDonald, *The Armageddon Factor: The Rise of Christian Nationalism in Canada* (Toronto: Random House Canada, 2010) at 207.
3 Canadian Press, "A Small Victory for Freedom of Religion" National Post (17 April 2006), online: canada.com www.canada.com/nationalpost/news/issuesideas/story.html?id=2d933a0a-f9c2-4912-8b52-f4201b9cdd2a.

Table 2: Litigation versus Deliberation

Litigation	Deliberation
adversarial	conversational
two sides	many sides
victory	compromise
argue	negotiate
exclusive	inclusive
lawyers	group leaders
interveners	citizens
legal remedies	policy decisions

Chapter 13

Fairness and the Freedom of Religion: Diversity and Pluralism in the Public Sphere

Iain T Benson[1]

A. Pluralism and the Secular

This article will examine two key terms in relation to our culture today — "pluralism" and the "secular" — and will discuss these against the background of diversity, freedom, tolerance, and the re-understanding of the public sphere. It will argue that both terms are generally insufficiently defined in popular contemporary usages, often frustrating rather than furthering the very principles they should represent. It will be argued that in order to maintain diversity and freedom, there must be a certain understanding of the role of law and a recognition of the *limits* of the law. After examining these, I would like to turn to discuss the fair treatment of beliefs in Canada today and why, as the title suggests, we should be searching for ways to maintain civil

1 This is a shortened, reworked, and re-titled version of a monograph entitled *Living Together with Disagreement: Pluralism, the Secular and the Fair Treatment of Beliefs in Canada Today* (Camrose, AB: Chester Ronning Centre for Religion and Public Life, 2010). The author would like to thank the director of the centre, David Goa, and Nicholas Wickenden for their assistance with that original publication. The views expressed are those of the author and not necessarily those of the firm, faculty, or various institutes or organizations with which he is affiliated. Parts of this paper will be used in the author's PhD thesis at the University of the Witwatersrand in Johannesburg, South Africa.

disagreement in many cases rather than seek a forced "agreement" that is often the result of using rights claims as trump cards where alternative viewpoints are legal to hold. What results from such forced "agreement" is not a *modus vivendi* of living together with disagreements but a sort of convergence that acts against the variety and pluralism that should define a vibrant multiculturalism. First, however, it is useful to note that religious beliefs (linked with "conscience" in section 2(a) of the *Canadian Charter of Rights and Freedoms*[2]) have public dimensions. That is why our notion of the nature of the public sphere and its relation to beliefs is so critical.

1) The Public Nature of the Rights of "Conscience and Religion"

It will be recalled that in the first decision of the Supreme Court of Canada dealing with the definition of the "freedom of conscience and religion" in section 2(a) of the *Charter*, Dickson CJC (as he then was) stated:

> The essence of the concept of freedom of religion is the right to entertain such religious beliefs as a person chooses, the right to declare religious beliefs openly and without fear of hindrance or reprisal, and the right to manifest religious belief by worship and practice or by teaching and dissemination.[3]

Note that the words employed are active, public words — "declare," "manifest," "practice," "teaching," "dissemination." We would do well to remember those words and their public dimensions at a time when many of the challengers wish to avoid a sharing of the public realm by seeking to privatize those rights that have a

---

2 *Canadian Charter of Rights and Freedoms*, Part I of the *Constitution Act, 1982*, being Schedule B to the *Canada Act 1982* (UK) 1982, c 11 [*Charter*].

3 *R v Big M Drug Mart Ltd*, [1985] 1 SCR 295, 18 DLR (4th) 421 [*Big M*].

genuinely public dimension. In recent years, some would choose to limit religion by finding it to be a private right only — something for home or church. Or else there is a suggestion, true in one way but which can be over-extended, that religious belief is one thing and religious conduct another.

2) Two Approaches to "Pluralism" under the Canadian Constitution

It is important to consider the nature of pluralism in Canada. Like so many terms in our public discourse ("values," "the secular," "liberalism," etc.) its common use can mask the fact that it is little analyzed. As such, if there are presuppositions in the term, or an ambiguous usage that is not discovered or discussed, we can be misled as to what is actually being said when the term is used. Pluralism can connote a kind of relativistic approach, as in "because we are a pluralistic society, such and such a moral position cannot have any public validity." It does not have to mean this, however, and in Canada our linkage of a language of pluralism with a firm commitment to group rights, for example, points us to a principled and what might be called structural or shared pluralism, rather than one that is relativistic or, perhaps, totalistic. This totalistic notion of pluralism views society as moving towards the articulation of only one public policy in contested areas, and such a view is antagonistic to the notion of plurality, freedom, and the tolerance of diversity. The political condition in Canada respects the *modus vivendi*, though, and as I shall argue with examples drawn from recent legal cases, whether it will continue to do so remains to be seen, as this foundational aspect is now very much under attack.

John D Whyte has noted that the Canadian Constitution has been framed on the basis not of any individualistic conception of liberalism but, rather, on one that respects and nurtures each person's communities. Moreover, the two kinds of rights protected by the *Charter*, group rights and individual rights (which, as with "religion," overlap as both personal and communal), derive from different conceptions of the proper role of the state, which are both reflected in the Constitution. In his words:

> There are two theoretical models for describing the modern democratic state. One derives from the political philosophy of liberalism, under which society is arranged without a particular conception of the good and in which individuals have claims of right to equal regard and respect. The other might be labelled the organic society, in which the primary focus is not the autonomy of the individual but the importance of nurturing communities or corporate life . . . . The truly effective way to respect life and to achieve a fulfilled life may be through identification with a group and having the assurance that one community or another recognizes one as having distinguishable substantive value.[4]

Consequently, as Professor Whyte observes:

> It is impossible to discern in the constitutional text either the clear direction to promote liberal values as wholeheartedly as possible or the direction to sustain communitarian values to the greatest extent possible.
>
> The Charter reflects the tension. Of course, it gives impetus to the nation's change to liberalism, but it does not reveal, in any precise way, where the limit should be drawn to protect other political values.[5]

---

4 John D Whyte, "Is the Private Sector Affected by the *Charter*?" in Lynn Smith, ed, *Righting the Balance: Canada's New Equality Rights* (Saskatoon: The Canadian Human Rights Reporter Inc, 1986) 145 at 174–75. For more on *modus vivendi* liberalism, see John Gray, *Two Faces of Liberalism* (New York: The New Press, 2000) discussed below [*Two Faces of Liberalism*].

5 Whyte, *ibid* at 177–78.

The Canadian model depicted above does not start with the proposition that either form of right is paramount, or will necessarily converge with or has a "trump" over other claims, but instead looks for the proper sphere of operation of each. We might also disagree with the separation of an "organic" from a rather individualistic form of liberalism as described by Professor Whyte and may wish to argue, as I do in this chapter, for a liberalism that is at once organic and communitarian in nature. A form of "structural pluralism" is possible and comports well with a description of ordered diversity given by American commentator James Skillen in these terms:

> [A] just society is one in which multiple institutions and diverse spheres of responsibility can function together in freedom, under protection of the law[; so] then part of the legal obligation of a just government is to recognize and protect that complex diversity of society. Closely related to this principle, and mutually inter-dependent with it, is the principle of religious freedom . . . . government should act in accord with the principles of justice by treating faiths and faith communities with equal public protection. Government cannot do this, however, without respecting the freedom and diversity of those faiths.[6]

Claims that are, therefore, totalistic, and which seek to represent in themselves all of "public policy" where recognition as such effectively delegitimizes other legally contestable perspectives, must be suspected of overreaching. Such totalistic claims for "recognition" by any particular advocacy group ought to concern us if we are moving towards developing a richer respect for structural pluralism that holds together notions of group as well as individual rights and a plurality of moral perspectives.

---

6 James Skillen,"The Theoretical Roots of Equal Treatment" in Stephen V Monsma and J Christopher Soper, eds, *Equal Treatment of Religion in a Pluralistic Society* (Grand Rapids: Eerdmans, 1998) at 72 [*Equal Treatment*].

I should like now to turn to another key term in contemporary society — the "secular" — because, as with "pluralism," how we use the term "secular" can hide what is actually going on in its use. What do we mean by the term?

3) The Nature of the "Secular" and the Illusion of "Neutrality"

The meaning of the term "secular" has changed over the last century and a half. The term in general usage now means, typically, free from religion, as in "we ought to keep religion out of the schools because they are secular." This was not the original meaning, nor is it a meaning which recognizes the *modus vivendi* aspect of pluralism referred to above or the public aspect of the freedom of religion set out above. Added to this is the fact that we are, as human beings, all believers, the question is not whether we believe but what we believe in. As we shall see below, our courts have, recently, come to acknowledge that any pre-emptive exclusion of "religion" from the category of "beliefs" that may operate in society is unfair to and intolerant of those beliefs that emanate from religious convictions, and gives a preferential position to the beliefs or convictions of atheists and agnostics. Such an exclusion is inconsistent with the principles of a free and democratic society. It is not simply a matter of how beliefs are expressed, but of what communities are nurtured and created by our analysis of pluralism that must be examined.

If we begin with the assumption (building it into our use of the term "secular") that religion has no place in the public sphere, then, of course, we shall tend to diminish the role of the religious in civil society. But this is really to adopt implicitly or explicitly the ideology of atheistically driven "secularism," since the term "secular," viewed historically, does not require, though it has come to imply, such a removal of the sacred dimension from the aspects of life it describes and, with it, the public role of religious belief and religious communities. The "secular," which is better and more clearly understood and examined as the "public," is properly understood as a realm of competing faith/belief claims, not a realm of "non-faith" or "non-belief" claims. Given the current dominance of the atheistic definitions of "secular" and "separation of church and state," it will take some time for them to be re-understood so as better to support the right (fair) ordering of freedoms in contemporary society.

Note how, in contemporary usage, "secular schools," "secular government," etc, are widely understood to mean "non-religious" or "not influenced by religion or religious principles." I would like to suggest that this is because we have adopted the atheistic or agnostic definition of "secular" in which the public sphere is preemptively stripped of religion and not a richer and more properly inclusive conception. The separation of church and state is, after all, a jurisdictional distinction important to both the church and the state. A valid separation should not preclude an equally valid *cooperation* between church and state. Most religious groups in the West, for example, do not in fact want the state to run the church or vice versa.

The historical change in the use of "secular" should be recognized.[7] It is tempting to ignore the change in meaning by acquiescing in the use of the terms "secular" and "religious" as if they described different worlds. But they do not describe different worlds. They describe different functions. What we most often mean by the "secular" is the public or the state, and by "religion" a set of practices carried on by religious adherents within the state. The beliefs of citizens, however, have, as we have seen,

---

7 The *Oxford English Dictionary*, 2d ed, *sub verbo* "secular," "secularism," and "secularity." All uses suggesting a meaning of "secular" that denote an absence of connection with religion postdate GJ Holyoake, *The Principles of Secularism Briefly Explained* (London: Holyoake & Co, 1859) and see also, *English Secularism: A Confession of Belief* (Chicago: Open Court Publishing Co, 1896).

public functions within the state. Therefore the separation of "religion" from something constructed as the "secular" serves, usually implicitly and often unintentionally, an anti-religious goal and is neither accurate nor just.

In fact, this more recent use of "secular," which we may justly call the atheistic or agnostic interpretation, is seldom viewed alongside alternative understandings. This is not helpful since an atheistic definition, if used as the meaning for a central term such as "secular," fails to give a proper place to religion in the private and public dimensions of society. The atheistic "secular" becomes, in effect, a blueprint for the naked public square. A more informed historical understanding, built upon a richer epistemological ground, better reflects both the reality of beliefs in society and the principles of freedom that ought to undergird a properly civil society.

4) Secularism Is Anti-Religious and Is Not Neutral

Secularism, as it is understood in what we may call the English tradition, is a particular ideology. It has a meaning historically. Usually the term is employed with no definition at all or with a definition that elides the history of its origins. When the term was coined by George Jacob Holyoake in the mid-nineteenth century, he and those who followed him had an idea of driving religion out of the public sphere and diminishing its public relevance. Thus, for the courts to suggest, without analysis or argument on the point, or for academics to suggest, without analysis of the term, that Canada and the *Charter* are based upon the principles of "secularism" (as some have done) indicates that they do not realize what they are dealing with.[8]

---

8 I have examined the origin and nature of "secularism" elsewhere. See: "Considering Secularism" in Douglas Farrow, ed, *Recognizing Religion in a Secular State* (Montreal: McGill-Queens, 2004) at 83–98 [*Recognizing Religion*]. This article is critical of the Supreme Court of Canada's

Equality in relation to all sorts of believers, religious and non-religious, means we have to think more deeply about the key terms we use to describe Canadian society going forwards. If we live, as we do, in a society that has no religious establishment and that allows public participation by all citizens (the term "secular" as most frequently used obscures these distinctions), it is one that is necessarily religiously inclusive and it is not one based upon the anti-religious ideology of secularism in which the public sphere is implicitly if not explicitly stripped of religion and religious influence.[9]

We need a new paradigm to deal with religious belief in relation to equality rights. Even if we look to reconciling, instead of "balancing," in certain areas, as Iacobucci J suggested in an article some years ago,[10] we still need to overcome the privatized

---

endorsement, in *Chamberlain v Surrey School District*, [2002] 4 SCR 710 [*Chamberlain*, 2002], of the term as part of Canada's constitutional understandings without any analysis of its history or meaning. The Court did not consider the term at all and it was not argued before them the way "secular" was. Their holding (as *ratio*) on "secular" is, with respect, inconsistent with the unconsidered endorsement (in *obiter*) of "secularism."

9 The trial judgment of Saunders J in *Chamberlain v School District #36 (Surrey)*, 1998 CanLII 6723 (BC SC) [*Chamberlain*, 1998] in which "strictly secular" was interpreted to mean "not based upon or influenced by religion," is a good example of a secularistic understanding of the meaning of "secular principles." For a detailed analysis of this decision in relation to the Court of Appeal judgment, *Chamberlain v Surrey School District*, [2000] BCJ No 1875 (CA) rev'd 1998 CanLII 6723 (BC SC) [*Chamberlain*, 2000], which overturned it, see Iain T Benson & Brad Miller, "Court Corrects Erroneous Understanding of the Secular and Respects Parental Rights" 40 LexView, online: Cardus Centre for Cultural Renewal www.cardus.ca/lexview/article/2284/.

10 Frank Iacobucci, "Reconciling Rights: The Supreme Court of Canada's Approach to Competing *Charter* Rights" (2003) 20 Sup Ct L Rev 137. The argument here is that "reconciling" has advantages over "balancing" as an analytical and practical tool in certain types of cases. The article

presumptions or the unrealistic expectations that undergird the false dualisms I have referred to already.

Social recognition is not something the law ought to promise to one side of legally contestable social debates. The law ought to be ensuring the open texture of civil society, not bringing its weight to bear on one side of the matter, for to do this risks tilting civil society against the freedoms that the law in general must protect for everyone. A leading American scholar on the law relating to religion, Michael W McConnell, has written:

> The beginning of wisdom in this contentious area of law is to recognize that neutrality and secularism are not the same thing. In the marketplace of ideas, secular viewpoints and ideologies are in competition with religious viewpoints and ideologies. It is no more neutral to favor the secular over the religious than it is to favor the religious over the secular. It is time for a reorientation of constitutional law: away back from the false neutrality of the secular state, toward a genuine equality of rights.[11]

This is consistent with the criticism of the use of the term "secular" presented in this article, however, observe that while Professor (later Justice) McConnell correctly identifies the "non-neutral" nature of the state, he perpetuates the false bifurcation between "the secular" and "the religious." Still, despite this error, McConnell rightly criticizes the notion that there is a "neutrality" that can be stripped of religious beliefs and claims in such a manner that what is left represents an adequate "consensus" for civil society.

---

reviews where reconciliation might be the best approach to what could, at first blush, appear to be a clash or conflict of rights.

11 Michael W McConnell, "Equal Treatment and Religious Discrimination" in *Equal Treatment*, above note 6 at 33.

5) The Meaning of "Secular" in Canadian Law: Enter the Religiously Inclusive Public Sphere

A most significant paradigm shift for the future of equality and how we understand accommodation and collisions of rights in law occurred in the *Chamberlain, 1998*[12] decision and this shift has not yet been sufficiently noted. The term "strictly secular" in the British Columbia *School Act*[13] had to be defined. Did it mean, as held at trial, that "any influence by religion" nullified the "secular" (better understood as "public") nature of the school trustees' role and decisions? When they took into account the concerns of local parents on the suitability of certain books as "classroom learning resources," and these concerns in turn were based, as some were, on the religious convictions of the parents, did this run afoul of the "strictly secular" aspect of the legislation? To hold this would have meant that, in effect, only atheists or agnostics had a right to have their beliefs fully respected in the public sphere.

Overturning the decision of the trial judge, Mackenzie JA for the British Columbia Court of Appeal held, against all contemporary uses, that the "secular" must *include* religious beliefs and not be understood or characterized so as to place impediments in the way of religious believers.[14] Understanding the "secular," public sphere in this way constitutes a shift of tremendous importance; it has relevance in various areas, such as, most recently, the question of the personal beliefs of marriage commissioners in relation to same-sex marriage. It has ramifications to all sorts of access and funding debates in the future.

The Supreme Court of Canada subsequently endorsed the holding of the Court of Appeal unanimously on this point, finding,

---

12 *Chamberlain*, 1998, above note 9.

13 RSBC 1996, c 412.

14 *Chamberlain*, 2000, above note 9 at paras 28–29. See also all of above note 8.

in effect, that Canada should have a "religiously inclusive" public sphere (though they did not select this term for it to describe the result as we shall see in the passages from the judgment that follow).[15] In a sense the future requires us to realize that the question is never one of religion *and* the public, religion *and* the civic, or religion *and* equality, but religious belief *within* the public, religious believers and groups *within* the civic, religion *as one aspect* of equality and so forth. The sharp dichotomies of anti-religious secularism should no longer hold sway, as they have for too long, in our analysis in Canada. This is easy to say, but to do the identification and nuanced analysis required to supplant them is difficult, since it requires rethinking our descriptions from first principles. What inclusiveness demands is making the scope for dissent larger, instead of making it smaller by invoking false dualisms to drive religion into the private and out of the public.

Justice Mackenzie, for himself and his colleagues in the unanimous three-justice panel of British Columbia's highest court in *Chamberlain*, 2000 analyzed the term "secular" in the following manner:

> Can "strictly secular" in s. 76(1) of the *School Act* be interpreted as limited to moral positions devoid of religious influence? Are only those with a non-religiously informed conscience to be permitted to participate in decisions involving moral instruction of children in the public schools? . . . . Simply to pose the questions in such terms can lead to only one answer in a truly free society. Moral positions must be accorded equal access to the public square without regard to religious influence. A religiously informed conscience should not be accorded any privilege, but neither should it be placed under a disability. In a truly free society moral positions advance or retreat in their influence on law and public policy through decisions of public officials who are not required to pass a religious litmus test.

---

15 *Chamberlain*, 2002, above note 8.

> . . . .
>
> In my opinion, "strictly secular" in the *School Act* can only mean pluralist in the sense that moral positions are to be accorded standing in the public square irrespective of whether the position flows out of a conscience that is religiously informed or not. The meaning of strictly secular is thus pluralist or inclusive in the widest sense.[16]

The Court of Appeal held that a contrary interpretation would not only be insupportable in principle but that it would raise immense practical difficulties and force inquiry as to the source of a citizen's moral convictions that would be "offensive and indefensible."[17]

Justice Gonthier for himself and Justice Bastarache, who would have upheld the Board's decision and therefore wrote in dissent on that part of the decision, but who wrote the reasons of the unanimous court (in effect) with respect to "secular" put their analysis in these words:

> *In my view, Saunders J. below erred in her assumption that "secular" effectively meant "non-religious." This is incorrect since nothing in the* Charter*, political or democratic theory, or a proper understanding of pluralism demands that atheistically based moral positions trump religiously based moral positions on matters of public policy* . . . . According to the reasoning espoused by Saunders J., if one's moral view manifests from a religiously grounded faith, it is not to be heard in the public square, but if it does not, then it is publicly acceptable. The problem with this approach is that everyone has "belief" or "faith" in something, be it atheistic, agnostic or religious. To construe the "secular" as the realm of the "unbelief" is therefore erroneous. Given this, why, then, should the religiously

16 *Chamberlain*, 2000, above note 9 at paras 28 and 33.

17 *Ibid* at para 29.

> informed conscience be placed at a public disadvantage or disqualification? To do so would be to distort liberal principles in an illiberal fashion and would provide only a feeble notion of pluralism. The key is that people will disagree about important issues, and such disagreement, where it does not imperil community living, must be capable of being accommodated at the core of a modern pluralism.[18]

Suggestions that, for example, the use of picture books in kindergarten classrooms to show that same-sex parents are just the same as heterosexual parent couples is "neutral," show that the concept of "neutrality" is incoherent where matters are foundationally contested.

To parents who view respect for persons (as distinct from "recognizing," "welcoming," or "affirming") as all that can reasonably be required of them by civil society, it is rather alarming to be told in cool and dispassionate tones that neutrality requires that their children be taught that what the parents believe to be wrong is, in fact, right. The case, however, did not require that the books be in every classroom but, rather, that they be available as learning resources should a teacher at the local level believe them necessary (presumably, though this is not stated, on a case-by-case basis in discussion with parents). What was at issue was a question of whether genuine respect is shown for religious adherents. The religious parents do not, after all, require that their "beliefs" be affirmed in the public school classroom.

Keeping in mind the nature of the *modus vivendi* and the danger of a totalizing or convergence liberalism (which assumes that some beliefs will simply slough away over time), it is interesting that the same-sex parenting picture books that were at issue in the kindergarten to grade two curriculum of the Surrey School Board in the *Chamberlain* case were viewed by a recent commen-

18 *Chamberlain*, 2002, above note 8 at para 137 (emphasis added).

tator as simply "to promote mutual respect and understanding."[19] The author shows no indication that such public classroom promotion that implies the complete equivalency of homosexual/lesbian sexuality and heterosexual sexuality (implicit in being "Mom" and "Dad") is anathema to mainstream religious adherents whether they are Sikh, Hindu, Muslim, Catholic, Protestant, or Jewish.[20] Whatever any of us may feel about it, such groups are, as a matter of law, entitled to their views.

Three relatively recent decisions, two from the Supreme Court

---

19 John Russell, "How to be Fair to Religious and Secular Ideals within the Liberal State" (2002) 60:3 The Advocate 345 at 352 ["How to be Fair"].

20 It is, of course, the case that there is divergence within religions as to the acceptability of homosexual and lesbian sexual conduct (and, for that matter, various sorts of heterosexual conduct as well — consider the requirement of celibacy for Catholic priests and non marriage for Orthodox bishops). This, however, says nothing about the respect that should be owed to communities that define themselves around one side of divergent beliefs. All belief systems imply divergence, and the fact that, for example, some feminists and some civil libertarians may disagree on a particular issue is not an argument against valid claims for respect that should be owed to feminists or civil libertarians. The Supreme Court, in decisions such as *Syndicat Northcrest v Amselem*, [2004] 2 SCR 551 [*Amselem*] or *Multani v Commission scolaire Marguerite-Bourgeoys*, [2006] 1 SCR 256 [*Multani*] has cautioned against trying to get "inside" religious beliefs yet, in one reading of *Chamberlain*, 2002, above note 8, to be quite willing to tell religions what they ought to accept in the public sphere they have a right to inhabit. Where matters are legally contestable (as they are with respect to same sex conduct and family structures) the inconsistencies in the approach indicate confusion about what are and are not properly public requirements in relation to religious freedom. A useful set of criticisms of *Chamberlain*, 2002 in this respect may be found in John von Heyking "Civil Religion and Associational Life" in Ronald Weed and John von Heyking, eds, *Civil Religion in Political Thought* (Washington, DC: Catholic University of America Press, 2010) at 318–20.

of Canada and another from the Ontario Superior Court, suggest that while a more nuanced balancing of rights is possible than was seen in the original decision and in some of the arguments of the Supreme Court judges in *Chamberlain*, the courts can still rule in ways that fail to give adequate respect for religious communities. Because the decisions go both ways it is perhaps too early to say whether religiously expansive or narrow decisions will come to predominate in future.[21]

---

21 *Multani*, *ibid* (wearing of kirpan in public school allowed, on the basis of freedom of religion; absolute ban overturned). For a comment on this decision see Peter Lauwers & Iain Benson, "Accommodating Kirpans in Public Schools" 57 LexView, online: Cardus Centre for Cultural Renewal www.cardus.ca/lexview/article/2476/; and *R v Khawaja*, [2006] OJ No 4245 (SCJ) (striking down section of the *Criminal Code*, RSC 1985, c C-46 requiring religious or political connection for terrorism charge to be laid creates an unacceptable "chill" on religious liberty). For a comment on this decision see Kevin Boonstra & Iain Benson, "Terrorism and the Law: Balancing Security with the Chill on Fundamental Freedoms" 60 LexView, online: Cardus Centre for Cultural Renewal www.cardus.ca/lexview/article/2128/. However, for recent decisions that fail to give adequate weight to the concerns of religious Hutterites, see *Alberta v Hutterian Brethren of Wilson Colony*, 2009 SCC 37 [*Hutterian Bretheren*]. Here the Supreme Court of Canada, in a narrow majority with three of seven justices in dissent, ruled that Hutterites, who, for religious reasons, may not have their photographs used for identification purposes, must nonetheless comply with the provincial law for reasons related to the public interest in identifying individuals in relation to driving licences. The decision has been widely criticized for not considering sufficiently that other means (such as fingerprints) could have been used to achieve the state's purposes which would allow recognition of the concerns of the religious community. See, for example, Kevin Boonstra, "Does Canadian Society Still Accommodate Religious Minorities?" 67 LexView, online: www.cardus.ca/lexview/article/2114/. Similarly, the most recent decision of the SCC touching on religion, *SL v Commission scolaire des Chênes*, 2012 SCC 7, is also subject to the criticism that it

6) *Trinity Western University*

An important decision on the scope of religious rights that, taken out of context, could be used to support a privatization of religion, is *Trinity Western University v British Columbia College of Teachers*.[22] The facts can be briefly stated.

The British Columbia College of Teachers (BCCT) is the governing body of the teaching profession in BC. Part of its statutory mandate is to establish standards for the education and competence of its members, "having regard to the public interest." Trinity Western University (TWU), a fully accredited private university founded on religious principles, sought (and was denied) full accreditation from the BCCT for its teacher training program.

The root of the dispute between TWU and the BCCT was the content of a statement of community standards which TWU requires that its students pledge to observe (although not necessarily agree with). The statement sets out the responsibilities of the student in contributing towards "an atmosphere that is consistent with [the] profession of [religious] faith."[23] As part of maintaining this atmosphere, one section of the statement requires that students "refrain from practices which are biblically condemned," including "premarital sex, adultery, and homosexual behaviour."[24] Despite a committee recommendation that TWU's teacher training program be approved, the BCCT ultimately

---

bent too far to accommodate state interests at the expense of parental concerns that a mandatory curriculum touching on culture and religion would negatively affect their children. The author acted for two different national coalitions that intervened in this case. See also Kevin Boonstra, "Whose Children are They Anyway?" 76 LexView, online: www.cardus.ca/lexview/article/3143.

22 *Trinity Western University v College of Teachers*, [2001] 1 SCR 772 [*Trinity Western*, 2001].

23 *Ibid* at para 10.

24 *Ibid* at para 68.

denied accreditation on the basis that "the proposed program follows discriminatory practices that are contrary to the public interest and public policy," on the basis of the statement that "homosexual behaviour"[25] is biblically condemned.

The trial judge overturned the Council's decision, and directed the BCCT to approve TWU's application. That decision was upheld by the British Columbia Court of Appeal.[26] Both Courts determined that there was no evidence to connect any particular graduate of TWU with any discriminatory conduct against gay or lesbian students. The BCCT appealed further to the Supreme Court of Canada.[27] An 8:1 majority of the Supreme Court of Canada denied the BCCT's appeal, and ordered it to approve TWU's education program, subject to the conditions set out by the BCCT's practice committee:

> In our opinion, this is a case where any potential conflict should be resolved through the proper delineation of the rights and values involved. In essence, properly defining the scope of the rights avoids a conflict in this case. Neither freedom of religion nor the guarantee against discrimination based on sexual orientation is absolute . . . .[28]

Differing beliefs will sometimes conflict; differing patterns of conduct relating to beliefs may conflict even more sharply. How such conflicting positions are balanced or reconciled is an essential issue in the kind of liberal, diverse, and pluralistic society we have. In TWU the Court (majority of eight judges) stated: "The diversity of Canadian society is partly reflected in the multiple religious organizations that mark the societal landscape and this diver-

25 *Ibid* at para 48.

26 *Trinity Western University v British Columbia College of Teachers*, 1998 CanLII 7054 (BCCA).

27 *Trinity Western*, 2001, above note 22.

28 *Ibid* at para 29.

sity of views should be respected."[29] If diverse views are to be respected, then claims for viewpoint or belief preference that amount to "trump" claims are suspect. Yet it is increasingly just such claims of trumps that are being seen frequently in constitutional litigation. When trump claims – such as the "visibility promotion" of gays and lesbians – are said to amount to "social policy" (this claim was seen in the *Brockie* case in Ontario[30]), it is

---

29 *Ibid* at para 33.

30 *Ontario (Human Rights Commission) v Brockie* (2002), 222 D.L.R. (4th) 174 (Ont Div Ct) [*Brockie*]. For a detailed review of this decision see T Peter Pound & Iain T Benson, "Court Overturns Key Aspect of Human Rights Board of Inquiry Decision: Religious Freedom Respected, but Narrowly" 51 LexView, online: Cardus Centre for Cultural Renewal www.cardus.ca/lexview/article/2318. Here the claim, by a gay rights group and the Ontario Human Rights Commission and Tribunal Counsel on appeal, that the advancement of gay and lesbian "visibility" was a formal government policy and that, in light of this policy, Mr. Brockie (the religious appellant) could have his views but only at home and in his church, was rejected by the Ontario court. The court held that Brockie (a printer) could not be required "to print [materials] of a nature which could reasonably be considered to be in direct conflict with the core elements of his religious beliefs or creed" (at para 58). He could refuse to do so in the public world of his printing business in downtown Toronto. As such, the Board's order was overbroad and conflicted with Brockie's rights to the freedom of conscience and religion. The attempt here by a governmental statutory agency to limit religion to the "private" realm was chilling. Fortunately the court struck down this attempt at administrative overreaching and, in so doing, an attempt to use trump-rights "liberalism" to enforce a secularist conception of the secular. For a case comment on the Tribunal's decision in the *Brockie* case see Bradley Miller, "*Brillinger v. Brockie*: Case Comment" (2000) 33 UBC L Rev 829, which shows how the Ontario Inquiry Panel failed to give any real weight to Mr. Brockie's religious beliefs. The present author, with Phil McMullin, acted as counsel for Mr. Brockie on the appeal to the Ontario Divisional Court but took no part in the cost appeal aspects that followed it. A simi-

important to note that a better approach, in accordance with the *modus vivendi* or "pluralistic liberalism" set out earlier in this article, is to look more closely as to how to share the sphere rather than "grant" dominance of the sphere to one viewpoint.

Since the *Trinity Western* case supported the distinction between "conduct" and "belief" as an operative conception in constitutional analysis, then this distinction must apply to all citizens. That is, the "beliefs" of gays and lesbians must not have superior or trump value as against the "beliefs" of other citizens. While, at the margins, a "belief" and "conduct" distinction may be appropriate (consider anti-Semitism as a religion or, for that matter, cannibalism — both of which can be justifiably restricted), it is also important to realize that the public manifestation, teaching, and dissemination of religion (referred to in the *Big M* decision[31]) anticipates a public dimension to religious belief that is also public conduct. This line will, therefore, have to be worked out on the facts of particular cases but cannot simply be reduced to a stark "you have the right to believe but not to act" formula, the way that is sometimes argued, or that one set of beliefs on contested areas (such as sexual conduct) requires that other beliefs be banished. So how useful a distinction is it? It may well be that its complexities and internal contradictions make its practical use rather limited.

It is also important to point out that while religion may be proposed, it ought not to be imposed, and that freedom *of* religion allows in certain respects for the freedom to be free *from*

lar narrowing by the court of an overbroad human rights panel decision against the proper understanding of the public nature of the freedom of religion also occurred in *Heintz v Christian Horizons* (2008), 65 CCEL (3d) 218, overturned in part on review by the Ontario Divisional Court in *Ontario Human Rights Commission v Christian Horizons* (2010), 102 OR (3d) 267. The author was counsel for an intervener, the Assembly of Catholic Bishops of Ontario in that case.

31 Above note 3.

religion. In this way, and by analogy, the freedom to believe what one wants about certain matters (say religion or sexual practices) must allow the freedom to dissent from or not approve of what others do about those religious or sexual practice claims. This means that care must be taken for a kind of tactical retreat at points where the beliefs are irreconcilable.

This notion of a "tactical retreat" or reduction of expectations should be learned by current zealots for certain sexualities who wish to impose their beliefs on others. Perhaps sexualities, like religious practices, ought to have a more private dimension. Certainly the claim to public "recognition," where recognition is shorthand for "acceptance," becomes very much like a theocratic claim to public sphere dominance for a particular religious tenet.[32]

If the appropriate place for the development of deeply held beliefs, such as religious beliefs, is the home and the church, then perhaps other deeply held beliefs, such as what is and is not appropriate sexual conduct, should also be reserved for the home?[33] Courts have yet to deal with this approach to sexually contested views the way they have with respect to religiously contested views in earlier days. Now would be a good time to embark on this kind of approach lest the totalistic claims of certain activists (the "new sectarianism" as one writer has called the new movement) lead to a new round of "[quasi-]religious wars."[34]

---

32 See Jean Bethke Elshtain, *Democracy on Trial* (New York: Basic Books, 1995) at 38 and 40 on the importance of maintaining a private/public distinction. She concludes her insightful analysis at 57 by noting that "the demand for public validation of sexual preferences, by ignoring the distinction between the personal and the political, threatens to erode authentic civil rights, including the right to privacy."

33 Of course religious schools, which are voluntarily chosen by parents, present a specific and principled distinction here. There it is not only appropriate but essential that particular religious teaching be provided.

34 Graham Good, *Humanism Betrayed: Theory, Ideology and Culture in*

B. The Fair Treatment of Differing Beliefs

1) The Nature of Liberalism and Diversity: *Modus Vivendi* or Convergence?

Though it is beyond the scope of this chapter to treat this next area in an extended way it is extremely important. There are several different theories going under the banner of "liberal" or "liberalism" and some recent writings warn us that one set of these conceptions actually poses a threat to religions and to properly plural, liberal society itself.

In *Two Faces of Liberalism*, John Gray suggests that there are two basic approaches to liberalism.[35] In the first, disagreements are assumed to be way stations on the road to eventual agreement and it is thought that emerging social consensus will eventually lead to a coalescence of viewpoints. This may be called "convergence liberalism," but Professor Gray calls it "rational consensus." In the second, disagreements and different beliefs are viewed as necessary accompaniments to living in a world of incommensurate (and incommensurable) beliefs and "values." Here the search is not for eventual convergence but for ways of coexistence or, as Gray calls it, the search for a *modus vivendi* or ways of living together.

Gray's work has provided a sustained analysis of the dangers to genuine freedom posed by the idea that there is only one form of liberalism itself. Gray suggests that the principles key to genuine liberalism must avoid "one size fits all" (monistic) approaches

---

the Contemporary University (Montreal: McGill-Queen's University Press, 2001) at 22–38.

35 *Two Faces of Liberalism*, above note 4. Peter Lauwers (now Lauwers J of the Ontario Superior Court) has commented insightfully on Gray's writings in a manner consistent with the themes in this article: see "Religion and the Ambiguities of Liberal Pluralism: A Canadian Perspective" (2007) 37 Sup Ct L Rev (2d) 1 at 12–45.

that foresee a common endpoint in a society that can and should be driven by law and politics. Genuine tolerance and genuine diversity must beware of counterfeits as they move towards the *modus vivendi*.

Gray writes that liberal thought "rarely addresses the deeper diversity that comes when there are different ways of life in the same society and even in the lives of the same individual. Yet it is the latter sort of pluralism that should set the agenda of thought about ethics and government today."[36] Gray also writes that:

> Liberalism contains two philosophies. In one, toleration is justified as a means to truth. In this view toleration is an instrument of rational consensus, and a diversity of ways of life is endured in the faith that it is destined to disappear. In the other, toleration is valued as a condition of peace, and divergent ways of living are welcomed as marks of diversity in the good life. The first conception supports an ideal of ultimate convergence on values, the latter an ideal of modus vivendi. Liberalism's future lies in turning its face away from the ideal of rational consensus and looking instead to *modus vivendi*.
>
> The predominant liberal view of toleration sees it as a means to a universal civilization. If we give up this view, and welcome a world that contains many ways of life and regimes, we will have to think afresh about human rights and democratic government. We will refashion these inheritances to serve a different liberal philosophy.
>
> We will come to think of human rights as convenient articles of peace, whereby individuals and communities with conflicting values and interests may consent to coexist.[37]

Gray cautions against a kind of illiberal "fundamentalism" that can hide all too easily in what looks like a liberal approach to

---

36 *Two Faces of Liberalism*, *ibid* at 12.

37 *Ibid* at 105.

tolerance and diversity but is not.[38]

It is difficult to read Gray's analysis and not think of the manner in which, in the *Chamberlain,* 2002 decision of the Supreme Court of Canada, parental concerns about legally contestable matters seemed to be shunted aside and clearer attempts at conceptualizing a shared public sphere were avoided. This decision tended towards doing precisely what Gray and another scholar, William Galston, former policy advisor to the Clinton Whitehouse, says is impermissible — making "valid for, and binding on, all a single debatable conception of how human beings should lead their lives."[39]

While the books portraying same-sex parenting seem innocuous enough, and did not, in the end, get into the classroom (once the matter was referred back to the trustees), the principles behind the decision could, as they no doubt eventually will, be taken much further — to suggesting that portrayals of the acceptability of same-sex sexual conduct are necessary in public education as a counter to "heteronormativity." Sooner or later greater attention will have to be paid to *modus vivendi* in this context if living together with disagreement is to become a reality.

2) Respect for Dignity and Disagreement about Beliefs, Religious or Sexual

You can respect my dignity as a religious believer even if you reject my religious beliefs, so why can I not respect your dignity as a homosexual or a lesbian even as I reject the validity of your beliefs regarding sexual conduct? Dignity ought not to be reduced to "forced agreement" about matters other than a gen-

---

38 *Ibid* at 20–21.

39 William Galston, *Liberal Purposes: Goods, Virtues and Diversity in the Liberal State* (Cambridge, UK: Cambridge University Press, 1991) at 301 and William Galstron, "Religion and Limits" in *Recognizing Religion*, above note 7 at 48 ["Religion and Limits"].

eral respect for the person. This is another aspect of the threat to liberty occasioned when the personal and private is dissolved into the public. We can live with each other in peace, in some respects, only because we do not have to force all our beliefs to arm wrestle for supremacy in public.

The manner in which religious doctrinal requirements were recognized in *Trinity Western* by reliance on ordering principles — rather than by the invocation of a "trump rights" approach (the removal of any "codes of conduct" outside of one universally acceptable one) — ought to be the kind of model that is used going forward.[40] Galston's conclusion about a more limited role for the government (and, by implication, law itself) is shared by Oxford's Joseph Raz, who stated that ". . . a government dedicated to pluralism and autonomy cannot make people good. To be autonomous they have to choose their own lives for themselves."[41]

---

40 *Trinity Western*, above note 22. (At issue was the constitutionality of a code of conduct for a Christian university that banned premarital or homosexual sex, amongst other things. The code of conduct was and there was no evidence of discrimination.) For a detailed analysis of this decision see Iain T Benson & Brad Miller, "Pluralism and the Respect for Religion" 46 LexView, online: Cardus Centre for Cultural Renewal www.cardus.ca/lexview/article/2308; see also David Brown, "Reconciling Equality and Other Rights: Paradigm Lost?" (2003) 15 NJCL 1.

41 Joseph Raz, *Ethics in the Public Domain: Essays in the Morality of Law and Politics* (Oxford: Clarendon Press, 1994) at 120. The original version of this article contained a more detailed discussion of pluralism in relation to the work of William Galston which has been cut for reasons of space. To that original discussion I would add that a very good review of versions of pluralism and recent scholarly work may be found in Mark Kingwell, *Practical Judgments: Essays in Culture, Politics, and Interpretation* (Toronto: University of Toronto Press, 2002) at 155–70. I am in substantial agreement with Kingwell's analysis of neutralist pluralism (citing Charles Taylor, Galston, Kymlicka, and others) and believe it consistent with the argument for *modus vivendi* briefly sketched out here.

Conflicts among basic liberties are always going to be present in law and politics. John Gray lists some examples of these and they will be familiar to most of us. These include: freedom of speech versus freedom from racist abuse; privacy for public figures versus freedom of expression for journalists; freedom of association and conscience in Catholic and Muslim schools (or more generally in relation to religious projects) versus freedom from discrimination in employment on grounds of religion or sexual orientation; freedom to proselytize versus the freedom to practice one's religion without fear of persecution. To this we might add the right of associations to have their own internal rules (with or without public funding) and the right of citizens to obtain employment without discrimination.[42]

Both Galston and Gray caution against illiberalism and warn that the search for grounds of cooperative non-agreement may all too easily be viewed as something else in which differing conceptions must be overcome by an overarching imperative. Charles Taylor, as well, has noted an important point in relation to politics, that touches on the kinds of conflicts we shall see more of as we constitutionalize norms that, in their nature (such as same-sex marriage), will not be accepted by, and legally need not be accepted by, large numbers of citizens. Too often the claims are framed in terms that focus on the "disadvantage" of one group to the exclusion of what the claimed advantaging will produce for everyone as opposed to the group itself. This, as Charles Taylor has written forcefully, is not good for politics or democracy as it can lead to political and cultural fragmentation.[43]

---

42 *Two Faces of Liberalism*, above note 4 at 76–77.

43 See Charles Taylor, "The Public Sphere" in Charles Taylor, *Philosophical Arguments* (Cambridge, MA: Harvard University Press, 1995) at 281. The call for *modus vivendi* articulated elsewhere in this article must deal at some point with concerns about fragmentation and individualism rightly noted by Taylor. It is important not to abandon the search for shared virtues and the adoption of programs to strengthen these in

3) The Jurisdiction of the Law and the State

Law is not and must not be everything in a free and democratic society. It is important for liberty that there are limits on the power of the state and the reach of law. Not everything should or can properly be the subject of law. This point needs to be worked through in much greater detail but I shall now turn to examine, in a broad-brush way, what some of the limits in this area might be, leaving more detailed analysis for another day.

a) What Is the Relationship between Law and Religion?

A signal exchange took place some years ago, when Beverley McLachlin CJC, at a conference co-sponsored by the Centre for Cultural Renewal and the McGill University Department of Religious Studies entitled "Pluralism, Public Policy and Religion," presented an article on the importance of conscience and religion. In the course of her remarks, the Chief Justice of Canada indicated her thinking at that time with respect to the relationship between law and the "religious citizen." Here is how she formulated the relationship:

> The modern religious citizen is caught between two *all-encompassing sets of commitments*. The law faces the seemingly paradoxical task of asserting its own ultimate authority while *carving out a space within itself* in which individuals and communities can manifest alternative, and often competing, sets

---

civil society. Nothing in this article about *modus vivendi* should be taken as supporting ethical or deep cultural relativism. It remains for other articles and initiatives to set out the principles and justifications for civic virtues and the common good. That not everything can or should necessarily be shared is not an affirmation that nothing can be and there is much to be said for a search for shared virtues since it is these that undergird the more general principles of the Constitution.

of ultimate commitments.[44]

Note the terms "all-encompassing" and "ultimate" here in relation to the law, as well as the fact that it is the law that carves out within itself places for what may be "competing sets of ultimate commitments." In this conception law is "bigger" than religion. Chief Justice McLachlin then developed this idea as follows:

> I wish to call this tension between the rule of law and the claims of religion a "dialectic of normative commitments." *What is good, true and just in religion will not always comport with the law's view* of the matter, nor will society at large always properly respect conscientious adherence to alternate authorities and divergent normative, or ethical, commitments. Where this is so, *two comprehensive worldviews* collide. It is at this point that the question of law's treatment of religion becomes truly exigent. The authority of each is internally unassailable. What is more, *both lay some claim to the whole of human experience*. To which system should the subject adhere? How can the rule of law accommodate a worldview and ethos that asserts its own superior authority and unbounded scope? . . . It is the courts that are most often faced with this clash and charged with managing this dialectic.[45]

Law here is viewed, frankly and openly, as a "comprehensive worldview" capable of competing with and even encompassing religion. Moreover, law is deemed capable of determining not only what is just but what is "good" and "true." It is able to lay claim "to the whole of human experience." Whatever else one can say of this, it elevates law to the status of transcendent determinations and therefore judges to the role of *de facto* clerics.

---

44 Beverley McLachlin, "Freedom of Religion and the Rule of Law: A Canadian Perspective" *Recognizing Religion*, above note at 16 [emphasis added].

45 *Ibid* at 21–22 [emphasis added].

It is starkly at variance with earlier decisions of the court that spoke of its inability to deal with "metaphysical" or "philosophical" matters[46] and with the common law tradition in which liberty, not law, is the primary condition. As Francis Lyall has noted with respect to liberty and law:

> As a general statement drawn from the common law, liberty is the basic position in law in Britain. Liberty is not conferred by a legal instrument: it is the normal condition, and infringements on that liberty can exist only as allowed by legislation or case law. Interference with the manifestation of traditional religious belief is therefore something which has to be justified in terms of public order or public good.[47]

---

46 *Tremblay v Daigle* (1989), 62 DLR (4th) 634 at 650 (SCC). The case dealt with whether the Quebec *Charter of Human Rights and Freedoms*, RSQ c C-12, provision saying "every human being has a right to life" provided protection for a third trimester infant *en ventre sa mère*. Near the beginning of its unanimous (and unattributed) reasons, the Supreme Court of Canada stated:

> The Court is not required to enter the philosophical and theological debates about whether or not a foetus is a person, but, rather, to answer the legal question of whether the Quebec legislature has accorded the foetus person-hood. Metaphysical arguments may be relevant but they are not the primary focus of inquiry. . . . *Decisions based upon broad social, political, moral and economic choices are more appropriately left to the legislature.* [Emphasis added.]

It is interesting to compare this conception of the role of law with that set out by McLachlin CJC in her McGill address (see above notes 44 and 45) some years later (discussed below). Clearly the role and nature of law as it is discussed and applied in Canada in the contemporary period is a very fluid set of concepts that can, at periods of time not so very far apart, be construed in radically different ways. One might be excused for asking whether, in light of the evidence, law's tiller is not sometimes rather unfortunately set to "full drift ahead"?

47 Francis Lyall, "Religious Law and its Application by Civil and Religious

On the other hand, and with respect, the Chief Justice's formulation tends towards a monistic or totalistic conception and is quite contrary to that kind of political pluralism referred to by other scholars, such as William Galston, in which there is a vision of "social space" and "spheres of autonomy" that must resile from claims to be a comprehensive good. On this reading, the Chief Justice's conception of law asks too much when it views itself as larger than the religious and other conceptions *alongside of which* it must operate as but one of several ordering frameworks within a constitutional democracy recognizing ordered and interlocking liberties.[48]

This limitation on the role of law was recognized by the University of Chicago's Jean Bethke Elshtain in her response to the Chief Justice's address:

> Surely, where the rule of law in the West is concerned, there is a great deal about which the law is simply silent: the "King's writ" does not extend to every nook and cranny. Indeed, a great deal of self-governing autonomy and authority is not only permitted but is necessary to a pluralistic, constitutional order characterized by limited government. In other words, the law need not be defined as total and comprehensive in the way the

---

Jurisdictions in Great Britain" in Ernest Caparros & Louis-Léon Christians, eds, *Religion in Comparative Law at the Dawn of the 21st Century* (Brussels: Bruylant, 2000) at 253.

48 In a recent essay, in the same volume as that containing the article of the Chief Justice discussed in this article, Galston succinctly sets out a history of the development of the notion of political pluralism from Aristotle through Hobbes to Rousseau and Rawls, showing the tensions between religious communities and the developed principles of political pluralism; see "Religion and Limits," above note 39 at 41–50. At 48, Galston states: "the common good of a pluralist society is not merely the aggregate of individual or group interests, but it is not and must not be a comprehensive good either."

Right Honourable Chief Justice claims.[49]

With respect, the way forward for constitutional adjudication in certain cases is to abandon entirely, or significantly narrow, the notion of the law's role in aid of forcing the approval of certain contested social conceptions with the implicit or explicit idea that we shall, sooner or later, come to agreement.

Interestingly, it may be that the Chief Justice herself had not finally settled on the relationship between law and religion, as she has since expressed a better understanding of this relationship than that articulated in her 2002 speech. In one of the Supreme Court's more recent decisions touching on religious liberty, *Amselem,* the Chief Justice noted that both the state and the law should be reticent to delve into personal matters related to the nature of religious belief, because

> the State is in no position to be, nor should it become, the arbiter of religious dogma. Accordingly, courts should avoid judicially interpreting and thus determining, either explicitly or implicitly, the content of a subjective understanding of religious requirement, "obligation," precept, "commandment," custom or ritual. *Secular judicial determinations of theological or religious disputes, or of contentious matters of religious doctrine, unjustifiably entangle the court in the affairs of religion.*[50]

There is a considerable difference between law "carving out within itself" a place for religion (as in the 2002 lecture) and law not wishing to "entangle itself in the affairs of religion" (as in *Amselem*).

In the West today no religions can, or do, claim priority over plural politics, yet in these earlier formulations of the Chief Justice (in her McGill address and the judgment in *Chamberlain,*

---

49 Jean Bethke Elshtain, "A Response to Chief Justice McLachlin" in *Recognizing Religion*, above note 8 at 36.

50 *Amselem*, above note 20 at para 50 [emphasis added].

2002), and in the writings of certain academic commentators, law (often spoken of as "equality claims" or "human rights" from one particular perspective) can all too easily claim a comprehensiveness that places it culturally in a position superior to the role of religions. In her judgment in *Amselem*, the Chief Justice subscribed to a better formulation of the relationship.[51]

There is another reason why law should not be elevated into a particular kind of religion or "community." In the first place, law and human rights are for all citizens, religious and non-religious, so the framework of both law and human rights ought not to be set up as a *de facto* replacement religion in some supposed "non-religious secular," however tempting it may be for some to view them in this way. In the second place, as both the BC Appeal Court and the Supreme Court of Canada decisions in *Chamberlain* noted, religions are, in some respects, *within* the public sphere.

Beliefs of whatever sort necessarily frame the work of all human beings in one way or another, and atheist and agnostic politicians have no special privilege in this respect. Of course the manner in which arguments are made based on beliefs has to be thought through carefully so that, in one's public role, they make sense to a wide variety of citizens. The personal beliefs of many important politicians, who may have been strong atheists, owed their galvanizing power not to, say, "gospel" pronouncements

---

51 I have been critical, in another article, of attempts to suggest that law constitutes a "community" as suggested by some commentators (most notably Benjamin Berger). Law as one of the ordering systems of the state must be available equally to all and must not be, even impliedly, understood to be the special province of some citizens but not others; see Iain T Benson, "The Case for Religious Inclusivism and the Judicial Recognition of Associational Rights: A Reply to Lenta" (2008) 1 Constitutional Court Rev [South Africa] 295 at 309 n30. If this is not what is meant by law being "a community" then perhaps another term should be used to avoid confusion as to what is meant.

better left to the pulpit but to the ability to speak persuasively about the common goods affecting all citizens.[52]

4) The Nature of "Dignity" and Asking Too Much in the Name of Toleration: Religious versus Sexual Dogma

One can accept the dignity of another person without having to accept their beliefs. In fact, to demand that one person accept the beliefs of another in order to accord dignity is an overreach that, again, asks too much from society out of the barrels of the law.

There are beliefs that we cannot rightly force others to share with us. Dogma, in this sense the deepest beliefs a person might

---

52 See Jonathan Chaplin, "Beyond Liberal Restraint: Defending Religiously-Based Arguments in Law and Public Policy" (2000) 33 UBC L Rev 617. Chaplin gives a useful review of the arguments of John Rawls and Robert Audi in terms of the discussion around what can constitute a properly "public" argument. Discussing the difference between public offices such as judges or ministers and so on, or between documents for use in church or by the state, Chaplin writes that

> both categories of actors (as Rawls rightly implies) share a duty to articulate their views in terms of the requirements of the "public interest." Yet, the difference of "office" . . . does impose different demands on the kinds of reasons they may publicly invoke . . . . Those [religious] believers who cannot resists [sic] invoking their comprehensive doctrines at every turn need not be regarded as irrational dogmatists but, rather, as political apprentices in need of guidance towards more focused and pertinent modes of political speech (at 643).

Consistently with the argument in this article, I would add to Chaplin's helpful insights that the same must be said of those (religious or non-religious believers) whose articulations, for example, quite often start out with erroneous dichotomies in relation to religion and/or religious belief and the civic, the public, or the "secular" and sometimes in highly dogmatic fashions.

have, has been bracketed out of public education as being inappropriate for non-denominational settings. Are there analogies to religious dogma with respect to other contested beliefs today? I believe there are. There is such a thing as "sexual dogma." Like religion, we allow citizens to hold differing beliefs about what constitutes valid sexual conduct and many other areas that are publicly debated. Citizens are free to believe what they want about them and, in respectful (non-violent) ways, say as much.

Understood this way, we can see that an issue such as "same-sex marriage," therefore, lends itself to treatment as *sexual dogma* akin to a *religious dogma* unsuitable for forced public school (or public sphere) affirmation, thus mirroring the wider social position of Canadian culture. The question of how to inculcate respect for citizens whether gay or straight, religious or non-religious must be dealt with in non-dogmatic ways whether that dogma is religious or sexual.

5) The Belief and Conduct Distinction

In *B(R)*[53] and again in *Trinity Western* the Court said that the right to hold a belief is one thing, the right to act on it in public another. This needs to be applied more consistently between religion and sexual orientation. As with the insistence that a person accept the beliefs of another in order to accord dignity, the idea that my conduct needs to be shown publicly and "affirmed" in a quest for "social recognition" asks too much of society, unduly pressures the scope of individual and group freedom, gives unrealistic expectations to certain other citizens, places unrealistic burdens upon the public sphere, and warps the proper role of the law.

The scope of this discussion, however, is being approached rather strangely at the moment. It is sometimes said that the

53 *B(R) v Children's Aid Society of Metropolitan Toronto*, [1995] 1 SCR 315 was a case involving the compulsory administration of a blood transfusion to a child against the parents' wishes.

failure to accept same-sex conduct or the "pro-choice" position on abortion, and to hold a view that same-sex sex or abortion are wrong, is an "ism" akin to racism. Why should this be? We do not say that the rejection of the views of a person as to religious conduct are akin to an "ism," so why should this be the case with sexual conduct or other legally contestable issues? At the moment the rise of new zealotry seems able to dominate public discourse because, at least in part, the conceptual categories needed to analyze the debates properly are badly confused.

C. Conclusion

The Supreme Court of Canada and the BC Court of Appeal decisions in *Chamberlain*, referred to above, in the way they handled the definition of "secular" (better imagined as "the public sphere") and pluralism as requiring the inclusion of religion and religious viewpoints, represent a model for the law, being the courts' first serious consideration of a non-atheistic/agnostic (or secularistic) "secular" in Canada. The approach found in these decisions, as in the Supreme Court of Canada decisions in *Trinity Western* and *Multani*, (but not *Hutterian Brethern* which failed to give respect for religion sufficient weight) provides the beginning outlines of ways to envisage both pluralism and the secular that will be superior to the pre-emptively non-religious and atheistic/agnostic concepts that preceded them. These decisions also correctly describe the nature of pluralism as one that encourages a diversity of beliefs and that resists the co-option of "secular" society by totalistic conceptions of liberalism that exclude diversity.

These decisions ought to lead to a reconsideration of how we view law and policies in relation to all public aspects of society, including public education. Pluralism can be and needs to be re-conceptualized within existing legal norms and the Canadian historical tradition, so as to foster a richer conception of diversity and genuine tolerance with an appropriately communitarian focus. For pluralism to be pluralism, however, it is important to rescue it from a pseudo-liberalism that hides its totalistic claims.[54]

The move to recognize two central versions of liberalism, one that is consistent with community and freedom (*modus vivendi* or "pluralistic liberalism") and one that ultimately negates genuine diversity ("convergence liberalism"), is a helpful tool when dealing with claims that hide their "trump right" aspects under the language of diversity and equality, while they in fact attack genuine diversity and the equality of all citizens. It could be that decisions such as *Trinity Western*, *Chamberlain* (the Court of Appeal decision more clearly, but also the Supreme Court of Canada decision on the meaning of "secular"), and *Brockie* (the Court of Appeal decision) signal the somewhat tentative and in some ways inconsistent beginnings of a new era in *Charter* jurisprudence in Canada. Time, other decisions, and a more nuanced public and academic debate in these areas, will tell.

---

54 Such totalistic claims can be exceedingly subtle. For example, the claim that "justificatory neutrality" is what is required in the public realm can amount to little more than that all beliefs are valid in public as long as they can make sense to non-religious people. This is hardly neutrality. See "How to be Fair," above note 19. In his clear and helpful article, Russell fails to deal with the historic shift(ing) of the term "secular" in an anti-religious direction, and in the title of his article bifurcates religion from the secular in a manner that I have argued elsewhere is both historically and philosophically suspect. Though he cites my article on the "secular" and describes it as erroneous, he does not, in fact, deal with its central arguments. See Iain T Benson, "Notes Towards a (Re) Definition of the 'Secular'" (2000) 33 UBC L Rev 519.

Chapter 14
Competing Rights in Context: The Rights of Persons with Disabilities

Lauren Bates

A. Introduction

It is an established principle of international human rights law that rights are *universal, indivisible*, and *interdependent*.[1] There is no hierarchy of rights: all rights have equal status and cannot be bargained or traded away. Further, the fulfillment of one right often depends, wholly or in part, on the fulfillment of others. For example, civil and political rights cannot be fully achieved without social and economic rights — poverty and lack of education will inhibit the ability of individuals to exercise their democratic rights. On the other hand, without civil and political rights, such as voting rights, individuals are unlikely to be able to press for the fulfillment of their social and economic rights.

---

1 See, for example, *Vienna Declaration and Programme of Action*, UNGAOR, 1993, UN Doc A/CONF.157/23, online: UNHCR www.unhcr.org/refworld/docid/3ae6b39ec.html, which states that

> All human rights are universal, indivisible, interdependent and interrelated. The international community must treat human rights globally in a fair and equal manner, on the same footing, and with the same emphasis. While the significance of national and regional particularities and various historical, cultural and religious backgrounds must be borne in mind, it is the duty of States, regardless of their political, economic and cultural systems, to promote and protect all human rights and fundamental freedoms.

This does not mean, however, that there may not be tensions between rights, and it is not uncommon to find situations where rights claims are, or are perceived to be, in tension with each other. Tensions are most acute when it may appear that one rights claim can only be fulfilled by abridging or denying another. In this sense, rights claims may be seen to compete with each other. This raises extremely complex issues.

Although it is not unusual for competing rights claims to manifest in the context of disability rights, these conflicts tend to receive relatively little attention compared to conflicts surrounding religious, gender, or sexual orientation rights. This paper will examine competing rights in the specific context of disability rights.

It is helpful to consider competing rights claims in the specific context of particular types of rights, such as disability rights, for two reasons. The first is that such a specific analysis may help to ground any approach to developing a framework to address competing rights claims. The second is that the challenges of competing rights may manifest differently in particular contexts, and that these varying manifestations may be an element in designing such a framework.

The approach of this paper is descriptive rather than prescriptive. It is not intended to evaluate any particular approach to addressing competing rights claims but to highlight some aspects of disability rights that may differentiate competing rights claims in this area from those in other areas, to identify the types of competing rights claims that may manifest in the context of disability rights, and to briefly identify some responses that have been made to such competing claims in this context.

B. Some Preliminary Considerations Regarding Disability Rights

1) Defining "Disability Rights"

As a preliminary step, it is useful to consider what is meant by the term "disability rights." The breadth or narrowness of one's approach to the concepts of "disability" and "rights" may determine whether a particular situation is considered to raise an issue of competing rights at all. That is, there is not necessarily agreement on which situations may be considered as raising competing rights claims: as some of the examples below demonstrate, in some cases, a particular issue may be seen as one of competing rights by some and not by others.

Defining what is included in the scope of "disability rights" raises a host of complex issues beyond the scope of this brief analysis, and can only be lightly touched upon here. There is by no means general agreement on what is meant by the term "disability," and depending on whether one adopts a bio-medical, functional, social, or human rights approach in a specific context, particular impairments or barriers will or will not be considered to fall within the scope of the term "disability." The Ontario *Human Rights Code*[2] contains a fairly expansive definition of disability as including physical, mental, developmental, and learning disabilities, as well as workplace injuries and past and perceived disabilities.[3] The scope of protection for persons with disabilities under domestic human rights laws has been interpreted broadly by the Supreme Court of Canada as including conditions resulting from physical limitations, ailments, perceived limitations, or a combination of these factors, the emphasis being on the *effect* of the distinction, preference, or exclusion experienced by the

---

2 RSO 1990, c H.19 [*Code*].

3 *Ibid*, s 10(1).

individual, and not on the proof of a physical disability.[4]

However, the *Canadian Charter of Rights and Freedoms*[5] and human rights caselaw provide many examples of situations where the scope of the definition of "disability" has been in dispute. For example, impairments such as temporary injuries, infertility, addictions, or obesity have in some situations been considered "disabilities" and in other circumstances not, and there is an ongoing debate as to whether genetic information that indicates susceptibility to particular diseases or impairments may bring an individual within the scope of "disability."[6]

Similarly, in considering "human rights" claims, it is important to note that the scope of "human rights" covered by domestic human rights laws such as the *Code* is considerably narrower than the scope of "human rights" embraced in international human rights documents, such as the *Universal Declaration of Human Rights*[7] and the new *Convention on the Rights of Persons with Disabilities.*[8] The *Code* references international human rights instruments in its preamble[9] and so should be read in that context.

---

4 *Quebec (Commission des droits de la personne and des droits de la jeunesse) v Boisbriand (City)*, [2000] 1 SCR 665 at paras 79–81.

5 *Canadian Charter of Rights and Freedoms*, Part I of the *Constitution Act, 1982*, being Schedule B to the *Canada Act 1982* (UK) 1982, c 11 [*Charter*].

6 For a detailed consideration of these issues, see Law Commission of Ontario, "Preliminary Consultation Paper: Approaches to Defining Disability" (June 2009), online: LCO /www.lco-cdo.org/disabilities/Disabilities%20 Threshold%20Paper%20-%20July%202009.pdf.

7 GA Res 217(III), UNGAOR, 3d Sess, Sup No 13, UN Doc A/810 (1948), online: UNHCR www.unhcr.org/refworld/docid/3ae6b3712c.html.

8 GA Res 61/106, Annex 1, UNGAOR, 61st Sess, Supp No 49, UN Doc A/RES/61/106 (2007), online: UNHCR www.unhcr.org/refworld/ docid/45f973632.html [*CRPD*].

9 The preamble to the *Code*, above note 2, states in part that "recognition of the inherent dignity and the equal and inalienable rights of all

Unlike the international instruments touching on disability rights, the *Code* is restricted to a limited number of social areas, such as housing, employment, and services. International documents include a wider range of rights, including rights to live independently in the community, to be free of violence and abuse, and to respect for home and family.[10] Further, domestic human rights laws are fundamentally anti-discrimination legislation, and while they may be read expansively, this imposes certain limitations, for example with respect to economic, social, and cultural rights which have been recognized in international instruments.[11]

While certain apparent competing rights claims may be resolved by restricting the scope of "disability" or "human rights" to those rights that are protected in domestic human rights laws, there are risks and limitations to this approach. As noted above, domestic human rights laws were developed in the light of international human rights instruments, and there have been some significant efforts to ensure that laws such as the *Code* are interpreted and applied in the context of the broader international human rights context.[12] A strategy that narrowly interprets the

---

members of the human family is the foundation of freedom, justice and peace in the world and is in accord with the Universal Declaration of Human Rights as proclaimed by the United Nations."

10 For example, the *CRPD*, above note 8, includes rights to live independently as part of the community (art 19), to access to mobility aids (art 20), to freedom of expression and opinion (art 21), to provision of health services as close as possible to the person's own community (art 25), and to habilitation and rehabilitation services and programs (art 26).

11 For a thorough discussion of these complex issues, see Ontario Human Rights Commission, "Human Rights Commissions and Economic, Social and Cultural Rights," Research Paper, Policy and Education Branch (OHRC, 2001), online: Ontario Human Rights Commission www.ohrc.on.ca/sites/default/files/attachments/Human_rights_commissions_and_economic_and_social_rights.pdf.

12 One example of this is the Ontario Human Rights Commission's (OHRC)

scope of human rights laws in order to avoid dealing with tensions between rights may be self-defeating in the larger context of the human rights movement.

2) Disability, Difference, and Universalism

As a further step in considering competing rights claims in the context of disability-related rights, it is helpful to consider the specific nature of disability rights. Central to disability rights is the challenge of according rights and respect to *difference.* As the Supreme Court of Canada pointed out in the *Eaton* case,[13] while most equality rights law and jurisprudence focuses on elimination of discrimination resulting from the attribution of untrue characteristics based on stereotypical attitudes, a key element of any approach to disability rights must be to take into account and accommodate the true characteristics of persons with disabilities:

> Exclusion from the mainstream of society results from the construction of a society based solely on "mainstream" attributes to which disabled persons will never be able to gain access. Whether it is the impossibility of success at a written test for

work on housing rights. The *Code*, above note 2, prohibits discrimination in housing on the basis of a number of enumerated grounds, but it does not contain broad rights to adequate housing such as are found in international human rights instruments such as art 11 of the *International Covenant on Social, Economic and Cultural Rights*, 16 December 1966, 993 UNTS 3, (entered into force 3 January 1976). However, the OHRC's *Policy on Human Rights and Rental Housing* deals at length with issues surrounding poverty and access to housing, with considerable reference to the provisions of international human rights instruments; see Ontario Human Rights Commission, *Policy on Human Rights and Rental Housing* (OHRC, 2009), online: OHRC www.ohrc.on.ca/sites/default/files/attachments/Policy_on_human_rights_and_rental_housing.pdf.

13 *Eaton v Brant County Board of Education*, [1997] 1 SCR 241 [*Eaton*].

> a blind person, or the need for ramp access to a library, the discrimination does not lie in the attribution of untrue characteristics to the disabled individual. The blind person cannot see and the person in a wheelchair needs a ramp. Rather, it is the failure to make reasonable accommodation, to fine-tune society so that its structures and assumptions do not result in the relegation and banishment of disabled persons from participation, which results in discrimination against them . . . . It is recognition of the actual characteristics, and reasonable accommodation of these characteristics which is the central purpose of s. 15(1) in relation to disability.[14]

There are a couple of elements of the responses that the disability rights movement has developed to this "difference dilemma" that are worth briefly highlighting. The first is an emphasis on the fundamental worth and dignity of all individuals, regardless of their abilities or impairments. Denise Réaume states that "[d]ignity refers to the ineffable quality that we ascribe equally to all human beings by virtue of which we accord them a special kind of worth."[15] She continues:

> To ascribe dignity to human beings as a moral matter is to treat human beings as creatures of intrinsic, incomparable, and indelible worth, simply as human beings. No further qualifications are necessary. Dignity is thus ascribed to human beings independently of their particular merits. The worth connoted is not contingent on being useful, attractive, pleasant, or otherwise serving the ends of others . . . . As something inherently "possessed" by human beings, there is a sense in which dignity cannot be taken away. It can, however, be dishonoured through

---

14 *Ibid* at para 67.

15 Denise G Réaume, "Dignity, Equality, and Second Generation Rights" in Margot Young, Susan B Boyd, Gwen Brodsky *et al*, eds, *Poverty: Rights, Social Citizenship, and Legal Activism* (Vancouver: University of British Columbia Press, 2007) at 282.

> a failure to show respect, in other words, through treating others as less than creatures of inherent worth.[16]

That is, the dignity and worth of individuals does not depend on their economic contributions, their intellectual achievements, or their ability to conform to the norm, but is intrinsic. Disability rights, as they have evolved, require us to rethink not just what we think of as "normal," but at their most profound, how we conceive of the experience of being human, and what it is that we value in each other. One of the challenges offered by the disability movement, in a society that is focused on economic productivity, and where other types of contributions tend to be under-recognized and inadequately respected, is to recognize the different types of contributions that all individuals, whether disabled or not, make and have the potential to make to their communities.

Another important response to the "difference dilemma" associated with the rights of persons with disabilities is the "universalism model," which aims to "establish a view of ourselves as individuals who exist at an infinite number of points on an infinite number of continua of ability levels,"[17] so that, rather than using difference to reinforce separation, we recognize that we are united in our variation. That is, the "difference" that is associated with disability does not separate persons with disabilities from others, but rather is simply part of the universal human experience. In this approach, persons with disabilities cease to be viewed as a minority group, and become part of a broader imperative for inclusiveness and flexibility in the design of social norms, institutions, and structures.[18]

---

16 *Ibid* at 282–83.

17 Doug Surtees, "What Can Elder Law Learn from Disability Law" in Israel Doron, ed, *Theories on Law and Ageing: The Jurisprudence of Elder Law* (Berlin: Springer-Verlag: 2009) at 102.

18 A helpful brief overview of the universalism model may be found *ibid* at 100–2. This model provides a counterpoint to what has been called the

This approach recognizes that all people can be characterized along a continuum of abilities and that the experience of disability is a normal and universal aspect of the human condition. Irving Zola argues that given the increasing prevalence of disability, we need to acknowledge that "[t]he issue of disability for individuals . . . is not *whether* but *when,* not so much *which one* but *how many* and *in what combination*."[19] He explains:

> It is more fruitful to conceive of disability as fluid, continuous, and holistic. In addition, populations are best conceived not as those who do have a disability versus those who do not, but rather (given the ubiquity of disability) as varying on a series of continua that cover the range of disabilities and degrees of disablement. Disability is thus not a fixed status but a continuously changing and evolving set of characteristics.[20]

In this view, disability is not static but instead is flexible, evolving, and constitutes "a set of characteristics everyone shares to varying degrees and in varying forms and combinations."[21]

Zola argues that this principle necessitates a recasting of disability so that there is a demystification of "'the specialness' of disability. By seeing people as 'different' with 'special' needs, wants, and rights in this currently perceived world of finite resources, they are pitted against the needs, wants, and rights of the rest of the population."[22] By contrast, through acknowledge-

---

"civil rights" model which aims to identify and overcome disadvantages that persons with disabilities face as members of an oppressed minority group.

19 Irving K Zola, "Disability Statistics: What We Count and What It Tells Us: A Personal and Political Analysis" (1993) 4:2 Journal of Disability Policy Studies 9 at 18.

20 *Ibid* at 24.

21 *Ibid* at 30.

22 Irving K Zola, "Toward the Necessary Universalizing of a Disability Policy" (1989) 67 The Milbank Quarterly 401 at 420 ["Toward the Universalizing

ment of "the near universality of disability and that all its dimensions (including biomedical) are part of the social process by which the meanings of disability are negotiated,"[23] we can reveal the social and political construction of disability.

Flowing out of this principle, the concept of universal design becomes centrally important. If all people exist along a continuum of abilities and the line is drawn to be the most inclusive possible, then designing infrastructure and social systems to facilitate maximum inclusion is a central goal of ensuring this principle is engaged. As Bickenbach *et al* state:

> Universal disability policy . . . merely expands the range of human normality to more realistically include empirically-grounded human variation. In particular, standards and codes should reflect a policy commitment to universal design, not merely for public buildings and transportation, but across the board for housing, workplaces and other human environments. Universal design is a blueprint for the creation of human environments and tools that can be successfully used by human beings given human variations. It means that, instead of catering to people who happen to fit within a relatively narrow range of the normal, we ensure that environments and tools are suitable to as many as possible.[24]

In this light, "a universal policy towards disability is not only a concern but in the interests of an entire society."[25] Similarly, Scotch

---

of Disability Policy"], citing D Stone, *The Disabled State* (Philadelphia: Temple University Press, 1984).

23 *Ibid* at 420.

24 Jerome E Bickenbach, Somnath Chatterji, & EM Badley *et al*, "Models of Disablement, Universalism and the International Classification of Impairments, Disabilites and Handicaps" (1999) 48:9 Social Science and Medicine 1173 at 1183.

25 "Towards the Universalizing of Disability Policy," above note 22 at 421. Similarly, Bickenbach *et al*, *ibid* at 1182, argue: "[r]ather than identify-

and Schriner assert that "[i]ncorporating individual variations requires greater initial effort than following rigid standard operating procedures"[26] but that this greater initial effort is justified by the benefits to the larger society. A universalistic approach therefore necessitates cooperation and facilitation to ensure that persons with varying human abilities are seen in a positive light as potential contributors to society.[27]

C. Identifying Types of Competing Rights Claims in the Context of Disability Rights

In the context of the rights of persons with disabilities, tensions or competition between rights claims arise in a variety of ways. Three commonly identified sources of competing rights are:

1) Accommodation of disability-related needs: in some cases, the accommodation of disability-related needs will have an effect or potential effect on others around them, and in these situations the affected individuals may characterize the situation as one of conflicting rights.

---

ing special needs that require special attention (and special legislation, special agencies and special experts), we need to see that all people have needs that vary in roughly predictable ways, over the course of their life span. Disablement policy is therefore not policy for some minority groups, it is policy for all."

26 Richard K Scotch & Kay Schriner, "Disability as Human Variation: Implications for Policy" (1997) 549 Annals, AAPSS 148 at 151.

27 *Ibid* at 158. In the context of employment, they argue that "[t]he human variation perspective acknowledges that some impairments may require an ad hoc definition of work expectations that may involve completely individualized facilities and practices" (at 157). Further, they say that "[a] human variation perspective on employment suggests that lack of access to employment by persons with disabilities be resolved by cooperatively maximizing each individual's productivity . . . [and] of having employers view individuals as potential contributors . . . ." (at 158).

2) Competing accommodation needs between individuals with disabilities: occasionally, two persons with disabilities will require accommodations that conflict.
3) Competition between different types of rights: these conflicts do not necessary involve accommodation needs, and often raise the most complex issues.

These different types of tensions have tended to evoke different responses. Each will be described and considered separately below.

1) Accommodation of Disability-Related Needs as a Source of Competing Rights

Perhaps the most commonly expressed tension in the area of disability rights arises from the perception that a particular accommodation for a person with a disability infringes on the rights of other persons. For example, in the context of rental housing, a person with environmental sensitivities may need other tenants in the same building to refrain from using certain materials or chemicals in the renovation or upkeep of their premises, thereby affecting the ability of those tenants to use their own spaces as they see fit. In the employment context, a person with a disability who uses para-transit for transportation to and from work may be restricted in the hours of work he is available, so that other employees may be required to work less preferred hours to provide necessary coverage for the employer.[28]

28 These kinds of tensions are not unique to disability cases, although they occur frequently in this context. The Supreme Court of Canada dealt with this type of tension in *Central Okanagan School District No 23 v Renaud*, [1992] 2 SCR 970 [*Renaud*], a case dealing with the accommodation of shift schedules on the basis of creed. In the accommodation of the applicant's religiously-based scheduling needs raised concerns regarding the impact of the necessary scheduling changes on other employees. The Court stated at para 30 that "The objection of employees based on

Whether these tensions are considered as issues of competing rights depends, as discussed earlier in this chapter, on what we characterize as "rights." In rare cases, accommodations for persons with disabilities will have effects on others who are recognized as rights bearers: these types of situations are dealt with in the following sections. In most cases, however, while effects of an accommodation are not infrequently perceived as impinging on "rights" by the persons affected or by the general public, these types of tensions have not been generally characterized as involving competing rights as the persons affected are not claiming legally enforceable human rights under domestic human rights laws.

In most cases, the affected individual does not have any legally recognized "right" at stake. For example, employees affected by a disability accommodation do not necessarily have any legally based "right" to particular hours. In some cases, employment contracts or collective agreements are in play, but human rights law generally takes precedence over other statutes, contracts, and collective agreements.[29]

There is a legal mechanism available for resolving these types of tensions arising from disability accommodations. This is the "undue hardship standard," which is found in all of Canada's domestic human rights laws, and which places an outermost limit on the extent of required accommodations. Under domestic human rights laws, accommodation needs related to disability must only be provided to the point of "undue hardship."[30] Most

---

well-grounded concerns that their rights may be affected must be considered. On the other hand, objections based on attitudes inconsistent with human rights are an irrelevant consideration."

29 See the *Code*, above note 2, s 47(2), which states, "Where a provision in an Act or regulation purports to require or authorize conduct that is a contravention of Part I, this Act applies and prevails unless the Act or regulation specifically provides that it is to apply despite this Act."

30 *Ibid*, ss 11(2) and 17(2).

domestic human rights statutes do not define "undue hardship," but the *Code* specifies that an assessment of undue hardship includes the factors of cost, health, and safety, and outside sources of funding.[31] For example, where an accommodation of a workplace disability-related need poses an undue risk to the health and safety of the disabled individual's co-workers, the employer is not required to implement the accommodation. Similarly, where the costs involved in an accommodation are so significant as to affect the viability or essential nature of a business, that accommodation will amount to undue hardship. "Employee morale" has also been identified as a potential factor for assessing undue hardship; however, given the unique wording of the *Code*, it is not clear whether this is a factor to be considered in Ontario.[32] In any case, the undue hardship standard provides a mechanism whereby certain types of rights or needs may be balanced against disability-related rights to accommodation. It is important to note, however, that the standard is a high one, and only a limited number of factors fall within the standard, so that many issues that are sometimes characterized as matters of competing rights are not addressed in this way.[33]

---

31 *Ibid*.

32 The caselaw regarding the consideration of these types of issues under the undue hardship standard is complex. The Supreme Court of Canada has included "employee morale" as a potential consideration in assessing undue hardship. Reflecting the unique wording of ss 11(2) and 17(20) of the *Code*, above note 2, the ORHC's *Policy and Guidelines on Disability and the Duty to Accommodate* excludes employee morale as a consideration in assessing undue hardship. See Ontario Human Rights Commission, *Policy and Guidelines on Disability and the Duty to Accommodate* (OHRC, 2000) at s 5, online: OHRC www.ohrc.on.ca/en/resources/Policies/PolicyDisAccom2 [*Policy and Guidelines on Disability and the Duty to Accommodate*].

33 See *Policy and Guidelines on Disability and the Duty to Accommodate*, *ibid*.

In those many cases where concerns regarding the impact of disability-related accommodations on others do not fall within the scope of recognized human rights claims or of the undue hardship standard, responses to such concerns tend to rely on the fundamental understandings of disability rights, as briefly outlined above. For example, a disability rights approach seeks to undermine the assumptions about the contributions of persons with disabilities in the workplace or in any other context, and to shift the norm to a more inclusive and respectful approach to persons with disabilities. A response to complaints from co-workers regarding the "special privileges" received by a person with a disability as part of an accommodation may therefore point to the importance of respecting the fundamental worth of persons with disabilities, and include a reminder of the many contributions that persons with disabilities, including the individual in question, makes to the workplace and to society in general.

Alternatively, a response may rely on the universalist approach and seek to reframe the emphasis away from accommodation of individual difference and towards the design of environments that minimize the effects of human variation. Flexible work hours, if instituted for the workplace at large and not only as a one-off accommodation for a particular individual with a disability, can benefit everyone. The announcement of transit stops on buses and subways makes travel by public transit easier for everyone, not just for those who are blind. And the chances are that everyone, at some point in her life, will need some accommodation, whether because of temporary injuries or illnesses or because of age-related changes, or because of the development of a long-term impairment: in this sense, accommodation is of benefit to all.

2) Competition between the Accommodation Needs of Two Persons with Disabilities

More difficult issues of competing rights arise where two persons with disabilities have different and conflicting accommodation needs. For example, one student in a classroom may have a sensory disability and use a service animal, while another student may have severe allergies that make it impossible to be present in the room with the service animal. In a housing context, one individual may need to use medical marijuana to cope with disability-related discomfort, while his neighbour has environmental sensitivities that are triggered by marijuana smoke. These types of conflicts are perhaps unique to disability rights, given the infinitely variable nature of disability-related needs and accommodations. The peculiar difficulty of such scenarios is that the rights are of the same nature and legal status, and are based on the same principles: rights may therefore be directly in competition.

The most obvious and frequent response to such scenarios is a procedural one, requiring the accommodation provider to explore all possible options for at least minimally respecting the rights of both persons with disabilities. For example, could one of the students be transferred to another class without unduly affecting her education? Are there alternative ways of supporting the person with a sensory disability in the classroom without the service animal, such as by the provision of a dedicated human assistant during class hours?

This type of procedural response places significant responsibilities on the accommodation provider, who is required to respond with creativity and flexibility to balance the competing needs of the parties. However, this is in harmony with existing human rights law, which holds that in demonstrating that accommodation has been provided to the point of undue hardship, the process engaged in by the person responsible for the accommodation is as important as the substantive content of the accommodation.[34]

This type of response may also require compromise and flexibility from the accommodation seekers themselves. In order to ensure at least minimal accommodation for both, neither accommodation seeker may receive the ideal accommodation. However, this notion of dialogue and flexibility is inherent in the notion of accommodation itself. As the Supreme Court stated in *Renaud,* "The search for accommodation is a multi-party inquiry" and all parties involved must work together to identify and implement appropriate accommodation.[35]

3) Competition between Different Types of Rights

The third type of tension involves competition between different types of rights, and may not involve accommodation of disability-related needs at all. As was brought to the attention of the LCO by the ARCH Disability Law Centre, a recent example involved labour action to resolve long-standing wage issues in the developmental services sector. In several instances, picket lines were set up in front of group homes of persons with developmental disabilities, in some cases resulting in considerable disruption, and in fear, disorientation, and humiliation for many residents. Arguably, the residents of the group homes had their "right to quiet possession" of their own homes disrupted by the exercise of labour rights by the workers.

Another example within the labour context involves labour actions by education assistants in the public school system: where the services of educational assistants are withdrawn due to a labour action, students with disabilities may be unable to attend school and be denied education, while the education of their non-disabled peers, who do not require the services of educa-

---

34 *British Columbia (Public Service Employee Relations Commission) v BCGSEU*, [1999] 3 SCR 3 at para 66.

35 *Renaud*, above note 28 at para 43.

tional assistants, continues with minimal disruption. In such a case, students with disabilities are denied equal educational services as compared to their non-disabled peers.

As with competitions between differing accommodation needs as described above, the first resort in such situations is generally to a procedural approach. Are there compromises or creative solutions that will allow at least the basic exercise of rights to all parties? Failing a procedural resolution, however, the tensions must be dealt with head on.

Such conflicts do not fall neatly within a human rights framework. In the examples above, where the rights of persons with disabilities are impaired by the labour actions of services providers, there is no clear mechanism within human rights laws for addressing the tension between the two types of rights. One might employ the primacy provisions of the *Code*[36] to assert the primacy of the rights of persons with disabilities over the labour rights of the workers. This might mean constraining the picketing rights of workers, or employing replacement workers to ensure that students with disabilities can attend school with their peers. The employer/service provider who does not act to constrain the labour rights of employees may then raise the defence of undue hardship, highlighting the effect of such an approach on employee relations and long-term service provision. At this time, human rights caselaw does not provide guidance in such circumstances, and cases would likely be resolved on a case-by-case basis.

The exercise of the *Code*'s primacy provisions may resolve the legal conflict within the relatively narrow confines of the *Code*, but does not address the broader social context in which there is a perceived competition between these kinds of rights. It also has implications for broader notions of the indivisibility of rights and of the status of socio-economic rights. In the examples raised, while labour rights are not *Code* rights, they are fundamental

36 *Code*, above note 2, s 47(2).

rights that are recognized and protected in the *Charter* and in international instruments.

From a disability rights perspective, in balancing such competing rights claims, one must consider not only the nature of the particular rights at stake for either party, but also the particular nature of the historical marginalization and oppression of persons with disabilities. Given the history of subordinating the needs of persons with disabilities to those of others, one must be particularly careful, where the rights of persons with disabilities compete with those of others, to ensure that the rights of persons with disabilities have been given at least equal consideration with those of others, and that the broader context of discrimination and exclusion of persons with disabilities has been taken into account. That is, any balancing of competing rights must take into account the approaches and social critiques arising from the disability rights movement, and must fully recognize and respect the dignity and worth of persons with disabilities.

D. Conclusion

It is clear from this brief description that the ways in which a particular set of competing claims will be dealt with in the disability rights context will depend very much on the nature of the particular claims at issue. There has been no single approach to balancing competing rights in the context of disability. The scope of "disability rights" remains contested, and therefore it is not always clear whether a particular situation truly raises a situation of competing rights. However, if one confines the scope of inquiry to the confines of the *Code*, this restricts the extent of competing rights claims considerably. Many situations that those affected may consider to be situations of "competing rights" are not so within the framework of domestic human rights laws, and can be dealt with relatively simply, at least from a legal perspective. From a broader perspective, to address perceptions of competing rights may in these circumstances require a non-legal approach that is founded in the basic insights of disability rights.

Where claims compete within the framework of the *Code*, a procedural response is generally the first resort, in keeping with the basic principles of human rights law. Such an approach requires patience, flexibility, creativity, and compromise. Where disability-related rights are in tension with other types of rights, the fundamental principles of disability rights require that, in attempting to balance or reconcile such claims, the particular nature of disability rights, including the history and context of marginalization and exclusion of persons with disabilities, be recognized and respected, so that the rights of persons with disabilities are not subordinated to those of others.

Chapter 15
Regulating Hate Speech in Canada

Richard Moon

A. Introduction

I was commissioned by the Canadian Human Rights Commission (CHRC) in the summer of 2008 to write a report on the regulation of hate speech on the Internet, focusing specifically on section 13 of the *Canadian Human Rights Act*.[1] Section 13 prohibits the repeated communication on the phone system or the Internet of any matter "that is likely to expose a person or persons to hatred or contempt by reason of the fact that person or those persons are identifiable on the basis of a prohibited ground of discrimination," such as race, gender, and religion.

I was asked to do this at a time when the CHRC was coming under significant scrutiny. There were, I think, two reasons for this increased scrutiny of the Commission. First, the CHRC (and other Human Rights Commissions (HRCs)) had in recent years received and investigated complaints about speech that seemed to reflect widely held views — notably, speech linking Muslims to violence, and anti-gay speech that rested on established religious views. Until recently, virtually all of the complaints received by the CHRC concerned postings on neo-Nazi or white-supremacist websites. Second, the CHRC, as well as several of the provincial HRCs, had investigated complaints against mainstream publications (or at

1 RSC 1985, c H-6 [*CHRA*]. The House of Commons voted to repeal s. 13 in June 2012, after this paper was written.

least their Internet versions), including *Maclean's* magazine and smaller publications such as the *Western Standard* and *Catholic Insight*.

I submitted my report to the CHRC in late October 2008. In the report I recommended the repeal of section 13 of the *CHRA* so that the CHRC and the Canadian Human Rights Tribunal (CHRT) would no longer deal with hate speech, and in particular hate speech on the Internet. I argued that hate speech should continue to be prohibited under the *Criminal Code*.[2] I took the position that state censorship of hate speech should be confined to a narrow category of extreme expression — that which threatens, advocates, or justifies violence against the members of an identifiable group, even if the violence advocated is not imminent — and that the restriction of this narrow category of expression should be dealt with under the *Criminal Code* rather than the *CHRA*.[3]

B. Hate Speech Law

Hate speech in Canada is currently restricted by both federal and provincial laws. The *Criminal Code* of Canada prohibits the advocacy or promotion of genocide, the incitement of hatred against an identifiable group, when this incitement is likely to lead to a breach of the peace, and the wilful promotion of hatred against an identifiable group.[4] Investigations into allegations of hate speech under the *Criminal Code* are conducted by the police. An individual may be charged under the wilful promotion of hatred provision only with the consent of the provincial attorney general.

---

2 Richard Moon, "Report to the Canadian Human Rights Commission Concerning Section 13 of the *Canadian Human Rights Act* and the Regulation of Hate Speech on the Internet" (Canadian Human Rights Commission, 2008), online: CHRC www.chrc-ccdp.gc.ca [Moon].

3 *Ibid*.

4 *Criminal Code*, RSC 1985, c C-46, ss 318 & 319.

If an individual is charged with promoting hatred, his trial will be conducted in a court of law. To be convicted under any of these offences, the accused must be shown to have committed the relevant act and to have done so either intentionally or with knowledge or awareness of the nature of her actions. If found by the court to have committed the offence, she may be sentenced to a fine or a term of imprisonment. The *Criminal Code* also includes a section that enables a court to order the seizure or erasure of material that the court determines to be "hate propaganda."[5]

The ban on hate speech in section 13 of the *CHRA* applies to telephonic or Internet communication that is likely to expose the members of an identifiable group to hatred or contempt. The purpose of section 13, and the other provisions of the *CHRA,* is to prevent or rectify discriminatory practices or to compensate the victims of discrimination for the harm they have suffered. The purpose is not to condemn and punish the person who committed the discriminatory act. In contrast to the criminal ban on hate speech, an individual may be found to have breached section 13 even though he did not intend to expose others to hatred or realize that his communication might have this effect. The focus is said to be on the effect of the act and not the intention with which it was performed. The ordinary remedy against an individual who is found to have breached the section is an order that she cease her discriminatory practices.

The process established under the *CHRA* is complaint-driven. Section 40 of the *CHRA* provides that "any individual or group of individuals having reasonable grounds for believing that a person is engaging or has engaged in a discriminatory practice may file with the Commission a complaint in a form acceptable to the Commission." The CHRC may also initiate a complaint "where it has reasonable grounds for believing that a person is engaging or has engaged in a discriminatory practice" but in the case of

5 *Ibid*, ss 320 & 320.1.

section 13, the Commission has done so on only one occasion. If the CHRC receives a complaint that falls within the general scope of the *CHRA* and is not trivial, frivolous, vexatious, or made in bad faith, it must investigate the complaint to determine whether it should be referred to the CHRT for adjudication. The CHRT is a separate and independent body from the CHRC. In contrast to other discrimination complaints, conciliation tends to play only a minor role in section 13 cases because the expression that is the subject of the complaint is often extreme in character, and because the parties ordinarily have no relationship prior to the complaint. In exceptional circumstances the CHRC has facilitated a non-adjudicative resolution of the complaint — most often an agreement by the respondent to remove the material that is the subject of the complaint from the website. If a complaint is referred by the Commission to the CHRT for adjudication, the CHRC may appear at the hearing "to represent the public interest." The complainant has carriage of the action before the Tribunal.

The human rights codes of British Columbia,[6] Alberta,[7] Saskatchewan,[8] and the Northwest Territories[9] include a provision similar to section 13 of the *CHRA,* although there is some variation in the scope of the different provincial and territorial laws and the procedures followed in each jurisdiction.

C. The Scope of Section 13

The *CHRA* prohibits several different forms of discrimination, including discrimination in employment[10] and in the provision of goods and services.[11] But while the ban on these other forms

---

6 *Human Rights Code*, RSBC 1996, c 210.

7 *Alberta Human Rights Act*, RSA 2000, c A-25.5.

8 *Saskatchewan Human Rights Code*, SS 1979, c S-24.1.

9 *Human Rights Act*, SNWT 2002, c 18.

10 *CHRA*, above note 1, s 7.

11 *Ibid*, s 5.

of discrimination has been interpreted broadly by the courts and the CHRT, the scope of the section 13 ban has been more narrowly defined. In *CHRC v Taylor,* a majority of the Supreme Court of Canada, in a judgment written by Dickson CJC, held that section 13 of the *CHRA* breached section 2(b) of the *Charter*,[12] the freedom of expression provision, but was a "reasonable" and "demonstrably justified" limit under section 1.[13] In reaching its decision in *CHRC v Taylor*, the Court drew heavily on its analysis in the companion case of *R. v Keegstra*, which affirmed the constitutionality of the *Criminal Code* prohibition on the "wilful promotion of hatred." In both cases the Court thought it significant that the law at issue prohibited only a very narrow category of extreme expression that could be shown to contribute to the spread of hatred in the community.

According to Dickson CJC, writing for the majority in *Taylor*, section 13 focuses on expression that contributes to "unusually strong and deep-felt emotions of detestation, calumny and vilification" and so is not "particularly expansive."[14] Chief Justice Dickson, however, noted that "the nature of human rights legislation militates" against an unduly narrow reading of section 13(1) and indicated that he had no "wish to transgress the well-established principle that the rights enumerated in such a code should be given their full recognition and effect through a fair, large and liberal interpretation."[15] While the absence of an intention requirement in section 13 means that "the section may impose a slightly broader limit upon freedom of expression than does section 319(2) [the hate promotion provision] of the *Criminal Code* . . . the conciliatory bent of a human rights statute

---

12 *Canadian Charter of Rights and Freedoms*, Part I of the *Constitution Act, 1982*, being Schedule B to the *Canada Act 1982* (UK) 1982, c 11 [*Charter*].

13 *Canada v Taylor*, [1990] 3 SCR 892 [*Taylor*].

14 *Ibid* at 928.

15 *Ibid* at 927.

renders such a limit more acceptable than would be the case with a criminal provision."[16] In the view of Dickson CJC, "as long as the Human Rights Tribunal continues to be well aware of the purpose of section 13(1) and pays heed to the ardent and extreme nature of the feeling described in the phrase 'hatred or contempt,' there is little danger that subjective opinion as to offensiveness will supplant the proper meaning of the section."[17]

In her dissenting judgment McLachlin J (as she then was) argued that the "absence of any requirement of intent or foreseeability of the actual promotion of hatred or contempt," while "consistent with the remedial . . . focus of human rights legislation,"[18] broadened the scope of the section so that it included communication that ought not to be prohibited. In response to this argument, that section 13 is overly broad in its scope because it lacks an intention requirement, Dickson CJC observed that the focus of the section "is solely upon likely effects, it being irrelevant whether an individual wishes to expose persons to hatred or contempt on the basis of their race or religion."[19] According to Dickson CJC:

> The preoccupation with effects, and not with intent is readily explicable when one considers that systemic discrimination is much more widespread in our society than is intentional discrimination. To import a subjective intent requirement into human rights provisions, rather than allowing tribunals to focus solely upon effects, would thus defeat one of the primary goals of anti-discrimination statutes. At the same time, however, it cannot be denied that to ignore intent in determining whether a discriminatory practice has taken place according to s. 13(1) increases the degree of restriction upon the constitutionally

---

16 *Ibid* at 928–29.

17 *Ibid* at 895.

18 *Ibid* at 962.

19 *Ibid* at 931.

> protected freedom of expression. This result flows from the realization that an individual open to condemnation and censure because his or her words may have an unintended effect will be more likely to exercise caution via self-censorship.[20]

It is important to remember, wrote Dickson CJC, that, in contrast to criminal law, the purpose of human rights legislation is to "compensate and protect" the victim rather than "stigmatize or punish" the person who has discriminated against her.[21]

The *Taylor* decision remains the touchstone for both the CHRC and the CHRT when applying section 13. In *Warman v Kouba* the CHRT identified certain "hallmarks of hate," factors that the Tribunal considered relevant in deciding whether the expression meets the *Taylor* test for breach of section 13.[22] The CHRT drew its list of "hallmarks" from "the growing body of section 13 jurisprudence." According to the Tribunal: "The hallmarks or attributes of hate messages are what distinguishes them from legitimate speech that is not subject to sanction under section 13 of the *Act*. All of these attributes involve an attack on the inherent self-worth and dignity of the members of the targeted group."[23] The list was composed of the following attributes: "(a) The targeted group is portrayed as a powerful menace that is taking control of the major institutions in society and depriving others of their livelihoods, safety, freedom of speech and general well-being"; "(b) The messages use 'true stories,' news reports, pictures and references from purportedly reputable sources to make negative generalization about the targeted group"; "(c) The targeted group is portrayed as preying upon children, the aged, the vulnerable, etc."; "(d) The targeted group is blamed for the current problems in society and the world"; "(e) The targeted

---

20 *Ibid.*

21 *Ibid* at 932.

22 *Warman v Kouba*, 2006 CHRT 50 [*Warman*].

23 *Ibid* at para 82.

group is portrayed as dangerous or violent by nature"; "(f) The messages convey the idea that members of the targeted group are devoid of any redeeming qualities and are innately evil"; "(g) The messages communicate the idea that nothing but the banishment, segregation or eradication of this group of people will save others from the harm being done by this group"; "(h) The targeted group is de-humanized through comparisons to and associations with animals, vermin, excrement, and other noxious substances"; "(i) Highly inflammatory and derogatory language is used in the messages to create a tone of extreme hatred and contempt"; "(j) The messages trivialize or celebrate past persecution or tragedy involving members of the targeted group"; and (k) the messages contain "[c]alls to take violent action against the targeted group."[24] This list, said the Tribunal, "is by no means exhaustive," but it may "provide a useful context" for the determination of whether the "material is more likely than not to expose members of the targeted group to hatred or contempt."[25]

Section 13 is breached only if an individual or group communicates its hate message "repeatedly." The requirement, standard in hate speech laws, that the communication be public is adapted to a technology that involves one-on-one interaction. Each time a phone message is played, it is heard by a single individual and so may be described as a "private" communication; however, as Dickson CJC in *Taylor* observed, "[w]hile conversations almost always take place on a one-to-

---

24 *Ibid* at paras 24–81.

25 The mainstream media are subject to non-legal or market constraints that ordinarily prevent them from engaging in the extreme expression that is the subject of hate speech laws — although not necessarily expression that stereotypes or defames the members of an identifiable group. These constraints include a reliance on advertising revenue and the need to attract a large audience. Section 13 of the *CHRA* applies to the mainstream print media in a roundabout way because most mainstream publications are reproduced on the Internet.

one basis, the overall effect of phone campaigns is undeniably public, and the reasonable assumption to make is that these campaigns can have an effect upon the public's beliefs and attitudes."[26] The requirement that the message be made "repeatedly" leads to a distinction between a private phone call, in which hateful views are expressed, and recorded hate messages which may be accessed by many different individuals and so amount to a form of general or mass communication. In *Citron*, the CHRT held that hate messages posted on a website were communicated "repeatedly."[27] The Tribunal found that a website posting, much like a recorded phone message, "waits dormant" until activated by the caller or browser. The CHRT noted that the Internet facilitates "the repeated transmission of material on a chosen site" and offers "an inexpensive means of mass distribution."[28] However, communication on the Internet takes many different forms, which are more or less controlled or accessible. The CHRT has addressed the issue of the private character of different forms of Internet communication on a case-by-case basis. Provided the communication is not widely accessible (that is, that access is restricted to a small group), it may be regarded as "private" or, in the terms of section 13, as not made "repeatedly."

There are two difficulties with the Supreme Court of Canada's attempt to reconcile the regulation of hate speech with the right to freedom of expression. The first is the claim that there is a causal link between the expression of hateful views and the spread of hatred in the community. The second is the claim or assumption that it is possible to isolate a narrow category of extreme or hateful speech that reinforces, or contributes to, hatred in the community.

In the *Taylor* (and *Keegstra*) judgment(s), the majority of the

---

26 *Taylor*, above note 13.

27 *Citron and Toronto Mayor's Committee v Zundel*, 2002 CanLII 23557 (CHRT) [*Citron*].

28 *Ibid* at para 113.

Supreme Court of Canada was prepared to treat hate speech as responsible for the spread of hatred and for increases in racist violence because they were skeptical that the audience would always exercise rational judgment when it considered racist claims. The concern was that those who hear racist views may come to view the target group differently and act towards its members in a discriminatory or violent way. Hate speech damages the group's position in the community because it changes or reinforces the way that members of the dominant group think about the target group and its members.

If some individuals are persuaded of certain views, which they then act on, we might say that the expression has "caused" the action. However, under most accounts of freedom of expression, the state is not justified in restricting expression simply because it causes harm in this way, by persuading its audience. The listener and not the speaker is responsible for the judgments he makes and the actions he takes. The familiar freedom of expression position is that ideas cannot be censored simply because we fear that members of the community may find them persuasive or that an individual's self-understanding or self-esteem may be negatively affected. It is often said that we should respond to racist claims not with censorship, but by offering competing views that make the case for equal respect or by creating more avenues for marginalized groups to express themselves. Faith in human reason underlies most accounts of freedom of expression and cannot simply be cut out and discarded from the analysis. The implications of downplaying this faith in reason are enormous. Upon what is our commitment to freedom of expression based, if not on a belief in human reason and its power to recognize truth? What restrictions on expression are not acceptable once we have lost faith in human reason? If we are unwilling to trust, or give space to, individual judgment and public reason, then the question of censorship will turn simply on whether the particular expression conveys a good or bad message or whether we think that public acceptance of the message will have good or bad consequences. But this amounts to a rejection of freedom of expression as a political/constitutional principle. A commitment to freedom of expression means protecting expression for reasons more basic than our agreement with its message, for reasons independent of its content.

The other difficulty with the Court's approach is its attempt to isolate a narrow category of extreme expression for restriction. It is difficult to see how a particular instance of bigoted or hateful expression, however extreme, "silences" the members of a target group (damages their self-esteem so that they withdraw from public discourse) or leads others to hate them or discriminate against them. The spread of hatred in the community is a systemic problem. No one instance of expression leads to hatred or silencing, but a wide range of discriminatory representations (some extreme and some more temperate and even commonplace) may contribute to hateful attitudes and discriminatory actions in the community or to the marginalization of an identifiable group. It is difficult to imagine that the bizarre views of Taylor or Keegstra would be taken seriously by anyone who was not already deeply mired in irrational hatred or prejudice or who was not limited in her capacity for reasoned thought, or who was not in a subordinate or vulnerable position in relation to the speaker. But if the problem is systemic, then there is no way to isolate a narrow category of extreme or hateful expression that "causes" or leads to hatred, discrimination, and silencing. The choice seems to be to restrict nothing or everything.

In the *Taylor* decision there is an obvious tension between the Court's affirmation of the larger purposes of human rights law and its narrow definition of the scope of section 13. The Court said that the purpose of section 13, as part of a human rights law, is "to prevent the spread of prejudice and to foster tolerance and equality in the community."[29] To advance this purpose, it might be necessary to ban any expression that encourages a negative view of the group or undermines its position in society — that defames or stereotypes the members of the group. However, the courts, and the CHRT, have limited the scope of section 13 to the most extreme and hateful forms of discriminatory expression. This has been necessary because a broader restriction on group defamation would involve a significant intervention into the conduct of public discourse and would severely compromise freedom of expression in the community. Yet the section 13 ban cannot be confined to extreme or hateful expression, if its purpose is to prohibit speech that negatively affects the dignity or status of the members of an identifiable group. The purpose of a narrow hate speech ban must be less ambitious.

D. The Repeal of Section 13

My recommendation to the CHRC that section 13 be repealed so that the restriction of Internet hate speech occurs exclusively under the *Criminal Code* rested on three claims.

1) The Restriction of Extreme Expression

The first claim is that the failure to ban the extreme or radical edge of prejudiced speech carries too many risks, particularly when it circulates within the racist subculture that subsists on the Internet. Despite our commitment to freedom of expression and our faith in public reason, we know that in some times and places reason does not always operate. Hate speech on the Internet is often directed at the members of a relatively insular racist subculture. When directed at such an audience, extreme speech may reinforce and extend bigoted views without being exposed to public criticism. Individuals, already weighed down

29 *Taylor*, above note 13 at 918.

by prejudice or susceptible to manipulation or already part of an extremist subculture, will see in these claims a plausible account of their social and economic difficulties and a justification for radical action. Because the Internet audience is highly fragmented, it is easy for a particular website to operate at the margins and avoid critical public scrutiny. While most Internet websites are public in the sense that they are generally accessible, the audience for a particular site is often self-selecting and sometimes quite small. Smaller hate sites (or those that are less easily accessed such as chat rooms) that link like-minded individuals are able to encourage a sense of intimacy and identity and to operate below the radar. Thus these sites can be an effective means for individuals and groups, who hold hateful views, to encourage others to adopt more extreme views or to take violent action. The extreme or radical edge of prejudiced speech — that which threatens, justifies, or advocates violence either explicitly or implicitly — carries too many risks, particularly when it is directed at the members of a racist subculture or occurs in a context in which there is little opportunity for response. The advocacy of violence may be a concern because, in the words of the Cohen Committee, "in times of stress such 'hate' could mushroom into a real and monstrous threat to our way of life"[30] or more likely because it may encourage "isolated" acts of violence against members of an identifiable group, acts such as "gay-bashing." Hate crimes are committed most often not by organized groups but by individuals who have immersed themselves in the extremist subculture that operates principally on the Internet.

If the purpose of hate speech law is, as some argue, to prevent the circulation of discriminatory views or the defamation of identifiable groups, then the size of the audience for a particular communication may be an important factor in the decision

---

30 Canada, Cohen Committee, *Report to the Minister of Justice of the Special Committee on Hate Propaganda in Canada*, (Ottawa: Queen's Printer, 1966) at 24 [Cohen Committee].

whether or not to censor; the larger the audience, the greater the potential for harm. However, if the purpose is narrower — to prevent the advocacy or threat of violence — then audience size is less important. Indeed, smaller hate sites (or those that are less easily accessed such as chat rooms) that link like-minded individuals and operate below the radar ought to be of particular concern because they may be more effective in promoting extreme views and encouraging others to take radical action. Hate mongers can use these sites to attract new recruits or encourage violent action, without exposing themselves to a broad and potentially critical audience. This is why some effort and expense is required to investigate hate on the Internet. Its complex public and private character makes the Internet a potent vehicle for the reinforcement of hateful views and the advocacy of violence.

Internet content is notoriously difficult to regulate because material can be posted anonymously and redirected quickly and because it can be generated anywhere in the world.[31] As long as hate speech remains substantially unregulated in the US, it will be accessible to Canadians on the Internet. Indeed, it is sometimes argued that there should not be a law prohibiting hate on the Internet for the simple reason that it will be ineffective. This argument, I think, rests on a mistaken or unrealistic understanding of the purpose and scope of hate speech law. Every instance of hate speech — every threat and every incitement — is harmful in itself and ought to be prohibited. Even if we are unable to prevent some, perhaps even most, instances of hate speech, we ought to prevent those that we can. I might add that a threat of violence or a call to violence will seem less abstract, and more immediate, when it comes from an individual or group within the same geographic area or political jurisdiction as those who are targeted. Moreover, a prohibition on extremist speech, even if it cannot prevent all such speech, represents an important affirma-

31 *Citron*, above note 27.

tion to minority communities of their right not to be subjected to intimidation.

A narrow understanding of the purpose of hate speech law has several advantages. First, it may provide a clearer rationale for the focus on extreme expression that has been adopted by the CHRC and the CHRT. Second, it offers a more practical standard for drawing the line between prohibited hate speech and other forms of discriminatory expression. While the line will sometimes be difficult to draw, it is possible to identify factors that characterize extreme hate speech, such as the "hallmarks of hate,"[32] and to make a reasoned judgment about whether a particular instance of speech is, or amounts to, a call for violence. In contrast, it is impossible to know where, or even how, to draw a line separating group defamation from ordinary public discourse, given the pervasiveness of racial and other forms of prejudice. Third, it provides a clearer justification for limiting freedom of expression: to prevent the risk of violence against the members of an identifiable group. Understood in this way, the ban on hate speech may be seen as an extension of the criminal law prohibition on the advocacy and threat of violence.

It would be naïve though to think that drawing the line between speech that advocates or justifies violence and less extreme forms of discriminatory speech will be simple. A decision maker may find it easy, for example, to see a violent purpose behind speech that is directed at a group that has in recent history been the target of an organized campaign of violence. Because phrases such as "the solution to the Jewish problem" or symbols such as the swastika evoke the Holocaust, it is easy to attribute a violent purpose to the individual who employs them. Because the act of burning a cross evokes the violent oppression of blacks in North America, it is easily understood as a call to violence. Yet in the case of harsh, vitriolic statements made about other identifiable groups that do not have the same recent history of

32 *Warman*, above note 22.

organized violent persecution, it may be harder to discern a violent purpose.

A narrowly drawn ban that prohibits speech that threatens, advocates, or justifies violence against the members of an identifiable group may be seen as inadequate by those who are concerned about the persistence of prejudice and inequality in the community. This narrow ban will not prevent the circulation in the community of unfair depictions and false or misleading claims. It is arguable that more moderate or mainstream forms of discriminatory speech are more harmful because their audience is larger and their discriminatory message more insidious (for example, the claim or assumption that there are genetically based differences in intelligence between "racial" groups). Indeed, once we recognize that extreme speech has an impact only because it builds on more common stereotypes and assumptions, it may be argued that less extreme forms of speech should be treated as part of the problem, as contributing to discrimination and violence.

2) Less Extreme Speech

The second claim is that less extreme forms of discriminatory expression, although harmful, cannot simply be censored out of public discourse. Expression that stereotypes or defames the members of an identifiable group is offensive, insulting, and harmful to the group's members. Nevertheless, because discriminatory views or assumptions are so widely held and circulate generally in society, they cannot be eradicated through censorship. Any attempt to exclude from public discourse, speech that stereotypes or defames the members of an identifiable group would require extraordinary intervention by the state and would dramatically compromise the public commitment to freedom of expression. Because these less extreme forms of discriminatory expression are so commonplace, it is impossible to establish clear and effective rules for their identification and exclusion. Because they are so pervasive, it is vital that they be addressed or confronted rather than censored. They are often spread or reinforced without a clear intent by the speaker or conscious acceptance by the audience. The only effective response, then, is to expose the prejudiced character of commonplace assumptions and bring it to clearer, and hopefully more critical, consciousness. We must develop ways other than censorship to respond to expression that stereotypes and defames the members of an identifiable group and to hold institutions such as the media accountable when they engage in these forms of discriminatory expression.

3) The Human Rights Process

The third claim is that a narrowly drawn ban on hate speech that focuses on expression that is tied to violence does not fit easily or simply into a human rights law that takes an expansive view of discrimination, emphasizes the effect of the action on the victim rather than the intention or misconduct of the actor, and employs a process that is designed to engage the parties and facilitate a non-adjudicative resolution of the "dispute" between them.

The language of section 13 is potentially quite broad in its scope. The section prohibits "the repeated" communication on the phone system or the Internet of any matter "that is likely to expose a person or persons to hatred or contempt by reason of the fact that person or those persons are identifiable on the basis of a prohibited ground of discrimination."[33] However, the courts and the Tribunal have interpreted the provision narrowly. According to Dickson CJC in *Taylor,* the words *"hatred or contempt"* in the context of section 13(1) refer only to *"unusually strong and deep-felt emotions of detestation, calumny and vilification"* that are

33 *CHRA*, above note 1, s 13.

"ardent and extreme" in nature.[34] (It is worth noting that the small number of section 13 cases that have been sent by the CHRC to the Tribunal, and in which the Tribunal has found a breach of the section, have all — or almost all — involved expression that is so extreme and hateful that it may be seen as advocating violence against the members of an identifiable group.)

Even though the scope of the prohibition has been narrowly defined by the CHRC and the CHRT, there are at least two significant problems with the current process. The first problem is that free speech interests are affected every time an investigation occurs, particularly since the investigation engages the parties and takes eight to ten months to conclude. This is a problem because the CHRC is required to investigate a complaint unless it is trivial, vexatious, frivolous, or made in bad faith. The CHRC therefore is bound to investigate some complaints that are unlikely to proceed to adjudication. Human rights commissions may be reluctant to exclude a complaint prior to investigation on the grounds that it is trivial, because such a finding may be seen as downplaying the genuine feelings of hurt or injury experienced by minority group members and will preclude the possibility of a facilitated resolution of the "dispute." Because section 13 is located in a law that seeks to advance the goal of social equality through education and conciliation, the CHRC may be inclined to err on the side of inclusion when deciding whether a complaint should be rejected prior to investigation on the grounds that it is trivial.

The absence of an intention requirement in section 13 is a problem, because it leaves the door open to a broader or more discretionary application. In the *Taylor* case the Supreme Court of Canada did not consider the absence in section 13 of an intention requirement (that the respondent intended to spread hatred or knew that his speech was likely to do so) to be fatal to

---

34 *Taylor*, above note 13.

the provision's constitutionality. Chief Justice Dickson held that the absence of an intention requirement did not undermine the constitutionality of section 13 because the purpose of human rights legislation is to "compensate and protect" the victim rather than "stigmatize or punish" the person who has discriminated.[35] Yet, despite the familiar claim that human rights codes are about harmful effects rather than wrongful intentions, the CHRC and the CHRT have not attempted to measure the effects of hate speech. It is in fact difficult to prove the impact of expression on the attitudes and actions of audience members, who may understand and react to the communication in many different ways. A wide range of discriminatory representations may contribute to hateful attitudes and discriminatory actions in the community. Indeed, less extreme, more commonplace, instances of discriminatory speech may provide the groundwork necessary for the spread of hateful attitudes and so might be caught by section 13 on an ordinary reading of its terms. In determining whether the communication at issue breaches section 13, the CHRT looks not at its actual impact, but instead at the extreme content and hateful tone of the communication. It is difficult to describe the wrong to which section 13 is a response without referring the meaning or intention of the communicator. Not surprisingly the language of intention frequently appears in the section 13 decisions of the CHRT.

The second problem is the burden that the process puts on private complainants. Hate speech is most often directed at a receptive, or at least interested, audience and is only known to the complainant because she has looked for it or stumbled across it. Hate speech necessarily targets a group rather than an individual. The complainant makes the section 13 complaint on behalf of the group or society in general. He may not even be a member of the group targeted by the speech but has simply

---

35 *Ibid.*

taken the initiative to bring a complaint. It is not accidental, then, that particular individuals have played a leading role in the initiation of complaints. Without the initiative of these individuals, section 13 might have no operation at all. The complainant carries responsibility for the complaint throughout the process, at both the investigation and adjudication stages. (While the CHRC has the legislative authority to initiate complaints under section 13, it has generally not acted on this. The CHRC is not required to appear at the CHRT adjudication, but may do so as representative of the public interest.) In addition to the burden of time and money that a complainant must bear, particularly if the complaint proceeds to adjudication before the CHRT, a complainant may be subjected to threats of violence. We should not expect complainants to bear such a burden. Moreover, searching neo-Nazi websites for hate speech, and engaging with individuals on those sites to determine their identity, involves ethical challenges that should not be dealt with by private citizens. Hate speech harms the group and the community. It is a public wrong. The state, not private citizens, should be responsible for the enforcement of the law.

The restriction of hate speech that threatens, advocates, or justifies violence is appropriately dealt with under the criminal law. In the words of the Cohen Commission, "[n]o civil statute can create a moral standard equivalent to that of criminal law."[36] Hate speech is a serious matter that should be investigated by the police and prosecuted in the courts and should carry a significant penalty. There are, of course, some potential drawbacks to an exclusive reliance on the *Criminal Code* hate speech provisions. These include the requirement that the Attorney General of the particular province consent to prosecution, and the lack of experience on the part of police and prosecutors in pursuing hate speech cases.

---

36 Cohen Committee, above note 30 at 64.

E. Changes to Section 13

In the report I also suggested changes that should be made to section 13 of the *CHRA,* if it is not repealed.[37] These changes would reshape section 13 so that it more closely resembles a criminal restriction on hate speech. They include: (1) changes to the language of section 13(1) to make clear that the section prohibits only the most extreme instances of discriminatory expression, and more particularly expression that explicitly or implicitly threatens, advocates, or justifies violence against the members of an identifiable group; (2) the amendment of section 13(1) to include an intention requirement; and (3) the amendment of the *CHRA* to establish a distinct process for the investigation of section 13 complaints by the CHRC. Under the amended process, the CHRC would receive inquiries and information from individuals or community groups but would have the exclusive right to initiate an investigation in section 13 cases.

The CHRC in a report to Parliament in June 2009[38] responded to the recommendations in my report. The CHRC called for a continuation of the "dual approach" to the regulation of hate speech "with both the *CHRA* and the *Criminal Code* being applied as appropriate." According to the CHRC, human rights laws are the appropriate mechanism "to deal with situations where the intent of the person posting the messages may not be as clear, but where the extreme nature of the hate messages and their impact" justify their removal even when there is no "moral blameworthiness" on the part of the person posting them.[39] The main difficulty I have with the CHRC's argument (that human rights

---

37 Moon, above note 2.

38 Canadian Human Rights Commission, *Freedom of Expression and Freedom from Hate in the Internet Age: Special Report to Parliament* (Canadian Human Rights Commission, June 2009) at 32, online: CHRC www.chrc-ccdp.ca/pdf/srp_rsp_eng.pdf.

39 *Ibid.*

code regulation is necessary to deal with hate speech that is not improperly motivated) is that it seems to assume that less extreme instances of "hate speech" will be caught by section 13. Yet the CHRC also argues that section 13 does not unduly restrict freedom of expression because it catches only the most extreme and hateful forms of discriminatory expression.

F. Press Councils

Because hate speech laws focus on extreme speech, they leave untouched expression that employs stereotypes, or makes misleading or unfair claims about the members of an identifiable group. The familiar refrain of those who oppose the censorship of hate speech or group defamation is that the answer to bad speech should be "more speech" — hate speech should be answered, not censored. But if we are serious about the "more speech" answer, then we must think about the real opportunities that individuals and groups have to participate in public discourse and respond to speech that is unfair and discriminatory. Groups within the community should have a meaningful opportunity to respond to expression that is not so extreme that it violates criminal or human rights laws but may nevertheless affect their position within the larger community. A "laissez-faire" approach to discriminatory speech fails the groups that are victimized and implicates the larger society in that victimization, because communicative power is inequitably distributed. This speech may be insulting and offensive to minority communities and may affect their position or treatment within the larger community. It may also provide the foundation for more extreme "hate speech," particularly when it appears in the mainstream media.

To advance this end, I suggested in my report that all major print publications should belong to a provincial or regional press council that has the authority to receive a complaint that the publication has depicted an identifiable group in an unfair or discriminatory manner and, if it decides that the complaint is well-founded, to order the publication to print its decision.[40] A decision by the council that its code of conduct has been breached results not in censorship but in "more speech" — the publication of a statement that the newspaper breached the code and, more particularly in this context, that it published material that unfairly represented the members of an identifiable group. I also suggested that if the major publications in the country are not all willing to join a press council, then the establishment of a national press council with statutory authority and compulsory membership should once again be given serious consideration. A newspaper is not simply a private participant in public discourse; it is an important part of the public sphere where discussion about the affairs of the community takes place. As such, it carries a responsibility not to defame or stereotype identifiable groups within the Canadian community.

G. Balancing Rights

Hate speech regulation is often said to involve the balancing of competing values or rights — the right to freedom of expression versus the right to equality. The assumption is that an increase or gain in one of these values involves a decrease or loss in the other. The issue then is how much weight should be given to each value.[41] Yet it is not clear that equality and free expression trade off in this simple way. It is true that when discriminatory views are expressed more widely in the community, the members of the target group may feel less secure, and others in the community may feel more comfortable engaging in acts of discrimination. However, an egalitarian society will not be achieved simply because the state has successfully banned the public expres-

40 Moon, above note 2.

41 For a discussion oF the challenges of balancing competing rights claims see Patricia Hughes, Chapter 10.

sion of prejudice (an impossible task, in any event). Prejudiced speech, although impeded, will survive in private exchanges and so must be addressed. But more importantly, an individual (and collective) commitment to equality will stand against the winds of change only if its rests on a judgment that all persons are deserving of basic respect and on a conscious rejection of prejudiced views. As I have already argued, it may sometimes be necessary to censor speech. When speech is extreme and occurs in a context in which it is unlikely to be examined critically, we should not take the risk that it may effectively encourage its audience to take extreme action. This is not the same, however, as attempting to expunge all instances of prejudiced expression from public discourse in order to advance a broad-based commitment to equality.

Chapter 16
Toleration and the Reconciliation of Conflicting Rights[1]

Stephen L. Newman

A. Introduction

Why drag John Locke, a seventeenth-century philosopher, into a discussion of conflicting rights in the twenty-first century? Well, for one thing, Locke is a famous rights theorist whose seminal contribution to the liberal political tradition is a justification of the state in terms of its role as guarantor of individual rights. Moreover, Locke is also famous for his defence of religious toleration, which he treats in terms of the right to liberty of conscience. While Locke does not concern himself with the difficulties arising from a possible conflict of rights, his theory compels us to think about the accommodation of religious diversity in the face of competing claims of conscience. And since on the terms of his own argument claims of conscience are put forward as a matter of right, the way Locke deals with these competing claims might well have something to tell us about how to handle rights in conflict. It is also relevant that Locke's philosophical construction of the state, rights, and toleration still inform our contemporary practices. As citizens of a modern liberal state, we

1 Originally prepared as "John Locke and the Right to Toleration" (Paper delivered at the Ontario Human Rights Commission/York Centre for Public Policy and Law, 5–6 March 2010). I want to thank my colleagues Martin Breaugh and Les Jacobs for taking the time to read my paper and offer comments.

are Locke's complacent heirs. Sometimes a backwards glance gives perspective on the present.

B. Locke's Right to Toleration

In the late seventeenth-century, dissenters from the Protestant Church of England made up approximately ten percent of the nation. The overwhelming majority of dissenters were themselves Protestant but differed with the established church over ritual, liturgy, and dogma. For this they were subject to persecution and faced a range of penalties that stretched from fines and imprisonment to physical torture and death.[2] Persecution was justified on religious grounds as being in the best interests of the dissenters themselves, whose descent into theological error jeopardized their chances at personal salvation. Not unimportantly in light of the recent Civil War, curbing religious dissent was said to serve the best interests of the nation by arresting the potential for further sectarian violence against the state.

In the texts now known as the *Two Tracts on Government*, written between 1660 and 1663, the young John Locke sided with the forces of persecution. The *Two Tracts* defended the magistrate's authority to compel uniformity in religious worship on grounds of public expediency. Locke opined that it was the magistrate's duty "to preserve the public good and keep people in peace and concord," a state of affairs he believed to be threatened by the proliferation of "enthusiastic" (fanatical) sects.[3]

---

2 See Henry Kamen, *The Rise of Toleration* (London: World University Library, 1967) at 201–5; and John Marshall, *John Locke, Toleration and Early Enlightenment Culture: Religious Intolerance and Arguments for Religious Tolerance in Early Modern and "Early Enlightenment" Europe* (Cambridge: Cambridge University Press, 2006) at 107–115 [Marshall].

3 John Locke, "Two Tracts on Government" in Mark Goldie, ed., *Locke: Political Essays* (Cambridge: Cambridge University Press,

A scant four years later, however, in the unpublished "Essay on Toleration" (1667), Locke maintained that "purely speculative [religious] opinions" as well as "the place, time, and manner of worshipping [one's] God" could neither disturb the state nor harm the worldly interests of anyone, and so "come not within the magistrate's cognisance." Speculative opinions and divine worship, he insisted, *"have an absolute and universal right to toleration."*[4] Some twenty years later, in the justly famous *A Letter Concerning Toleration* (1689), the mature Locke affirmed this judgment, declaring that "Liberty of Conscience is every man's natural Right."[5] He went on to defend the right to toleration in two further, book-length "letters" written in reply to objections posed by Jonas Proast, chaplain of All Souls College, Oxford, who asserted the establishment view that the government had the right to use "moderate" force to compel dissenters to consider the merits of Anglicanism, the truth of which Proast thought would be obvious to any reasonable person. Locke was at work on

---

1997) at 60 [Goldie]. For a discussion of Locke's anti-tolerationist argument in context of the times, see Kim Ian Parker, *The Biblical Politics of John Locke* (Waterloo, ON: Wilfrid Laurier University Press, 2004) at 11–12; and John Marshall, *John Locke: Resistance, Religion, and Responsibility* (Cambridge: Cambridge University Press, 1994) at 13.

4 John Locke, "Essay on Toleration" in Goldie, *ibid.* at 136–37 [emphasis added]. Locke's change of heart may have been influenced by his recent association with Lord Ashley (later the Earl of Shaftesbury), who favoured the toleration of dissenters for political reasons. The sheer amount of time and energy Locke devoted to the subject of toleration over the length of his career suggests, however, that his conversion was principled rather than politically expedient.

5 John Locke, *A Letter Concerning Toleration* (Indianapolis: Hackett, 1985) at 51 [Locke, *Concerning Toleration*].

A Fourth Letter for Toleration when he died in 1704.[6]

Lockean toleration is a negative right largely consistent with how we think about religious freedom today, as enshrined in the *Canadian Charter of Rights and Freedoms* and the First Amendment to the United States Constitution. For us as for Locke, the right to liberty of conscience means that religious believers may entertain whatever conception of the divine seems true to them and engage in whatever manner of public worship they think appropriate without encountering coercive interference from the state or their fellow citizens. Although several of Locke's arguments for toleration explicitly draw on his understanding of what is required of Christians in their conduct toward one another, the regime of toleration he proposes extends to Jews, Muslims, and "Pagans."[7] To this extent, then, the Lockean right to toleration

---

6 Locke's four letters on toleration can be found in *The Works of John Locke*, vol. 5 (London: Routledge/Thoemmes Press, 1997; originally published in London, 1794) [Locke, *Works*]. Richard Vernon assesses the Locke-Proast exchange in *The Career of Toleration: John Locke, Jonas Proast, and After* (Montreal and Kingston: McGill-Queen's University Press, 1997) [Vernon]. John Marshall situates Locke's argument in the context of the early modern European debate over toleration in Marshall, above note 2 at 470–71.

7 At the very beginning of *A Letter Concerning Toleration* Locke writes, "Since you are pleased to inquire what are my Thoughts about the mutual Toleration of Christians in their different Professions of Religion, I must needs answer you freely, That I esteem that Toleration to be the chief Characteristical Mark of the True Church" (Locke, *Concerning Toleration*, above note 5 at 23). He goes on to argue that scripture provides no warrant for persecution and moreover that toleration hews to the example set by Christ and his disciples. Micah Schwartzman explores the contribution of Locke's expressly religious arguments to his overall case for toleration in "The Relevance of Locke's Religious Arguments for Toleration" (2005) 33:5 Political Theory 678.

is deliberately inclusive.[8] It acknowledges the social identity of minority religious groups and creates a space for them within a religiously pluralistic civil society.[9] The antagonisms born of religious differences are muted by assigning politics and religion to separate spheres. Within the political sphere all persons share a common civic identity and a common set of "civil interests," which Locke enumerates as "Life, Liberty, Health, and Indolency of Body; and the Possession of outward things, such as Money, Lands, Houses, Furniture, and the like."[10] Religion, on the other hand, is assigned to a non-public sphere where like-minded individuals are free to come together in voluntary associations — churches — for the purpose of worshipping God "in such a manner as they judge acceptable to him, and effectual to the Salvation of their Souls."[11] The Lockean right to toleration

---

8 "[T]hose whose Doctrine is peaceable, and whose Manners are pure and blameless, ought to be upon equal Terms with their Fellow-Subjects. Thus if Solemn Assemblies, Observations of Festivals, public Worship, be permitted to any sort of Professors; all these things ought to be permitted to the *Presbyterians*, *Independents*, *Anabaptists*, *Arminians*, *Quakers*, and others, with the same Liberty. Nay, if we may openly speak the Truth, and as becomes one Man to another, neither *Pagan*, nor *Mahometan* [Muslim], nor *Jew*, ought to be excluded from the Civil Rights of the Commonwealth, because of his Religion" (Locke, *Concerning Toleration*, *ibid.* at 54).

9 Compare to Ingrid Creppell, *Toleration and Identity: Foundations in Early Modern Political Thought* (New York: Routledge, 2003) at 121: "Locke's position indicated, first, an individuation of belief. It also pointed crucially to a 'space' in which presentation of one's religious identity in public was protected from interference or coercion by others and by the state. Finally, this juridical space of protection (a cold, formal state of affairs) was much more than that because it involved expression and recognition . . . ."

10 Locke, *Concerning Toleration*, above note 5 at 26.

11 *Ibid.* at 28.

assures that the particularity of the individual's religious identity can be preserved alongside her non-denominational civic identity. At the same time, it rules out the pursuit of religious ends by political means, thus neutralizing the threat posed by religious sectarianism. T.M. Scanlon captures the essence of Lockean toleration when he says, "What tolerance expresses is a recognition of common membership that is deeper than [group] conflicts, a recognition of others as just as entitled as we are to contribute to the definition of our society."[12]

C. Civil Authority and Claims of Conscience

A parallel might be drawn here with John Rawls's idea of public reason.[13] Locke's magistrate is required to confine his actions to measures that will protect and promote the civil interests common to all citizens. Accordingly, he must be able to describe his actions in light of that purpose in order to avoid having their legitimacy called into question. Inevitably, difficult cases will arise. Locke gives the example of a law forbidding the slaughter

12 T.M. Scanlon, "The Difficulty of Tolerance" in David Heyd, ed., *Toleration: An Elusive Virtue* (Princeton: Princeton University Press, 1996) at 231. It is debatable, however, whether Locke believes that a person's civic identity (and civil interests) can or should outweigh her faith-based identity. Given the supreme importance he attaches to the individual's interest in her personal salvation, it seems more likely that he hopes to mitigate the social frictions that create an unbearable tension between the requirements of civility and the demands of faith.

13 See John Rawls, "The Idea of Public Reason Revisited" in John Rawls, *The Law of Peoples* (Cambridge, MA: Harvard University Press, 1999) at 129–80. On the parallel between Locke and Rawls, see Vernon, above note 6 at 35–51; and compare to Steven Lecce, *Against Perfectionism: Defending Liberal Neutrality* (Toronto: University of Toronto Press, 2008) at 36–45.

of calves imposed to replenish the nation's livestock after the supply of cattle had been greatly diminished due to some "extraordinary Murrain." He thinks this objective is well within the bounds of the magistrate's just authority, but observes that it will have a differential impact on believers whose religion requires the weekly sacrifice of a calf as part of their worship service. Need these believers be accommodated by making an exception to the general law temporarily forbidding the slaughter of calves? Locke thinks not. He explains that "in this case the Law is not made about a Religious, but a Political matter: nor is the Sacrifice, but the Slaughter of Calves thereby prohibited."[14] What matters to Locke in this example is not only the magistrate's language of justification, but also his intentions. By acting only for a valid public reason, the magistrate shows respect for the believers whose weekly sacrifice is blocked by the law. It is, of course, possible to doubt the sincerity of the magistrate, and Locke is well aware of the temptation to make duplicitous use of political language. Accordingly, he cautions the magistrate "always to be very careful that he do not misuse his Authority, to the oppression of any Church, under pretense of the public Good."[15]

Might Locke have opted for accommodation in this example? There is no apparent reason why not. If the magistrate were to decide on reasonable evidence that a religious exemption from the ban on the slaughter of calves would not injure the public by defeating the goal of the general ban, it is arguable that in light of the Lockean right to toleration, he is in fact obliged to grant the exemption. To do otherwise would only encourage the suspicion that he had acted out of prejudice "under pretense of public good," which would justify conscientious disobedience on the part of the affected worshipers.[16] The fact remains, however, that when reasonable accommodation is not possible, Locke

---

14 Locke, *Concerning Toleration*, above note 5 at 42.

15 *Ibid.*

16 *Ibid.* at 48.

allows the public good, as interpreted by the magistrate, to trump the claims of conscience. That said, he also acknowledges that whether or not in any particular case the public good truly requires that the magistrate's action is always contestable, and since there is "no judge on earth between the Supreme Magistrate and the People," a resort to arms may be necessary to break the impasse. Locke thinks the consequences of this are usually so horrific that it gives both the magistrate and the people reason to pause.[17]

D. Toleration and Identity

Modern critics of Locke sometimes complain that the terms on which he allows religious and cultural minorities into the political sphere deny them the public recognition necessary for full inclusion.[18] The critics claim, in effect, that religious and cultural minorities are allowed a universal civic identity by Locke (and those liberal theorists who follow in Locke's footsteps) only if they hide their particular religious and cultural identities. This might prove less galling if the political sphere were truly a neutral zone devoid of religious or cultural referents, but the critics contend that it invariably carries the imprint of the majority.[19] This imprint may be invisible to members of the dominant religious and cultural groups, but it rarely escapes the notice of minority group members and only serves to remind them of their outsider status. A more inclusive form of toleration would acknowledge minority groups for who they truly are by welcoming them into the political sphere in all their religious and cultural particularity on equal

---

17 *Ibid*. at 49.

18 See, for example, Anna Elisabetta Galeotti, *Toleration as Recognition* (Cambridge: Cambridge University Press, 2002).

19 See, for example, Bhikhu Parekh's critique of Rawls in *Rethinking Multiculturalism: Cultural Diversity and Political Theory* (Cambridge, Massachusetts: Harvard University Press, 2000) at 81–90.

terms with the majority. Where Locke would have the magistrate treat a person's religion as something largely irrelevant to his civic identity, Locke's modern critics would have the state regard a person's religion as a one aspect of his civic identity and entitled to the same concern and respect as his non-denominational civil interests.

This critique is not without merit, but arguably it misconstrues the purpose of Locke's carefully crafted separation of politics and religion. Assigning religion to the non-public sphere is not intended to hide it away in private, but rather to create a social space for the (unthreatening) public display of religious identity. Disallowing state action intended either to promote or impair religious ends serves to protect this space and keep it open.[20] The conditions for society's recognition of particular religious identities on equal terms with one another are made possible by the state's regard for liberty of conscience and the right to toleration, making it impossible to exclude the members of minority religious groups from, for example, public schools or public office, simply on account of their religion. Granted, the right to toleration does not and can not guarantee the minority more than a social presence; lingering prejudices may prevent the majority from embracing the minority in the manner hoped for by Locke's modern critics. But it is far from clear that official state recognition of religious minorities, whatever form that might take, would do any more to combat social prejudice than a zealous regard for minority rights. Ultimately, it is to be hoped that general recognition of the right to toleration (and its enforcement by the state) will encourage the development of mutual trust, eventually leading to the dissipation of prejudice and full social acceptance of

---

20 Compare to Brian Barry's account of the depoliticization of religion in *Culture and Equality: An Egalitarian Critique of Multiculturalism* (Cambridge, Massachusetts: Harvard University Press, 2001) at 24–32.

the minority by the majority.[21]

E. The Intolerant Locke

Locke has also been faulted by modern critics for denying toleration to Catholics and atheists. His denial of toleration to atheists rests on the now discredited notion that a belief in supernatural rewards and punishments is the essential underpinning of morality.[22] Locke seems to have believed that human beings simply cannot be trusted to be good without God, something few moral philosophers are likely to affirm today.[23] His denial of toleration to Catholics rested on their supposed allegiance to the Pope, who claimed a worldly authority superior to that of the magistrate. Locke's objection to Catholicism, then, is political, not theological. His concern is that good Catholics cannot be good citizens. (Given England's relations at the time with its Catholic adversaries, France and Spain, Locke's apprehension concerning the loyalty of England's Catholic subjects was understandable, if not fully defensible.) Notably, however, Locke holds no brief against what he describes as the purely "speculative" opinions of any church, because he is persuaded that speculative religious opinions pose no threat either to the state or its citizens.

> If a *Roman Catholick* believe that to be really the Body of Christ, which another man calls Bread, he does no injury thereby to his Neighbour. If a *Jew* do not believe the New Testament to be the Word of God, he does not thereby alter any thing in mens

---

21 On the relationship between trust and toleration and the conditions for generating trust, see Richard H. Dees, *Trust and Toleration* (London and New York: Routledge, 2004).

22 Locke, *Concerning Toleration*, above note 5 at 51.

23 The unreliability of atheists was disputed in Locke's own time by Pierre Bayle, who saw no reason why unbelievers could not be good persons and good citizens. See Edward G. Andrew, *Patrons of Enlightenment* (Toronto: University of Toronto Press, 2006) at 84.

> Civil Rights. If a Heathen doubt of both Testaments, he is not therefore to be punished as a pernicious Citizen.[24]

What Locke finds unacceptable about the Catholicism of his day is certain "practical opinions" admixed with its religious doctrine, such as the notion that kings excommunicated by the Pope forfeit their crowns and kingdoms. Were English Catholics to abjure these opinions and accept his conception of a church as a voluntary association, Locke would no longer have any reason to deny them toleration.

This concession would appear to temper Locke's anti-Catholicism; however, the conditions he would impose on Catholics in order to make them candidates for toleration raise the possibility of a more subtle theoretical bias. Locke, who freely interweaves expressly religious arguments for toleration with his more philosophical, rights-based arguments, draws on a broad-church, Protestant vision of Christianity emphasizing the centrality of the Gospels, and making the individual's personal experience of saving faith, the "inward perswasion of the mind," the key to God's favour. It is because faith cannot be compelled, but must proceed from "light and evidence," that Locke dismisses Proast's reliance on "moderate" force to get dissenters to "consider" the doctrines of the established church.[25] The notion that personal faith arises only through the individual's sincere quest for religious truth underwrites Locke's conception of a church as a voluntary association. In Locke's ecclesiology, churches

---

24 Locke, *Concerning Toleration*, above note 5 at 46.

25 Throughout his second and third letters on toleration, Locke repeatedly accuses Proast of being deceptive when claiming that force is to be used only to ensure that dissenters will give due consideration to Anglican doctrine. Locke thinks Proast's real aim is to enforce religious conformity, regardless of whether or not those persons forced into the established church sincerely adhere to its doctrine.

exist solely for the purpose of allowing their members to engage in public worship. The ultimate fate of any individual, however, has no bearing on the fate of her co-worshipers or anyone else for that matter. As Locke puts it, "The Care . . . of every man's Soul belongs unto himself, and is to be left unto himself."[26] The point to consider here is whether Locke makes toleration available to Catholics, Muslims, and Jews only on the condition that these religious groups become more like (Lockean) Protestants in their church polity and religious self-understanding.

F. Lockean Toleration and Liberal Multiculturalism

This is precisely the accusation, albeit rendered in secular terms, that present-day communitarians and some multicultural theorists make against the Locke's liberal heirs. Even allegedly "political" versions of liberalism, which eschew reliance on any comprehensive moral or theological doctrine, are said to sneak in through the back door a commitment to individualism and personal autonomy. If true, this would suggest that despite its nonsectarian appearance, modern Anglo-American liberalism cannot escape its Protestant roots. Of course, it never would have occurred to Locke to separate his religious ideas from his politics. So far as he was concerned, both were in accord with right reason.[27]

What follows from this? Is the Lockean right to toleration a hollow promise for those who take *works*, the outward acts that characterize a life lived in accordance with one's religious beliefs, to be as or more important for attaining salvation than an inward

---

26 Locke, *Concerning Toleration*, *ibid*. at 35.

27 "The Toleration of those that differ from others in Matters of Religion, is so agreeable to the Gospel of Jesus Christ, and to the genuine Reason of Mankind, that it seems monstrous for Men to be so blind, as not to perceive the Necessity and Advantage of it, in so clear a Light." Locke, *Concerning Toleration*, *ibid*. at 25.

faith? To put the question more concretely, are the rights of, say, a conscientious Catholic for whom there is religious imperative to oppose abortion given short shrift by a modern Lockean polity that treats abortion as a matter of personal choice and requires him to tolerate the practice? Are orthodox Jews whose religious sensibilities are offended by the immodest photos featured in advertising posted in their neighbourhood denied religious freedom because they are prohibited from tearing down the advertisements? It is likely that anyone who thinks of religion not as an easily compartmentalized set of personal beliefs (inward faith), but as a complete way of life for an entire community (outward works), would answer these questions in the affirmative.[28]

Locke might respond, as modern liberals do, by saying that people are free to conceive of their religion in any manner they please and to live their lives accordingly, so long as they do not intrude on the rights of others. Thus, the Catholic Church may forbid its own members from having abortions on pain of excommunication, but the church may not issue commands to non-Catholics. Catholics are at liberty, of course, to attempt to persuade non-Catholics that abortion is a sin. For Locke, this is how toleration operates. Respect for the religious point of view is institutionalized through a multi-faith dialogue where the object is to win hearts and minds by means of reasoned argument. The problem is that Locke conceives of this religious dialogue as

28 Knud Haakonessen notes that while High Anglicans and Roman Catholics were inclined to view both church and state as divinely ordained aspects of the same historical body, some Low Anglicans and most dissenters tended to look on both as purely conventional bodies created by compact. The two views are diametrically opposed, explaining the natural reluctance of the former to accept the Lockean argument for religious freedom at face value. See Knud Haakonessen, ed., *Enlightenment and Religion: Rational Dissent in Eighteenth-Century Britain* (Cambridge: Cambridge University Press, 1996) at 5–6.

being about speculative theological opinions, whereas the hard questions that give rise to so much religious strife in the present day concern practical moral opinions bearing on the conduct of life. Catholics object to abortion not only because according to Catholic theology it is a sin, but also because they consider it to be a grave moral wrong. It is the admixture of speculative (religious) and practical (moral) opinions in Catholicism that fuels opposition to abortion.

Locke is aware that all religions combine speculative and practical opinions in their doctrines, but his arguments for toleration focus on the former, perhaps because in his day dissenters were persecuted chiefly on account of what they professed and not for how they lived. Still, Locke acknowledges that the pursuit of a good life is "not the least part of Religion and true Piety." Problematically, how individuals choose to pursue the good "concerns also the Civil Government."

> Moral Actions belong therefore to the Jurisdiction both of the outward and inward Court; both of the Civil and Domestic Governor; I mean, both of the Magistrate and Conscience. Here therefore is great danger, least one of these Jurisdictions intrench upon the other, and Discord arise between the Keeper of the public peace and the Overseers of Souls.[29]

It is not easy to share Locke's confidence that the limits his argument places on the authority of both church and state "will easily remove all difficulty in this matter."[30] The difficulty will remain unless church and state see eye to eye on moral issues at least most of the time. And indeed, Locke, who has a puritanical streak, seems to think that a broad societal consensus can be

---

29 Locke, *Concerning Toleration*, above note 5 at 46.

30 *Ibid*. at 47. Compare to Eldon J. Eisenach, *Two Worlds of Liberalism: Religion and Politics in Hobbes, Locke, and Mill* (Chicago: University of Chicago Press, 1981) at 78–83.

expected on moral questions.[31]

With the breakdown of that consensus, liberalism after Locke inclined toward greater acceptance of moral pluralism, which it sought to accommodate by enlarging the number of speculative and moral opinions assigned to the non-public sphere protected from outside interference. J.S. Mill, for example, expands the boundaries of personal liberty far beyond the range Locke would have found tolerable, and modern liberals go further still. As the state retreats from policing morals, persons, and groups who, for religious reasons, take a strong interest in the moral quality of public life, are likely to feel increasing aggrieved. It should come as no surprise, then, if when told that they must respect the rights of those who take a different view of religion and morals and refrain from interfering with conduct they find objectionable, they protest this as a denial of their religious freedom and a violation of their own rights. This is the paradox inherent in Locke's construction of the right to toleration: in the name of conscience, individuals and groups are expected to tolerate conduct they find grossly immoral, which is itself an affront to conscience.

Conclusion: The Duty of Civility

Insofar as the modern liberal state still conceives of the relationship between politics and religion in Lockean terms, it can be said (with just a hint of irony) that Locke's doctrine has made Protestants of us all. Who today seriously argues that church and state are one organic body divinely ordained for the enforcement of divine law and the salvation of souls? Who seriously disputes the voluntary character of religious affiliation or questions the legitimacy of religious pluralism? But the general agreement to tolerate diverse modes of worship and all manner of speculative

---

31 Compare to Marshall, above note 2 at 715–16. See also Greg Forster, *John Locke's Politics of Moral Consensus* (Cambridge: Cambridge University Press, 2005).

religious opinions does not preclude dissension over the reach of practical moral opinions, which transcends the boundary Locke established between church and state. Sincere believers who campaign to make abortion illegal or to prevent the legalization of same-sex marriage do so not in order to impose their religion on the state, but rather to prevent the state (through morally lax laws) from doing injury to their religion *as a way of life*. In fact, on both sides of these issues, sincere believers demand the same thing of the state — that it respect their right to live as conscience dictates. Absent a new moral consensus, which seems an unlikely prospect at this juncture, these claims are bound to generate conflict that appeals to the right of conscience cannot resolve.

Does Locke's doctrine have anything to offer us in the face of this dilemma? Locke recognizes that to sincere believers nothing is more important than religious obligation, a perspective he apparently shares. "The principal and chief care of every one ought to be his own Soul first," he writes, "and in the next place the public Peace." But he immediately adds that "there are very few will think 'tis Peace there, where they see all laid waste."[32] Locke's words are a caution to believers, who in his time were all too familiar with the devastation caused by wars of religion.

Chastened believers have ample incentive to embrace what Locke has to say about the duty of civility. In one place, Locke describes civility as a duty consisting in "outward expressing of goodwill and esteem or at least of no contempt and hatred," and he ranks it second only to justice among the virtues which relate to society.[33] His belief in the efficacy of civil discourse was shared with other European advocates of toleration in the early Enlightenment's emerging Republic of Letters, which set itself against both the intransigence of religious dogmatism and the bellicos-

32 Locke, *Concerning Toleration*, above note 5 at 49.

33 Locke, "Morality," believed to have been composed between 1677 and 1679, in Goldie, above note 3 at 269.

ity of religious fanaticism.[34] Locke and his colleagues may have been overly optimistic about the chances of settling religious and moral controversies on terms that all reasonable persons could agree to, but they were surely right to think that the willingness to engage those with whom we disagree without rancor vastly improves the chances of a peaceful outcome.

The duty of civility receives support from Locke's insistence that beliefs grounded in religious faith are not subject to demonstration and hence cannot be shown to be true in a manner convincing to all.[35] The lesson he would have us draw from this seems similar to what Rawls intends by "the burdens of judgment."[36] Since according to Locke, the beliefs people do hold are a result of their experience and associations, which vary from one person and one group of people to the next, it is only reasonable to expect a diversity of religious opinions. Thus, although "every one is Orthodox to himself," as Locke puts it, no one has a reasonable basis for declaring others to be heretical.[37] Recognition of the Lockean burdens of judgment makes mutual toleration the

34 Compare to Marshall, above note 2 at 501–22.

35 Locke associates knowledge with that which can be "demonstrated" by means of a deductive argument or logical proof. In contrast, belief or opinion may be based on either probability or faith. This makes the scope of our knowledge very narrow. In most everyday concerns, we have to rely on probability, in matters of religion, on faith. For a fuller account, see E.J. Lowe, *Locke* (London and New York: Routledge, 2005) at 52–57. In *A Third letter for Toleration* Locke writes, "This is the highest the nature of the thing will permit us to go in matters of revealed religion, which are therefore called matters of faith: a persuasion of our own minds, short of knowledge, is the last result that determines us in such truths" (Locke, *Works*, above note 6 at 144).

36 John Rawls, *Political Liberalism* (New York: Columbia University Press, 1993) at 54–58.

37 Locke, *Concerning Toleration*, above note 5 at 23.

default position for competing orthodoxies. It is not much of a stretch to apply his version of the burdens of judgment to controversial moral issues as well, once we have discarded his notorious claim that moral propositions are capable of demonstration in a way religious beliefs are not.[38]

Accepting the duty to be civil will not prevent clashes between conscientious believers or the collision of competing rights claims, but it should help keep a lid on things and make it less likely that hard feelings will poison relations between the contesting parties. It should also promote a general willingness on the part of individuals and groups to accommodate one another insofar as this is possible without compromising a fundamental interest. But like all of Locke's arguments on behalf of toleration, the appeal for civility is addressed to persons who already recognize the religious "other" as a fellow citizen possessing the same rights and deserving the same consideration as themselves. What is to be done, then, about the genuinely intolerant, those who out of sincerely held religious beliefs would deny religious freedom to others? Locke writes, "those that will not own *and teach* the Duty of tolerating All men in matters of meer Religion . . . have no right to be tolerated by the Magistrate."[39]

---

38 Locke asserts in *An Essay Concerning Human Understanding* (1690) that it should be possible "to place morality amongst the sciences capable of demonstration," proceeding from the idea of an omnipotent God whose workmanship we are and the idea of ourselves as rational beings. He never abandoned this claim, but he never made good on the demonstration. John Locke, *An Essay Concerning Human Understanding*, vol. 2 (New York: Dover, 1959) at 208.

39 Locke, *Concerning Toleration*, above note 5 at 50 [emphasis added].

List of Contributors

Shaheem Azmi is the director of Policy, Outreach, and Education of the Ontario Human Rights Commission.

Lauren Bates is the staff lawyer for the Law Commission of Ontario.

Iain Benson is senior associate counsel, Miller Thompson, LLP, Canada.

Janet Epp Buckingham is an associate professor at Trinity Western University.

Lorne Foster is an associate professor of public policy and equity studies as well as director of the Graduate Program in Public Policy, Administration, and Law at York University.

Barbara Hall is chief commissioner, Ontario Human Rights Commission.

Patricia Hughes is the executive director of the Law Commission of Ontario.

Lesley Jacobs is professor of law & society and political science, as well as the first director of the York Centre for Public Policy & Law at York University.

Errol Mendes is a professor of law at the University of Ottawa and a commissioner of the Ontario Human Rights Commission.

Richard Moon is a professor of law at the University of Windsor.

Stephen Newman is an associate professor of political science at York University.

Miriam Smith is a professor of law & society at York University.

Shauna Van Praagh is an associate professor of law at McGill University.

B. J. Wray is a lawyer for the Department of Justice, Government of Canada, in Vancouver, British Columbia.

Gary Yee is chair of Ontario's Licence Appeal Tribunal.

Kolibri 360 GmbH
Ferdinand-Jühlke-Straße 7
99095 Erfurt, Deutschland
produktsicherheit@kolibri360.de